For Coni & John —
Who spread
Christmas Cheer
All Year.
Happy Holidays   12/13
From the Blazes,

CHICAGO QUARTERLY REVIEW™

Volume 17
The Chicago Issue
2014

Senior Editors
S. Afzal Haider, Elizabeth McKenzie
Managing Editor
Sean Chen-Haider
Fiction Editor
John Blades
Non-Fiction Editor
Jim Stacey
Assistant Poetry Editor
Jake Young
Contributing Editor
Umberto Tosi
Staff Editor
Mona Moraru
Graphic Designer
Caroline Webster
Editorial Assistants
Nick Forbes, Arthur Fox, Peggy Townsend,
Vito Victor, Dan White
Interns
Nora Mathison, Angela Zhang
Legal Consultant
Kathryn Vanden Berk

Cover Illustration by Laura Williams

This publisher is a proud member of

COUNCIL OF LITERARY MAGAZINES & PRESSES
w w w . c l m p . o r g

TABLE OF CONTENTS

NON-FICTION

POETRY

ART

BUDDING LITERARY MASTERS

Introduction
345

EDITORS' NOTE

Back in the spring of 1994, when the *Chicago Quarterly Review* published its first issue, the Editors' note said, "This is probably your first issue of the *CQR*, as it is the first one we have produced. If you've got the feeling you have picked up an issue before, it's either déjà vu or the result of something amorphous from the back of your refrigerator you ate instead of tossing it out." Now, nearly twenty years later, we are amazed and humbled to look back at the hundreds of writers who have lent their work to our pages.

Literary journals have been essential to Chicago's robust writing life and its preeminence in letters for more than a century—some of these internationally renowned, like *Poetry Magazine* founded in 1912 by Harriet Monroe. The *CQR* doesn't go that far back, but in our twenty continuous years, we have justly earned a respected place in Chicago's vibrant literary scene. We salute all of our fellow asteroids, past and present, in the literary cosmos of Chicago, including *TriQuarterly, Chicago Review, MAKE, Rambunctious Review, Other Voices, Fifth Wednesday, The Point Magazine, after hours,* and *Another Chicago Magazine,* among many notable others.

In this special Chicago Issue, we present the work of fifty-four writers and artists who live and work in Chicago or reflect the city of Chicago in their work. If ever there were a testament to the exuberance of the Chicago writing scene, and the Chicago influence on the mind and psyche of those touched by the city, this is it. To all who are gathered together here, we thank you.

We would like to give special thanks to former *CQR* Managing Editor Natalia Nebel for her generous help with this issue.

We'd also like to thank Donald G. Evans, director of the Chicago Literary Hall of Fame, for asking us to support the CLHOF-sponsored Budding Masters competition, honoring and encouraging young Chicago writers. We are proud to publish the winning entries here.

You are holding Volume 17 of the *CQR,* and you are not lost in the cosmos, it is not déjà vu all over again, this is the real thing—the *Chicago Quarterly Review,* a nonprofit, independent literary journal publishing the finest short stories, poems, translations, essays and art by both emerging and established writers and artists. We rely on the support of the Friends of the *CQR*; between us it is a labor of love for the printed word, keeping this tradition alive and well.

Enjoy.

THE WORLD LEFT BEHIND
Paul Skenazy

"I am preoccupied with feelings and longings."

"Somewhere in my Jewish and immigrant blood there were conspicuous traces of a doubt as to whether I had the right to practice the writer's trade."

"It was up to me to find ways to reconcile the Trojan War with Prohibition, major-league baseball, and the Old Country as my mother remembered it."

Saul Bellow

I first met Saul Bellow on a dormitory wall. Pierce Hall, 55th Street, University of Chicago, September 1962. I was eighteen, child of Jewish working-class parents who finished high school in the 1930s and went to work to support themselves and their families. Mom was a secretary until I was born and again after I started high school. Dad worked for his uncle as what was called an "installment dealer": he sold goods to poor immigrant families like his own, mostly Spanish-speaking like his own, then collected a dollar or two a week, on installments, driving all over the city to their fourth and fifth floor apartments to collect his payments, perhaps sell them more merchandise. When I learned to drive, I started working part of his route on Saturdays, and continued to go home periodically all through college to help when he needed me.

Dad and the other installment dealers–there were more than a hundred that I can remember, working out of stores along Roosevelt Road before the businesses there were torn down to make way for the University of Illinois Chicago campus–were like human credit cards, I would explain to friends in later years when I talked about his work. Which I never did at college, embarrassed by my background among over-educated university students from professional families. I had one cousin who went to teacher's school; otherwise I was the first in my extended family to study beyond high school. The University of Chicago was a stretch for my folks; they were hoping for a local school that would let me live at home. They couldn't see the reason to spend so much. When a scholarship came through for a third of the expense, they were willing to let me try it for a year. I covered another third of the costs by working all four years (renting and delivering TVs at night in a hospital; recording data from stress experiments for a psychologist) and every summer (supplying transistors on an assembly line; stacking metal Christmas trees in a warehouse). My confused but loving parents scrambled to find the money to handle the rest.

* * *

Pierce Hall had just been built; we were the first class to occupy rooms. I wandered down the corridor to meet other freshmen, walked into Greg Bellow's room, introduced myself. Above his bed on the right side of the room he had already put up a plaque: The National Book Award for 1954, awarded to Saul Bellow for *The Adventures of Augie March.* I didn't know who Saul Bellow was, what *The Adventures of Augie March* was, what a National Book Award was. It was a prize Greg's father won, as a writer, for a novel he wrote, Greg explained.

When I was in sixth grade I won a free dinner for my dad and me for writing an essay about my father. I was part of our school quiz team that won a few rounds of a city contest on the local radio station. I went to a technical high school because I wanted to be an engineer and wrote a poem that was printed in the dance card for our senior prom. (By the time I started college my ambitions had changed: I had given up on engineering and wanted to be a psychiatrist, though I had no idea what either of those careers involved. A man who led our local Jewish youth group had training in psychology; the time I spent learning from him, at the synagogue, was my first separation from family. That was enough to help me create a new ambition for myself.)

We didn't have many books at home. I remember a complete Shakespeare my parents bought off a remainders table, a book of street maps of Chicago, a set of prayer books for the Sephardic Jewish temple that we attended, and the popular novels my parents read before bed. I don't remember being read to as a child, nor does my sister. Mom and Dad both read the morning and evening newspapers, the *Sun-Times* and *Daily News,* cover to cover. My mother read magazines and best sellers she took out of the library, which adorned the glass-covered top of the dresser that served as her nightstand. My dad read detective novels: paperbacks with lurid covers promising violence, sex, mayhem. He kept one flattened, open to his place, rubber-banded to the sun visor in his car and would pull it out during the day when he had to wait for a customer. He kept more buried in the bottom drawer of the dresser on his side of the bed under his socks and underwear, a private stash. When I was alone in the house I would sneak into their bedroom and pull out book after book looking for sex scenes, descriptions of voluptuous women, whatever titillation I might find. They were my introduction to literature, along with the *Black Stallion* novels my friend Mike Hoffman introduced me to.

But this notion Greg introduced me to, of a father who wrote novels and won awards, was a foreign country. So was the university. Before classes started all entering students took ten exams in math, writing, chemistry, physics, history and art to determine our background knowledge. Based on our scores we could place out of up to eight of the required courses for the two year general education curriculum. The assumption was that people accepted to the University of Chicago would already know enough to place out of three to five of the classes, allowing them to begin their major concentrations during those first two years. Though an all-A high school student at what was considered one of the better Chicago public schools, I failed all ten exams, while other students on my dorm floor were passing out of five, six, eight classes. (One guy who went to Eastern private schools became famous for placing out of all ten exams. There was some odd satisfaction in the fact that he left before the first quarter was over, victim of too much alcohol, not enough interest in his studies.) Our first essay in an introductory Humanities course required us to travel downtown to the Art Institute, look at an El Greco painting ("The Assumption of the Virgin"), and write about it. I did, in the flowery, purple prose that had worked in high school. The paper came back with a "C" on it and "Bull Shit" scrawled in the margins of every page.

I don't remember ever opening my mouth in class that whole first year. But I do remember only a few weeks into that same Humanities intro reading Faulkner's *The Sound and the Fury.* Somehow it made sense to me, I could figure out the shifts in time, in voice, in story. I could write about it. The teacher who dismissed my art criticism liked the paper; he would become a mentor. In my second year another teacher approached me:

"Why don't you ever say anything in class when you write so well, and obviously think about books so well?"

"I find it easier talking to my typewriter than to people," I told him.

"Well, so do I," he answered, "but look at me, standing in front of your class, talking all the time. Try it."

I think I smiled, turned my head down, as was my way then, blushed, as was also my way. But I started to talk. I would become a literature major, I would go on to graduate school and spend more than thirty years as a literature teacher.

Bellow was the one who helped me turn my face homeward, inward, outward to the world of books, all at once. Sometime that first winter, 1963, I found a copy of *Henderson the Rain King* on a remainder table in the college bookstore; because of the plaque on Greg's wall, I bought it. It would take me until that summer to actually sit down and read it. I learned that Bellow himself was teaching at the University; he'd accepted a position on the Committee of Social Thought that fall. But I couldn't take his classes and had no contact with him.

Still, by the time *Herzog* was published in 1964, when I was a Junior, I had devoured all his earlier novels: *Dangling Man, The Victim, Augie March, Henderson*, the stories collected in *Seize the Day*. Bellow not only was a Jew, he was a thinking Jew. He helped me discover the world of books, culture, and the arts. But he also helped me look back to where I came from: back to my working-class dad driving all over Chicago; to his work that shamed me; to his sisters who spent years selling perfume and jewelry and women's clothes behind the counters at Mandel Brothers and lived at their parents' home with their husbands long after they married. Back to their husbands, my uncles, installment dealers all, loud-talking bossy men all, who showed affection with a painful pinch on the cheek, a hand slammed on the back, an extra piece of salami they threw at you while cutting some up for a sandwich.

Herzog was the book I, unknowingly, longed for: an intense mixture of unkempt desires and philosophical speculation; of misdirected passions and self-destructive impulses; of deep thoughts and a heartfelt recognition that no ideas–however lofty, however wise–were going to bring contentment. The touch of self-deception and venom that I noted years later rereading were lost to me then next to the vision of this schlemiel from Chicago, witty and charming and lost, who could stumble and fall and come out the other end, at peace with himself. *Herzog* was sacred script those years when I was filled to overflowing with my high-minded university education, higher-minded political intentions, confusing physical longings; when I was in love and not with my college sweetheart and trying to decide what to do with all the parts of me that warred with each other. I wrote my senior thesis on Bellow's *Seize the Day* under the direction of the College Dean, Wayne Booth, a noted scholar and, it turned out, friend of Bellow's. The paper itself burned up years ago in a fire but I still have my copy of the novel from that year, with my round-lettered thoughts littering the margins.

If the university was a foreign country, Bellow was my translator. He spoke Chicago, a mix of heady sentiment and coarse skepticism that I didn't realize until then was the language of my past: of my dad, his buddy Dave who owned a dry cleaners, Dick who worked at a currency exchange, my Uncle Max who sold furniture. Of my Uncle Abe, the playboy bachelor who parlayed a life selling cameras into connections with the rich and famous; who came over to dinner Monday nights with stories of schmoozing with Jerry Lewis, Buddy Hackett, Sammy Davis Jr.

There's a moment in *Herzog* when Herzog tires of listening to someone's pomposity and mutters to himself, "Shame on you. Your father sold apples in the street." That unuttered rejoinder caught it–caught the edge that kept me honest, kept me me, kept me separate from that university world I came to love and distrust and live in my whole life. I didn't mention Bellow's name when I went back to my parents' home, didn't say much about my schooling until well after graduate school. The divide between home and university was nearly complete those college years. I grew up on the other end of the city–at 5700 North versus Pierce Hall on 55th St. South. To go 'home' to work for my dad or borrow the family car for a date, I got on the El at 55th, got off at Lawrence or Bryn Mawr, where Dad was waiting to pick me up. My parents were embarrassed by their lack of schooling; I didn't realize I needed to help them bridge the gap, explain it didn't matter. Because then, alas, it did matter, somehow, to me, seeking release from that world I would eventually come to miss and cherish. My folks seldom asked about my school life, I seldom volunteered information. But at some point Bellow's name did come up, one Sunday dinner over ribs and steak in the usual too-noisy restaurant. My dad and his buddy Dick told me they knew him a little when they were growing up. They didn't like him much. He was a little older. Stuck-up kid. Stunk at stickball.

But there it was again, this serendipity. Bellow was born in 1915, Dad 1918. Bellow went to the same schools as Dad and his gang. Like Bellow's father, my grandfather was itinerant: he repaired shoes for awhile, worked on an assembly line; then sold caramel, fudge and other candies on the street when he got too ill for the hard labor. That generation of Jewish immigrants worked their way up, made some money, and raised children who bought homes across the city, sent their kids to college; who counted happiness in cash, nice sports jackets, jewelry for their wives.

That plaque on Greg's wall was the beginning of what has been a lifelong one-sided friendship with Saul Bellow; an essential part of my lifelong life in literature. He got to me at the right time, in that first year of college when the world of books cascaded before a willing but unenlightened and naïve set of eyes. He was there in person, if distant, those years and that somehow mattered. He was a Jew. He was my friend Greg's father; Greg who soon coupled with JoAnn Henikoff, a girl I had a crush on in high school when we were both part of the same Jewish youth group and who eventually became Greg's wife.

* * *

If you lead a reader's life, as I have, you discover that certain books, and certain writers, and certain friends you talk to about those books and writers, are as intimate as lovers or family. They shape the contours of your mind, give it boundary and dimension, direction and substance. And intimacy involves change: shifts in perspective, fights and feuds, arguments, contested territories.

As a reader, and as a teacher, I eventually, sadly, parted company with Bellow awhile back, somewhere between *The Dean's December* and the birth of my first son in 1983. For all the acclaim it garnered and awards it won, *Mr. Sammler's Planet* felt like invective to me. *Humboldt's Gift* was more inviting, but baggy, old-fashioned, cloaked gossip more than fiction. In the late 1980s came the series of novellas, Bellow the ventriloquist back at his business, talking his way through despair. But the books seemed slim in intention, range, story. By the time Bellow collected his essays in *It All Adds Up* (1994), including many of the public statements that accompanied Bellow's fame after he won the Nobel Prize (1976), I dismissed him as a rearguard prose-lytizer. I blinded myself to the way that Bellow had broken ground, in our national literary life as well as my own biography; let myself cozy up to a portrait of him as the keeper of the gates. I dismissed him, or so I thought. I was looking for younger, more radical, inclusive, multi-cultural accents. Feminism made me suspicious of his manhandling of the women in his novels–made me unforgiving of my own lecherous pleasure in peeking in on Ramona in *Herzog,* for example. PC concerns about colonialism and cooptation kept me from rereading *Henderson the Rain King.* I taught *Herzog* sometimes, worked with graduate students over *Seize the Day,* which I find a more abundant book than Bellow himself or others do. I was writing about detective novels, he was arguing from Tolstoy; I was working with the writings of women of color and he was reminding us that there were no great Zulu classics in a statement that has long been misunderstood but remains a thorn in the side of his reputation for openhearted attention to the possibilities of literature.

But hard as I tried I couldn't get rid of him. I loved Bellow, it seemed, in that way I loved my annoying relatives–my misanthropic cousin, my penny-pinching uncle. In the same way I slowly realized I was, proudly if also sheepishly, a son of working-class Jewish parents from the Midwest; realized I shared that viewpoint on the world even as I tried on others. I gradually understood that there would always be something compelling about Bellow, however much we parted ways politically or culturally. His rants, his voices, his characters; the rush of language rash and undigested; the cacophony; the mass of material life he collected in every paragraph: these outlasted my intellectual hemmings and hawings.

Then came a piece Philip Roth published in *The New Yorker* in 2005. Roth quoted comments from Bellow about his early years as a writer. At the very end comes this reminiscence from the 1950s, working on *Henderson the Rain King:*

> Those years were the grimmest years of my life. My father had died, a nephew in the Army had committed suicide. My wife had left me, depriving me also of my infant son. I had sunk my small legacy into a collapsing Hudson River mansion. For the tenth time I went back to page 1, beginning yet another version of "Henderson."

That tenth time, that 'another version,' that process of sinking misery into beginning again: it's the image of a man and writer who has moved very far from his initial sense of himself as an outsider I quote at the beginning of this essay. Moved to a realization that writing is his soul, his entrance inside and out; to himself and to his culture. Maybe not salvation but as close as he, or most of us, can come to knowing salvation; what he can return to amid collapse. Bellow was there again, as he always had been, read or ignored: reminding me, teaching me, extending me.

I kept in touch with Greg over the years, but I only met Saul Bellow in person once. Late in his life, in the 1980s, he published his series of brief novellas. I was reviewing fiction for the *San Francisco Chronicle* and got the chance to interview him on one of his book tours.

We met in his hotel lobby, sat beside each other on an uncomfortable couch amid the noise. He was nattily dressed in a handsome grayish suit, brightly colored tie knotted tight over a fine yellow cotton shirt. He was all smiles when I introduced myself, explained my connection with Greg and JoAnn and my years of admiration for his work.

He was an easy interview, and a flat one. I felt from the first that I was being played with by someone so secure in this kind of situation he didn't even need to memorize his lines anymore. I asked questions, he answered, his phrases crafted by years of experience. Until one moment near the end, when I actually sensed him listening to himself with pleasure, or surprise, as if he perhaps was saying something he hadn't said a hundred or more times before; as if I actually was helping him think, as he had for all these years been helping me.

It started when I asked him about the endings of his books. I'd long loved the way Bellow moved through a final scene, the narrative strands left to drift off rather than bound together tightly, the reader released from the tensions of the story in a way that offered both lighthearted freedom and emotional charge. So I asked about the end of the novella in a way that made it clear I had read it carefully.

"Oh," he said, startled. "You finished the book. Most interviewers don't."

Yes, I said, going on to explain that what interested me was a cadence I responded to in the depth of me; a cadence I read for, and found, so often at the end of his fiction–a tamping down of emotions; a breath of quiet that led a reader out of skirmish.

He looked at me as if I had dug up some secret bone. For answer he described the ferries he once took from Chicago across Lake Michigan as a child. When the boats left, the seagulls followed in their wake, floating within the draft of the boat until it reached a certain distance from shore, when the birds turned back and the ship went on.

"That's what I am trying to get with the sentences," he said, "that quality of the birds' effortless flight, their wings extended on the air currents from the boat, that float and freedom."

"And that point when the air current ends, and there is a return to the world left behind?" I wondered.

"Yes, that too."

That too: the free ride out across the water, the work to return to shore. To the streets of Chicago: the city that made me; the city that Bellow revealed to me; the city we share. ☐

BLACK WAS MISSING
Don De Grazia

"I dreamed a dream that made me sad
Concerning myself and the first few friends I had."

And I was on the Belmont bus heading toward Lake Michigan. It was ten at night. I had taken an Adderall. I didn't take Adderall, but I had heard such amazing things that when this chatty blonde bartender offered me one, I decided to go home and experiment. It seemed like cheating, but I wasn't pure like that anymore, and now my brain was rotating gyroscopically in my skull; I was wired and at the same time deflated over the fact that Adderall wasn't really a magic inspiration pill but just the clenched-up clammy whirl of speed.

I had been sitting at my desk when Rocha called me, all worried about Black. It creeped me out a little, to hear the cloying vulnerability in his voice. It made me wonder about him and Black. When they got all fucked up, did they…my mind's eye went to static when I began to picture it. They were both pushing forty and out of shape; tall, spindly, beer-gutted, and ugly. But maybe I'm trying to make it seem like their unattractiveness was what sent a shiver through me, when it was primarily the idea of them doing something gay together. Then again, I got the same feeling when I was a little kid, on the two or three occasions I saw my parents kiss, so. Anyway, Black and Rocha were both lonely and hopelessly fucked up sensualists and I don't think it was that crazy of me to wonder.

I stood like a twitchy, overzealous doorman at the front of the bus and gripped a silver pole, lost in a reverie about Black's smarmy face—of my fist hammering down on the spot where his glasses rested on the bridge of his prominent nose. "Prominent nose?" Did I just say that? Oh, boy. It was a boorishly giant *schnozz* that said everything there was to say about Black. His nose and glasses made him look like he was wearing a nose-and-glasses disguise. Back when we lived together, there was a TV commercial for some nasal decongestant that featured a guy who, instead of a head, just had a gigantic nose. Whenever it played and we were lazing around on the ratty living room couches, I'd go, in a mocking, mentally challenged voice:

"Blaaaaaaaaaaaaaaaaaaaaaaaaaaaa—aaaaaaaaaaaaaaack... kk-kk-unghhhhh!"

It was pretty hilarious, let me tell you. He got me just as good plenty of times, don't worry. Strange relationship we had. He was part of that first group of Loyola kids I moved in with, and I immediately hated him, but every year, when our lease was up or we got kicked out of a place for throwing parties and pulling pranks and such, a few of us would move to some new shithole apartment together, and Black was always part of the group. He was an English Lit major, and I was gonna be the next Bukowski (only way better, of course) so I guess it was inevitable we'd butt heads, and we did, often, him absolutely insufferable and delivering platitudes like they were drops of glistening truth on the inescapable web of argumentative brilliance he had just woven—between massive hits of skunk he had just pulled from the three-foot Graffix bong which stood perpetual guard on the execrable coffee table, adorned with old English decal lettering Rocha had used to spell out: "Li'l Chernobyl." And me, red-faced and belligerent, probably well into my third forty-ouncer of Big Bear Malt Liquor, saying things like:

"Sorry I don't have the *magic decoder ring* that makes *Ulysses* good! Guess I should pay forty grand so a bunch of Loyola professors can tell me what I should *like*."

And him smiling with a superiority that had never known doubt (it was, in fact, the smile of a professor's son) and looking all the way down that nose. At me.

I jumped off the bus at Sheridan and saw a cabbie looking at me like *come on man, times a-wastin'!* and the speed in my brain had me feeling like I was in an action-adventure film, so I ran to him and then I was heading south on Lake Shore Drive and thinking the exact same thing I always thought as the coast of Lake Michigan slid by: "Every year, I resolve to spend more time taking advantage of the city's wonderful lakefront, yet here it is, the end of another summer, and I haven't been there once..." But the regret quickly passed. What was there to do there, anyway? It was a giant bowl of toxic soup. Plus, now an invasion of primordially hideous Asian Snakehead "Fishzillas" was supposedly threatening to devour what ecosystem still existed. No way was I getting in that water. And I didn't see the value of just sitting around staring at shit. Black disagreed. He valued "beauty" more than I did, but

I always thought it was kind of part of his English-Major-with-a-specialty-in-Elizabethan-poetry pose. In looking back at it, though, I think he actually found the contemplation of nature a genuinely useful excuse to get high. In my mind, you'd have to be stoned to find a jagged shoreline made of giant concrete blocks, and the long, blue vein that outlined the lake's horizon interesting for more than a few seconds. When it stormed, though, and wild iron waves whipped up and smashed into each other and took crazy fraying leaps over the shoreline, I'd secretly admit, he was right, it was beautiful. But only for an instant, in passing, framed by car glass and you safe and warm and dry.

The crazy thing about Black and me is that we ended up living with each other in all those apartments for eight straight years. And we hated each other even more by the end than when we first met. Like, he would say he wasn't going to pay one quarter of our phone bill because of my 411 Information calls, and I'd be like, all right, motherfucker, but you're the one with the fucking air conditioner hanging out your window and the goddamn towel under your door so as to not let us enjoy any of your refrigerated air, so here's one dollar for the electric bill. That kind of stuff. We finally split up. When we rented a truck to move our things to separate places, he wasn't wearing his glasses and he tried to re-park the U-Haul after I had opened the back door up, and the only piece of real furniture I owned—a six drawer cedar dresser I had stolen from one of our previous apartments—fell off the back and crashed to the street. As I contemplated its cracked frame, Black backed the truck up and crushed the dresser beyond repair. We had a screaming match and didn't speak for a year.

But, eventually, we started crossing paths, and we were actually glad to see each other, for some reason, and then he got a job bartending at a little bistro called The Compass Lounge, over on Clark, and I'd stop in to see him and the owner was a smarmy, poodle-haired, 80s-looking, trust fund jagoff, so Black had no qualms about pouring me out glass after glass of hundred-dollar-a-bottle Cabs and Red Zins. The place instantly became my new local, and we started hanging out some. The funny thing was, now he was all into Bukowski and kind of trying to live that bohemian life, whereas I had renounced him. I was going to be the next Camus, now. Black was shooting avant-garde guerrilla film shorts, and living in a dark, Wrigleyville basement studio crammed from floor to ridiculously low ceiling with second-hand editing equipment. We became pretty good friends.

But then one night I went into The Compass Lounge with a girl and we got fucked up on all that good red wine after hours and when I went to take a piss, Black apparently made some snide comment to her hinting that I was an unfaithful asshound, which was, perhaps, the truest insinuation ever made, but it caused me a great deal of trouble, and I was furious. He was dead to me. Again.

* * *

My cab got to the entrance at North Avenue Beach, just as Rocha came riding up on his mountain bike, wearing his eternal outfit of Buddy Holly glasses and Docs and Dickies, with a chain on his wallet, and then I remembered that I had gone to a street festival with him a couple weeks before, where we ran into Black, and everything was cool. So, we had actually stopped being enemies. Again.

As we walked toward the parking lot, Rocha filled me in. Black and Rocha and a bunch of other idiots made plans to go to the Santana concert on Friday, but Black never showed up. On the Wednesday before that, Black mentioned to Rocha that he was taking his inflatable kayak out on the lake. That was his thing now—getting all fucked up and paddling out there and floating around while the fireworks blossomed above Navy Pier and showered down over him.

"I think he might be dead, dude," Rocha said, and it struck me as melodramatic and childish for some reason. Black was not fucking dead, and I was about to say as much when we came upon his old blue beater Camry, sitting there in the empty parking lot cold and lifeless and festooned with a veritable headdress of bright orange parking tickets.

* * *

We badgered the maintenance man to let us into his apartment the next morning, and found the Santana ticket on his desk, next to a small bag of shrooms. Rocha called the police. Then he phoned Black's parents back in Des Moines and they weren't too worried, but the next day something changed and they said they were going to hire a detective. Then Rocha got a call from the cops—they'd pulled a body out of the lake and would we come down to Belmont and Western and identify it?

I hopped in a cab and met Rocha in the parking lot and isn't it weird how people get during stuff like that? I think we were a little excited. A black woman in a patrolman's outfit brought us to a dreary little office and a tired looking, red-faced police detective came in and handed us a manila file folder and then the big moment was at hand: We held our breath as Rocha opened the folder. There was a Polaroid photo inside of a corpse's swollen face.

"Did… Black grow a mustache?" I finally asked.

"No…" Rocha said, and then asked, with what sounded like a small laugh, "Could that be him?"

"I don't know."

"That's not him."

It was some other guy. The next day the detective that Black's family had hired called and said the cops had found another body. He picked us up and we drove to the morgue on the South Side. He was a retired Chicago cop, with a gray, slack face and a big gut that strained the fabric of his buttoned sport coat.

"Did he have a girlfriend?" the detective asked us.

"No, she cheated on him and they broke up a few months ago. He was dating a young girl," Rocha said.

"Mmf. *Young* girls," the detective said. He looked through his windshield, and scowled, apparently recalling his own personal young girl apocalypse.

They showed us via video camera. Black lay on a table, naked and horribly bloated and decaying. Giant flaps of skin were starting to peel up off what we could see of his torso. It didn't look like the real Black, it looked like some Macy's parade inflatable caricature. But it was him.

The detective walked to his car and called Black's parents from his cell phone, and Rocha turned his sinewy back to me and started calling our friends. I walked behind a stucco-surfaced pillar and wept for about ten seconds, and then stopped. I wasn't sure if the tears were genuine. I felt like a device with faulty electrical wiring. I wiped away the tears and walked over to Rocha.

"Fucking answering machine," he said. "I don't know what to say."

"Say: 'One of those Fishzillas got Black, and we all need to meet at a bar. Tonight. To plot our revenge.'"

* * *

Back in the 90s, when I was down on my luck but reluctant to sell out and get a straight job, my stomach and my landlord conspired to remind me that, genuine artist or not, I needed cash. So I took a job working at my uncle's private detective agency. My uncle had been a bookmaker for The Outfit, and when he saw the money that PIs were making tracking down deadbeats, he made a career switch—right as the first tremors of the housing market collapse began to register. Before you knew it, he had the biggest agency in the Midwest.

The job consisted mostly of wearing out shoe leather all over the broken and battered West and South Sides of Chicago, slinging paper. Foreclosure, Divorce, Summons. I was The Grim Reaper's *non-mac-*

tabilis little brother, and I soon realized the job was actually *costing* me money, seeing how it drove me to leave prodigious amounts of cash at every North Side dive bar I was still allowed in. I told my uncle I wanted to work on a *real* case, so one day he took me out with him to the seedy old Motel Row on Lincoln Avenue, where the standard rate for beds was still hourly.

We pulled over and parked beneath The Spa's decrepit and psychotic burned out neon sign, which promised Free TV and something else six decades of Chicago winters and air pollution had rendered a mystery. It wasn't a motel, it was a depravity bazaar, and a year later the place was demolished by a decree from Richard II, and a cop shop built in its place. The history of Chicago, in one sentence.

The building manager greeted us in the lobby in exactly the manner you would expect from a former officer in Saddam Hussein's Republican Guard—solemn, canny, and heavily mustached. My uncle had dealt with this guy before. Plenty of times.

"How ya doin', Adib? Man... how long you been working here now?"

Adib shrugged, slightly.

"A long time, Meester Swanson."

"I'll bet you got some stories, hunh?"

Adib shrugged again and said: "It is a motel. It is not a church."

He led us up a flight of revoltingly carpeted stairs to room 209, our client's previous address before he was relocated to the Cook County Jail. He was a Mexican and had been dealing pot out of that room for about a year, but then he missed a payoff or got cut out by a rival, and the cops kicked his door in without a warrant and dragged him off to a minimum ten years in the big house. It struck me as so cruel and extreme that just thinking about it stung my face. Like the way it feels when the wind is blowing off the Lake in January and it's sleeting out and you forgot to wear your hat and suddenly you realize you're a long way from home and on top of it all, you're out of smokes.

"No, no," Adib was saying to my uncle. "No one could kick this door in, it is very solid. See?"

The fact that he actually tapped on it was what convinced me he was a liar. My uncle began asking Adib what he knew about our client, and while Adib made evasive answers, I tapped on the door myself. It was solid oak. I wandered down the hall and tapped the next door, and by comparison it seemed like balsa wood. I tried another door. And another. And it was clear—door 209 was a bad apple.

"You know something, Adib?" I said, walking right up between him and my uncle. "You're right, nobody could knock this door down.

I mean, I can pretty much run down this hallway just pounding my fist on each door as hard as I can…"

I pounded my fist on 209 and winced with pain. Then I trotted to the next door and there was a splintering of wood as I punched a hole in the outer panel. I calmly walked to the next door, punched a hole in it, then stared at my fist like I'd just discovered I had super powers. I crossed the hall to another door, drew back my fist, and looked at him.

"Care to reconsider your answer, Adib?" I asked. "There are an awful lot of doors in this place, and I've got all afternoon."

On the drive back to the office, I could tell my uncle was proud of me. Damned proud. But he masked it by pretending to be pissed off. "Godddammit," he said. "I never shoulda taken you out on this case! Your blood is still too hot! You seen too many goddamned movies! You don't 'crack the case' with one big clue! You nurture relationships! You make them *like* you. You keep them talking, and eventually they just *tell* you everything you want to know."

That story, of course, is total bullshit. It didn't really happen that way at all. Actually, that's not true. It happened pretty much exactly that way, except I didn't punch any holes in any doors. I had a plan, at one point, to write a hardboiled detective novel under an assumed name and make a million dollars to fund my career as a writer of fine literary fiction, and that seemed like a cool way to end that scene.

In reality, I just waited until we were back in my uncle's car and told him that the door had obviously been replaced. My uncle went back to the motel on another day and got Adib to spill the beans, and the Mexican was off the hook. This filled me with an enormous sense of pride and justification for my existence. I didn't work as a detective much longer—I started getting part-time teaching gigs at colleges, and it paid better. But I decided that I *would* have been an *exceptional* detective, if I'd stuck with it—that I had a real knack for gumshoeing. I'm telling you all of this to illustrate why and how I took it upon myself to prove that Black committed suicide. No one else thought it happened like that. They figured a speedboat hit him or something. But they couldn't do a legitimate autopsy after he'd been in the water that long, so it was officially a mystery.

I made a point to individually interrogate every single misfit bustout who showed up at that long-gone nameless dive on Buena the night we gathered to commiserate over Black's death, and continued my surreptitious sleuthing at his funeral in Des Moines. Here is a compilation of the key evidence I unearthed:

*Black had undoubtedly become a full-fledged alcoholic and weed-addict. By all accounts, in those final days, he was always drunk or high or both or asleep—the fate of many who work in the bar industry to support their artistic aspirations.

I worked in bars for years, before my heavy smoking and drinking and poor diet finally landed me in the emergency room with red spots covering my entire body and a 105 temperature that did not abate for two weeks. Before going to the hospital, I wandered into my dark living room to find Black sitting on a couch watching Twin Peaks. I sat down next to him for about half an hour, drenched with sweat, forehead aflame, and I remember nothing about the show other than the fact that watching it that night remains the single most unpleasant event of my life. Finally, I told Black a bit about my situation, and he suggested I take an ice bath. That didn't help. After two weeks in the hospital, I spent two more weeks sleeping in a tiny closet in my mother's Roger's Park apartment. She spoon-fed me yogurt and fresh squeezed juices until I was well enough to go outside and walk half a block. Then I took a cab back to my apartment. Black did not seem particularly moved by my story. But he did show a great deal of interest.

*While following the mythic blueprint for indie-film success, Black maxed out several credit cards to buy second-hand equipment to shoot a feature-length documentary about a wild-eyed, crazily bearded old beatnik photographer Black had decided was his spiritual mentor. The man was an ex-con who used his avocation primarily as a means to get barely legal runaways and poor little rich girls to disrobe for him. He ran an underground coffee shop in his Lincoln Park basement. After several years of filming, the photographer came to suspect that the story would not be shaped exactly to his liking, and he made veiled threats to Black via email and phone messages warning that if Black presented an unflattering portrait, he would be sorry. Black briefly mentioned the situation to me, and I told him to tell the guy to go fuck himself. Black was reluctant to do so and seemed to enter the type of spiritual paralysis some children fall into when a parent withholds approval.

*Black began to do strange things while drunk and in the presence of his co-worker and friend, a kind-hearted gay waiter. Two incidents stood out to the waiter. Once, after a drinking bout, they were watching an old Twilight Zone episode, where death is represented by a character's crossing of a river. The dead character is able to call out to the living. "If I called you from the other side," Black asked the waiter, "would you answer me?" On another occasion, Black sat on his couch, pulled out a big wad of cash—his tips for the night—and began to burn ten and twenty-dollar bills with his lighter, until only a pile of ashes remained.

*Black called Rocha one night and confessed to having sunk to an unprecedented and frightening depth of depression. He felt that he had almost no true friendships. Rocha brought me up, and Black said: "I've called him a few times now. He hasn't called me back. What kind of friendship is that?"

*Black's mother, the quintessential Des Moines housewife, was in love with proto-celeb-chef, Rick Bayless. Shortly before Black's disappearance, his parents came to Chicago to visit. They loved Black unconditionally, but they were worried about him. They had generously assisted his starving artist lifestyle for a long time now, but concluded that they weren't doing him any favors by enabling what was at core an unhealthy lifestyle. On their last night in Chicago, Black took them out to Frontera Grille.

Halfway through dinner, Black excused himself to go to the restroom. Black used this opportunity to slip into the Frontera kitchen. A few minutes later, Black's mother felt a tap on her shoulder, and turned around to see Bayless himself, smiling broadly. Black's mother was red-faced, flustered, and mute. After a long moment of stunned silence, she finally just said: "Whoa."

The next morning, before they left for the airport, Black asked his parents to walk over from their hotel to Oak Street Beach. Black met them there, and they said their goodbyes. "I just want you both to know that I love you very much," were the last words he ever told them. Face-to-face, that is. A few nights later, Black called his mother, and when he got her answering machine, he allowed about ten seconds of silence to tape, before saying: "Whoa," and hanging up.

* * *

I compiled entire notebooks (mostly pocket spiral) of that kind of evidence, but there isn't really any point in going on. I was just being thorough. Perhaps I just wanted to prove to myself that I really would have made a top-rate detective, I don't know. But I didn't care about changing anyone's mind, and I didn't need any more proof than the last time I saw Black to know. Running into him that night was the type of gift you sometimes get even when you don't deserve it, and it makes you re-consider concepts like the benign indifference of the universe. I agreed to go to a Lincoln Park street fair with a few friends and Rocha showed up and I drank Bud Light from plastic cups and smoked weed from Rocha's one-hitter. Rocha found a stolen Jewel grocery cart in an alley and began pushing it down the sidewalk, past the venerable, ivied brownstones, looking deep in thought until we got to the bar district on Armitage. He pulled the cart over in front of a 7-11 and I followed him inside and stared at a few, lonesome taquitos as they rotated on their silver rack and I felt sorry for them. Then, after a few minutes of this addled, misplaced emotionalism, I decided to eat them.

I walked out of the 7-11 with my greasy bag to see Rocha had emptied a case of beer cans into the shopping cart and was placing a bag of ice on top of them.

"ICE COLD TRAVELERS!" he began shouting at all the preppie passersby and then the Indian guy from 7-11 came running out of the shop frantically as I gnawed on a spicy chicken taquito.

"What's wrong?" I asked the Indian guy. He focused on me and then his eyes got big.

"Sir, you did not pay for your taquitos!"

"ICE COLD TRAVELERS, LADIES AND GENTLEMEN! Three

dollars for one, or two for five bucks."

A line was forming in front of his cart as I dug into my pocket for money.

"Sir! You cannot sell beer in front of my store!"

I examined a crumbled five dollar bill and then looked up and saw Black there on the corner, smiling like a father watching his sons kick ass on the football field. It probably brought him back to that summer when we were still just kids and made our living this way, selling beers at music festivals in Grant Park and the Sunday blues shows down on Maxwell Street. Rocha was just doing it to make a spectacle now, to draw attention to himself in an environment where he did not belong, which, more and more, was every environment. I gave the Indian man my money and Black and I followed Rocha down a side street as he sold his wares. Black kept looking at him and then at me, gesturing, as if to say: "Oh, man… isn't this wonderful?" And he was being so sincere that I couldn't help but like him very much right then, even though his behavior was puzzling me. He was glowing like the Buddha himself. He looked so genuinely unburdened and light and joyous. And he displayed such unaffected affection for Rocha and me. He kept looking at me, smiling, like he was about to say something. I began to fear he was going to bring up the whole thing with the pigeon again.

One night, in the winter before our last estrangement, Black and I had been bar hopping late at night in Lincoln Park and Old Town and smoking weed and snorting cocaine and walking down twisting little alleys of frozen cobblestone and we came upon a pigeon who was stuck up in some chicken wire above the doorway to a bank. The wire mesh had been strung up there to keep the pigeons away, but this one had been undaunted, and now the smartass was trapped and fluttering around frantically and Black couldn't stand it and neither could I.

"We've got to free him!" Black exclaimed, reading my mind.

"Yeah, man," I said, firmly, as if telling an audience of naysayers that they'd better not try and stand in our way. "We're not leaving here until he's free."

The pigeon's jail was about ten feet above the sidewalk. We tried to figure out ways to climb the polished marble wall, but finally I got down on all fours, bare hands on the ice cold sidewalk, and Black, all 220 pounds of him, stepped up on my back and stretched his 6'5 inch frame up toward the wire and the pigeon started going berserk, unaware of our benevolent intentions. The heels of Black's boots were gouging into my back muscles, and I was glad, because I wanted to suffer for this pigeon.

"Can you arch your back just a little bit more?" Black asked, panting heavily.

I did my best, but my body was shaking with cold and fatigue and I didn't know how much longer I could last.

"Just a…. Ahhhhh!" Black said before slipping and falling down—I absorbed the full force of his body and he crushed the breath out of me. It hurt. A lot. But he had hooked the wire with his fingers before he fell, and I saw the unmistakable off-white and gunmetal blur of escaped pigeon. Black broke into exuberant laughter and I huffed like an asthmatic on the concrete, but when I could breathe again, I began to laugh, too.

"We freed him!" Black kept exclaiming, like the drunken, stoned goon he was, and I kept saying, "Right, man! Fuckin' A right we did!" and we embraced and laughed, like noble victors.

Sober, the memory made me cringe. But whenever I went out drinking with Black, and he reached a certain level of fuckedupedness, he would invariably lean over to me, with a significant look, and say, in confidence:

"Remember when we freed that pigeon, man?" And I'd say, "Yeah. Yep. I remember." The thing was, Black was such a cynical know-it-all that I felt he should have been able to see the hackneyed quality of his attempts to affix some sort of beauty to the freeing of that pigeon. To me, it was just another story about two drunks being cornballs.

He must have sensed how I felt, because he didn't bring it up that last night I saw him. He just kept telling me with that smile *I love you, friend, so much, and I can not begin to describe how happy it makes me to bear you no ill will.*

Not even for that. □

IT HURTS
Natalia Nebel

C hris was working at an ad agency over the summer; it was just the sort of appalling job an appalling person like Chris would take, I thought. I saw Chris mornings, when I ate my cereal. He'd run through our communal kitchen, always doing something with his hands like smoothing down a loud tie in a collection of loud ties he had, or brushing his short hair into place, and a feeling of repulsion combined with repulsion would come over me as he ran out the door.

Chris and I were among nine college students spending the summer in an old sorority house. For two hundred dollars a month you got use of the kitchen, a bedroom, bathroom, and a telephone in the hallway which refused to make out going calls. The phone was on the wall near my room and across from Chris', and from overhearing his conversations I gathered certain things about him — he was loud, he was self-confident, he was persuasive in a sick sort of way; also, he was cheating on his girlfriend. I knew this because he took two phone calls every night at around eight o'clock. To the first woman he always said, "Goodbye. Yes, I love you. Sweet dreams." To the second woman he said, not nearly as loudly, "I'll be over in fifteen minutes."

Chris was good looking in an all American way, he knew it, and he apparently got away with murder because of it. I'm sure I would have hated him, regardless.

The morning of my internship search, Chris ran through the kitchen smirking and tucking a turquoise blue shirt into a pair of perfectly faded jeans.

"Ciao," he said, without looking in my direction. The door slammed shut behind him before I could say ciao back.

I was anxious because I was eating cereal with milk that had gone past its expiration date, and of course there was my internship to worry about too, but seeing Chris, oddly enough, made me feel better, put things into perspective, as they say, for I couldn't help thinking, whatever happened, at least I was not Chris. At least I was not going out in the world and selling sugar coated cereal to children. Or third rate vacation spots. Or kitty litter. I was going to find work with a nonprofit organization, in the art world probably, to the general benefit of people besides myself. The more I considered it the better I felt, I even forgot about the milk's expiration date, and when I left the house that morning to meet my college's internship coordinator, I felt good; up and down and all-the-way-through good.

* * *

It was a small, unpromising room Ms. Darre showed me to; it was a small, unpromising file Ms. Darre handed me: Internship Opportunities, Humanities. Ms. Darre said, "I'll be back in a bit," and smiled distantly, then left the room. I watched her go; she was young to be so middle aged, I decided. If she got rid of her polyester shirt and took her skirt up above the knee, it would have made a huge difference; who knew how her life might change?

Ms. Darre gone, I didn't open my file right away, thinking what a pity it was Ms. Darre's youth and looks were wasted, and only gradually did I notice that there was something missing in that building—activity. I listened more carefully—not a sound. It seemed to me a summer jobs room, even at a small liberal arts college in St. Paul, Minnesota, should be more bustling, shouldn't feel deserted or worse, abandoned. Already I'd been shocked that morning to learn you actually had to interview for an internship; I'd been under the impression they were given to you automatically, part of the twelve thousand dollar a year package, so to speak. As I became aware of the complete quiet of the building, I also noticed that my file was rather light. This was the summer of 1981, and if I'd paid attention to the news I would have known there was a recession going on, and the situation would have made some sense to me. Although I didn't pay attention to the news, I did know who our President was, and to my credit, to my very great credit, I felt, I had voted against him. This single vote of mine, in fact, was what made me confident in my social conscious; it was why I was opening a slim file labeled, Humanities.

I counted seven worn sheets of paper in the file. The first three organizations needed Art History majors—if only I'd majored in Art History instead of English, I thought, depression and regret coming over me. I turned to the fourth page. Wanted: Editorial Assistant. Good typist ... I didn't have to read further. Three pages left. I slowed down. Teaching Assistant. If only I liked children! Again a depression came over me. I hated the way children stared at you and asked you rude questions, besides which, their energy seemed borderline pathological to me. Two sheets left. Editorial Assistant, experienced in ... But I'd no experience in anything except working in my father's law firm for my father, compiling all the possible versions of an arcane tax law, and doing an enormous amount of xeroxing. I hadn't even had steady baby-sitting jobs, and I couldn't swim so I'd never been a life guard like the other half of my friends. To realize that people had experience in things other than baby-sitting and life guarding was, in fact, my second shock that morning. There was only one page left, I had to turn to it and I did so, reluctantly. It read: seeking dedicated writer to help with biannual newspaper which addresses the needs and concerns of homeless people. We are a local community organization ... looking for someone who cares...

That was me! I hadn't voted for Reagan, I hadn't dreamt of voting for Reagan, and I was a writer and English major, obviously I hadn't given my own welfare top priority when choosing what to study. I scanned the job requirements. No experience necessary.

Ms. Darre entered the room. I realize now she must have known exactly how long it took to read those seven pages.

"Anything?" she asked. Her smile didn't connect with her eyes, and I think that was one of the reasons she alienated me, besides her clothes and, in all honesty, the questions she had asked me that morning: "Any extracurricular activities? You haven't worked for the literary magazine here? Hmm."

"Yes," I said. "I found something."

* * *

"You're dressed up," Chris said. He'd stopped his morning dash midway through the kitchen and was standing in front of the stainless steel refrigerator doors, his back to me, squinting at his reflection while trying to tie a knot properly. He had a nice back, actually, broad shouldered and slim at the waist.

"Where did you get all the ties you have?" I said. "Did you go to an auction or something?"

He stopped tying his tie, I could see his hands arrested near his collar. "Ha ha, very funny," he said, and then began fiddling with his tie again.

"I'm serious. Did you go out and buy them all at once or did someone buy them for you or what?" My obnoxiousness at the time didn't surprise me.

Chris was having problems with his tie and, at my last question, in fact, he yanked it from around his neck and turned to face me.

"What's wrong with my ties?"

"Nothing," I said. "I was making a joke. I didn't know you were sensitive."

"I didn't get them at an auction."

"Fine," I said.

"What are you all dressed up for, anyway? Job interview?" He spoke sarcastically, as though an interview was improbable, but I pretended not to notice.

"Yes, as a matter of fact. With a newspaper for homeless people."

"Oh. Well. Isn't that nice. Florence Nightingale herself." Then he stuffed his tie into his perfectly faded blue jeans' pocket, and rushed out the door.

* * *

I entered a navy blue room that was empty except for three plastic chairs; they were remodeling their offices, and they hadn't yet moved the furniture back. In retrospect, I wonder, if there had been anything besides those three plastic chairs in the room, and if it hadn't smelled intensely like cheap carpeting, I wonder whether I would have felt differently about the organization, and in that case, perhaps I wouldn't have done what I did. I'll never know. I was directed to one chair, Mr. Mack sat in another, and John, he preferred to be called John, sat in the remaining one.

Mr. Mac was obese, while John was painfully thin, a thinness emphasized by his almost waist length beard, his long thin hands, and the long thin seeing stick he propped next to him; he was legally blind. John sat down, folded his long fingers together on his lap, smiled at me encouragingly, and the depression and regret which had come over me while I looked through the Humanities file swept over me again, but more forcefully.

Mr. Mac said, "I know John and I make a funny pair, but we've been together for a long time now."

"How long?" I asked.

"Almost fifteen years," he said.

"Wow," I answered. I actually said wow during the interview.

Again, maybe things would have been different if Mr. Mac hadn't been a chain smoker. I would have listened to what he said, and then I'd have left the interview with some idea of what they wanted me to do. As it was, Mr. Mac took a cigarette from his inside jacket pocket, (he was wearing a three piece suit), lit the cigarette, breathed in deeply, and I began obsessing. He is obese and he smokes! I obsessed. He's a coronary disaster! He won't have a chance when the heart attack comes, it's going to be total heart failure it's going to be fast and it's going to be soon! Mr. Mac lit one cigarette after another while he spoke, dropping them when he was done in an ashtray next to his feet so that smoke began rising up all around him, something like incense.

"We've made a lot of progress in the past five years, but our current President can only mean disaster for programs like ours. We feel..."

Doesn't he know? I wondered. Doesn't he realize? He's going to die. Not like everyone else, in the distant future, the fact is that every day is a miracle for this guy, he is a living, breathing miracle. Then he mentioned his two boys, and the picture I was forming of his story became complete and tragic—I could see a funeral, his crying wife, their poor wide eyed children and the casket. What would they do for money? Belatedly, I realized I couldn't breathe.

"Is there something in here, some smell, not the cigarette smoke but there seems to be something," I found myself saying, interrupting Mr. Mac.

"The new carpeting," John said. "It's making me a little nauseous too." He smiled the sweetest smile you could imagine towards me, and that's when I realized what depressed me—he was a naturally generous person, one sensed that immediately, while I was not. Mr. Mac got up, sighing deeply, opened the door, then stood in the doorway, arms crossed.

"If my cigarettes bothered you you should have said so. We're all friends here, we're family."

"Mac," John said, "she's not going to tell you that at an interview."

"You're from Winnetka," Mr. Mac said, ignoring John. He leaned back on the heels of his loafers. "That's one of the most exclusive neighborhoods in the country."

"Is it?" I said. I hoped that I sounded surprised.

"Rich people," Mr. Mack said, thoughtfully. "I met a woman from Winnetka on the train once. When she heard I was a social worker she told me she knew the Kennedys. How's that for a non-sequitur!"

"What do you write, mostly?" John asked me, proving right there what a decent person he was.

"Short stories."

"I write also. Country songs. I've sold two of them."

"That's fantastic," I said. "I wouldn't know where to begin."

"This job," Mr. Mac said, "will require someone who can write well and who is socially committed. We're looking for a self-starter. You'd be out on the streets, finding stories, talking to homeless people." He dug into his jacket pocket and pulled out his cigarettes, put one in his mouth and looked at me intently.

I swallowed hard and said, "Well, that would be me. I'm socially committed." And then for emphasis I added, "Very. Very."

Mr. Mack grinned, took the cigarette out of his mouth and said, "We like you, Stacey. Welcome aboard."

* * *

If I left the house at seven-thirty in the morning and came home at eleven at night, I could successfully avoid ever talking to Mr. Mac again. My only tight moment was dinner time, when I had to go back to the house to eat; I couldn't afford to eat every meal at the Student Union. Otherwise, I could more or less live in the library, and I did, for five days. There, I began reading newspapers, dozens of them every morning. Our country was in much worse shape than I'd imagined, and yet the possibility of working for Mr. Mac in a job which would have addressed the problems I'd been reading about, filled me with panic. When I tried to picture myself out on the streets drumming up stories, the carpet smell of the interview room came back to me so intensely I became convinced I emanated it, and I had to go into the library's air conditioned reference room to breathe again.

On my sixth day of Mr. Mac avoidance, I went back to the house for dinner and then ran upstairs to grab a sweater as usual before going back to the library. I was ready to go when Chris knocked at my bedroom door and cleared his throat.

"Someone keeps calling for you. Something about the internship you're starting next week, they need to talk to you," he said, pushing open my bedroom door slightly so I could see half his face. "Could you call them back? I'm sick of answering the phone."

"Actually," I said, "if they call again, tell them I'm out of town."

"What?" Chris asked. And then, with a gleam in his eye: "You're going to blow off those homeless people?"

"I'm not blowing off homeless people. I just — it's hard to explain."

The phone rang.

"It's been ringing like this for two nights now," Chris said. "You really should talk to them, anyway."

"I'm not answering it," I said.

The phone continued ringing and I began counting ... four, five six ... I could tell Chris was counting too. The rings took up the entire hallway, as one faded another began. Surely they'd stop eventually! Chris raised at least the one eyebrow I could see, and then left my doorway. I could hear him answering the phone, hello? and then, "Yes, she's here. Just a moment. Stacey!"

The same physical things always happen to me when I go into shock. First, I freeze. Then, my heart begins pounding hard, and I find it difficult to breathe. Finally, maybe because I'm on the verge of a sort of auto-asphyxiation, I react and, because of my physical condition, invariably do the wrong thing. In this case I went out into the hallway and took the phone from Chris, without even the presence of mind to say something nasty to him. I put the phone up to my ear, knowing only that I was about to do something desperate.

"Stacey?"

"No," I said.

"This isn't Stacey?"

"This is her sister."

"This sounds an awful lot like Stacey."

"Naturally" I said, "we're sisters. Everyone gets us confused."

There was a pause, I thought I could hear Mr. Mac lighting a cigarette, and then he began explaining that he was under the impression that my sister was going to report for work next Monday. I had to tell him that my sister, unfortunately, had gone to Europe, there was a once in a lifetime opportunity for her there. Also, she was sick. She had never enjoyed the best of health since she'd had mononucleosis in high school. There seemed to be some sort of relapse and then there was this trip to Europe. Mr. Mac would have liked to talk more, but I said goodbye. Then I wiped the palms of my hands on my jeans, went to Chris' room and pushed his door open. He was lying in his bed, reading, or pretending to read, actually he was laughing quietly, and he burst into open laughter when he saw me.

"You had no business, no business at all making me answer that phone. Especially, especially! when you're cheating on your girlfriend," I said, trying to control my voice. Chris stopped laughing.

"What makes you think I'm cheating?" he asked.

I picked up an imaginary phone, put it up to my ear and said, "I love you. Sweet dreams." I then put the phone down, waited a second, picked it up again and said, "I'll be over in fifteen minutes."

"You don't understand," Chris said, looking back to his book which, I noticed, was upside down. I thought I saw a hint of blush under his tan.

"I understand very well," I said, and then, still trying to keep my voice calm, I said, "You're an asshole," and I left the room.

* * *

I imagined many things about myself when I was young, obviously, and

I also imagined many things about how adults conducted their lives. One of the things I believed was that when adults suffered deep humiliation they went out and bought liquor, then drank it, straight up, while listening to music or watching TV. Where I'd gotten this impression I'm not sure; my parents had a puritan hatred of any substance which bettered your mood even momentarily, and the people I knew who drank too much drank socially. But I was young and my ideas about what one did were vivid and fixed. So I walked six blocks to a liquor store, bought a six pack of beer, a bottle of wine and a pint of Southern Comfort because Southern Comfort is sweet and Janis Joplin used to drink it.

The guy behind the counter rang up my purchases and then, as he was putting everything in a bag, he said, "Party?"

"Yes," I lied, trying to smile as though I were looking forward to a party. It's come to this, I couldn't help thinking sadly as I went out the door with my package, I'm lying to check-out people even.

* * *

The phone rang just as I reached the top of the stairs. I put down my bag and ran, getting to it before Chris. I knew exactly who was going to be on the other end, and I knew exactly what I was going to say to her. I would tell the poor woman that Chris was out for the evening with someone else, he was never home after eight; the best thing she could do was get rid of him.

"Hello?" I said. My eyes met Chris'. He had rushed to a spot directly across from me. I held his pleading gaze and smiled what I considered a vindictive smile. And then, inexplicably, I said, "Yes, Chris is here, I'll call him."

He grabbed the phone from me before I could change my mind.

* * *

I went to our communal living area and turned on our ancient TV. I opened a beer, drank from it and became bored, something I thought inappropriate, so I opened the bottle of Southern Comfort and drank from it directly. It made me nauseous, and that seemed right. I considered calling one of two friends I had who was also spending the summer in St. Paul, then thought better of it; the whole point of the ritual was to be alone. I alternated between beer and Southern Comfort, and began watching a movie about an idealistic lawyer who defends a boy who has confessed to killing his mother—it was a blatantly coerced confession. Everyone in the movie was terribly dressed, and the boy played folk guitar songs badly. Still, I wanted to know who had really killed his mother, and I'm surprised I fell asleep watching the movie, especially because I had the idea that the movie's lawyer would be a good role model for me.

Chris woke me up.

"Stacey. Stacey."

When I realized it was Chris shaking me awake I sat up and pushed him away. He then sat down on the floor in front of me, cross legged.

"What the hell?" I said.

"You fell asleep here on the couch, watching TV. Stacey, this is the couch that was left outdoors all last summer. No one uses it."

Chris smelled like beer, cigarettes and something else I couldn't place. I had a fleeting image of my father in the kitchen opening some sort of can.

"What time is it?" I asked.

"It's late. Stacey," Chris said, "I have to talk to you. Thank you for not telling my girlfriend about, you know. I don't really love either of them. Things just take on a life of their own, you know?"

"No," I said.

"And I'm sorry about what I did," he continued, ignoring my answer. "I was just sick of answering the phone. You know how it is living near that damn phone. It just rings and rings."

"Chris, no offense, but you really smell."

"Oh my God!" Chris put his head in his hands and rocked forward, began laughing loudly, the way he had in his bedroom. "I forgot. I ate a can of sardines. Just half-an- hour ago I was in my car, eating sardines. The whole steering wheel is covered with oil. I'm lucky I got here alive."

"You ate the entire can? The tails and everything?"

"Yes, yes. I was so hungry." Chris stopped laughing and smelled his hands. "Oh my God," he said. And then he said, "I'm such an idiot. You hate me, you hate my ties."

Chris seemed genuinely upset, and for the first time since I'd known him, as I was looking at him sitting on the floor—drunk, apologetic, his hair sticking up around his head like he'd slept on it and his tee shirt untucked—it occurred to me that he was human, and that he was suffering. In my half sleep I decided I wanted to help him.

"Chris," I said. "You're cheating on two women, okay, that's despicable. But I just blew off a blind guy and a community of homeless people. These people have nothing, they don't even have a change of clothes. I pretended to be my sister to get out of it. I don't even have a sister. I don't see how you can talk to me seriously."

My voice actually broke at the end of my speech; I felt all the disappointment I'd tried not to feel that afternoon; I remembered my dumb panic when I picked up the phone.

"Stacey," Chris said. He uncrossed his legs with some difficulty and got to his knees, then took both my hands in his. "Stacey. You're a beautiful, very nice woman. It's just, you're middle class, you know? I went through this myself last year. Look, your dad's a lawyer, right?"

"Yeah."

"So the fact is, you're pretty much doomed. My dad's a lawyer too. We're just this way, is all."

"What way?" I asked. I wanted to know precisely what he meant. What way were we? If he could answer me I thought everything about my life might change. Chris paused, as though collecting his thoughts, opened his mouth, then closed it and shrugged.

"Just this way," he said simply. Then he smiled at me, his white teeth glowing in the dark, and he said, "We're made for each other, basically."

"That was cruel," I said.

"I know it hurts. The truth hurts. Then you live with it. I've thought everything out though. Listen. This agency I'm working for will hire me next year, I'm going to make partner there before I'm thirty, I'm sure. When I make partner we'll marry and we'll live happily—" He brought my hands to his mouth, kissed them, and then said, "I've got to rest for a second."

Saying this he leaned back, then lay down on the floor and fell into a dead sleep. Now I know this is typical of him. I stood up, went across the room to the couch people used, and lay down. I looked at Chris sleeping. Even with his mouth open there was something attractive about him, and he had a great back. He could buy new ties, I found myself thinking. Amazingly, that night, I fell asleep again without getting sick.

That summer I ended up taking a Creative Writing class instead of working. The woman who took the internship I refused worked for Mr. Mac and John beyond that summer, and today she runs an established community action group. Chris made partner at his agency before he turned twenty-eight, an unprecedented promotion, we married, and I teach a night class called "Journal Writing for Accountants." Chris and I have money, I can't deny that, but we do give a lot of it away to charity, because the fact remains, no matter what we are, we still wish the world a better place. ☐

DARES
Joe Meno

Dani dared Ben to hold his breath. They were in the front seat of Ben's father's station wagon—Ben, who, like everyone else their age, still lived at home, even though he was twenty-two—when Dani said she liked people who were willing to do dumb things for her. He grinned and said Okay and then held his breath for two and a half minutes before he began to cough, his face turning blue. Afterward, as a kind of consolation, Dani smiled, closed her dark green eyes, and placed her mouth against his. This was their second date and Ben was genuinely amazed when she climbed into the backseat and began to pull off her t-shirt. The t-shirt was yellow and said "Bummer" on it and Ben stared at it for a few moments, crumpled there on the carpeted floor, before pulling himself into the back of the car in an uncoordinated hurry.

* * *

Two days later they were at a convenience store when Ben dared Dani to steal something. After all, they were still kids; Ben had only recently finished his B.A. in communications—a degree his prudent father and safety-minded mother had mistakenly decided would be "useful one day," while Dani, an oldish twenty-one, was just beginning her masters in art therapy. It was a Tuesday and they were on their way to a movie and had stopped to get some candy because they could not afford it at the theater. Together, they stood, side by side beneath the fluorescent lights, neither of them amounting to much of anything.

Ben, for his part, had been overweight most of his life. Now he was in better shape but his head, his brown hair, his chest, all still seemed a little too big for his body. During the last few months his father had been trying to get Ben to join the aluminum siding business. He was thinking about becoming an elementary school gym teacher but had done nothing yet to explore this option. His face, at the moment, beheld its usual expression of monumental uncertainty.

Dani, on the other hand, smiled quizzically at her options. She had been Danielle until she had started college. Now her hair was long, dark blonde, and her limbs had become tawny. She had been shy in high school but was trying on the idea of being a libertine; everything was now some new form of amusement to her. Her face wore its typical bemused-looking smirk. Ben glanced over at her, saw her smile, saw all that it might imply, and then looked up at the foreign-looking clerk and whispered, "I dare you to steal something."

"What?" Dani asked, rolling her eyes. "That's totally stupid."

"Why? Come on, it'll be awesome."

"Are you serious?" she asked and a childish dimple appeared on her left cheek.

"Go on," he said. "You have to. You are under my command."

Dani made a decision to ignore the word "command" and all that it suggested. She had taken too many women-studies courses to do anything than to pretend it never happened. She looked up at Ben's goofy smile and rolled her eyes once more, then picked up a candy bar, and quietly slipped it into the back pocket of her jeans.

From her deliberate, quick, confident movements, Ben realized she had done this sort of thing before.

* * *

A week later Dani dared Ben to eat an entire lemon. It turned out he was willing to eat awful things for fun—garlic, uncooked hot dogs, packets of hot sauce. They parked Ben's dad's station wagon, ran into a half-price supermarket, spotted the most dazzling lemon they could find, then gave the elderly check-out clerk two quarters before hurrying back outside. The faces he made in the parking lot, the wincing, the drooling, the groans, Ben doubled over, foaming at the mouth, Dani's laughter as bright as the discarded rind. Though there was something about the other each found extremely attractive, there was also a slight repulsion—the fear of liking someone more than you ought to, more than they liked you—that expressed itself as an antsiness, a willingness to torture and be tortured, to tease and be teased.

* * *

Two days after that, they were eating at a fast food taco joint, when Ben asked Dani to take off her bra. Dani blinked at him with a half-frown, set her food down and then disappeared into the bathroom. When she came back, she picked up her burrito again and began eating. "Did you do it?" Ben whispered. Dani only nodded. "Well, where is it?" he asked. Dani glanced up and gave him a spooky look. "In my purse," is all she said. Ben turned and stared down at the purse for the rest of the meal, grinning dumbly.

* * *

A few days later they were in Dani's bedroom—lying in the same four-poster Dani had slept in since she was four, purple drawings and pictures of high school friends adorning the lilac walls—both of them in their underwear; Ben's smudgy white, Dani's a sleek gray. After some thoroughly decent making-out, after some sustained and prolonged petting, Dani dared Ben to shut his eyes.

"Why?" he asked.

"Because. Just because."

He could feel her hair hanging in his face and thought there was something pretty primeval about it, something he could have written a decent composition paper on back in college: something about the Cave of Man, etc. He shrugged and laid back and closed his eyes as tight as possible. Immediately, Dani put a pillow over his face. He thought he might black out and did not want to, as he knew that would probably ruin the moment and call his entire manliness in question, thereby putting the future of their relationship into some sort of peril. He definitely did not want to do that. Even though Dani worked at a corporate sandwich shop as an assistant manager during the day, she went to grad school at night. He felt he still needed to impress her. He tried to remain still as she roughly pulled off his briefs. For a few seconds, he waited for the touch of her hand, her mouth, her hair to fall across his bare stomach. But there was nothing, just the sound of the air-conditioning blowing on his limbs. After a couple of minutes, he sat up and saw she was gone. Protectively placing the pillow against his groin and midsection, Ben crept out into the hall. Dani's mother was a RN and worked days—but still. He slowly climbed down the carpeted stairway and found Dani sitting on the couch, watching TV, eating a bowl of cereal and laughing, still in her underwear.

* * *

All summer there were those kinds of moments, those sorts of provocations, childhood games with an air of adult menace, the distant circling of two people, inching closer and closer together. Finally, at the end of the summer, Ben dared Dani to cut his hair. She agreed with a shrug of her shoulders. He was sitting in his underwear, on top of the toilet seat, in her mother's pink and yellow bathroom. He did not feel self-conscious even though he did not look his best semi-naked or sitting down. With her characteristic concentration, Dani carefully snipped at the back of his neck with a pair of sewing shears. She was trimming the unruly hair above his ears when she suddenly said, in an almost off-handed way, "You know what? We should totally get married."

Ben's eyes went wide as he stared straight ahead, afraid to move an inch. "What? Are you serious?"

"I dunno. Why not? What's the worse that could happen?"

Ben's mouth dropped open. Dani still hadn't looked at him. She finished evening out the hair along his neck and then glanced up. The look on her face was more a dare than a question.

* * *

They told their parents and a few of their friends. Ben's father, happy to see his son take some—even a stumbling—step toward adulthood, sprang for the wedding, which took place on a weekday night at an out-of-date country club. After the brief, informal ceremony, Dani's mother kissed Ben on the side of his mouth and asked where they planned to live. The bride and groom both looked at each other and then shrugged. They were twenty-two and were now married. Theirs was a future where there was nothing else to fear.

* * *

Without ever really discussing it, they moved into Dani's mother's house. Dani's mother liked having a man around, or so she said. She began cooking the adventurous varieties of *Hamburger Helper.* Ben finally took the plunge and started selling aluminum siding with his dad. He went out and bought a tie and briefcase, both the same curious shade of brown. The briefcase remained empty, except for some old *Sports Illustrated*s Ben stole from a doctor's waiting room. Dani was pleased. A month after the wedding, she cashed in a savings bond and used some of her student loans to pay for a honeymoon: five days and nights in Costa Rica. It was a trip Dani had been planning for years, ever since a coworker at the corporate sandwich shop had gone backpacking through the rain forest and had come back with blurry snapshots of howler monkeys, of jellyfish, and three-toed sloths. Dani had always imagined going on a trip to some exotic location at the start of her adult life. Ben seemed excited. They looked at a few photographs online and then booked a trip for October.

* * *

October, it turned out, was not a good time to visit. Apparently October was the rainiest month of the year. Ben and Dani took a four-hour bus ride to the coast over roads that had never been paved, except for the ones owned by the United Fruit Company. They stared off into the Caribbean Sea, which was impenetrable, murky. It did not look like a snapshot, or a postcard; more like a place to dispose of some bodies. Everything was either black or gray. Dani gave Ben a frown. She was wearing a green t-shirt and a pair of green bikini bottoms. She was barefoot, her white legs puncturing the beach. Ben looked down. Their footprints—the shape of their toes and heels—somehow revealed exactly how young they both were.

"Now what?" Ben asked. Dani picked up a handful of seaweed and threw it at him. He frowned and picked the slime off his shirt. There was a whole conversation there, in that moment that went unsaid. Neither of them knew it was going to be the rainy season and so there was no one to blame but they ended up blaming each other anyway. Was this a sign of what was to come? Was this how it was going to be with them? Dani leaned over again and found a pink and white seashell, a conch, and held it up. She blew into it like a trumpet and then an enormous spider crawled out. She screamed and then tossed the shell back into the ocean. Ben bent over laughing. Dani turned and called Ben a fucker and then kicked sand at him. They had been married for five weeks now and apparently this was exactly what being married meant.

* * *

All Dani had wanted to do was to see a manta ray, which Costa Rica was famous for, or at least according to an internet post she had read. But apparently the manta rays were on the other side of the country, the Pacific. Still Dani did not give up. She decided they would go swimming with the turtles instead. They tried all the cafes and bodegas asking for a tour guide but all the palm-roof huts were unoccupied. Finally, they found a booth operated by a sixty-year old man named Mr. Big, whose leathery face looked like tree bark. As he talked—his syllables a jumble of Caribbean dialect and Spanish—there was a sudden flash of silver. They were surprised to discover Mr. Big could afford braces; as far as they could tell, there was no doctor, let alone an orthodontist anywhere in town. "No trips today. Or tomorrow. More rain. Maybe Friday," he muttered.

"But we're leaving on Friday," Dani said.

Mr. Big shrugged his shoulders and went back to his game of solitaire.

* * *

As they were walking back to their crumbling hotel, a boy—no older than twelve—ran up to Dani and said something in Spanish. It took several tries to realize he was saying he had a boat: he would take them out.

"When?" Dani asked.

"Now," the boy said and Dani was so happy she clapped her hands together twice. Ben glanced up at the sky and a saw a purple gray crease: there was definitely more rain on the way. But still they followed the boy down to the beach. Ben helped the boy drag the boat out into the water; it got stuck a few times in the black sand but they finally got it out to sea. Then the boy had a hard time getting the small motor started. Finally, in a blast of sulfuric smoke, the boat lurched forward, skidding out over the coal black water. The waves were choppy, the surface as cloudy as the little outboard engine. If there were turtles somewhere in the water at the moment, they were impossible to see. The boy swung the boat around and around, searching for a spot that was clearer than the rest, but there was nothing. No visibility. After a few more tries, he shrugged and throttled the couple back to shore. Ben gave him twenty bucks American and told him they'd like to try again in morning. The boy nodded and then walked off. Ben realized he was never going to see the kid again. He looked over at Dani's face, seeing how disappointed she was, and then wondered at the stupidity of their decision-making. "That was actually kind of dumb," Ben said as they walked back to the hotel. "I mean, what if he said it was okay to get in the water? Who knows what the hell's in there? I mean would you have gone in?"

"Probably," she said and he knew she was not lying.

* * *

It was raining again the next morning and the day after that so they decided to go on a tour of the nearby jungle. They hiked for about a half-mile into the deep foliage, but in the end, the jungle was just a sheet of green precipitation. Somewhere above there were howler monkeys. Ben thought he could smell their urine, but apparently the animals had more sense than to be standing out in the rain.

* * *

Later they headed back to their hotel and decided to go in the pool because it was still raining and no one else was around. Dani asked,

"Do you think if I tell them I'm the niece of Jacques Cousteau they'll take me to swim with the turtles?" Ben said he didn't know; he didn't think so. Dani offered to give him a handjob as a sort of apology. They poked their fingers around inside each other's swimsuits but nothing much happened.

* * *

It rained again later that evening. The TV only worked intermittently and so they acted out episodes of their favorite television programs. It was a guessing game, like charades. Ben did "Dallas" and Dani did "TJ Hooker." They fell sleep with their limbs knotted together and awoke a few times to stare at each other's faces.

* * *

On the last day, Friday, it finally stopped raining. Ben followed Dani over to Mr. Big's booth in a hurry. He looked up from his cards and asked if they were still interested in swimming with the turtles and they said yes and Ben gave him their money. They followed another darkly tanned boy, this one about fifteen years old, down to the beach. For a moment something like the sun peaked out. They climbed into a rickety silver boat and the guide ran them out to a brown and pink reef, then pointed to a clear patch of water. "Turtles," he said. Then he threw an anchor overboard and took a seat in the prow and began peeling a grapefruit.

Ben frowned at Dani. She looked at him and grinned dumbly. To-gether, hand-in-hand, they both leapt in. Underwater, everything was beige and brown, even the fish. "Where are the turtles?" Ben asked and Dani only shrugged. They paddled around without direction for several minutes. Suddenly there was a small pink cloud, glittering along the surface. Ben squinted for a moment before figuring it out: a jellyfish. Ben turned and spotted another one. Then again. Everywhere there were jellyfish, an entire, seamless mass of them. When Ben turned around, Dani was nowhere to be found. Ben began to panic and kicked back over towards the boat. Dani was already sitting in it, looking sullen. He swam over and said, "There's jellyfish all over the fucking place!" He pulled himself into the boat and saw Dani's legs were covered with bright red stings.

"Why didn't you say something to me?" he shouted, pointing at the water angrily. "I mean it's like full of jellyfish."

"It looked like you were having fun," she said.

"Fun? Some fun," he said, looking down. He saw Dani's bare left thigh was now swollen up with three different stings. She kept poking at them, saying, "Ow," each time.

"Don't keep touching them," he said.

She shrugged and the guide tried to start the engine. Ben looked over at Dani's legs again, at the spots and red marks, and was completely terrified. Because twice now she was willing to get them killed. For what? Just to say she saw some fucking turtles? And this was who he chose; she was the one he was supposed to be spending the rest of his life with? With that thought, Ben felt an inexplicable thrill, a sort of soft panic, because he suddenly realized the girl was capable of anything; the future, his life, their life; there was no telling about any of it now. □

AUTOMATIC
Cecilia Pinto

Tricia stood in the boys' bathroom. It was the only one at her all-girl high school and she had never been in it before. She could hear the voices of girls and boys who were attending the school's Friday night mixer outside in the hallway. She had hoped, standing in the quiet, tiled bathroom, not so very different from the girls' room, to glean some tangible information about the opposite sex; something that would explain not them, but her interest in them. But nothing in the bathroom offered information, not even the urinals, which held the embodiment of the mystery, suggestive somehow of sex, and odorous, but not informative.

She stared into the mirror which she noted was exactly like the one in the girls' room except for a crack that ran through the center of the glass. Absorbed in assessing her flaws, she was startled by a boy entering the bathroom. They stood staring at each other until he said, "I gotta take a leak." Tricia hurried past him and was met in the hallway by several girls including her best friend, Mary Carol, who shrieked with laughter.

Tricia composed a serious face. She told them that she had been getting a drink of water when she heard a noise that sounded like some sort of explosion. Then, two boys dashed past her out of the bathroom, one of them holding something that looked like a gun.

"I swear to God, you guys," she said. "I am not making this up."

Her friends encouraged her to tell the principal, Sister Alistair. When Tricia hesitated they dragged her down the hallway where the principal stood in conversation with another teacher.

Tricia told her story to Sister Alistair changing it slightly to include an additional boy who swore at her as he passed. Tricia knew Sister Alistair was an adult that many students felt comfortable spending time with. She also knew that Sister Alistair would never be privy to the secrets of adult life that she was anxious to learn. Tricia felt that this made her superior to Sister Alistair whom she could only assume lived a life far less important than her own. It didn't occur to her not to lie to Sister Alistair.

She told Sister Alistair that she had gone into the bathroom to check on a friend.

"A male friend or a female friend?" Sister Alistair asked.

"Female, I mean, male, I mean, I don't know," said Tricia vaguely. Behind her, the other girls stood like back-up singers.

The boy who had actually entered the bathroom exited and they all turned and stared at him. "That wasn't him," Tricia said quickly. "It was some other guys."

The principal told the girls to return to the cafeteria saying she would investigate the washroom herself. When the girls entered the cafeteria it seemed an announcement had already been made about a possible incident. The DJ stopped thumping out top forty hits. The chaperones turned on all the lights in the cafeteria and the few couples who had found places to hide and grope were scattered like birds.

Sister Alistair arrived and stood on a chair in her black sweat suit and white turtleneck, explaining that all students and visitors would remain in the cafeteria until an investigation had been made. A groan went up from the crowd.

The adult chaperones replaced the cafeteria tables and insisted that students sit at the tables with both hands in front of them on the table top. It was suspected by the adults that what had occurred was at best a prank but it was deemed necessary to take certain precautions and so the police were called.

Tricia and Mary Carol found seats at a table with a boy they did not know. The girls sat across from each other, the boy sat to Mary Carol's left. Tricia wondered if she would have to talk to the police and even as she rolled her eyes at Mary Carol she refined the story she would tell them.

She would say that a girlfriend, an unidentified one, had gone into the boys' room with some guy and she was worried that perhaps the friend should not be in there at all. Then she heard the noise. Then the boys came out and shoved her out of the way. Then she went into the boys' room where she saw the broken mirror. She had no idea how the mirror had been broken or for how long it had been that way. But she gambled that her explanation was better than the truth.

Tricia felt the agitation she experienced when an adult inquired as to her plans for the summer, or what books she was reading, or what she and her friends liked to do. It felt as if she was constantly being judged by adults who were scrutinizing her for defects and failings. She did not feel guilty about lying. This lie cast her in a far better light than the stupid truth. It was not her fault anyway. She felt sure of this sitting with Mary Carol who was really more responsible for the whole business since it had been Mary Carol who wanted her to talk to Sister Alistair in the first place.

Mary Carol chattered on about the police, the gun and the general excitement, turning her attention to the boy seated with them. Mary Carol's perky greeting was met with a sidelong stare that could have been interpreted in many ways. Tricia thought it was sexy and crossed her legs and edged forward on the bench.

Mary Carol pressed the boy for information and without enthusiasm he gave up his name, which was Chris, his age, which was almost eighteen, and the information that he attended the local public high school and was not Catholic.

Mary Carol guessed she might know people that Chris knew and she began questioning him in what Tricia thought was an increasingly idiotic way.

"Do you know Katie Shannon?" Mary Carol asked. "She dates Rob Walsh."

"No," said Chris.

"Do you know Jake, oh you know, he works at Uncle Frankie's? You know, he's got really curly, black hair? Jake, Jake...I can't remember his last name."

"I've seen him," said Chris, "but I don't know him." He was looking at Tricia as he spoke. She rolled her eyes to indicate how annoying Mary Carol was.

"What about Nick Healey?" Mary Carol persisted. "He's a swimmer."

"Yeah, I know him," said Chris, leaning back and placing his hands on his thighs. He looked away from the girls around the room.

"Really? You know Nick? Really, isn't he cute? I mean, well, oh my God, don't tell him I said so." Mary Carol fiddled with the chain around her neck, swinging the small gold cross that hung on it back and forth while she talked. "Well," she added, "he is cute. But he doesn't even know me, like I'm sure you'd go and say this girl thinks you're cute and stuff and he doesn't even know who I am, God."

Chris turned slowly back toward Mary Carol, his face empty. "What?" He said. He drummed a rhythm on the tabletop with both hands, his body bobbing slightly. This called him to a chaperone's attention and she repeated in a formal, general way that everyone must keep their hands firmly on the table top. Chris complied but under his breath he said, "Fuck."

Tricia thought he was again looking right at her as he said it and she was warm and excited. She wished both that Mary Carol would disappear into thin air so that she was alone with the boy, and also keep talking, so that she could continue to observe him and appear as cool as he was so that he would notice how, well, how cool she was.

"Are you a swimmer too?" Mary Carol whispered.

"I got kicked off the team," Chris said, suddenly more animated. "It sucked."

"What?" said Tricia. Her heart was racing, "What sucked?"

But Mary Carol interrupted, "This is Tricia, she saw everything that happened tonight."

"Then Tricia's the only one that needs to be here," Chris said, again scanning the room. He raised a hand to someone at a table across the gym.

Both of the girls watched him. "Who's over there?" Mary Carol craned to see.

"Just a buddy," Chris said, shrugging.

Two police officers entered the cafeteria and stood in the entrance way looking around. News of their arrival traveled through the crowd in spasms. Someone had brought them coffee and after glancing around the gym, they stood examining some plaques on the wall.

"Maybe there's somebody really dangerous here," Mary Carol said. Tricia could feel her jiggling her legs up and down under the table. Tricia looked at the police officers; vague nervousness wormed its way around her stomach. Glancing back across the table she saw Chris put a quick hand inside his jacket.

"What's in your jacket?" she asked.

"A gun," Chris replied coolly, "a big gun." Leaning towards her, he said, "You want to see it?" Tricia thought she caught some scent off of him; sweat, deodorant, cigarettes. She wasn't sure what it was, she paused thinking about it. She wanted to close her eyes and just live there for a moment.

"God," said Mary Carol elbowing in, "where'd you get it?"

"I'm kidding," said Chris, shaking his head and looking away.

"I knew that," Mary Carol said sitting back again. "Actually, I don't think that anything really happened. I think Tricia was in the bathroom with some guy."

"Shut up Mary Carol," Tricia snapped. In her mind she had been saying yes, to Chris, to whatever he was offering. Now he was looking at her with open curiosity and she was embarrassed.

"No, you shut up," Mary Carol said and gave the boy a little nudge, like they were in on something.

Sister Alistair appeared quietly at the table.

"Girls," she said gently, "this is not an appropriate time for loud conversation."

"Sorry, Sister," Mary Carol said smiling brightly. "Do we have to talk to the police, Sister?"

Sister Alistair turned towards Tricia. "Tricia I'd like to speak with you in my office. Can you come with me now?" She held an arm out towards Tricia in an offer to support her down the hall.

"Okay," said Tricia getting up slowly. She sucked in her stomach. She couldn't tell if Chris was watching but if he was, she wanted to look as thin as possible. She hated leaving him there with Mary Carol who might reveal something embarrassing about her or talk him right into a date. She went the long way round the table so that she passed behind Chris. She ran the fingertips of her left hand across the back of his jacket. She couldn't even be sure if he felt it.

Sister Alistair motioned her from the doorway of the gym and Tricia moved towards her, away from the boy at the table, wishing time would stop and leave her there.

The school hallways were cool and quiet as Tricia walked with the principal to her office. She didn't listen to the principal's small talk but dragged her hand along the tiled walls imagining that when she touched his back Chris had turned and grabbed her around the waist and pulled her to him.

"Were you enjoying the dance?" Sister Alistair asked pleasantly as she unlocked her office door. Tricia tried to focus on what Sister Alistair was saying.

"Oh, yeah, I guess. The music was pretty good." She wondered what the principal really meant, what was she really asking?

Sister Alistair was fiddling with her keys and didn't continue the conversation as they entered the office.

Sister Alistair's office had sea blue carpeting and two green upholstered chairs facing a broad cherry desk. There was a large window which looked out on what was called the prayer garden. The garden's spring flowers were in bloom and even in the evening light the promise of new green was evident.

The principal cleared her throat. "Tricia, the police officers are convinced that the incident was at most a prank. And after checking with our janitorial crew I believe that the crack in the bathroom mirror has been there for some time. So you must have been mistaken. But I thought that you and I should talk. I'm wondering if you can tell me what you heard or saw again. I'd like to be absolutely sure that I understand."

"Um," said Tricia. "Well, actually..." she hesitated. Behind Sister's desk was a large wooden fish. It was hand carved with blue-green scales and fins flecked in gold. Tricia stared at it thinking about a fake gold bracelet she'd lost at a movie theater. She'd purchased the bracelet two years ago, the summer she was thirteen. The bracelet which featured hearts and skulls had cost six dollars and ninety-nine cents and was part of a line of jewelry promoted by a popular singer. She had thought it was the height of sophistication but now it seemed juvenile and tacky and she was glad she'd lost it.

"Isn't that grand?" Sister Alistair followed Tricia's gaze. "A friend brought it from Thailand. I had to think of all sorts of scripture passages with references to fish in order to justify it." She smiled at Tricia. "Of course, there are quite a few, aren't there?" Waiting a beat she tried again, "Tricia, I need to know what happened."

"Well," said Tricia again, "nothing happened really. Mary Carol has a big mouth and I was just joking but somehow she thought I was serious and I wasn't even in the boys' room. I was just getting a drink."

She said this very quickly looking at Sister briefly and then back at a spot on the floor. Honesty now seemed the quickest way to expedite things and hopefully she could catch up with Chris or at least Mary Carol before they left.

"I'm sorry," she added. "They were making fun of me."

"They were making fun of you for getting a drink of water?" Sister questioned.

"No, for being in the boys' room."

"What were you doing in the boys' room?"

"I was just looking." Tricia said this more loudly than she intended. "I just wanted to see." It irritated her that adults required such specific explanations for everything. Why couldn't you just do things without always having to say why you were doing them? Who cared why she was in the boys' bathroom? What did it matter? The problem with telling the truth was it really didn't make any more sense than the lie.

"And, when the girls began teasing about the bathroom, you lied," Sister insisted, leaning forward in her chair.

"Yes, look I'm really sorry Sister, I am. I made a mistake. I didn't think the police would come, gosh." Tricia just wanted out. This boy, Chris, would leave and she would have no way of meeting him again. She only wanted to get back to the cafeteria.

Sister Alistair sat staring at her. After a moment she picked up the phone and spoke with someone regarding the police

Then Sister Alistair stood, leaning her hands on the desk. "Tricia, curiosity is an important quality and I would be the first to advocate most forms of educational exploration. However, one has to be responsible for one's actions and one has to have the confidence of one's convictions. You disappoint me tonight by having neither. I suggest that you consider the company that you keep, both in terms of your friendships and your spiritual self. And there will have to be some consequences but I'd like to think about what they might be over the weekend."

"Yes, Sister," responded Tricia. She looked Sister straight in the face for as long as she could. She was thinking that the drowsy white blossoms in the garden were bobbing in an annoying way and something about them made her feel frantic.

"Adult life, Tricia," Sister Alistair said ushering her to the door, "is a question of balance. Sometimes it can be a bit tricky juggling all the pieces but I'm sure a bright girl like you can handle the task. We all make an occasional error in judgment." She paused. "Well, that's enough I suppose. How are you getting home, may I call your parents?"

Tricia's response was panicked. "Oh no," she said quickly, "I've got a ride."

"All right then, in the future, if something makes you feel uncomfortable or unclear, please come and talk with me. I'd be happy to listen."

Tricia looked at Sister Alistair's hands as the nun held the door for her. They were young and smooth looking, unused. Aloud she said, "Okay sure, thanks. Um, I'm sorry about all the trouble. Goodbye, good night."

She backed out of the office and ran down the hallway to the gym feeling more excited and alive than she had ever been. But the gym was emptying and in the loud and crowded room Tricia couldn't find the boy she hoped to see.

Out in the parking lot the spring air was cool, moist on her skin and she stood staring at the dampness on the hoods of cars. Her heart beat slowed to its normal rhythm. She shivered as the adrenaline that had so instantly energized her left her body. There was nothing to do but walk home as she was unable to find Mary Carol and she wasn't answering her phone.

She walked quickly. It was almost eleven o' clock and she was not accustomed to being out alone on foot. The lights were mostly out in the homes that she passed. An occasional car rolled by or a dog barked.

She would go home, she thought, and get into bed. Maybe she would watch TV first. Maybe she would lie in bed and think about what might have happened between her and the boy and touch herself. She would hug her pillow and pretend it was him. He would tell her how beautiful she was.

Nothing Sister Alistair had said made much sense to her. Nothing that had happened that evening seemed very important. As she walked she decided that the whole night, her interest in the boy, and especially her curiosity about the boys' room, had been stupid.

Her street was arched with large trees that bent to her and as she walked towards her house she slammed her shoulder into each tree she passed.

A car pulled up alongside her; it was Mary Carol. There were others in the car.

"Hey you!" Mary Carol shouted, laughing.

"Hey, Slinky," said a male voice.

There was some laughter from the car and Mary Carol could be heard saying, "Slinky? What?"

Then she poked her head out. "Come on, Tricia," she encouraged, "we're going for a ride."

A boy she did not recognize stuck his head out the passenger window and said hoarsely, "C'mon, we're going to party!"

Tricia opened one of the rear doors and slid in. The car radio was playing noisily. There was Chris, the boy from the dance. "Hey," he said moving closer to her and offering her the joint he had been smoking. "I was looking for you in the bathroom."

Everyone in the car laughed a lot and though it didn't seem that funny Tricia laughed too. She accepted the joint from Chris, their hands bumped and sparks dropped in the dark. Tricia took a long hit off the joint. Chris put his hand on her thigh. Finally, she thought, finally. □

THE PARADOX OF BEN HECHT
Jan Herman

I f Ben Hecht is remembered at all today, it is not for his novels. It is not even for his journalism or the movies he wrote, credited and uncredited, but for a more general reputation as the most successful screenwriter of his time. He was the fastest, most prolific, and highest paid. By his own account, he wrote sixty movies, including Hollywood landmarks as diverse as *Scarface, The Front Page, Notorious* and *Wuthering Heights.* According to his informative and judicious biographer William MacAdams, he had a hand in one hundred. He rewrote the first half of *Gone With the Wind* for $3,500 a day over nine days. Complete scripts on average took him two weeks, none more than eight, earning him fees during the 1930s of as much as $125,000.

Hecht's novels are so totally forgotten that when I asked Richard Lingeman, the biographer of Theodore Dreiser and Sinclair Lewis, what he thought of Hecht's fiction, he drew a blank. All he could remember was the title and nothing else of Hecht's first and best-known novel, *Erik Dorn.* I suppose it was unfair to coldcock Lingeman with a question out of the blue like that, and I don't mean to embarrass him here by telling the story. It's meant merely to illustrate how removed Hecht's fiction is from the literary canon.

A sadder story: when I managed to find my favorite Hecht novel, *Humpty Dumpty*, his fourth of ten and the one I consider his best, I saw that the copy I'd borrowed from a university library had never been read. The pages were uncut. A check of the records showed that I was the first to borrow the book since the library acquired it in 2003. It was a first-edition copy printed in 1924, so surely it must have passed through other hands. Had it been unread all those years because of the title? *Humpty Dumpty* sounds comical, absurdly so, for a serious work.

Another question: why would anybody be curious to read any of Hecht's fiction? Despite his ubiquitous presence among the writers of the Chicago School during the years it flourished and an outpouring of novels afterward—*Erik Dorn* (1921), *Gargoyles* and the novella *Fantazius Mallare: A Mysterious Oath* (1922); *The Florentine Dagger* (1923), *Count Bruga* and the novella *The Kingdom of Evil* (1926);

A Jew in Love (1931); *The Book of Miracles* (1941); *I Hate Actors* (1944); *The Sensualists* (1959)—let alone a handful of plays, including Broadway hits such as the enduring and spectacularly successful *The Front Page*, and more than a dozen short-story collections, he's been largely dismissed as a literary figure of any significance.

In a review of Hecht's autobiography *A Child of the Century* (1954), Louis Berg calls Hecht "a word slinger rather than a stylist, master of invective rather than wit, poetaster rather than poet, crackpot philosopher and calculating crackpot, romantic cynic and cruel senti-mentalist, third-rate Mencken and fifth-rate Rochefoucauld."

Never mind that Mencken himself was an early admirer who pub-lished Hecht's stories in *Smart Set* or that Hecht's writing had already appeared in the Chicago-based ur-literary magazine *The Little Review*, alongside poetry by Ezra Pound, T.S. Eliot, Hart Crane, and Carl Sand-burg, stories by Hemingway and Sherwood Anderson, prose by Ger-trude Stein, and chapters of James Joyce's *Ulysses*.

Never mind that Hecht touted his friend Anderson's *Winesburg, Ohio* stories before they were ever published; that Hecht drew deft por-traits in his novels of Dreiser, Anderson, and Sandburg (a newsroom colleague whose poetry he revered), as well as indelible depictions of *The Little Review* founder Margaret Anderson (no relation to Sher-wood) and the Chicago School poet Max Bodenheim, a close friend who collaborated with him on the satirical novella *Cutie: A Warm Mama* (1923).

Never mind that Hecht published and edited his own "little" maga-zine, *The Chicago Literary Times* (1923-24), and wrote the city's most entertaining daily newspaper column, "1001 Afternoons in Chicago" (1922), much of it fiction passed off as journalism and still unequaled for color and verve.

In other words, Hecht's obscurity is part of an academic feedback loop designed to ignore Hecht. Historically as well as literarily, the grandest oddity of all is that he himself diagnosed the issues that would come to haunt his reputation.

"I'm a victim of too plastic a vocabulary," says the protagonist of *Humpty Dumpty*, a cynical young writer named Kent Savaron clearly modeled on the author. "Its ability to defend any action of mine has deprived me of a conscience." Savaron knows so well how to manipu-late the language of simile and metaphor that he gives a contemptuous demonstration of his skill. "Writing is a bastard art," he tells Helen Dean, who is modeled on Margaret Anderson.

It is dependent for its effects upon its least important asset—technique. I imagine you would like the imagist method. No emotion. Allegedly passionless translations of phenomena. A very jaw-breaking sentence. I'll let you read some of my rain mathematics some time. Rain, like frightened diagonals, covering the sidewalk with Vs. Rain beating like a wing against the roofs; rain like domino lines, like ramrods, like hair, like strings of a towering harp. Gusts of rain like gray flags disappearing in the wind. Rain that tiptoes down the street like a phantom. Rain smelling of hazelnuts and well water, turning the walls of buildings into dark mirrors. Rain like ghost-ships riding over the chimney.

A wolfish philanderer, Savaron is intent on seducing Dean. Although he regards her as "a redundant and make-believe aesthete," she is nevertheless "a stimulus that hoisted him onto a pedestal of rhetoric and started him shoveling adjectives into her lap." More than that, he sees her as an antidote to his romantic involvement with the conventional Stella Winkelberg, whose philistine family he despises for its bourgeois conformity. He serenades Dean not only with his technical brilliance but lays on his aesthetic judgments and vents his rage against the moralistic clichés of the booboisie, even against what he regards as the clichés of the avant-garde:

"Look how the afternoon gleams with rain." He smiled. "Why don't you play the piano when it rains? Scriabin played in the rain becomes a lonely child weeping for its mother's return. Satie, Prokoffief, Schelling—try them. Let's hear how the rain distorts their modernistic tonal algebraics into variations of 'Home, Sweet Home.'

"Oh yes," he went on, "the third approach. Our old friend the moralistic calciminer. No, they don't overlook anything, these life haters. They see in every phase of nature a mystic cleansing fluid for man's spotted soul. The purifying rain. The rain like a benediction. It rained and he grew sad remembering his sins. The virgin rain. The dark herald of rainbow. Every cloud is silver-lined. The sweet and invigorating rain. [...] What filthy decadents these moralists are! What a race of befouling egomaniacs! They see in the swing of the stars, in the mind-exhausting mysteries of nature—what? Proofs of their little swinish idealizations. Sermons in stones and tongues in babbling brooks.

"It's one way to write successfully. Reduce lie and nature to mystic vindications of Americanism. Honest as the day. Noble as the sun."

Is it surprising that the avant-garde was no less inclined to forgive

Hecht than the academics? Furthermore, his brief against "Americanism," expressed throughout his books, didn't help with the wider audience. His libertarian politics in general also ran counter to the liberal-left establishment. During the Depression his anti-communist mania made him something of a raving neoconservative avant la lettre.

And there were other problems. For example, when Savaron confirms what he has suspected—that Helen Dean is a lesbian (her virginity "a bit more involved than the usual hymen complex")—his homophobia rises to the surface. It turns out that he's as narrow and conventional in his attitude as any conforming moralist. Although the homophobia is applied with a fair amount of subtlety in *Humpty Dumpty*, Hecht's own queer bashing can be so overbearing elsewhere in his writing that it's hard to stomach. This would support the view that Hecht's personal limitations infected his fiction, that the characters in his novels are a reflection of them. Savaron can rant all he wants about the Winkelbergs and the artist bohemians both, but he is as flawed as they are and in the end defeated by his own inauthenticity. "I'm a theory that has refuted itself," he says on the point of suicide.

"A bag of wind with a hole in it. Ha! That's me. Words. All kinds of words. Home and fireside. That's what I want. Goddamn them. I can't keep on. I'll go back. I'll kneel. Sure. Why not? Let me in, I'll say. Here I am, the prodigal. Bring on the feather bed. And an ice pack. Let me in, I'll say."

Nelson Algren understood that this was the problem. When the University of Chicago Press asked Algren for an introduction to its 1962 reprint of *Erik Dorn*, he took the view that "no American yet has written a novel this good yet this bad." The least academic of critics had qualms worthy of Berg—not because of the word-slinging (if anything, he admired its pungency) but because he believed Hecht lacked the conviction to back it up. "This is the one work of serious literature we have that by the same token stands as a literary hoax," he wrote. "*Erik Dorn* is so true that nobody but his creator could have made him so spurious. No other writer has written a novel anything like it—and yet it resembles many novels."

One has to wonder why the publisher chose to use Algren's pan for an introduction to a novel it was trying to sell. Certainly Hecht wondered. When he learned of it, he refused to help market the book, failed to show up at the publication party, and pretended that Algren was so far beneath him he couldn't recall reading anything of his. (This, despite having worked on the screenplay of *The Man with the Golden*

Arm.)

Algren's opinion of *Erik Dorn* helps to explain why it never became the iconic novel of the period that Sinclair Lewis's Midwestern novels *Main Street* (1920) and *Babbitt* (1922) did. Other reasons, I would suggest, are that *Erik Dorn* is more acid in style and more opinionated, more introspective in tone and more intellectual, its concerns narrower and its targets more elevated. Although "*Erik Dorn* is a man who seems, to himself, to be a perfect translation of his country and his day," as Algren noted, he is nevertheless a sophisticated if bored-with-himself newspaper editor, which was a more rarified breed of creature than a middle-aged, suburban real estate agent like George F. Babbitt. Also, the milieu of *Erik Dorn* is big-city Chicago and fashionable Michigan Avenue. For the period, *Main Street*'s small-town Gopher Prairie and *Babbitt*'s midsize Zenith were more representative of America.

The opening pages of these novels show an immediate difference between Hecht and Lewis. In the first lines of *Main Street* we meet its protagonist, Carol Milford. She is a college girl standing on a hill by the Mississippi River not far from Minneapolis and St. Paul, and is seen "in relief against the cornflower blue of Northern sky." She is "meditating upon walnut fudge, the plays of Brieux, the reasons why heels run over, and the fact that the chemistry instructor had stared at the new coiffure which concealed her ears."

A breeze which had crossed a thousand miles of wheat-lands bellied her taffeta skirt in a line so graceful, so full of animation and moving beauty, that the heart of a chance watcher on the lower road tightened to wistfulness over her quality of suspended freedom. She lifted her arms, she leaned back against the wind, her skirt dipped and flared, a lock blew wild. A girl on a hilltop; credulous, plastic, young; drinking the air as she longed to drink life. The eternal aching comedy of expectant youth.

In *Babbitt*, again in the opening lines, Lewis introduces the protagonist, who is "beginning to awaken on the sleeping-porch of a Dutch Colonial house in the residential district of Zenith known as Floral Heights."

His name was George F. Babbitt. He was forty-six years old now, in April, 1920, and he made nothing in particular, neither butter nor shoes nor poetry, but he was nimble in the calling of selling houses for more than people could afford to pay. ... He was not fat but he was exceedingly well fed ... prosperous, extremely married and unromantic;

and altogether unromantic appeared this sleeping-porch, which looked on one sizable elm, two respectable grass-plots, a cement driveway, and a corrugated iron garage. Yet Babbitt was again dreaming of the fairy child, a dream more romantic than scarlet pagodas by a silver sea.

When Hecht introduces us to the title character of *Erik Dorn*, he sets an entirely opposite scene.

The crowds moving through the streets gave Erik Dorn a picture. It was morning. Above the heads of the people the great spatula-topped buildings spread a zigzag of windows, a scribble of rooftops against the sky. A din as monotonous as a silence tumbled through the streets—an unvarying noise of which the towering rectangles of buildings tilted like great reeds out of a narrow bowl, seemed an audible part.

The city alive with signs, smoke, posters, window; falling, rising, flinging its chimneys and its streets against the sun, wound itself up into crowds and burst with an endless bang under the far-away sky.

And Dorn himself is as far as one can get from either a college naïf or a dream-dazed realtor.

Moving toward his office Erik Dorn watched the swarming of men and women of which he was a part. Faces like a flight of paper scraps scattered about him. Bodies poured suddenly across his eyes as if emptied out of funnels. The ornamental entrances of buildings pumped figures in and out. Vague and blurred like the play of gusty rain, the crowds darkened the pavements.

Dorn saluted the spectacle with smiling eye. As always, in the aimless din and multiplicity of streets he felt himself most securely at home. The smear of gestures, the elastic distortion of crowds winding and unwinding under the tumult of windows, gave him the feeling of a geometrical emptiness of life.

Here before him the meanings of faces vanished. The greedy little purposes of men and women tangled themselves into a generality. It was thus Dorn was most pleased to look upon the world, to observe it as one observes a pattern – involved but precise. ... Things that made pictures for his eyes alone diverted Dorn. Beyond this capacity for diversion he remained untouched.

Shrewd and alert, Dorn has been hardened and made cynical by disappointed expectations:

At thirty he had explained to himself, "I am complete. This busi-ness of being empty is all there is to life." Intelligence is a faculty which enables man to peer through the muddle of ideas and arrive at a no-where.

It is this hardness, amounting to a form of self-pity, which Algren objected to. And self-pity is what ultimately defeats Dorn, though it is never expressed as such. He doesn't kill himself, like Savaron, but is drawn back to the mothering arms of his wife.

Babbitt, too, having had an extra-marital affair, ends up back in the bosom of his family. He has made peace with himself, however, and with the conformity he tried to escape from, finding redemption of a sort by counseling his son to go his own way. In the melodramatic words that end the novel, he says: "Don't be scared of the family. No, nor all of Zenith. Nor of yourself, the way I've been. Go ahead, old man! The world is yours!"

As for the young college girl in *Main Street*, she marries and moves to Gopher Prairie with her doctor husband, but eventually leaves because her life is miserable in a town she has so desperately and un-successfully tried to reform. She, too, returns—and Lewis makes the same point again: Older and wiser, she is not defeated. (Neither were readers. *Main Street* was a phenomenal best-seller. It sold 250,000 cop-ies, far outstripping *Erik Dorn*.)

By the beginning of the 1930s, Hecht was already writing screen-plays for Hollywood. The fabled tale goes that his friend Herman Mankiewicz, who was recruiting writers for Paramount, sent him a tele-gram: "Millions are to be grabbed out here and your only competition is idiots. Don't let this get around." Hecht hadn't given up on novels, though. In 1931 he published another major work. This time, instead of a silly title like *Humpty Dumpty*, he chose a provocative one: *A Jew in Love*.

Conceivably, he was trying for an association with D.H. Law-rence's *Women in Love*, perhaps hoping to capitalize on that novel's scandalous reputation. Hecht had already courted notoriety as a por-nographer with *Fantazius Mallare*, an erotic novella vividly illustrat-ed by his newsroom buddy the artist and writer Wallace Smith. This had resulted in a highly publicized lawsuit brought by the U. S. Postal Service. Accused of sending "lewd, lascivious and obscene" literature through the mail, Hecht wanted a show trial with Clarence Darrow as his attorney, but finally agreed to a plea of *nolo contendere*. (He and Wallace were fined $1,000 each.)

Given Hecht's disdain for Lawrence's novels, which he claimed were full of hot air, and given the anti-Semitic tenor of the times—the Ku Klux Klan was in poisonous flower and a little man named Hitler was on the rise—it's more likely that Hecht was merely looking to make trouble. If you didn't know Hecht was Jewish, you'd think he was a Klansman in training. *A Jew in Love* begins like this:

> *Jo Boshere (born Abe Nussbaum) was a man of thirty—a dark-skinned little Jew with a vulturous and moody face, a reedy body and a sense of posture.*
>
> *The Jews now and then hatch a face which for Jewishness surpasses the caricatures of the entire anti-Semitic press. These Jew faces in which race leers and burns like some biologic disease are rather shocking to a mongrelized world.*

In fact, Hecht was a non-practicing Jew who scorned all religions. Later in life he became a secular Zionist, denouncing Franklin Delano Roosevelt for failing to rescue European Jews who had escaped the Holocaust. He also raised large sums of money for the paramilitary Irgun and the underground Stern Gang in their drive to oust the British from Palestine and wrote manifestos to help establish an Israeli state. But that doesn't minimize the bile of *A Jew in Love.*

> *People dislike being reminded of their origins. They shudder a bit mystically at the sight of anyone who looks too much like a fish, a lizard, a chimpanzee or a Jew. This is probably nonsense. The Jew face is an enemy totem, an ancient target for spittle and, like a thing long hated, a sort of magic propagandist of hate. Its persistence in the world is that of some repulsive and hostile fauna, half crippled, yet containing in its ineffaceable Yiddish outline the taunt and challenge of the unfinished victim. This, of course, is true only of the worst looking Jew faces and the worst Jew haters.*
>
> *Boshere was not quite so bad as this. The racial decadence which had popped so Hebraic a nosegay out of his mother's womb was of finer stuff than that glandular degeneration which produces the Jew with the sausage face; the bulbous diabetic half-monsters who look as if they had been fished out of the water a month too late.*

The "brooding, ironic smile" he wears is meant to convey "superiority to his Jewishness." Boshere is someone to be envied if not admired. As disdainful of having "won a million in the stock market" as he is of being an eminently successful book publisher, he considers his wealth and his vocation pure accidents. But what is he? In short, not a nice man. He is a snobbish, egotistical, deceitful skirt-chaser with a parasitical need to enslave any woman who falls for him. He is also complicated.

> *The niggerish delight of the Jew in the blonde was no part of Boshere's enthusiasm in his new conquest. His egomania with its neurotic underlayer of inferiority had long outstripped the simplicities of Jew-Christian reaction.*

The novel might be more accurately titled *A Jew in Lust*. And it did cause a scandal. It also became a best seller. Banned in Boston, it was "reprinted five times in six weeks" with sales, MacAdams reports, of 50,000 copies.

Although Boshere was modeled on a friend of Hecht's, the legendary Broadway producer and notorious cocksman Jed Harris (born Jacob Horowitz), the character actually reads with devastating force like a psychological self-portrait of the author. Inevitably, the protagonists of Hecht's key novels were all self-portraits.

This was the true paradox of Hecht: he was an author so brilliant at observing others but so self-absorbed that in writing about them he could only write about himself. Hecht's "smiling and swaggering savageries" (to quote Dorothy Parker) may have been aimed at friends—to keep them entertained, he said. But in the same way that "his immeasurable vanity made him always determined to dominate any conversation" (to quote Bodenheim), he couldn't help dominating the protagonists of his novels.

Characteristic of them all are probing internal monologues, which Hecht spins for pages on end. He captures the logic of deluded human beings as well as any author I've read, offering insights into their motives, frustrations, philosophies, and emotions. But because the intensity of the analysis is unrelieved, monotony can set in—there is rarely any humor—and so the novels are less than completely satisfying. The pleasure I get from them, however, is the feeling that some kind of genius must have written them—a malicious genius who didn't give a damn. Compared with the tons of novels that don't have the slightest touch of genius of any kind, that is satisfaction enough.

Has any novella opened with a more prodigious sentence than the one that begins Hecht's *Fantazius Mallare*?

> *This dark and wayward book is affectionately dedicated to my enemies—to the curious ones who take fanatic pride in disliking me; to the baffling ones who remain enthusiastically ignorant of my existence;*

to the moral ones upon whom Beauty exercises a lascivious and cor-
rupting influence; to the moral ones who have relentlessly chased God
out of their bedrooms ... who flatten themselves upon prayer rugs, who
shut their eyes, stuff their ears, bind, gag and truss themselves and offer
their mutilations to the idiot God they have invented (the Devil take
them, I grow bored with laughing at them); to the anointed ones who
identify their paranoic symptoms as virtues ...

And ten pages later ends like this:

... to the intellectual ones who play solitaire with platitudes, who
drag their classrooms around with them; to these and to many other
abominations whom I apologize to for omitting, this inhospitable book
... is dedicated in the hope that their righteous eyes may never kindle
with secret lusts nor their pious lips water erotically from its reading...

Did Henry Miller, De Sade, Celine, Poe, Evelyn Waugh, Bukowski, Burroughs, or the Comte de Lautréamont ever write a sentence as
delicious as that one for mockery?

If Hecht is ignored by the academics, and therefore not in the canon, he's also off the radar for all but the most curious contemporary
readers. With a few minor exceptions his approximately forty books
are out of print, including his autobiographical *A Child of the Century*
and the equally charming, often fictitious memoir *Gaily, Gaily* (1964).
Unlike Algren's work, which has seen a recent groundswell of new editions, Hecht's is probably not going to be revived.

In some cases his fiction is too antiquated. *The Florentine Dagger: A Novel for Amateur Detectives* is an archaic potboiler. *Gargoyles*,
set between 1900 and the beginning of World War I, is no worse than
Babbitt and in many respects better. But it feels timebound despite a
masterly evocation of the petty affairs and phony dreams of a Midwestern politician and his middle-class circle of family and friends. In other
cases, his fiction is little more than light reading. *Count Brugia*, the one
novel of the 1920s not dominated by a disguised self-portait of Hecht,
is a seductive but pitiless hatchet job that exposes his friend Bodenheim
as a lecherous drunk with the temperament of an eccentric snob. The
story, however, is weightless. *I Hate Actors!*, a screwball comedy about
Hollywood in the 1940s, has a farcical murder plot and is deliciously
droll. Today, however, it might be more resonant as a witty period piece
adapted for the stage. *The Sensualists* (1959), Hecht's last novel, has a
polished hard-boiled 1950s flavor. The story involves a long-married
husband and wife who discover she has a sexual preference for his les-

bian mistress. I was entertained, but the book was roundly panned when it appeared, and I'm betting it will remain condemned to dusty shelves forever. *A Book of Miracles*—which Hecht was especially proud of, according to MacAdams—has the inherent problem of dated content as well. It would make an excellent candidate for a new edition, though, if anyone were interested in reprinting a protean collection of seven novellas about the follies of mankind. Hecht is not showing off for a change. *Miracles* is written in winning prose with fairytale simplicity. I'd like to think it would have a market. But that's an unlikely fairy tale too far-fetched even for such an incurable fabulist as Ben Hecht. ☐

PILSEN
James Paradiso

DREAM TUNNEL
James Paradiso

SIDEWALK MAN
James Paradiso

THREE DOGS IN THE WINDOW
James Paradiso

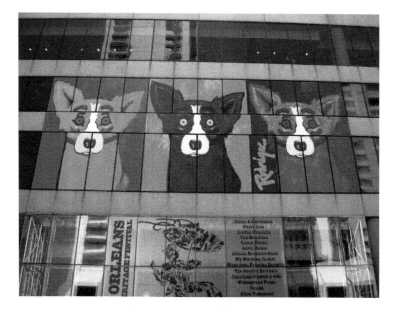

THE DERMATOID "I"

James Crizer

The boss of my imaginary self,
that stoic dermatologist, loves me, I guess—
born to rash, to bathe in vague gray water
sprinkled with oatmeal. Reminded always of lungs,
of cough—the aquatic superhero imprisoned by skin,
the family forever on me. When I ask
questions, they don't proclaim a uniform wisdom,
only answer in a wash of pitches.

Don't scratch, just breathe.
I clip fingernails—holler at the anemic banana chips,
cut back the groves of lush keratin. I
will not feed an itch from my own claw. The face
replaces steam. Today *eczema* russets a perfect symmetric hue
over opposing cheekbones. And like other gravelly dawns,
this is somebody's anniversary. So I'll *dress in cotton*—
a civil return from a long trip.

I comb the jaw-line and shadow beneath my chin,
but rarely the hair I've tired of— grooming
teeth held in a pinch, the straight going-over, past coils,
grating invisible nails down an unseen face— my pompadour a mess.
Breathing, once an intro to cello, now passes silently—
a mortgage, I think, or a debt—
earthbound this way until a lung or two clatters,
a couple of tulips flash.

I used to wish for black eyes,
some vicious punctuation, only to wake pink—
pajamas lined with rash. *Commonly called Fifth's disease.*
Stay home, dress in a lime nightshirt, run a bath
with *lukewarm water.* Now bare the neck,
pull it clean once a month in winter—fur, no animal secret
the dry air spins to fertilize—a fresh strip of poultry-song,
a live weed beneath the snow.

PANACEA
James Crizer

I'm seeking a painless existence
probably wasn't the best response.

But I am. Thumb over a comb,
the inkling of reverb slight.

Outside, she holds the low branch
of our live oak. A swath of bees

covers the arms past her sun
dress. I feel a welling

like tears, but cannot open the ducts
behind my eyes. Inside, the mirror

catches my hair, the steam on the window
and everything. She butts

the trunk against her back, smiles
like a monk on a tightrope.

I veil my head, glove my hands
and meet her. She unzips me.

We laugh. I consider a proposal and
touch my stomach—

plates shift back to Pangaea.
Danger comes like a sneeze.

She falls with scarecrow arms and plays dead.
I fetch another lozenge.

THIS IS THE PRESIDENT'S SON
Gina Frangello

D iane has missing lights down to a science. When Eli is here in Bogotá with her, he always drives, and Diane is stuck in the passenger's seat watching her husband drive like a Midwestern American Pussy. Diane, though, who is from New York and never drove a car until she started living overseas, drives native. She runs red lights to avoid stopping, since the area around the airport is famous for car-jackings, robberies and kidnappings. She was born to drive this way, and in that sense as in many others, Bogotá brings out the essence of a person: the stripped down version of who you were meant to be if placed in some godforsaken *Lord of the Flies* battleground where anything is permitted.

Even as Diane swings up to let Mary in the car, she doesn't collect any dust. Mary, her fresh-faced American colleague at Colegia Nuevo; Mary who vomited aguardiente the first night Diana and Eli partied with her at the onset of the school year and they had to hold her overly full, yellow hair over their rusty toilet; Mary, now just back from a Christmas trip to Mexico where she apparently took ill and so needed her ass fetched from El Dorado to be shuttled to some Colombian hospital where surely a shittiest-shift-of-the-year doctor will do his best to kill her, tonight being New Year's Eve, and Diane will have to ring in the New Year standing guard. Diane pulls up to arrivals and barks at Mary, "Get in!," not stopping long enough to help Mary, whose skin looks waxy and slick, with her luggage or someone is sure to come over and try to scam them out of something. At best, some cop pretending they've committed a parking infraction and wanting a bribe, which if they could pay it right there on the street wouldn't be so bad. Diane's Colombian friends have told her never to go anywhere *near* a police station. Her friend Maya's husband's sister was gang raped at the District 1 station, according to Maya, who teaches at San Bartolome, the antithesis of the posh Colegia Nuevo.

Bogotá is a web of complex negotiations, the rules varying enormously depending on the street on which you happen to find yourself. Up on the hill where Colegia Nuevo is located, teachers have maids, cooks—are not intended to worry themselves about issues like "security," which is the concern of those lower on the social hierarchy; at the Colegia, it is bad form, a social violation, to fear for one's safety even though in private, in the crappy, living-room-sized tienda Diane and her fellow teachers have dubbed "The Club," she and Eli jokingly coach new teachers to point at whatever kid happens to be standing next to them and proclaim, "Este es el hijo del Presidente!"—*this is the President's son!*—should FARC rush the classroom. Even FARC, though, is something of an "elite" concern; when Diane goes to visit Maya, she has to drive down 5th Avenue, in one of the crappiest neighborhoods in the city, and the traffic always sucks on 5th, so if you don't want to be stuck waiting at lights forever just begging to get carjacked, you have to take all these circuitous routes through the run-down, vaguely Eastern-European-looking squat gray buildings, some painted that hideous concrete pink, through the shanties, down the trash and shit-littered street (on streets like this, it's not just dog feces you're likely to find either, Diane knows), just to get wherever the hell you're going. FARC doesn't care about you here, but still you have to drive fast and not stop for anything until you see what you came for: the place or person you know.

Once upon a time, Diane found all of South America glamorous. Lately, though, her forty-sixth birthday passing without fanfare and the new teachers at the Colegia young enough to be her and Eli's children, Bogotá increasingly seems just one volatile minefield of shit, stretching out between the places you need to be or the people who keep you sane when you get there.

Mary slams the car door, desperate and gasping like a fugitive, not meeting Diane's eyes. They are not close, and Diane takes her for (rightfully) embarrassed for calling in a fellow-American favor on a holiday, though in truth she's glad enough to have something to do on New Year's Eve, Eli gone and the other, younger teachers probably out trolling for local action tonight. Still, a trip to the ER isn't anyone's idea of a good time. Plus, Mary looks like hell. It's all Diane can manage not to do a double take as Mary sits there hacking into her elbow. Typhoid Mary, Diane thinks, and cracks the window a little for fresh air. Generally, Mary is a cute girl, barely twenty-five—hell, even girls who aren't that attractive are pretty when they're twenty-five, though you can't convince them of it at the time. But today. Wow. Mary has that watery, red-faced look of a sickly baby, one with scabies or a perpetually crusty nose. Her hair, which is usually full and curly, looks limp and frizzled out. Diane pats her knee. "Geez," she says. "There's nothing worse than being sick far from home." Then she laughs. "Not that this is *home*, exactly…"

Mary murmurs, "When we get to the hospital, do you think you could—" then coughs like a motherfucker—Diane feels herself gaping in horror—"can you stay with me for awhile?"

"Nah, I was planning to ditch you so I can go buy some slutty outfit for tonight," she says sarcastically. "Eli's out of town—he's visiting his sociopathic mother in Florida—so I've got my eye on some local stud for midnight."

Mary giggles a little, which makes Diane feel slightly better. Diane is never sick. Eli does sick sometimes, but not her. Her ancestors are from Russia and Poland—peasant women who probably worked in the fields until the minute they squatted down and pushed out a kid. She may not do the kid part, but that's her to a T: hale and hearty. Sick people make her nervous. Like the kind of morbidly obese people you see on morning talk shows in the States, Diane cannot help thinking the sickly are somehow to blame for their own fate.

They are stuck at a stop sign. Diane doesn't do stop signs, but some dolt in front of them has halted, so there they are, waiting. Diane says, "Did you have a good holiday at least before you got sick?" and the obvious effort Mary puts in to her inhale and the beginning of her answer makes Diane wish she'd just kept her mouth shut. (Diane doesn't do *quiet*, either.) Mary is saying something, but Diane is no longer listening…

Four youths, maybe between the ages of twelve and fourteen, have surrounded the car. Diane barely has time to cry out Mary's name in warning before one of them smashes the passenger's side window with a pipe—glass flies everywhere, straight at Mary's face, scattering and sticking in her hair. Mary screams; she seems to have ducked fast enough that the pipe didn't actually hit her—Diane can't see any blood. She tries to get the car in gear and take off, but the kid who smashed the window has his arm inside the car, has Mary by the hair—the one on Diane's side is trying to open the driver's side door but Diane always locks her door. Mary's door is open, though, and they've pulled her out—*dear God are they going to kidnap her? Rape her?*—Diane thinks for a minute about slamming on the gas and shooting the hell out of there but her foot won't obey, won't leave Mary there on the street, and in the less than twenty seconds she spends trying to decide what to do, her own window has been smashed too and she's let go of the wheel, is belly down on the seat and screaming, but two of the boys reach in and drag her from the car, fling her body right into the middle of the road.

A passing car drives around her as though she were a pothole.

The boys—they are dressed almost identically in gray or black T-shirts with jeans—have already lost interest in Mary, too. One has

Mary and Diane's purses clutched to his body and another has Mary's suitcase open and is looking through it, tossing useless items out the open car door. It occurs to Diane that they must not know how to drive—they don't actually know *how* to steal the fucking car or they'd already have taken off. Un-freaking-believable. After all this time in Colombia, worrying about FARC kidnappings, she's being held up by four pimply pre-teens who can't work a bloody stick shift! Priceless. Diane walks around to the sidewalk and takes Mary by the arm, says in disgust, "They'll be gone in a second—just hang tight."

She expects Mary to nod, maybe whimper or cower a little in her pneumoniac, hair-grabbed state. Shards of glass still hang in Mary's hair, and Diane sees a long slash on her shoulder and another on her upper arm, where some of the pieces must have hit with some impact after Mary had already ducked. Blood leaks right through Mary's shirt, dribbles down her uncovered elbow below where her sleeve has been pushed up, drips off the fingers of her right hand. Diane tries to get a better look, assess the bleeding (though of course they're headed to a hospital already), but Mary yanks her arm away, and for a second Diane thinks she's hurt her—then blinks hard.

Mary is gone! She's bolted—not in the opposite direction of the boys, rather straight at them, grabbing one by the hair and pulling him out of the car, kicking him in the stomach. Holy shit. This is not happening. This cannot be happening. Skinny little Mary, coughing her skinny little lungs out, has jumped inside the car and is shouting at the remaining three boys in Spanish, hitting them in the faces with her bloody hand, trying to grab her suitcase. Immediately one pulls out a knife—Diane can see the glint of it through the unbroken windshield, Mary and the three other boys frozen in its thrall. They are ordering Mary out of the car, shouting *"hembra rica!"* The boy Mary threw to the ground and kicked begins to rise—Diane dashes over and kicks him again, this time in the face, feels blood gush onto her shoe. Oh God! The kid is down again, his body hidden by the open car door—his buddies don't seem to have even noticed.

Then it is over. They push Mary out of the back seat by barreling her own suitcase into her chest—she catapults out backwards, landing on her ass. The boy clutching the purses has already taken off, and the other two hold the knife out in front of them while they help up their bloody mouthed friend, cursing Mary and Diane. They sprint off in the same direction as the purse-wielder, laughing like hyenas. Mary and Diane stand, relatively unscathed, staring at the wreckage. Throughout the entire ordeal, Diane has counted at least eight cars that passed by, not one stopping to help or—she bets—even call the police. On the street, there are a good ten people milling about, a few of whom have even stopped to watch the action from across the street, the rest ignoring the situation entirely, literally averting their eyes as they pass bloody Mary, stepping over the car's broken glass and the spilled entrails of her luggage.

Diane squats and begins retrieving Mary's discarded belongings. The kids threw out most of what they didn't want: Mary's girl-clothing, her make-up. Diane doesn't know what they were looking for in the suitcase—something of value they probably didn't find, though no doubt Mary's passport, Colombian ID and all of her cash were in the purse, so now she'll be fucked, with no identification, when they get to the hospital. Mary is sitting on the pavement, clutching the body of a broken doll—the doll's head, apparently made of glass, was smashed by the running foot of one of the boys. She clutches the doll, sobbing inconsolably; it must be her favorite childhood toy, Diane thinks, though it seems a weird toy for a little girl to play with, being made of glass. Still, Diane feels bad for her. She lost her own childhood teddy bear in a youth hostel in Paris more than a decade ago, and the memory of the loss still smarts—she and Eli even went back to the hostel all the way from Switzerland, but the thing was gone, probably not even stolen but thrown away. Diane contemplates going to Mary to comfort her, but the way the girl is bleeding and coughing she needs to get to the hospital more than she needs emotional support, so Diane needs to get the clothes and open suitcase back in the car, needs to brush the seats free of glass, needs to get Mary's bawling ass back inside so she can take off. She bends again, gathers more clothing in her arms.

That is when she sees it.

Eli's sweater.

Eli's sweater, strewn onto the pavement with the rest of Mary's belongings.

It is Eli's airplane sweater. The sweater he always wears to travel, so he won't have to use one of the scratchy, probably unsanitary airplane blankets.

He had it on. He had it on his body when he left for Florida.

Now, here it is, on the ground.

Mary, oblivious, keens for her broken doll. She is lying on the concrete now, tapped of all energy, her face flushed red, eyes mad with some grief or fever. It occurs to Diane for the first time that the girl is sicker than a person ought to be. That maybe she will die right there, on the shitty Colombian pavement. Maybe the shattered glass hit something major. Maybe the pneumonia is actually something worse. Maybe Diane just *wishes* these things, clutching Eli's sweater in her aging hands.

"¿Qué mira usted? ¡Anos!" She shouts at the residual crowd, gawking from their doorways, their windows. In their oppositional grief, she and Mary have both become spectacle, and Diane can only think of getting them out of here as soon as possible. "¡Le blasfemo!" She throws the remainder of the clothing into the car, onto the back seat or the floor, rushing with purpose. Eli's sweater, though, she tosses under the car, where Mary will not see it—where no one will see it until they drive away.

She imagines then, the neighbors coming out one by one. She envisions them—though she knows it will not happen this way—in a line, a procession, each trying on Eli's cable-knit, taupe-colored Irish sweater, bought in Dublin during his junior year abroad, before Mary was even born. Before Diane ended their accidental pregnancy that would, had she kept the baby, have set her life on an entirely different course so that, wherever she might be in that alternate life, she would not be *here*, with Mary, with Eli's empty sweater, right now. And so she imagines a neighborhood matriarch, stocky and strong, rolling up its sleeves and claiming the sweater for herself. She imagines Eli—wherever he is that his lovers' tryst with this sick little girl could have ended badly enough for him not to accompany her home—unable to ever board an airplane again without his Irish flying sweater, and therefore stranded, lost to her now. Wherever he is, there he will remain, unable to ever clarify how his most treasured item of clothing ended up in the suitcase of another woman—unable to ever be confronted, to affirm or deny. For twenty years, after all, Diane has been living in Limbo, without family, without a home. It only makes sense that Eli should be part of the Limbo too—that in this Limbo of dichotomies, Mary is both her enemy and her charge to save.

There is no time, though, to think of this for long. Even to Diane, the air of Bogotá suddenly feels dangerously thin. On the street, Mary is still bleeding. In the windows and the doorways, the locals have all heeded her witch's warning and are gone. ☐

THE CANDIDATE
Steve Trumpeter

The channels on this boxy hotel TV cycle with maddening sluggishness, and they all seem to be airing commercials. My first piece of advice for running a successful Senate campaign would be to find yourself a fresh-faced young eager beaver at each local party HQ and enlist him or her to load up your BlackBerry with a spreadsheet listing the channels for that town's network affiliates. The time you save could mean a twelve minute head start for that Ambien to kick in. That extra twelve minutes of sleep may save you from going off the rails at a sparsely attended Chamber of Commerce fundraiser the next morning.

I shouldn't even bother with the ten o'clock news. It's barely October, and my goose is cooked. I'm a sacrificial lamb. A lame duck with a clipped right wing. To the Bible-thumpers and tea-totalers that have warped my party's platform beyond logic and reason, I am a Republican-In-Name-Only RINO: too soft, too secular, too subtle. I'm not sure why I agreed to this in the first place. Conservatism is not what it used to be.

If elected, I solemnly swear that Creationism can be taught in schools, but only in English class.

I land on Fox News Channel to see myself bloviating, red-faced with a sharp finger puncturing the air. The sound is muted, but I know it can't be pretty if they have to blur my mouth. There's no such thing as bad press, they say, but that cliché must predate f-bombs. More pixelation onscreen as the middle fingers come out and three of my own security guards have to physically hold me back from whatever I had it in my head to do. I am briefly relieved by the fact that my wife is not here to witness this debacle, then realize that I wish to Hell she were. It was not my finest hour.

I call down to the front desk and ask them to send up a bottle of Jameson and a BLT. My BlackBerry shows that my calendar has been cleared tomorrow. We'll play duck and cover, sleep late and sip Starbucks while the hysteria burns itself out.

If elected, I solemnly swear that anyone who spends more than three dollars on their morning coffee will be legally prohibited from complaining about the price of gas.

In this bluest of the blue states, a Republican is going to poll somewhere in the range of jack and shit, even a pro-choice centrist with a proven record of fiscal responsibility and social moderation. But there were a few in the party who decided I was sympathetic and chipped away until they had me convinced I could at least elevate the discourse and give Jackson a run for his money.

They said my narrative would bring the women in droves, because it's all about sympathy for today's voting masses, about which candidate you'd want to have a beer with. I poll strongly among retirees who winter in the South, rail commuters, golfers and, for some reason, Episcopalians and Jews. They say I've got a telegenic haircut that might appeal to young centrist voters who didn't get brainwashed by the cult of Obama. When asked whom they would vote for in a Republican Senate primary, nearly seven out of ten registered voters who identify themselves as left of center or farther would choose me over any other candidate in the state. Unfortunately for me, in November, seven out of ten bleeding hearts still vote for the Democrat ten times out of ten. It's something akin to asking a straight man which NFL quarterback he'd blow if he had to choose – the kind of far-fetched hypothetical for the wee hours at a dive bar, not a poll commissioned by CNN/Gallup, interrupting your dinner, begging you not to hang up.

If elected, I solemnly swear to keep gay marriage illegal, but I'm also going to outlaw straight divorce and see what's a bigger threat to American families.

My room service arrives with a knock at my door, only it's not the bellhop, but Molly, the *Westcott for Senate* campaign's Assistant Communications Director. She is still wearing the badge around her neck that grants her access to all the private areas that get cordoned off each day, but has changed out of her pantsuit and into hip-hugging capris and a tank top. She wears a silver bracelet around her slender ankle and a tiny stud in her nose that sparkles when she tilts her head. I don't see the sandwich, but thank Christ, she's carrying whiskey.

"Long day, Congressman?" she asks. I shrug my shoulders. Despite all the hullabaloo, today really doesn't even crack the top ten, if I stop to think about it.

My chances now hinge on an October surprise or a Christmas miracle, and though I might say I no longer believe in miracles, Molly has just wrapped her lips around the bottle and taken a sizable swig, and Hallelujah, I'm beginning to see the light. She hands me the whiskey and shoots me an emasculating look when I reach for a glass from the table next to the coffee maker. She is like no Young Republican I've ever met. I take a pull straight from the bottle and let the liquor burn its way down.

My second piece of advice for running a successful Senate campaign would be to hire Molly.

"I'm mortified about this morning," she says. "We should have spotted them earlier."

"It's okay," I say. I don't want to dwell on it, despite the fact that I haven't been able to turn off the TV, where the caption now says, "Westcott Washed Up?"

"Well, I feel terrible," she says, and I hand her back the bottle. She regards it as though she's studying the ingredients, then takes another heavy gulp.

I want to reassure her, but honestly, I've had it with feelings. This whole campaign has been about feelings. Nobody's interested in facts or logic anymore. Undecided voters just want to hear which politicians will most pander to the tenets they cling to, parrot their slogans, give them the warm fuzzies. They want me to promise that the decisions I make will fix all their problems and make them feel better about their lives. And if that's all they're looking for, they might as well stay home on November 6.

If elected, I solemnly swear to repurpose Guantanamo Bay for voters who are still undecided by the first week of November.

Molly sits on the corner of the bed and takes off her badge. She's made it this far; no one's going to check her credentials now. A thin red stripe marks the skin where the string has pressed into the back of her neck.

"You can bounce back from this," she says, and I just scoff.

The footage now documents this morning's protesters holding up placards as they push their way to the front of the crowd. The benign ones just say, "Abortion is Murder" or "Judas" or "Life Begins at Conception." But there are others. Pictures of fetuses, EEG printouts, graphic depictions of surgical detritus and the grotesque aftermath. They are shouting "baby killer" and "burn in Hell," and it's not the first time these people have crashed one of my campaign events. I used to be on their side, or at least sympathetic to it, so they hate me that much more. I could explain my stance. I've got gigabytes of statistics ready to spout off, startling population facts, heartbreaking anecdotes, dollars and cents details, and plenty of nuance and eloquence to go with it. But this fucking issue, it touches a nerve deep in our cores and facts don't stand a chance. It's too personal. I guess in this, I'm a hypocrite, too, though I know I am right. I've lost any shred of doubt. This is the politician's burden: we must know that we are right, and it's harder than it looks. We're either preaching to a choir or adding fuel to a fire.

I watch this footage of myself ignoring the heckling until a few of them unroll a new poster and push their way to the front of the audience. The camera doesn't seem to have picked up the front of their placard, but it was impossible for me to miss. I swear, they shoved it right in my face. It featured a picture of my wife, Janet, with flames along the borders and a caption: God Punishes Sinners. After that, it happened just as it's been playing out on TV, feeding the news cycle at the top of every hour.

Molly steps behind me and offers the bottle over my shoulder. She has a small five-pointed star tattooed inside of her wrist. When I take the bottle, she begins to knead my shoulders. "You can't give up," she says. "Maybe you'll pick up some votes from the 'wishes-they-could-assault-a-fundamentalist' demographic. It's bigger than you think."

She is twenty-two years old, but old enough to know better. Old enough to know what happens in a Congressman's hotel room just shy of midnight after he's well into a bottle of Jameson, having torpedoed his career earlier in the day.

I click off the TV and turn toward her. Her hands slide from my shoulders and come to rest on my chest. "Molly," I say. "You shouldn't be up here."

She smirks at me, a half smile turned up on her right side, offset by the stud in her nose that catches the dim hotel lamplight like a sign from God. "Do I have to twist your arm?" She gives my tie a gentle tug and kisses me like she's about to board a plane. She grabs my wrist and gives it a playful turn, but I don't need any convincing.

"Let me make you feel better," she says. And God love her, for a while, she does.

If elected, I solemnly swear to support abstinence-only curriculum in Junior High, but sooner or later, a well-rounded education has to include some of the tricks Molly knows.

Later I feign sleep, watching through one eye as Molly shimmies back into her hip huggers and picks up her shoes. She tiptoes through the dark, waving an arm side to side in front of her. She slips out the door and pulls it shut behind her, with one hand against the frame to keep it quiet.

I feel guilty – always – at times like this, though it's fleeting. This is something I'll never be able to let go of. I do still love my wife.

I'm not sure what happened to the BLT I ordered and find myself starving, but it's too late to call for another, so I'll have to settle for an Ambien and another splash of whiskey. While I wait for it to bring me down, I turn the TV back on. It's the rally again, now yesterday's news.

This time, they found footage that has captured the poster with its caption that set me off. God Punishes Sinners. If only He limited it to them.

But I know for a fact God punishes all of us. Even Janet, who just shook her head when the doctors told her she wasn't likely to make it through the delivery; that there was only the slimmest of chances for the baby. You're facing a difficult decision, they said, but there was no choice for us that hadn't already been made, no prognosis so dire as to override what we knew to be good and just and righteous. We had ruled it out before we ever even imagined it'd be something we'd have to decide. And of course those protesters didn't know this, not the whole story, because some things you don't bring into the arena. They didn't know what we endured, what we paid. They only knew the bullet points: that I used to believe unequivocally in the sanctity of life, then, at some point after Janet died, decided I don't. I'm a flip-flopper and a heretic and all the other labels they want to throw at me. It's all true.

If elected, I solemnly swear to lie awake at night wishing we had chosen to save you, that you could still be here with me.

I stare at the old photo of Janet on the TV now and feel my temper rising again, and I know I won't go back out there. My campaign is over. Let someone else deal with the important issues of the day. Someone who knows all the right decisions, who doesn't lie awake, haunted by the nuances, the grey areas, the consequences. There are plenty to go around.

If elected, I solemnly swear that I don't know the answers.

If elected, I solemnly swear that I'll never stop paying for being so wrong.

If elected, I solemnly swear that no one's going to feel any better. □

composite character
Robert Brown

fourth grade boy slides a coltrane solo [of a body] in to the seat
nearest the door not knowing that it would have been proper to
raise a wand in the air. a thin tree managing shadows across the
floor like charlie brown's christmas. piano begins, or does not
begin, it's all a pantomime. fourth grade boy believes he will be
counted amongst the dead for being early and bright. teachers
will think it worthwhile to conjure a corpse. sing promises into
the red dirt like it's a diary. *i will explain the horror thing* the
absence of his hand, his eyes and fourth grade boy heart will
not stay with him instead he will lift a concrete block awaiting the day or night the good lord falls from heaven that glass
menagerie, wet with oil, which he had thought to visit when the
bubbling block was lighter

SNOW
Robert Brown

Snow

The powder did not stick to the stick on the ground, the awkward ladybug below, or on the ground. The ground was wet and cars passing spilled paintings from their backdoors. Undone paintings. Paintings that had trouble fitting in on their respective canvasses, no real lungs you see, and needed lungs to breathe, so they spilled onto the ground. In order of period. Out into the snow and mated passionately with the snow and the snow gave new paints with the potential for taking breath away.

Snow

This rectangle was all white once. All snow with nothing but glass underneath. Beautiful. Then four fingers slid a wide U into the center: from the top left a courageous dive, wobbly line, upward sag. Four new fingers, maybe not quite as cold, add four new letters in cursive A FAG. The snow is a fag? Is that why fingers wiped it out to make new spellings? The snow is magic still. The snow is not afraid of little fingers with meaty sacks attached at the wrists. The snow is made of water too. Mostly. The snow is a brain. Emily Dickinson wrote all about it. Said "the brain is just the weight of God."

Snow

We pass by the bus stop where members of his ensemble wrote TTS @ DePaul onto the brick wall. There is snow in the crack of a brick; it's so small it's hiding its gender: water. We pass the snow, even as it kisses our faces affectionately. Cleaves to our legs crying " " as we march on. Snow is so " " and also " " Sometimes I want to take " " of it because it takes mere " " to die.

Snow

Inside water is life. Inside life is God. Inside God is love. Inside love is pain. Inside pain is memory. Inside memory is a birthday cake around which stand two women I love alive and taking care of children who grew

old and had their own. Inside a birthday cake is chocolate. Inside chocolate is milk. Inside milk is water (87.3%). Some water is snow.

fourth grade boy plays out the window too much his teacher writes somewhere in red ink like she's building *too much* from thin air.

from The Illusion That Is With its Costume On

Robert Brown

I. A.
Different sizes of wood, around them rooms that *are*
to *be*
clean dust kid, folding sonnets into birds
that do slit
on set. Birds with fourteen wings "that are" not patient at all.

B.
What's *instress* mean? Oh, wiry appendages of the everyday *beam* from
dinner bells,
fireworks, whenever one on the grand proscenium *sees*
personal face *become* The Great Repetition there is one who knows a little
pink oil to slide
the patient tin man *forward*.
To make him a pink house

C.
of equipment red high heels, lists with pizza on them, a wedding dress
with pearls stitched. Sudden as the
flash
of emerald upstage he
the actor hears a voice say "give them hell" so he
questions
"is this real
if you must break the fourth wall
to give it to your audience?" The Illusion that is, racing, with
its costume on.

II. A.
If you remember something ancient
recalls. Whether it is or is not
The Lord on your side, the reddest fabric,
smallest gels, wonderfully executed
executed wonderfully pathos.

B.
you don't love me as much as you say
you don't love me as much as you say
you don't love me as much as you say
you do because if you did you would say
something natural. Or, the Complete Works
of William Shakespeare Abridged. It's obvious
smoking dense cigars with an owl outback
is a bad way for literature to go. I will always be
for you for you is the subject. You is a sonnet
or a pun chickened out.

C.
One day I will be forced to tell the hardest stories of my life. Because
I know those will be stories with the most love. The easy solution is to
affirm that, that day is not today. But then what is at stake? Not the whole
world. And if the whole world isn't at stake, or isn't affected, I will pout
and pout and not take any deliverance from anybody. Here—bow. It is
your bow. It is your bow. If I could I would wear it like a shape.

(To frame and claps. Exit The Illusion That Is With Its Costume On).

WAITING
Marcia Cavell

Before me is a picture of Stanley leaning into a very large window at Logan Airport, his hands cupped at the sides of his eyes to shield them from the glare of the sun. His shoulders are hunched and he is intently staring at something in the distance. Even though his face is turned away from us, we know that this man is grieving. Stanley was my first husband, and after one of her frequent visits to him in Boston, he is sending our five-year-old daughter, Rachel, back home to me in New York. With a nametag around her neck and accompanied by a stewardess, she is boarding the plane. Perhaps a few minutes ago she had her arms around his knees, snuffling "Papa Daggy" through her tears, and he had picked her up and said, "I'm mad about you, baby girl, and I'll see you in two weeks. It may seem like forever but it won't really be so long."

The day my father left when I was eighteen months old was just a normal Saturday. It took a long time to realize that the leaving that day wasn't itself the catastrophe. The catastrophe was his total disappearance after he left. He hadn't moved; he hadn't died. He just disappeared. Many years later, my therapist, Bob, announced an imminent departure and I, embarrassed to be enacting 'the patient' protested, as always. He added that he would be going away again several times in the coming months. He smiled as he said it, and I realized I was missing some subtlety. Oh. Of course. He couldn't go away *again* unless he had come back. And he did come back. The cycle continues until – I am always certain it will happen – disaster strikes. Leaving becomes disappearing.

The story of the circumstances in which my birth was embedded is still scarcely credible to me. In brief: within the span of two years and some months my parents married each other twice, divorced each other twice, and gave birth to me. In the first few months after the divorce my father visited me once a week. Then those visits abruptly ended.

As a mature woman I was skeptical of this whole account that my mother, in bits and pieces, gave me when I was growing up. So during that period in my life in which I was moved to open previously locked doors, I wrote to the Bureau of Records in Cook County, Illinois, asking them to send me copies of the relevant documents. I possess proof of the following:

July 6, 1930: first marriage of my parents.
December 4, 1930: annulment of first marriage.
January 4, 1931: second marriage of my parents.
December 4, 1931: my birth.
October 1932: my parents' divorce.

This is the synopsis I will be fleshing out.

* * *

I used to tell myself stories about my mother and father. In one, my courting father drives her along the shores of Lake Michigan to the Indiana dunes where he knows she had loved to go with her father. I have a photograph of my curly-headed mother and my grandfather atop a dune, my grandfather smoking his pipe beside her. She is looking up at him adoringly while he gazes steadily across the lake. I make something of the fact that he is not looking at her, nor is he bundling her close to him. He elicits love, but I have gathered that he was too self-absorbed to be able to return it.

My parents' matchmaker was my Uncle Hardin. From work he knew Malcolm Jennings, or Bill, my father, who would have seemed in many ways a suitable partner for my mother. The economic reasons for the marriage were the most pressing. My grandmother Helen, who was so parsimonious that she saved and carefully folded birthday and Christmas wrappings, had been in straitened circumstances since her divorce from Lee, my grandfather, and was now supported largely by Hardin and Aunt Madeleine. Bill was doing very well and could take care of my mother, who was a worry to Helen. My mother was twenty and my father thirty-six when they married.

Like Lee, Bill valued self-reliance. Like Lee, he came from Midwestern farmer stock and 'good blood', as my grandmother would have put it. In addition, Bill was an artist, or so my mother thought when she married him. That is, he was an *advertising artist*, a qualification that mattered a great deal to my mother, who grew up idolizing 'the real thing': her famous father, the poet Edgar Lee Masters who wrote *Spoon River Anthology*, and his artist friends – Carl Sandburg, Theodore Dreiser, Percy Granger – artists who are still remembered, who established for themselves a secure place in the lineage of American artists, but who were never considered first-rate, though my idolizing mother would have put my grandfather closer to Keats than to Sandburg.

But Bill's wish to study at the Chicago Art Institute had been thwarted by his need to support his mother – a story parallel to my mother's who had wanted, as an aspiring poet, to go to the University of Chicago to study English, but couldn't because for her too there wasn't enough money. So my father went into business. Now I wonder what he felt about his sacrifice and about the work that took its place. As a child I didn't know what an advertising artist was, and my guess is that Mother didn't either, though her tone of voice when she spoke of it betrayed contempt. Would he have been a painter? A sculptor? And what artists did he admire? Like many others, these questions about him occurred to me only much later in my life.

Lee was not only a famous poet but also the law partner of one of America's most famous lawyers, Clarence Darrow, who defended Loeb and Leopold (one of whom had lived near the house in which I grew up on Kenwood Avenue), and John Scopes, who was on trial for teaching evolution in a public school. Darrow was a defender of the poor and those whom nobody else would defend, of rebels, and unions. Despite the familial havoc that he caused and the genuine cruelty of which he was capable, I am still proud of my grandfather for sharing these moral convictions. Then, after five years of partnership between the two men, there was a thunderous falling out.

The *coup de grace* was a sonnet sequence called "The Return" about his wife that was published in *Poetry Magazine* and several newspapers in 1923, around the time of their divorce. Once or twice the sonnets were mentioned in my house with the same whispered horror that in those days one spoke, or didn't quite speak, of cancer. My mother never described the sonnets to me, and there was no copy in the house. Again in that period in which I began opening myself to the past I tracked them down in the public library.

The day the Chicago papers announced the divorce, photographers surrounded the house – *our* house, for it was the house in which he also grew up — with their snapping, blinding lights, branding my mother, who was thirteen, with shame. The following two sonnets are no worse than the other eleven:

I.

When he returned he saw the porch at first
    Where cornices and pillars showed decay.
The entrance door was scaling, seemed accursed;
    The water troughs had rusted quite away.

Then it was raining, and the house was cold;
　　And over wires for lights, the telephone,
A vine hung thick as moss, and the rain tolled
　　The minutes in a monotone.
He stood beside a window and looked out
　　Into a yard of tangled grass and leaves.
And the rain swishes from a half broken spout,
　　And gusts of wind blew water from the eaves.
She came in and was singing, asked him then:
　　"Are you not happy to be home again?"

II.

He turned to see how yellow was her face
　　Creased where the collops met along her cheeks;
And see her greasy jacket with torn lace,
　　And the drab hair that crossed her brow in streaks...
Then looked again at this autumnal morgue
　　Of long neglected bushes; then away
His fancy hurried to the Luxembourg,
　　And Chopin's waltzes he had heard that day,
Only a month ago. Then there was rain,
　　But lyric rain that mingled with nocturnes
And no pain then save as delight is pain,
　　And not the ache of clouds and broken urns.
She still was standing in the door and said:
　　"If you are ill, you'd better go to bed."

Granny probably did say, "Aren't you glad to be home again?" a question that in its extraordinary obliviousness to the present conditions for them all must itself have maddened Lee. Decorum was one of Granny's principal values, and defenses. Perhaps there is a story that would make what Lee did not merely understandable, but forgivable, though I can't imagine what it would be. It's impossible that he was unaware of the effects of his fully conscious, deliberate, actions, not only on his wife, but also on his children. While he was not an evil man, his sonnets tell us that he could be heart-stoppingly cruel.

It was Clarence Darrow, incidentally, whom my grandmother Helen engaged as her lawyer when she sued Lee for divorce. He must have been enraged beyond endurance by the two of them. In his auto-biography (*Across Spoon River*) Lee tells us, in a voice both admiring and resentful, how canny she was. Indeed. What an ingenious, coolly impersonal, perfectly decorous way of expressing her own fury, and spearing him. In my growing-up years with my grandmother I never saw this side. But when I did, so much later, I was relieved, for her, and proud. I'm sure my mother ambivalently saw her mother's action in a different light.

Many critics praise Masters for finding a new cadence and a new subject for poetry – elevating the everyday life of everyday Midwestern Americans. And perhaps in order for him to tell the blunt truths he wanted to tell in the particular way he wanted to tell them, the women in his family paid a heavy toll – even I, a generation removed from the earlier traumas.

Compared to what Lee had done, my father's leaving me was a mere peccadillo. Perhaps the lingering effects of the misery that her father had caused her was one of the reasons my mother divorced my father when I was so young, and soon told him that he couldn't see me again.

In my imagination Bill was smitten with my mother from the first. She was a larky young woman with mirthful brown eyes, affectionate, with an easily aroused sense of humor, and guileless. As a child I loved the stories she told me about her own childhood, and the massages she gave me with warm eucalyptus oil when I was sick. And when I was older, going with her downtown to Marshall Field's to try on hats, which we did with a sense of mischief and hilarity, and sampling testers on the perfume counter, smelling each other's wrists, our vocabularies for smells getting sillier and sillier.

Shortly after her marriage Mother fled to Granny in tears and she and I stayed with her for a couple of months. She told her that the first night of their honeymoon my father asked her to call a woman named Stella. Why didn't he do it himself? I don't remember what Mother said when I was old enough to be told this part of the story, but presumably it was because Stella, too, was married. Mother did call the first time he asked. After that she balked. Why did she consent in the first place? Perhaps fear of him, together with a permanent sense of how little she was worth. The final insult was that her husband didn't want to make love to her. Why? Because she was a virgin. When mother requested an annulment she told the judge about the incident with Stella, that her husband beat her, and that he spurned her sexually. The request was formally granted on December 4, 1930.

A couple of months later Bill called on her and begged her to give him another chance. Would she at least have dinner with him? I suspect that Granny and Hardin again played a large role in the baroque scenario that followed. Granny was always the family pragmatist and I can imagine her saying something like, "Marcia dear, perhaps you should give him a second chance. He may have learned his lesson, and it's clear he loves you. He just needs the love of a good woman." Whatever the reason, Mother agreed. But when they went to the Cook County courthouse to get a license, she couldn't go through with it. Bill was furious and left her standing tearfully on the street.

Yet they did begin again. Bill told my mother that on New Year's Eve he was taking the train to New York with two good friends. Would she come with them? They could be married in New York, with his friends as their witnesses. She told me this story several times, and when I grew older I wondered why she wasn't insulted that this proposal was tacked onto a pleasure trip with someone else.

One of the dramatic details in Mother's story was that they were married in New York on New Year's Eve, and that when the marriage was announced in the New York papers, Hardin called to congratulate her. But the Cook County records show that they were married in Chicago on January 4, 1931, exactly eleven months before I was born. Mother divorced him six months later. This sort of confabulation was among the things that motivated me to check the official records about the crucial dates of my early history.

The more precise coincidence is between my birthday and the annulment December 4. I realized now that the coincidence must have had a profound significance for them. For my mother it was an annual, rueful confirmation of what she already knew but had ignored when she annulled the marriage, and a poignant premonition that I, too, would grow up without a father. I don't know what the coincidence meant to my father, but it must have been a sad reminder of a failure for which he knew he was responsible. My guess is that he never had any doubts about that.

At the divorce proceedings she told the judge that they had sex just one time, the night of my conception; that Bill hit her; that he didn't give her enough money to run the household, let alone enough to buy clothes, though he had a fancy wardrobe; and that more than once he had dragged her in her nightgown around the bedroom floor by her heels, the windows wide open to the winter wind, while I was screaming in my crib. It is one of that cluster of images from my past that I feel are engraved in my brain. Madeleine, Mother's witness at the divorce proceedings, confirmed that Bill had hit her. She saw the large bruises on her face. My father was given the right to see me once a week. When I was eighteen he would be free to see me when we both liked.

Why did Mother agree to that second marriage? She always said that she was "forced" into it. I can certainly believe that she was pressured. But the annulment and the divorce themselves tell us that she was quite able to say No when No was called for. So something else was going on. She agreed because, despite everything, she still loved him? Or was excited by him, perhaps in part because she feared him, but – and – also sexually? As a child I had never seen a picture of my father. I think I asked, but there were none in the house. The first I saw was many years later when I got in touch with Anne, his second wife. It was a large photograph, taken, perhaps, when he was in his forties. He is a seductively beautiful man who is looking straight at me with clear, warm eyes. He has a broad brow, like mine, and his aspect is interested and slightly amused. I had always thought I looked like my mother, and I do, but equally like my father through the lower half of my face. He is wearing a white shirt and a solid tie, and between two fingers he snugs a cigarette from which, like an artist's fading signature, a barely visible line of smoke is curling. He looks like a man who is capable of intimacy, the thing I demand most urgently from a lover or a friend. He looks like a man with whom I might fall in love. A few years ago Rachel asked to borrow the photograph and framed it for me as a Christmas surprise. She clearly picked up my mute longing, of which even I was not quite aware. I have the photograph on the wall behind my bedroom door so that I can hide or examine it at my pleasure.

When I asked Mother why my father wasn't coming to see me any more she said that they had had a fight and decided that it wouldn't be good for me to be torn between them, that he might want to have me some of the time, or even all the time – a surprising and exciting idea, and that she wouldn't be able to stand it if I were taken from her. It wouldn't be good for either her or me. Perhaps, as I remarked earlier, the ghosts of her own childhood hovered in the background, and in banishing my father for good she thought was saving me from her fate.

The coincidences don't end with the annulment of my parents' first marriage and my birth. Not long after their divorce my father married Anne, who gave birth on December 4th, 1934, to a little girl they named Joan. Again, the coincidence must have had meaning for those it concerned. It couldn't have been merely a notch on the world's time-line. Perhaps for my father Joan's birthday was the annual commemoration of mine. Or so I like to think. Anne told me years later that it annoyed her because it took some specialness away from their own child. She didn't want Joan to be a perpetual reminder for my father of me. When I was a child my mother said that perhaps I had a sibling, but she didn't know for sure. And she said nothing about the eerie December 4th coincidence.

I realize now for the first time in the very act of writing about it that throughout the early years of my childhood my mother must have been reeling from what she'd been through. In addition she was working as a full-time journalist for the *Chicago Tribune*. My daytime 'mother' was my grandmother Helen. If Mother talked about her feelings about all this to me then, or ever, I don't remember what she said. But I was surely always aware of them. And I must have reassured her that she was good, and that, after all, something wondrously beautiful had come from her disastrous marriages.

Perhaps Mother's explanation that my father might want me to live with him all the time opened a secret door to alternate realities. I had sometimes wondered what it would be like to be my friend Jane, or my grandmother, but it hadn't occurred to me to wonder, consciously, what it would be like to live with this stranger who was my father. Where would we live? Would it be just the two of us? And in what kind of a house? In the city? In the country? Would my father be strict with me? Or also affectionate, indulgent, and adoring, like my friend Elizabeth's father, who often, as the bad gorilla, romped with her in the living room and taught her geography and chess? These are questions I explicitly ask now. Perhaps, if also then, I imagined Tom's dark, unfathomable cave, or Mary's secret garden, or at the back of the enchanting, terrifying, North Wind. As I became old enough to put such questions explicitly to myself, the larger questions of the 'philosopher', who *might* I have been? Would I still have been me? Who would I be if I had grown up with my father? Who would I be if my father had not left? As a child, the fundamental questions to which there were in fact answers, though I didn't know them, were, Where is he? Why did he leave? And why didn't he ever come back? My mother's one-sentence answer – we had a fight – told me only that she didn't want to talk about it. All I knew was that he had just disappeared. When I asked her where he lived, she said in a town not far from us (Lake Forest, a suburb of Chicago), which made the puzzles of why he never visited me, why I never heard from him or got birthday or Christmas presents from him, yet deeper.

There were two stories about what happened on the day my father left. The first is the one I knew as a child, and even though I later learned that it was false, and could even have seen that it was full of inconsistencies, until a few years ago it was still the first answer that came to my mind. In this story it is a usual Saturday morning and my father is coming to see me. It is spring. Cicadas are singing their scratchy songs of love. I am dressed in my best white dress and my ankle-high white shoes. I am so excited that I shit in the entrance hall and smear the shit around the floor in a fit of lavish generosity. When I greet my father in the midst of my mess, he is disgusted with his fecal child, and leaves. I see that the story explains things, and it puts the blame on me, leaving him clear to be the strong, perfect father I need him to be. Yet at the same time it puts the power in my hands. I am not being left, I am driving him away. I am both, *the abused* and *the abuser*. Of course I don't mean that these ideas were conscious, but that something like them was working somewhere in my mind.

In the second story I throw a tantrum. I remember once standing in the bathtub when I was about six and screaming, and Mother telling me "You will be a force for great good or great evil, it's up to you," a prophecy that weighed heavily on my childhood soul. In this second story, too, with my anger I drive my father away. When children asked me where my father was, I told them that I didn't have a father. Of course I did. Though, in a way, it's true that I didn't. And thinking that I didn't protected me from acknowledging that I had a father who didn't want to father me. Saturday became the recurring day of disappointment, mourning, sad bewilderment, and again the urgent question, What have I done?

Years ago, after telling one of my many analysts about my father's 'abandoning' me when I was so young, she said, "You must still be very angry with him!" Each time I undertook an analysis, or therapy, it was because of a sense of worthlessness, and guilt, and because I was acting in self-destructive ways, not finishing my dissertation, hopping into bed with inappropriate men, driving appropriate men away.

After my divorce from Stanley there was a mostly meaningless string of lovers, some of them with men I didn't even find attractive and who were demeaning to me. Brooke was a handsome, talented, and charming man whom I met at a Saturday night party of Nina's, a good friend of mine, and who invited me to go home with him. I was tempted, but also uneasy. I had met this man only just now. Sometimes I could say to myself that perhaps this would be a lasting affair, but this time I knew it wouldn't. I asked Nina for advice. Of course what I really wanted was permission. I wasn't so much afraid as a little ashamed to be giving in to the impulse, once again, to indulge in what would undoubtedly be a one night stand. "He won't hurt you," she said after a moment's thought, "and you'll have a good time." We went to his house, and the sex was physically good. He was a prolific lover. But when, in the middle of things, he said, laughing, "Sex is the best game in town," and erupted inside of me, I blindingly envisioned myself as a dead animal. I had been looking forward to reading the Sunday paper with Brooke over a cup of coffee in the morning. He told me that he had a lot of work to do and that I would have to go home. He didn't even take me to the train. I was angry and humiliated. But like a cow to slaughter I followed orders and numbly called a taxi. Now I see that

I set the whole thing up, as I did other demeaning sexual relationships. Why would I want to do such a thing? Perhaps it goes something like this.

If I think of myself as the horrid child who drives her father away, then he is in the clear and she can hold onto my fantasy of the perfect father, the one who protects her from all harm and pain. I am the one at fault. And as I become smaller and dirtier, he becomes larger and more radiant. My fecal badness becomes a condition for having the golden father. I wonder if my father could have had any idea how his loss would cripple me, causing me to look for men who were super-stars in a desperate attempt to repair the original loss, men to give me a sense of my own value, which, because it was borrowed, so easily shattered in the mirror of their eyes.

"I know. You'd think I'd be furious. But I'm not. And I never have been. I think he did a very bad thing that really harmed me. But it's a thought, and not an angry thought."

"Just you wait," she said.

Stanley and I separated when Rachel was two-and-a half years old. Stanley was that very talented, powerful, seductive man who would tell me who I was and to whom I would feel beholden. But there was a big difference between the effect on Rachel of her parents' divorce and the effect of mine on me. Both Stanley and I were committed to Rachel's maintaining a close relationship with him throughout her childhood. It was easy for us to do. He and I had parted amicably, both of us feeling sad that we were not still together. In fact, we didn't quite understand how the parting had happened. He was a man of deep integrity and commitment and he loved Rachel dearly from the first. I have a small picture of him holding her over his shoulder with an expression on his face close to ecstasy. For a couple of years while the three of us were still in Berkeley, Stanley often walked Rachel to nursery school and came to our house for dinner. When he moved to Boston, before and after Rachel and I also moved east, we made sure that she would see him every two weeks. She didn't have a father she could see every day, but she saw him often enough to maintain a genuine relationship.

In my thirties I belatedly wanted to know more about my father. I searched my memory for the name of his business partner. To my surprise I came up with it, McFarland, and I looked him up in the Chicago telephone directory. He was dead, but Mrs. McFarland was alive, and she put me in touch with Joan, who happened, like me, to be living in New York. She and I had lunch together several times and we talked about the father that she had known, and the father that I hadn't. She said he was a very good father, stern when needed, but loving. As for

Joan and me, I think we found each other nice – I had the feeling that she was nicer, kinder, more thoughtful, than I – but basically incompatible. I was 'an intellectual', and like her father – our father – Joan lived in the world of business. Anne invited us down to Saratoga, Florida where she still lived in the house that she had shared with my father, and she told me why my father never came back. I tell the story this way.

It is a Saturday morning. Anne and my father drive up to my house in South Chicago where I am waiting on the front porch. They come up the steps to get me, and we three go down the walk to my father's car where they nestle me between them. But something is wrong. Claudia, the maid we have had since before my mother, comes slowly down the steps with a troubled look. "Miss Marcia don' wan' you take the baby off the steps," she says, and lifts me away from my father and Anne. My parents agreed that he would not come again. I imagine that pride and fury played at least as large a part in his concurrence with my mother as did concern for me. Anne told me that she didn't approve of his decision and often told him so.

She told me many other spellbinding things as well. One day I appeared unannounced at my father's office on Dearborn Street. His secretary opened his door and told him that Marcia Jennings was in the waiting room. Should she show her in? He assumed it was my mother (after whom I was named) and was taken aback when it turned out to be me. Perhaps he asked me where I was going to college and I said, "Smith." "Good for you!" he said. Then some talk about what I wanted to major in. Perhaps I said something like, "I'm not sure. Right now it's English literature, but I used to want to be a concert pianist and a composer. Now I'm not sure. I think I'm giving it up. I just don't I have the talent." "Maybe you do. Go for it," he said, "if that's what you really want to do. I wanted to be an artist when I was your age, but my family didn't have the means to support me. I had to make money." But of course the conversation couldn't have been anything remotely so candid, on either side. What on earth did we talk about? Nor can I remember whether I told Mother about this meeting, but I think I did, and that she reported I had been disappointed.

This was a meeting I impulsively made on my own initiative. The second meeting was the one that had been long promised. My memory of it is hazy, at best. But I do remember a large hotel, or something like it. Oh. Like suddenly hearing the third voice in a string trio, I recall 'The University Club' – here is another of those times in which I suddenly remember something in the very moment of writing about it. It was a luncheon, but I have no idea how it was arranged, or by whom, or what was said. The party turned out to include not only my father but also his wife and Joan, my now undeniably existent sister. I think I remember my father's telling me not to eat so fast, a chiding that pleased me since it was addressed directly, and accurately, to me.

Anne phoned me shortly after that lunch. Mother answered the phone. Anne was inviting me and Joan to Florida for a weekend. Mother and I talked about it. I didn't know what to do. I was curious. But I also knew that my going would deeply upset her, and I was afraid of feeling intense loneliness, afraid of feeling that I was on the wrong side of a window looking at the happy family inside. I think I felt that it would make my father too real, real as a man who had his own ongoing life, which now included another daughter. I said No.

Again, what did he feel? What did he make of the fact that I turned them down? Was he relieved? Disappointed? Was he curious about me? Guilty? He must have been all these things. The questions expand: What were his demons and how did they get there? What was the world of his childhood like? Was his father belittling? His mother overbearing? Or were the dynamics of his family not those at all? Writing this I find I have begun to let him in as something other than a wind-filled ghost, a simulacrum of a human being – no history, indeed no human present. He will always remain a mystery. But I can no longer hope to know him. He's dead. Anne is dead. And so is my mother, whose memory I wouldn't trust in any case. Joan is alive, and still precisely three years younger than me. But she wouldn't be able to give me a lot of the answers I want.

I do remember, some weeks or months after that luncheon, sitting in a red velvet chair in my bedroom with the white wallpaper patterned with blue cornflowers, a room I loved and without thought of cost had lavishly decorated myself, now that my mother had married a man who was generous with his substantial salary. For a while I thought of calling or writing my father, which for my sake I certainly should have done. But I put it out of my mind with the angry thought that it was his place to call, not mine. – At first, just this minute, instead of 'angry' I wrote 'proud.' It is still easier for me to apologize than to scream. – and that was the end of the business with my father.

On that visit to Saratoga, Anne told me other things that slowly changed my understanding of my past. She had kept in a box all my father's cancelled checks against the time, she said, when she and I might meet. I was impressed that she had been so thoughtful of me. From my mother's requests to the courts that my father give her more alimony, requests that were denied, Anne knew that money had been an issue. The checks told me that the alimony was not thirty dollars a month but thirty dollars a week. I don't think Mother lied. Her imagination had made this conversion and it soon became for her the truth. But to me, the difference between the sum she had reported and the actual sum was the difference between a stingy father who cared nothing for us, and a father who may have given my mother all he could, both because we were living in the Depression and because he was supporting his mother.

Anne said that my father needed gentleness and trust in the early years of his marriage, that he came to it feeling like "a very bad man," guilty about his failure with my mother and guilty also about his desertion of me. For some reason the only other thing I remember her telling me about him was that he had suffered unspeakably as a soldier in the war. He told her only one war story, about a man in the bed next to him in the hospital at Verdun who had a wound in his leg that had to be kept clean, which, because the hospital was out of medicine, it did by gorging the wound with maggots. She always wondered if the man was my father himself.

Anne's temperament was sunny and full of a sense of fun, which apparently my father appreciated. When she met him she was one of a trio of pretty young women who sang popular songs on the radio. My father courted her and she was immediately attracted to him, for his masculine beauty, and for the good man she could see beneath the temper, which with her help he learned to constrain. He needed "taming," she said. Once, before they were married, he struck her, and she told him that if that ever happened again the engagement was off. It never did. He never lied to her. He never strayed. And he never kept money from her, either when she needed it for household expenses or for her personal needs. He was a man almost the opposite from the one my mother had described. He was a *husband*, and a *father*, which made my loss, my envy of Joan, the more acute. What had happened to transform him so? Was it Anne? Or chagrin over his marriages to my mother? Or perhaps both, abetted by a belated growing up.

The germs of my fantasies about my father included my Uncle Bart, whom I feared and adored in just the right daughterly proportion. Every Christmas he gave each of his two daughters, my beloved cousins, an enormous doll or stuffed animal, which I desperately wanted. I could scarcely bear my envy. One Christmas he gave me one too, an enormous Raggedy Ann doll with her long red-and-white striped stockings and her white pinafore, and I wept with joy. I adored the doll. But more, Uncle Bart had now included me among his daughters.

One incident with Ann and 'our father' is burned into the deepest level of my memory. The upstairs hall is filled with light. Ann and I have taken off our shorts and our underpants and are standing on our heads when Uncle Bart comes up the stairs, pauses for a moment, and then says soberly, but without anger, "Put your clothes on girls." I am embarrassed, and greatly relieved that he didn't scold. In retrospect I think he behaved just as a father should. He didn't ignore the gravity of the incident but he didn't scare us, and it was clear that our shameless-ness made no difference to his love.

My picture of a father was also constructed from the wartime mov-ies, many of which were about absent fathers, all of them good, kind, authoritative, protective men: Gregory Peck in *Keys of the Kingdom*, Walter Pidgeon in *Mrs. Miniver*, and Joseph Cotten in *Since You Went Away*. In some additional movie from that time – I was around thirteen – that I vividly remember, though I can't recall its name or its stars, a woman is about to give birth and no other woman is around to help her deliver her baby. Some man – husband, friend, stranger? – plays mid-wife. He is at the foot of her bed. She is screened from our view, but not his, and we know she has her legs spread wide. I could feel a new, surprising heat spreading my own. She is so completely helpless and exposed, and he is so deeply absorbed in what he sees and does with her.

At the end of *Since You Went Away* I was sobbing. I had gone to the movie with a friend and her mother, whom I worried and who sug-gested that I needed to spend more time with my friends. Even I knew that my feelings were exaggerated. I also knew that they were probably evoked by my father. I am now pleased to realize that despite my seri-ous lapses of memory, my father was in fact always inside of me.

The scary father surfaced in dreams, or at least that's how I inter-pret them. When I was about eleven I had the following dream, images which have been part of the cluster all these years. I know my age because the *mise-en-scene* was the house on Kenwood Avenue that we sold when I was eleven.

Mother and Granny are having a big party. We are in the kitchen and Mother asks me to take out the garbage. I go to the front of the house where the garbage alcove is [there was, in fact, the one I envi-sioned]. I stop just inside the archway and am scared by a man half hidden in the dank gloom, a man wearing a hat slouched down over his eyes, smoking a cigarette, and with red finger nail polish. I scream and run upstairs, shouting "Something bad is about to happen. Everyone get out!" I fly across the street to a neighbor's house. When I go home in the morning a woman dressed in white with a strange expression on her face opens the door. She says that my mother will be all right but that she can't have any visitors now. She closes the door and I am alone.

After many years of analysis I still have no understanding of that dream. Why the sexual ambiguity (the red nail polish)? What has he done to my mother? What is the awful thing he intends to do to her, and does? He injures her in some mysterious way. The baby? The pregnancy? Or am I on the wrong track altogether?

I am still surprised at the sight of fathers taking care of their little children, holding babies close to their chests in a sling, playing with their older children, teaching them. Surprised – after all these years – and envious.

I am on the bus, looking out the window. On the sidewalk is a father with his little girl who is about a year-and-a-half old. It's drizzling. He picks her up and settles her in her stroller, carefully lowering the plastic cover that will protect her from the rain.

A father is walking hand in hand with his child, asking her 'Which side am I on?' She is baffled. "Am I on your right side or your left?"

On his own back a father carries his daughter's pack with a stuffed bear sticking out.

A small child stumbles as she balances herself along a curb. "I lose my balance."

"Where did you lose it?" he asks her. She giggles.

A father puts his finger to his lips. "Cool it. You're being too loud."

A little girl is sticking her finger in her father's nostril, tugging at his ear.

A man and a woman are in a crosswalk with a gaggle of three little kids mindlessly careering behind them. "Follow Daddy," the mother says to them. Then again, imperiously, "Follow Daddy."

A father picks up his little girl with the scraped knee and dries her tears while the two of them inspect her wound together.

A boisterous little black girl, her hair dressed in blue-beaded cornrows, chattering non-stop, stumbles up the steps of the bus with her father. She can't sit still and is bouncing back and forth from one side of the bus to the other. "Baby, you gotta stop that," her father says gruffly, but with no effect. A man on the other side of the bus and I are smiling at the little scene. "Babe, you do what I say." Finally he grabs her. She buries her face in his lap giggling. Then, "Mommy!"

I am surprised again and again, not only by the attention these fathers pay to their little daughters but also that they are paying it to *daughters*. Aren't fathers interested only in little boys? My friends comment that we didn't see fathers doing such things when we were growing up because the roles of men were so different. Yes. But that misses my feelings of envy of these little girls, and my sadness.

My sister Joan told me that when she learned her father was dying she drove to the hospital as fast as she could and found him on a gurney in a hall, an I-V in his arm, waiting for a room. "Hi Daddy," she said. He took her hand and squeezed it. She said she had the feeling that he had been waiting to see her before he died. Again I am envious. Would he have done that for me?

My second husband, whom I married in 1984 when I was in my fifties, died unexpectedly in 2003. Strange – yesterday, for just a moment, I figured that the time that has elapsed between Donald's death and now is determined in the same way as it is between two dates in the past, say December 4th, 1931, and July 16, 1932. If the distance between the dead and the living were like that, the time of Donald's death to 'now' would always be nine years. My period of mourning would always be the same. There would be no more grieving, no more fantasizing, no more re-constructing the past as it lives for me in the present, and he would not be slipping further and further away from me. I knew something was wrong with my way of thinking but for a brief moment I didn't know what it was.

The afternoon they took my husband off the life-support machines I knew I would wake up in the middle of the night not only unbelieving that the man who had always been a breath away from me was not, but also in an agony of dread, about dying, about the possibility that I had mis-lived my life, and about something else that was nameless, like the "falling forever" that is D.W. Winnicott's attempt to describe the anxious infant. I was desperate for the warm body whose contours I knew so well, for the smell of the back of his neck, wondering who I was and how was I going to continue from now on. What was my life about? Who, now that Donald was dead, who would hold it together, would hold me together? I was stranded in a landscape to be forever whipped by a nettled wind. The waiting would never end.

When we are waiting there is, necessarily, something we are waiting for: the mailman, the promised ring, the bus, our wedding day, the doctor's word. The grammar of waiting, like that of 'wanting' and 'hoping for' and 'fearing', gives it an object. All are conditions of lack. They live partly in the present, more, obviously, in the future, and of course also in the past, which is where we learned what to want, or dread. But as is not the case with wanting and hoping for, the object of our waiting need not be something we think of as good: one can wait for – await – the executioner's song, the teacher's reproof. Nor need we know that we are waiting, or what we are waiting for, and so we may accept, even look for, surrogates that we do not recognize as such and that furtively maraud our souls: wealth, or fame, or a man like Brooke. Sometimes, for a while, reality, the healthy self, and luck, prevail. Stanley truly had much of what I needed and he was a good man, though less able to be the husband that might have helped me heal than I could have known, both because I was unaware of my own wounds and because my inexperience and my scars kept me from seeing his.

Since one may have experienced the object of waiting as both painful and pleasurable, she may, unknowingly, seek, accept, the pain as promise and condition of the pleasure. To wait, in full consciousness that you are waiting, so, in a condition of lack, and fully conscious of what you are waiting for, demands patience, and courage, and perhaps faith. I think of Kierkegaard's 'Knight of Faith,' who continues to hope for the little treat at the end of the day, though he knows there will be none. Are Vladimir and Estragon (*Waiting for Godot*), whose lives consist of acknowledged waiting, examples of such holy fools? It depends on whether they know who or what they are waiting for. Are they so fractured from the world, themselves, and sense, that their waiting – their hoping – has no particular object? Would they recognize him if he came? Since prolonged waiting is so painful, we make believe that we are not waiting, or that we're waiting for this, the loss of which would not much disappoint us, rather than that, which would be devastating.

'Ladies-in-waiting' and other such persons whose business is to service us, wait differently: they 'wait on' the demands of others. Between the two senses there is, however, an important kinship: both kinds of agents are passive in an essential way. How difficult to accept that passivity without assuming deformity in oneself. How irresistible to inflict deformity on others. How easily we become executioners or toads. My father was supposed to come on Saturdays and I waited for many weeks, not knowing that my waiting was in vain; then months; then years, inexorably 'forgetting' what I was waiting for, 'forgetting' even what I felt.

For a confused moment I have sometimes murmured "Mother" when I was frightened, or sad. I wanted something beyond words, like what babies want when they cry, a surrounding warmth, a heartbeat that isn't the baby's own, a familiar soft melodic voice. Like all of us at my age, I find myself distressed by the gradual loss of my friends, the ideas of inevitable illness, possibly irremediable pain, the failure of my organs, first the little failures of well-being that come padding toward me, and then the big ones, shouting the names of their decay, and, inevitably, death. I am lonely, and I will only get lonelier. Perhaps death wouldn't be quite so terrifying if it didn't resonate with one's first loss. But then I remember the father who waited to see his daughter before he died. And instead of calling for my mother, unthinkingly I now find myself sometimes whispering "Daddy."

I have discovered my missing father as someone who is not a two-dimensional wall-sketch from an ancient cave, but a man with a mind enlivened by memories, longings, painful feelings of regret, remorse, shame about his mistakes, love, loss, ecstasy, fear, surprise, rage, regret, whether or not I know something about the content of his feelings. And slowly I begin to see my father in the objects of my fury. Sometimes, to my surprise, these fathers are returning my fury with kind words and faces. Bob smiles at me with his usual warmth as I tell him, my anger rapidly fading, that this time I did not miss him at all and that in fact felt that my appointment with him today was an irritating interruption. I tell him that I find his frequent little lectures on medical conditions, which he himself always acknowledges as self-indulgence, both annoying and unprofessional. Perhaps it is time for me to leave. I say.

I was promised anger. I did not expect to find also love.

Memory has its way. I know that my father, the real father, not the man who from time to time seems a more-or-less suitable embodiment of my father, will always be beyond me. But I think that in a primitive recess of my mind it is always Saturday morning on a bright spring day, and I am still waiting. ☐

TRUE WITH TIME
Jack Fuller

After the customary period of apprenticeship following law school, Mark Jacobs decided to specialize in the representation of creditors in bankruptcy. There was money to be made on both sides of the table, but debtors were often just too intense for him. To be counselor to businessmen about to see their life's enterprise go belly-up would have immersed him in emotional turmoil. He preferred his work at the law firm to be what studying in the great gothic law library at the university had been, a respite from the more personal part of life, where he had no choice but to let himself be drawn into the deep.

For many years Mark had, in the main, managed to keep his two worlds as separate as reason and passion. He had, that is, until he encountered Barbara Rose.

"See if she has plans for lunch," he told his secretary when she told him Barbara had been on the phone first thing, asking for time.

"Should I make a reservation?"

"Twelve-thirty," he said. "An out of the way table. What do I have after?"

"Just the Paxton Group at three. But you know about that."

"Two and a half hours," he said. "Do you think that will be enough for her?"

His secretary controlled her smile.

"Shall I bill it to the firm?" she said.

"If she were a paying client, we'd be rich."

From his windows he could see the weather rolling in from the west, an imposing shelf of clouds sending a shadow across the grid of streets that stretched flat to the horizon. When the firm moved to the new building, he had lost his lake view, but he had never regretted it. The worn side of the city was an acquired taste—the railroad tracks angling out from the center, the old gray warehouses, the smokestacks. He could almost imagine himself back in the old Chicago where hard work was called industry: the Depression ending, things beginning to gear up, people having learned to be careful.

Mark was the kind of man who has patience with compound interest in insured accounts. When the firm elected him to partnership, instead of taking Anne out for a glorious night on the town, he had gone home and reviewed their financial circumstances with her, projecting out income and making decisions about how much to increase his life policy and the savings they were putting away each month. He always told prospective clients that there were two ways to do business: you could either hug the legal line and try to leap across the places where it disappeared in a fog, or you could take a step or two back from it and be sure.

He was not a man of his times. Now that his generation had taken "Forever Young" as its anthem and begun to worry about finding gray in their hair, Mark actually wished he had been born earlier. He just did not fit the Baby Boom. He was too undemonstrative, saw duty too much and right too little. He was made for another era, for stability not change. But despite all that, he did believe in progress, and he wanted to do what he could to advance it. Carefully.

That was why he had decided to take a calculated risk with Barbara Rose. The firm had been looking to recruit women, with an eye toward one day welcoming some into the partner ranks, and Mark had gone interviewing at his alma mater with that very much in mind. There were plenty of safer prospects who signed up to see him, pleasant young ladies dressed for success who questioned him closely about the relative merits of a litigation practice versus straight corporate or tax. Barbara Rose was different.

Her resumé stood out when he read it on the plane east. Excellent grades, law review, undergraduate honors in a drama program known for its rigor and the roster of stars it boasted among its alumni. In addition to the academic side, she listed some other, unique accomplishments. During the war, for example, when Mark was in the Central Highlands of Vietnam yearning to return to a world steadily governed by law, she was in college making a reputation as a leader of the New Mobilization. He rather looked forward to meeting Miss Rose.

They assigned him to a small office. The applicants came at half hour intervals. All who paraded before Mark were ambitious and quite intent on making an impression. He had trouble keeping them straight.

Barbara Rose was his first appointment of the afternoon. She arrived punctually, slinging her book bag off her shoulder onto a chair by the door. The faded yin-yang stenciled on the back of the canvas sack had been kissed by the sun of a lot of demonstrations. She was not dressed in the usual job interview uniform. She was wearing khaki slacks, the kind Mark wore when he was going out on Saturday errands or doing chores around the house. The turtleneck jersey did not hide her figure, but neither was it cut to show off. Around her neck was a string of graceful shells alternating with what looked like claws.

"Where do you want me?" she said.

He was standing next to the desk, and after he shook her hand he pulled the chair out just a bit for her convenience. She looked at him as if she did not know quite how to sit down.

As she settled herself, she brushed her long black hair back over her shoulders. It hung straight, in the fashion of a decade before. He glanced at the top sheet of the resume. She was older than the others, only a few years younger than Mark himself. There was a gap in her history. At some point Mark needed to discuss that.

"What leads you to have an interest in Dakin and Will, Miss Rose?" he asked.

"I've always kind of liked Chicago," she said. "It has a lot of good associations."

"Trade associations."

She laughed easily.

"I was in a theater company there for a few years after college," she said. "People always seemed more gentle in Chicago."

"Yes, well, I guess in the practice of law we may see a somewhat different group," he said.

This time her laughter was a little less easy.

"They weren't all saints at the stage door either," she said. "There were always a few who wanted to hit on you."

"You were an actress?"

"For a time."

"Then you decided to change professions. Why?"

"Have you ever been on the stage, Mr. Jacobs?"

"Can't say that I have."

"It's by definition unreal. Hard to harmonize with the here and now. All the different roles, I mean. I wanted something I could actually be."

He didn't know exactly what she meant, but she seemed earnest about it. He remembered the way people talked back in the Dark Ages of war and opposition. Earnest and intense and a little off, just like Barbara Rose.

"I'll need to have a list of all your previous employers," he said.

"The theater types thought I was utterly bonkers, of course. I mean, well, they don't exactly have a high regard for lawyers."

"Unless they find themselves needing one," he said.

She had not decided about a legal specialty, which he said he appreciated. It was a recipe for disenchantment to channel yourself too early. At Dakin & Will they put first and second year associates through a rotation of all the departments. It gave them a pretty good handle on their options, he said.

She was attentive and bright, but she did not put the usual questions about compensation or the gestation period for partnership. Nor did she quiz him on the percentage who made it, nor even on the absence of female partners. Self-assured, he decided.

He touched only briefly on her political background. Even though he did not let on where he had been during the bad years, she was quick to tell him that as far as she was concerned when the troops finally came home the movement lost all its lovely, yeasty passion. It did not escape his notice that she used a lot of loaded words.

"Miss Rose," he said, "I mean no criticism by this. But in the practice of law there are certain conventions, and you have to be sure you will be comfortable with them before making a career decision."

"You mean the way I dress."

"The conventions can be quite binding. There is not a lot of give. We deal with business people, and they have expectations. They seek vital advice from us, and they need to be reassured by more than our wit.

"Bearing. Style. Voice. These are the elements of our bedside manner, Miss Rose. And at Dakin and Will we take it very seriously."

"I'm used to costumes," she said. "I wore one today, didn't I?"

"I'm afraid I don't know what you mean."

"You can tell a lot by the way people react."

"We don't put our clients to that kind of test."

For the first time in the interview she bristled.

"I wouldn't be marrying them," she said.

"And what exactly would you be looking for?" he asked.

Whatever had come over her suddenly blew away and she lighted up with a sly smile.

"Why happiness, of course," she said.

On the strength of Mark's recommendation, the firm flew Barbara Rose to Chicago a few weeks later for a further round of interviews. He was a bit nervous about what kind of figure she would cut, but she didn't let him down. She wore such a tasteful blue suit and white blouse that he hardly recognized her. She greeted him as if he were her confidante.

Not knowing exactly what she had encountered in her conversations with other partners, Mark felt that before she left he should bring up the overwhelming maleness of the firm. He assured her that the partners were determined to change with the times, and that meant opportunity. At Dakin & Will being a woman was actually an asset. Still, some of the older men were not used to the new ways, so she should keep that in mind if they used the wrong words or seemed too solicitous.

"They come from a different era," he said. "We've made it pretty difficult for them."

"To say nothing of what they have done to us," she said.

In the end Mark had to overcome a certain amount of resistance, but the reasons for it were so vague that he was able to make the argument that the qualities in Miss Rose that troubled some of the partners were the very characteristics that would serve her best in practice: energy, toughness, and a certain independence of mind. The firm finally voted to give her an offer, and after several long telephone calls with Mark running over her questions—about the organization of the place, who had influence, who to be careful of, the usual sort of thing—she accepted.

Anne was wary of her from the very beginning. You're going to regret it, she said. She's used to making demands. She probably thinks that's what ended the war.

Mark heard this as jealousy, which was not like Anne. He felt flattered.

But there was no reason for Anne to have worried. Barbara Rose had no unworthy interests, and his own were purely, painfully professional. In fact, he had to overcome a certain amount of awkwardness before he could even think of serving as her mentor, which was clearly what she had in mind. At first when she came by with some problem or another, he was exceedingly formal. It was an agony to find the words to compliment her. When she asked him to lunch, it threw him into what could only be described as an extended argument before the appellate bench of his conscience.

It wasn't long before Barbara Rose invited Mark and Anne over to dinner at her apartment to meet her fiancée, and that made everything a lot easier. He was a pleasant enough fellow, an actor she had known since her first stay in the city. In the course of the evening Barbara Rose let him hold center stage from time to time.

* * *

The problems did not start during her first year. Barbara Rose was a good, solid worker. She was bright and eager to learn. Sure, maybe just a little too eager at times, but that did not hurt her at the firm. The only complaint he ever heard was that she was a little rough on her secretaries and the paralegals. A perfectionist, he said. All in all, Mark's judgment in bringing her in was vindicated, and he was asked to triple his recruitment trips the next year.

She did consume a lot of his time, but he did not really mind. Of course, there were some moments when she would stop by his office with a list of points she wanted to go over and he had to fight the urge to tell her she had better learn to figure them out on her own. But as time passed, she did not actually seem to want his advice. She needed to be heard. He supposed she had gotten used to constant feedback when she was appearing before an audience, or perhaps it was the habit of receiving a grade once a semester. In a professional organization it was not always possible to know exactly where one stood. This, he told her, was one of the attractions of litigation practice. It had clear victories and defeats.

Late in her second year, she went through the crisis almost every young associate did as he tried to make up his mind what specialty to pursue. Mark noticed that her visits became more frequent, her lists longer. The note of sadness he had detected in her manner early on grew more pronounced. Her wedding was only a few months off, and yet she did not seem excited. It was as if she could only focus on what she did not have or was afraid she would lose. This made it especially difficult for her to light. If she went into general corporate or tax, she would rarely see the inside of a courtroom. But a pure diet of litigation wasn't what she wanted either. The peaks were high enough, but the valleys were too deep.

He told her that he would be pleased if she came in with him in the bankruptcy practice, but that only made her feel worse.

"That's so sweet of you," she said.

"Has nothing to do with kindness," he said. "A straight business proposition. You're good at your work."

Perhaps secretly he hoped she would show enough spunk to go off into some other area, but he never mentioned it. And in the end she rewarded him by choosing to join his team. They celebrated by going out for a drink. Anne joined them. Barbara's husband did, too; he did not say anything that Mark could remember.

By the time she had reached her fourth anniversary with the firm Mark had begun to feel moments of regret. She burdened him with everything, including the difficulties she was having at home, what with her husband finding it so difficult to get decent parts. She said he was pushing for her to have a baby, but of course that was out of the question for financial reasons, not to mention the rhythm of her career. Her husband was understanding, but he would not let the matter go.

And then there was the matter of his allergies. It seems he had started to react badly to cats, and she had three of them.

"Anne has been wanting a pet," said Mark. "We could take one of them off your hands."

"It isn't that easy," she said.

By then, nothing was.

The quality of her work on behalf of clients never deteriorated. It was the way she dealt with the internal situation that put the firm in turmoil. Barbara began by circulating a petition to all the associates demanding a roll call vote on partnership and compensation decisions, with the tally made available to all lawyers of whatever rank. Naturally, Mark heard about this and was expected to speak with her.

"It's not done, Barbara," he said.

"Hasn't been, you mean," she said.

"Isn't."

"Things are different now."

"There are certain procedures we follow. Civilities. Things that make it possible for us to stay together and do our work."

"Is it unreasonable to want to know where everyone is?"

"That isn't the point."

"You think it's fair that the partners can destroy a person without even having the courage to confront her?"

"Nobody's trying to destroy you," Mark said.

"That's not the way it feels."

"Until this foolishness came up, your work had nothing but rave reviews."

"And now I've gone and screwed it up. That's what you're saying."

"I don't know what we did to make you feel uncomfortable," Mark said. He rubbed at his forehead where it had tightened up. It was always so much more businesslike when you were talking about a client's business.

"A certain coldness," she said. "A chill."

"It's your imagination," he said. He wanted to say, grow up.

"Don't tell me you didn't notice," she said.

"I'm telling you that if you don't repair the damage, you won't find what you are looking for here."

"Are you speaking as a boss or a friend?" she asked.

There it was. The bad old days. Which side are you on?

"I'm boss and friend both," he said. "In this case they're exactly the same."

Within days she was back to him in an excess of contrition. She asked him what she could possibly do. Had she ruined it for herself? Was redemption out of the question?

"Just go about your work," he said as gently as he could. "You have three years before you're up for partner. It'll be forgotten by then."

But it wasn't, because she refused to allow it to be.

For a while there was nothing dramatic. She failed to show up at the annual firm outing, but she had an excuse. Her husband would have been uncomfortable, she said. Then she began to slack off in her billable hours. Though she never slipped below the average, it did not go unnoticed, because until then she had always been near the top. The change was reflected in her annual bonus, and she went into the throes of doubt and anger.

"Behavior has consequences," he told her. "It's just as simple as that." It felt ridiculous to have to put it to her this way.

"I've been pulling my share," she said. "You know that."

"And you've received an average reward," he said. "It's just that you've become used to more."

"I'm talking about quality. It isn't all a matter of the time you put in on the clock."

"Not all. But part of it is. That's the way it works."

"You're still satisfied, aren't you?" she said.

It was not about him. It had never been about him.

"The decision was by consensus, and I concurred," he said. "We're a family. We all have a say."

"Mom and Dad and Buddy and Sis," she said.

"That's not fair, Barbara. You know what I mean."

"Here's a news flash: Father doesn't necessarily know best."

"I want you to settle down now," Mark said.

"You're furious. You don't like to show it, but you are."

"Disappointed," he said. "I thought we had an understanding."

"Till death do us part," she said.

"Nobody takes an oath here," Mark said, stiffening.

"Maybe I should leave," she said.

This was the first time she had ever mentioned the possibility, and she put it forward with all the gravity of a suicide threat.

"Nobody's saying anything like that," he said.

He did not tell anyone else at the firm about their conversation; there were a few partners who would have taken her comment as an offer and accepted it before she had a chance to revoke. But everyone knew that something was up, because Barbara Rose went on the offensive. Oh, she worked hard enough, but she was a spitting fountain of complaints: Her secretary was a thoroughly inadequate typist. How could anyone do first rate work under such conditions? If she was going to continue to produce at a high level, she needed a summer associate assigned to her to do her research. Mark was not ready to fire a secretary or poison the relationship with a law student they might eventually want to recruit. He listened to her arguments and politely but firmly turned her down.

She tried to go around him with a memo to the management committee. He intercepted it and saved her the embarrassment of a rebuke. She went into a weeping fury.

"The universe does not revolve around you," he said. "That's Copernicus." He resolved to himself that if he and Anne ever did succeed in having children, they would not leave home without learning this vital bit of astronomy.

Then suddenly Barbara Rose became calm. She stopped inviting herself in to review the travails of her day late in the afternoon when Mark was trying to catch his train. She handled her cases with a minimum of consultation, and when he did go over her work, he saw that she was performing competently. A few clients even went out of their way to praise her judgment and tell him that he had trained her well.

In a busy practice it is easy to let management matters slide. Though it was the pride of a good attorney to be able to read the papers memorializing a deal and imagine all the future ambiguities that might challenge it, the same man could fail to notice an obvious problem gathering darkly close to home. It was not unusual for a successful, respected lawyer to go years without filing his taxes. When it came to personnel matters, if there was no crisis, attorneys were notorious for letting them slide. This tendency was commonly blamed for the incidence of divorce.

Mark did chat with Barbara Rose whenever they bumped into one another in the hall. He shared a thought or two with her after client lunches and occasionally even went out of his way to poke his head into her office to say hello. He had the impression at the time that he was staying in touch, though in retrospect he realized that he hadn't said a dozen words a day to her for months.

He was out of town when the disaster struck. John Hawkins called and pulled him out of a meeting in New York to tell him the news.

"She's done it again," he said.

It seems Barbara had walked into a management committee meeting and dropped on the group a memo of grievances, embellishing them liberally in an oral argument that Hawkins described as quite coherent, considering. Mindful of precedent, the sages on the management committee had adjourned.

"What do you think we should do about this?" Hawkins asked.

"I'll be back tomorrow. I'll talk to her."

"What is the cause, exactly?"

"I'm not sure I know," said Mark.

"She's your responsibility."

"Yes," Mark said. "Of course."

He did not tell Anne when he arrived home from the airport because he was not in the mood to be reminded of what she had warned. The next morning, he pushed himself to be pleasant at the breakfast table, and Anne asked him what was wrong. He did not lie. He told her not to worry; everything was under control.

His first order of business when he arrived downtown was going to be to summon her. But Barbara Rose had gotten there ahead of him. When he stepped into his office, his secretary was waiting with Barbara's request for time.

When it was quarter past twelve, he put on his suit jacket and walked briskly to her office, where he found her sitting idle at the desk. Framed playbills and dramatic posters hung on the walls, and among the plants stood a vase with half a dozen red roses in it. She was as stiff as if her back were in a brace.

"Ready?" he asked.

"I suppose."

"Good."

They were spared small talk in the elevator by the presence of Norm O'Rourke, who wanted to tell them all about his misadventures with a sporty new convertible he had bought upon turning forty. He walked two blocks with them to finish the tale of accidents, recalls and thefts. "The damned thing's trying to tell me something about acting my age," he said before peeling off at a corner and heading west.

The maitre d' greeted them warmly and showed the way to a table in a corner where they could speak frankly. Barbara Rose asked for a wine spritzer, and Mark settled on plain soda. She picked up her menu and used it as a wall against him, so when the waiter finally brought the drinks, they were both ready to order.

"I think I'm going to have to leave you," she said as soon as the waiter was gone.

Mark made a move to stand up, but then he realized that she wasn't talking about going to freshen up.

"Leave?" he said, returning the napkin to his lap.

"It isn't you," she said, "anything you've done or haven't done. It's me."

"What is, Barbara?"

"I've felt confined."

"That's a common reaction among associates," he said. "It changes once you get an equity stake."

"It isn't the money."

"You could have fooled the management committee. They thought you were trying to negotiate a raise."

"I admit I was confused. Something didn't feel right, and I was foolish enough to think that if I talked about it, I could make it better."

She leaned forward when she said this, and he thought for a moment she was going to take his hand. He slid it slowly back toward him, but it turned out that she was only reaching for an ashtray. Then she eased back in the chair, as far from him as she could be and remain at the same table. She lighted a cigarette with a stagy flourish, tilting her head back so she could blow the smoke toward the ceiling.

"I wanted to tell you first," she said. "I'll take responsibility for notifying the others. I don't expect you to have to do that."

"But why?"

Suddenly tears welled in her eyes, though they did not overflow.

"I'm just not satisfied," she said.

"That's the wrong question."

"Maybe for you," she said. "Not for me."

The waiter arrived with two large salads. He placed them down carefully before them and raked the table for crumbs, even though neither of them had touched the rolls. Barbara brought her napkin to her face and dabbed lightly beneath her eyes.

"Have you found something else?" Mark asked.

He wasn't sure how he wanted her to answer.

"There's nobody else," she said.

"This isn't wise. You know, you've got a lot invested in this firm. Are you sure that you want to throw it all away without knowing what's next?"

The tears welled again, but again she was able to hold them back.

"Forgive me, Mark," she said. "I hate it when I get so angry that this happens."

"Angry?"

Suddenly he felt something rising in his own face.

"I thought you'd understand," she said.

"Understand an associate marching into a management meeting with a list of non-negotiable demands?"

"They weren't demands," she argued. "Points. Issues. Not demands."

"And doing it without so much as a word of warning."

"You were always so busy," she said.

"When did I ever fail to make time to talk with you," he said, a little too loudly. He lowered his voice and repeated, "When?"

"That's the point," she said. "I always had to come and ask."

"Well, you're going to find a damn sight less handholding wherever you go next," said Mark. "I guarantee that."

His voice had risen again, and by the time he caught himself, the people at several nearby tables were looking his way.

"We're a spectacle, for God's sake," he whispered.

"Speak for yourself."

Instead of responding, he picked up his fork and speared some lettuce, sending croutons caroming off the other side of the plate.

"I didn't want it to be this way, Mark," she said, leaning forward again.

"I just can't figure you," he said. As it came from his lips, he heard regret. At bottom he was sorry for the mistake she was making. He wished he knew some of her friends well enough to ask them to talk some sense into her. But that never worked, did it.

"Look," she said. "I guess you've been as decent as I had any right to expect. It just isn't working, that's all."

"I'd like you to take the night to think about this. I'm not going to say anything to anyone until tomorrow."

"I've made up my mind," she said.

Already he felt himself withdrawing from her.

"Let me know first thing," he said.

"I suppose we have to think of the details," she said.

"I'd better get one of the other partners to handle all that," he said.

"In other words," she said, "you're telling me to deal with your lawyer."

"You'll be properly treated," he said. "There's no need to make this bitter."

"Amicable," she said.

He allowed her to leave first and gave her plenty of time to get in and out of the office before he returned. He knew that some of the other associates would be upset when they heard. Mark would be expected to have an explanation. While some men might have been tempted to make it painful for her, he wanted only to do the decent thing. That meant saying that Barbara Rose had been a valuable asset, that he was sorry to lose her, that there had been mistakes made on both sides, and that for some reason they had just not been able to make it work. Like many such gracious gestures of complicity and mitigation, this one had the virtue of feeling truer with the passage of time. □

TIME MACHINE
Christine Sneed

His name is Fred, which is not a name I would have chosen for him if I had been present on the day of his birth. Aside from the improbability of this scenario, it is also impossible – Fred is four years older than I am. But unlike many people, I don't think that the future possibility of time travel is something we should dismiss. We might not be able to book a trip on a time machine right now, but I do feel confident that if the right scientists devote enough brainpower to inventing such a machine, it will become a fact of our lives, maybe relatively soon.

If time travel were possible, things would certainly get interesting. Maybe, for a change, history wouldn't repeat itself (and deliver us onto the doorstep of one bloody tragedy after another – war being the most enduring industry ever created by personkind. An intrepid time traveler might make it his [or her] mission, for one, to smother Hitler and Stalin at birth). Still another traveler would likely want to go back and figure out just what Jesus and Mary Magdalene got up to on washing day when their tunics were on the line and they were walking around in their makeshift underwear, or maybe no underwear at all because underclothes (and modesty) are a fairly modern invention.

Regarding Fred, he is a friend who has recently told me that he would like to be more. He has been divorced for a year from a woman named Misty who, two years ago, fell in love with the man who gave her riding lessons over in Harms Woods, a few miles from where she and Fred lived. She moved to Montana with the horseman, leaving Fred behind to care for their dog and cat, but no children.

I'm not divorced, but I am a widow and have been since I was twenty-nine. At the time my husband died (in a cross-country skiing accident, as improbable as such accidents are supposed to be – no high-speed descents down steep mountain slopes, in most cases), I didn't know that I would remain a widow so far into the future, but it's fine that I have. Ian died almost fourteen years ago, and I have chosen to raise on my own our one child, Victoire, who is a freshman at the big university near the center of our state, where unfortunately, she's not having a very good time. If they accept her, she might decide to transfer to the University of Chicago, but I would prefer that she transfer to Northwestern; she would only be a mile from home and could live with me again if she wanted to, though I'm sure she doesn't. She might never again live with me, not for more than a few months at a time – only during her summer breaks, unless she finds a way to leave town and build houses in Honduras or follow a boyfriend around Europe until it's time to go back to campus. She is tired of me, the part of me, in any case, that insists on telling her that her life will be an extraordinary one, that she is gifted and beautiful. (If anyone other than I were saying these things, she would be more than happy to hear them, I'm sure.)

There was a boy not long after the semester started whom she fell for for no reason other than his arrogance and generic good looks, one who did not treat her with decency and respect after she went to his room and did some things with him that people everywhere are doing at all hours of the day. How can this boy blame her for wanting to be touched? I know the answer: women are supposed to be sexy but not want sex, and it drives me nuts that this double standard endures. Since then, since Victoire fell for his cocky talk and bland, handsome face, and I told her that I didn't have a good feeling about him, she has not been particularly willing to talk to me about the things she cares about most. I love her too aggressively, Fred recently said.

That is, I smother her.

"You have no children," I reminded him. "So kindly refrain from giving me parenting advice."

He had the grace to blush. "I'm only saying—I only meant—if you give her a little more breathing room, she'll come around."

"Maybe, but even so, it's going to take her a while."

"That's not okay?"

I shook my head. "She's my closest friend."

He gazed at me for a long second. His eyes are clear blue—beautiful, preternatural eyes, that, if he knew where and how to look for them, would see ghosts. Possibly quite a few.

Finally he said, "That's sort of an unconventional way to think of your daughter, isn't it?"

"Maybe, but it's true. She is my closest friend. You're one of my closest friends too, by the way."

"Thank you." He smiled. "But that's a lot of pressure to put on Victoire, isn't it? Being a daughter is hard enough, I'm sure."

"Being my daughter, you mean."

"I didn't say that."

"You didn't have to."

He laughed a little, not meeting my eyes. "How long will she be home over the holidays?"

"About a month," I said. "Unless she goes back early, but I don't think she will. She's not very happy down there. I wish this weren't the case, even if it'll be nice to have her closer to home if she does transfer to the U of C. She's been talking about it, and I think she's already started the application process."

"She'll leave behind a trail of broken hearts down in Champaign, I bet."

"Urbana," I said, not sure why I felt this compulsion to correct such a small error. "A lot of the university is in Urbana. That's where her dorm is too."

He blinked. "Oh, sorry."

"Her heart's the one that's been broken, but she doesn't say much about it to me. I've sent her flowers twice since we had a little argument about the boy who disappointed her. Those bouquets haven't helped my cause though."

"It's the boy who should be sending her the flowers," he said. "Not you. She probably expected them to be from him, but then she opened the card, and well, you can imagine how it must have been for her."

I stared at him, stricken. Why I hadn't thought of this myself, I still don't know. "Oh God," I said. "My poor baby."

After a moment he said, "I'm sure she'll be fine, Anne-Josée. Just give her a little breathing room."

Fred is one of the 187 male subscribers to the journal I founded ten years ago and continue to act as editor-in-chief for, *The Spider Lady Quarterly*. The other 2,796 subscribers are either libraries or women. He probably subscribes because he thinks I'd be mad at him if he didn't. I have no idea if he actually reads what's in each issue (maybe the recent article [not our typical fare] about female v. male orgasm? or the op-ed about newborns and circumcision?), because I don't often ask him and he rarely brings it up. He started subscribing after his wife left him, though we met two years before that, when he helped me with a flat tire I managed to acquire by running over a nail when I was out grocery shopping. He was unlocking his bicycle from a parking meter, about to ride home with his artichokes and rice flour and 14-grain bread, when I galumphed over with my ailing tire.

For a health nut, he's pretty sexy. He isn't too skinny from his fat-free, high-fiber diet; he shaves most days, showers regularly, does not wear unsightly or smelly clothes made of hemp or burlap or raw wool, and sometimes, to my surprise, he even wears an expensive French cologne. Maybe I should be sleeping with him, but the last man I had sex with, which was a couple of weeks after Victoire left for college, suggested that he move in with me. We went out on three dates, had sex once, and then, aggressive romantic that he was (or else he had money troubles), he wanted to move in together.

But I'm happy with the status quo. If I had money problems, however, it's less likely that I would be. Most women will be as pragmatic as necessary when faced with the prospect of having to rely on the local food bank's stock of baked beans and white rice rather than a blank check made out to their favorite boutique grocer. If I hadn't been able to sell my parents' canning company about eleven years ago, a year after my mother followed my father to the grave (and only a couple of years after Ian met his end in a cluster of pine trees), I probably would have had to remarry or else sell the house because I couldn't have kept up with the mortgage with only my feeble salary from the high school where I taught Spanish and French, even with the small life insurance policy Ian had taken out when we learned I was pregnant with Victoire.

As is probably obvious, I have spent quite a bit of time over the years thinking about women and their place in the world. One of the more controversial op-eds published in the *Spider* in recent years is a piece that I wrote, one with the artless title "The Pros and Cons of Marriage." A summary:

Cons:

- Both members of many married couples believe that they put more in than they get out.

- In general, money is not independently earned, spent and/or saved. His debt becomes your debt, and vice-versa. N.B., gentle readers and friends: how much money you have and where (or whom) it comes from is a fundamental component of your identity. Do not forget this.

- One member almost always has a lower sex drive than the other, often much lower.

- Arguments are likely, after the first year or so (possibly sooner), about every conceivable topic.

- Adultery is also more likely than not. (There's a reason why so many marriages end in divorce, and often, as you probably know, adultery is this reason).

- The same is true of boredom. It is the scourge that often leads to all of the problems noted above.

Pros:

- Decreases the likelihood of an attacker following you home and successfully assaulting you (but to be frank, a good guard dog would probably be even more effective in dissuading a potential rapist than a husband).

- Shared responsibility for household bills and chores (again, at the price of your financial independence).

- Sex generally available (even if it's not as available as you might like).

- The end of blind or otherwise bad dates.

- If you want children, here, ostensibly, is a man whose DNA will be available to you when you deem it appropriate.

- Easy-to-locate companion for dinners out, concerts, vacations, employment-related functions, appointments at the abortion clinic (Did I really just say that? Yes, it seems I did. Remember, young goddesses, that you do not have to have the baby just because your husband says you do. If he does say this, you would be better off asking a friend to accompany you to the clinic. Your body really is your own. It's also quite likely that he believes his body is his own).

The backlash to "The Pros and Cons" was immediate and unsurprising. How cynical I was! How irreverent and downright obscene. How predictable this clichéd attack on the holy institution of matrimony! Subscriptions immediately dropped from about 2,500 to 1,800. But then, because a number of prominent feminists and scholars, among them Susan Frankenweiler (*Yes! I Am Me*), Billie Kennedy (*The High Road Is Rocky but Scenic*), Jacqson Rivers (*The She-Monster and Other Men-Made Myths*), praised me for my obscenity and irreverence, subscriptions increased to 3,300 for a few years but now average about 3,000. (The pro-lifers among my readers didn't renew their canceled subscriptions, but I do think it's true that you have to pick, with cynical intelligence, your battles, and I wasn't about to start writing pro-choice screeds to show, fruitless as it would have been, these previous subscribers just how much I opposed their point of view. *Spider Lady* is certainly political – all printed matter is in some way a political statement, but I am more interested in publishing articles covering issues about which it is still possible to change someone's mind.)

Regarding "The Pros and Cons," the irony is, as I wrote in response after response to the readers who had written in disappointment or outrage or both, I married my own husband hopefully, as most brides do, and I also happened to love him until he died. I had felt very lucky to marry him too – no one forced me, not even Hollywood, which a film critic once labeled "a machine dedicated to the manufacture of the heterosexual couple."

So why such a jaded view? readers wanted to know. Fred eventually asked me this too, even after his wife had left him and my incendiary op-ed was five years in the past.

"Probably because when Ian died, I was still in my twenties. I hadn't yet seen so many of our friends' marriages implode. Not to mention the marriages of people who weren't my friends but heard about anyway."

"There's no shortage of pessimism on your end," he said.

"There's no shortage of bad news either. If you were covering some of the topics that I do in *Spider Lady*, you'd probably wonder how anyone gets out of bed in the morning."

"You have to figure out what to ignore if you want to be happy."

"Yes," I said. "And you have to learn how to suppress your conscience."

"Some marriages last."

"Sure, and some of them are happy too. But the odds are against it, against Us instead of Me."

Tonight, his half-birthday, which his mother made an occasion of until he was sixteen, and for which I've prepared two of his favorite foods, shrimp paella and a citrus salad, he brings up the topic of marriage again.

"It's been a year since I signed my divorce papers," he says softly, looking down at his empty salad bowl.

I try to catch his eye. "Are you okay?"

He nods. "Sure. Misty called me last night and asked me the same thing. We hadn't talked in about five months."

"Were you happy she called?"

"I don't know. No, probably not. It makes me feel a little weird to know she's still with that horse guy."

We are sitting at the kitchen table, and because he still won't meet my gaze, I glance at the sliding glass door that overlooks the backyard. Because it's past sunset, I can only see our reflections, not the rose garden and the small vegetable garden further back in the yard. In the summer, my favorite season, if I turn off the lights in the kitchen, I can see the neon scribbles of lightning bugs in the evening air through this same door's screen. These bugs are like little glowing ghosts but are more charming than most ghosts. Real ghosts, from what I can tell, do not like the light. They literally shrink from it, like cockroaches – an unfortunate comparison but more or less apt. Something I am pretty sure of is that if you shine a flashlight on a ghost, you can paralyze it. This is a good thing for everyone to know, especially those of us who are afraid of ghosts, but it's not something I go around advertising. Like the biomass beneath the earth's surface, something said to be filled with more creature life than what lives on top of it, the spirit world is truly vast and populous. Therefore, I suppose, it is terrifying for most of us to contemplate.

"Did you tell her that you were having dinner with me tonight?" I ask.

He finally looks at me. "Yes."

"What did she say?"

He hesitates. "She was jealous, I think."

"What a surprise," I snort.

"It was for me," he says. "I didn't expect her to be jealous at all."

"It doesn't matter that she's with someone else. She feels like she should always own some part of you."

"Well, she probably will. Don't all wives, whether they're exes or not?" His smile is self-deprecating. "I'm probably bringing you down. I don't mean to."

I shake my head. "You're not. You should always say what's on your mind."

He laughs. "Well, not always. I'd get arrested if I did."

"You know what I mean. But if you ever did get arrested, I'd arrange for bail."

"That's more than Misty probably would have done."

"Which is one reason why you're divorced."

"Yes," he says, reaching for more paella. He has a small star-shaped mole above his right eye. Sometimes I can't stop staring at it. He catches me and waggles his brows. "Is it winking at you again? Didn't you say it did that once?"

"I was making a wish on it."

"Am I in it?"

"You know you can't tell your wishes if you want them to come true."

"If it does, you have to tell me."

"Maybe," I say, though I probably wouldn't tell him, even if I had made a wish and it came true. Wishes are like a pretty face or broad shoulders – they shouldn't be bragged about.

A little while later, when we're at the front door saying goodnight, he asks, again unable to meet my gaze, if sometime I might let him stay the night. "Or part of the night?" he says.

I don't think so. But I don't say this. It would hurt him too much, on a night when he's already hurting. Instead, I say, "I need some time to think about it, Fred. Is that all right?"

"Yes," he says softly, leaning close to kiss my cheek. He holds the kiss for a few seconds, and in spite of myself, I stiffen a little. When he pulls back, he's blushing, not having noticed my discomfort, it seems. "Talk soon?" he says.

"Yes. Thanks for coming over."

"Thank you for dinner," he says, smiling boyishly. "It was a lot of fun."

I wait until he's in his car and almost out of the driveway before going back inside. It is mid-December and cold, only three more days before Victoire is due home on the Amtrak from Urbana. She was home for five days over Thanksgiving and took the Amtrak then too. I offered to drive down and pick her up after finals because she will have a big suitcase and probably a backpack full of books, but she wouldn't allow it. "Everyone takes the train or the bus or else they carpool. I don't want you picking me up like I'm still in fifth grade," she said when I offered again on the phone last week.

"Wouldn't you rather have a door-to-door car ride than sit on a train for three hours with a bunch of noisy people? I'll be coming down to meet you at Union Station anyway. It would only be a couple of more hours from there to U of I in the car."

"No, Mom, don't come downtown to pick me up. It'll be rush hour. I can take the purple line home. It'll be running express at that time of day."

"If your train isn't late."

"It won't be."

"You don't want to have to wrestle your suitcase up the steps to the el platform."

"It's not a problem," she said mulishly.

"At least let me go down there to pick you up. You don't need to ride the el home."

"I know, but I want to. You can pick me up at Dempster. I'll call when I'm getting close."

"How's Ashley getting home? Couldn't you ride with her?"

"I have no idea."

"Maybe you should call her."

"Maybe, but she could call me too if she wanted to talk to me."

There was no malice in my daughter's voice, instead, resignation, which I found sadder. "I knew she shouldn't have joined that sorority," I said.

"Yeah, Mom, me too. But let's not talk about this right now, okay?"

"I hope she's all right."

Victoire exhaled quietly. "She has a lot of new friends now. I'm sure she's just fine."

The Dempster purple line station is six blocks from our house, a twelve-minute walk or a two-minute car ride. I knew that my daughter was doing her best not to let me help her with anything. This trend began when she was still in high school, and I do understand it – she has a right to be an independent woman – but it became a little ridiculous in its extremes after she got involved with Kyle, the ungrateful boy from Lake Forest whom I know she still thinks about and has probably seen again. I suspect that she had sex with him but has found that it wasn't enough for him to declare her his girlfriend publicly. I doubt, however, that she'll tell me if I'm right. To be right is what everyone wants, and this, of course, is the problem because someone has to be wrong. I'm right most of the time, and I can't blame her for being irritated by this, but her life really would be easier if she took my advice. All of it.

When she fell under Kyle's spell, I knew it was bad the first time I heard her voice, two nights after it happened. The marks were on her – the sighs, the impatience, the inability to concentrate – the kind of desire that makes it hard to sleep, to read a book, to return phone calls. I also worried that she wasn't eating enough, and I was able to find her roommate Charlene's email address in an old message with a goofy article from *The Onion* that Victoire had sent to a number of her friends and to me just after she moved down to Urbana when she was still sending me those kinds of emails. I sent Charlene a note asking if she would make sure that Victoire wasn't starving herself. Charlene promptly wrote back saying, "Of course I will! You count on me! No problem! Victoire is such a great roommate! I hope we can room together all four years! Btw, I think it's so cool that you edit a magazine. Especially one that's in our library! :) luv, Charlee"

Charlene, a well-meaning but not very discreet girl, told Victoire that I had emailed her, despite my request that she not, and not surprisingly, Victoire was angry. "I'm old enough to take care of myself," she said the next time we spoke, her voice rising dangerously. "I don't need you or Charlee to remind me to take my vitamins and clean my plate. You never did when I was still living at home."

"Because I could see for myself that you were doing those things."

"Stop trying to control everything, Mom. You can't, so just stop," she said. "Why can't you be happy that you don't have to worry about me anymore?"

"Is that how you think it works?" I said. "Because I don't know any mothers like that."

"Some mothers are like that," she said. "Charlee's mother isn't sending me emails to make sure she's still eating."

"I'm sure Charlee is very good about making sure that she doesn't starve herself."

"What's that supposed to mean? Are you saying she's fat?"

"Nothing at all. I'm simply confident that Charlee is looking after herself."

"You think she's fat."

"No, I don't."

"Yes, you do."

"I think we'd better talk when you're in a better mood."

"Okay, goodbye," she said and promptly hung up, leaving me with unspoken words that went back down as jaggedly as a horse pill.

Now, three days post-half-birthday dinner for Fred, my daughter is coming home for Christmas break. From where I am parked next to the café across the street from the Dempster station, I watch her appear in the illuminated doorway. She doesn't notice how people are looking at her, my child who is also a woman in possession of her own heart and mind, both of these forces intent on having their say, and so, of course, conflict is inevitable. She has not yet realized this, has not yet figured out how to silence one and listen to the other.

Victoire wasn't wrong the time we argued about the email that I sent to Charlene. There are mothers more than happy to see their children grow up and leave the house. They want to be bothered less by the demands a child always makes. But I'm not like that. Victoire has been my best friend since she was a little girl, when she would charge into my study three times a day to ask for facts that she could report back to her friends, impressing them with whatever unusual or spooky scrap I offered (*There are fish called ghost fish. They are blind and live in water found in mountain caves not far from here. You can find them in Missouri and Arkansas, where there are mountains named the Ozarks*). Maybe, according to some psychologists, it isn't healthy to be best friends with your child, but our closeness never kept her from befriending other children. I know that this is one of the reasons why Fred thinks that I make it hard for her to feel carefree and untethered like a girl her age should. I have told him that girls never feel untethered, something he doesn't quite believe, though he nods, pretending to understand.

I roll down the car window and call my daughter's name, waving her toward me, smelling bus exhaust and incipient snow. The air tonight is heavy with cold humidity, a time of year that since girlhood has always felt to me like Christmas. It is dusk and the people who have gotten off the train with Victoire quickly scatter toward their homes on neighboring streets with our newly skeletal trees, voices growing faint as they disappear with their cell phones into the night. Victoire's thick, dark blond hair is captured in a clip at the nape of her neck and she wears a knit purple hat with her long black down coat and high-heeled black boots, both new and purchased with money I sent to her in early October.

She looks like she has just arrived from New York instead of a small city downstate where the most famous people for miles are the college football coach and his players. When she sees me, she waves and smiles, her face pink with cold. She has the most colorful aura, the intuitive, sensitive blues and violets; the passionate, angry reds; the intelligent yellows and earthy, tranquil greens. She has always had a complex personality, something most people believe they have, like good judgment and generous hearts, but obviously, that's not the case.

I pop the trunk and get out of the car as she's crossing the street. She looks at me, happy but a little reluctant to let it show. "Mom," she says, stepping into my arms. "Thanks for picking me up."

She smells like the night – cold and sweet. "I'm so glad you're home, honey," I say, tears springing to my eyes. "Pinkie and Penny will be so happy that you're back for more than just a few days. They were so depressed when you went back to school after Thanksgiving."

"I'm sure they were fine. Cats aren't like people. Lucky for them." She heaves her suitcase into the trunk, not letting me help.

"They are and they aren't," I say, but I really don't want to argue and instead tell her when we're both in the car what I've made for dinner – salmon with dill, lemon rice, a green salad with hothouse tomatoes and raspberry vinaigrette.

"Sounds good, Mom," she says dutifully. "Thanks for making it."

"You don't have to thank me. Of course I'm going to cook for you."

I turn onto Dempster and almost cut off a cyclist who isn't wearing a helmet nor is he using a bike light. My heart leaps, but he speeds past us unscathed, not even bothering with an angry glance.

"What are you working on right now?" asks Victoire, not bothering to comment on the cyclist.

This is her failsafe question. When she can think of nothing else to say, she resorts to questioning me about *Spider Lady*. It's nice that she does, but I wish we could talk about her instead – about what she has been experiencing these past four months with all of the other bewildered and homesick students. Victoire has made it clear to me several times that she doesn't like to drink and that she isn't really tempted to drink when she goes out. The night she met Kyle she wasn't drunk but what good did sobriety do her, I wonder. The body has its imperatives, whether we have anaesthetized the mind with alcohol or not.

"I'm writing a piece on wolves," I say. "Hunters are killing them right and left because a few weeks ago some National Parks employee said on a syndicated radio show that they were proliferating and the population needed to be culled. This isn't the case everywhere, but people are using it as an excuse to mow down as many as they can."

"Why do we have to kill everything?"

"If I knew the answer to that, I'd probably be the most famous armchair psychologist in the world."

"Did you invite anyone over for dinner tonight? Is your boyfriend coming over?"

I glance at her, noticing her smirk. "My boyfriend? Do you mean Fred?"

"Who else?" she says.

"You know that he's not my boyfriend, Victoire. And no, he's not coming over. He does want to see you before you go back to school though. I think he has a Christmas gift for you."

"He does? Am I supposed to get him something too?"

"No, not unless you want to."

She snorts. "That would be a little weird, wouldn't it? He's your friend, not mine."

"You can do whatever you want. Fred's easy. You know that."

"Is he still in love with you?"

"He's not in love with me."

"Whatever you say," she says, still smirking.

"He's not, honey. He's not over his ex-wife yet."

"So? He can be in love with two people at the same time, can't he?"

I look over at her but she's facing the window. Some of the trees in the yards near ours are festooned with colored lights, snow having fallen last night, everything glistening and crystalline. "Yes, I suppose he can, but I don't think he is."

A minute later when I turn pull into the garage, Victoire jumps out, car still running, leaving a glove on the seat. "Where's the fire?" I call after her, reaching for the glove.

"I have to pee," she says, already half inside the house.

"You're going to trip if you don't slow down," I say, but she is already gone.

Pinkie, a grey shorthair with black stripes, and Penny, black with a white sun on her throat, are waiting in the hall, meowing a frenzied greeting when I come in from the garage, probably having been brushed aside by Victoire in her haste to get to the bathroom. When Fred is visiting, I have to quarantine the cats upstairs because sometimes Pinkie hisses viciously at him, probably smelling Fred's own cat on his clothes. But the one time she and Penny escaped, schizophrenically, she suddenly loved him, her furry face staring up at him adoringly, her body caterpillaring against his legs. While Victoire is away, they have the run of her room, and often when I haven't see them roaming around the house in a while, I can find them under her bedclothes, two warm, kittenish mounds that mew in surprise and sleepy outrage if I pull back the quilt to peer down at them. They are the fifth and sixth cats of my life. We had a dog, Peanutbreath, when Ian was alive but she died a few years after he did. Like me, she was never quite able to get over the fact that Ian hadn't returned from his ski trip.

* * *

A surprise my daughter springs on me near the end of dinner, as children returning from college are known to do: something has happened between her and the fraternity boy that I didn't foresee.

I'm about to offer her some homemade chocolate ice cream, her favorite dessert since she was a little girl, when she says, "Don't get mad, Mom, but Kyle is taking me out tomorrow night. We're going out for dinner and a movie."

I look up sharply. If she had said that she was dropping out of college to become a snake charmer, I almost couldn't be more surprised. Her face is flushed, her hands jittery on either side of her plate, the rubbery skin from her salmon all that remains of her dinner. I'm happy to see that she has an appetite; at least the boy from Lake Forest hasn't robbed her of that. "Do you think he'll let me read his palm when he picks you up?" I finally say.

She grimaces. "Mom, don't even think about asking him. He'll think we're both wackos."

"Does that mean he thinks you're the only wacko in our family right now? Or am I the wacko?"

"He doesn't think either of us is a wacko, as far as I know. Not yet, anyway."

"How did this happen?"

She regards me. "How did what happen?"

"How did you end up with a date with this boy? I thought you weren't speaking to him."

"I never said that."

"No, but you never said that you were either."

"I ran into him a few days ago and he asked if I wanted to go out when we were home for break and I said yes."

"He's coming down here to see you, I hope. You aren't going to him."

She hesitates. "No, I'm not going to him. We're meeting in Highwood."

"Where in Highwood? Not some friend's house."

"No," she says, irritated. "At this Mexican place he likes, Casa de Ivan or something."

"That hardly sounds Mexican."

She shakes her head. "Casa de Isaac. That's what it is, I think."

"It's supposed to snow again tomorrow."

She laughs in a hard burst. "So? Unless it's a blizzard, I'm going, Mom."

I don't say anything. My heart is working too hard, sending out foreboding messages to the rest of my body.

"What?" says Victoire, incensed. "Don't look like that. It's just a date. I don't think there's anything wrong with seeing him while I'm up here for Christmas."

"Is this the first time you've gone out with him since you met at that party in October?"

She falters. "On an official date?"

"Yes, of course. What else? An unofficial date?"

"We've hung out a couple of times. We went out to dinner once."

I don't reply. I can't help but see what's there in front of me: she has had sex with him but only when it has suited him.

"What?" she says, her cheeks coloring. "Don't give me that look."

"I'm not giving you a look, Victoire."

She gets up from the table, takes her plate and dumps it in the sink with a violent clatter.

"Be careful," I say. "You'll break it if you throw it around like that."

"It didn't break," she says flatly. Without a word, she leaves the kitchen and stomps upstairs. The chocolate ice cream will sit untouched in the freezer unless she comes down later and eats it after I have gone to bed. I don't want any of it now, and the remaining rice and salmon on my plate look wholly unappetizing.

I put the pan I used to cook the fish in the sink and the plates and silverware in the dishwasher before following my peevish daughter upstairs. Her bedroom door is closed and probably locked but I don't bother to knock and go instead into my study where I don't turn on the light after shutting the door. A lot of people underestimate the benefits of sitting alone in a familiar dark room, the intention to sleep as far away as China. If you look out the window, you can see what's out there instead of only your haunted face peering back at you. If there is a quiet, uncluttered yard beyond the window, you might catch a glimpse of tomorrow morning. It is there, a tiny book waiting to be opened and read aloud, but it isn't easy to find. Often I can't.

Tonight when I stare out the window and into the yard that I pay a fourteen-year-old boy down the street forty dollars to mow during the months when the grass grows, I see something that is undoubtedly tomorrow's book. My daughter is on the first page, her happiness and the suspense of her date with the boy from Lake Forest sending out rays of jubilant light. I want her to be happy. It is a pedestrian wish, maybe, considering all of the miseries in the world, ones that might be better to focus this wish on, but it is what's most important to me. She believes, however, that I am jealous of the possibilities ahead of her and has said as much – all of the boys and men to love and places to travel and jobs to try and clothes to wear and thrilling new people to meet. She thinks that I spend too much time alone, inside my head, up here in my office with a swarm of half-formed thoughts and intentions. The solitary spider lady spinning her sticky web. *You can't be happy unless you're sucking the life out of someone else!* College and its anxieties have turned her tongue sharper than it has ever been. I tried not to be hurt by it, but I was. I am often alone, yes, but I do not often allow myself to feel lonely, something that my daughter doesn't believe or else can't understand.

What she doesn't know, what I have tried to keep from her, is that her father's death, long ago as it was, has been hard to recover from. I don't ever talk about this, not with friends or with her. What would my readers say if they knew that the editor of *The Spider Lady Quarterly* is a fearful sentimentalist? *Spider Lady* has always been a refutation of the sentimental, of the illusions that allow some people to believe that all is right with the world because their problems are rarely the kind that keep them awake at night. Since I was a child, I have had some ability to catch glimpses of the future, but I had no sense that Ian's death was coming. The heart clouds one's vision. It is not the eyes that do this, but the heart. It is the same for me with Victoire – sometimes I know what will happen but other times, I can't see a thing. If I fell for another man, Fred or someone else, how would I know that he would not abruptly be taken from me too? I like the way things are right now, though I do wish that I could restore Victoire's faith in me. Aside from my dead husband, there is little that I am missing.

I knew him for seven years before he died. In the span of a lifetime, that is not very long – only one-eleventh or -twelfth of the average life expectancy. I had believed that I would have him until we were old and arthritic, so ossified in our ways that if one of us went, the other would have to follow because it would be too difficult to pry us apart. This will sound strange, probably perverse, but it's nonetheless true – in a way, Victoire was fortunate to have known him for so little of her life, to have lost him at five, when she had not yet formed a mature attachment to him.

If a time machine were invented right now, if I were allowed to climb inside and program it for thirteen years and ten months ago, I would – consequences, repercussions, cosmic disturbances – all of them be damned. I am selfish, but who, to be frank, isn't? I would go back to the morning Ian left for the stand of woods up near Kenosha where he liked to ski and had skied many times before. ☐

E ntering a big city like Chicago for the first time can be both an awe-inspiring and slightly frightening experience, which I tried to capture in my photograph of Chicago Avenue at night, near the Brown Line elevated, looking east. The dark, shadow-like buildings suggest gigantic, looming creatures. The moon was unusually large when I took the picture and the comings and goings of the cars and people seemed to me to have a kinship with Japanese prints of the pleasure districts of Japanese cities.

CHICAGO AVENUE NIGHT LIFE
Robert Kameczura

T aken during a rainstorm while wandering on the spit of land near North Avenue.
(Model is tapestry artist Marzena Ziejka.)

CITY RAIN
Robert Kameczura

I meant the photo to be suggestive of a kind of mystical rapture we experience in dreams. In the photo I intended vague suggestions of the Cretan Earth Goddess figures (the ones who hold the snakes aloft in some sort of magic ritual), implying mystical powers to make new realities out of our dreams. The photo was taken in the rear of an old historic building dating from 1831, which inspired thinking of the resonances of the lives and dreams of the many people who lived there over the years.

(Model: artist Christa Wellman)

DREAM, DREAM, DREAM
Robert Kameczura

A mother goddess like figure performs a ritual to pass on her magic powers to her acolyte daughter. The setting suggests a sacred place with a stone cairn and enchanted vines and a sky full of stars. The mother seems to gather the light of the stars and the power of the blowing winds with a spinning tapestry that focuses the powers of the universe.

(Models: Patty Rhea, then Curator of the Rockford Museum of art, and her daughter dancer Alex Rhea.)

PASSING ON THE LEGACY
Robert Kameczura

THE EXPLORER KNOWS
L.M. Kell

What does the edge of an abyss look like?
Some dark rock chasm,
sheer rock rising higher than sight
falling lower than hell.
The broad footpath of this morning
dwindled in daylight
to a sudden slight ledge.

The ledge on the edge
of an abyss you can't miss
dead trees and other skeletons
waiting below.

If only.

Then the explorer might carefully turn around
retrace the way
to the familiar footpath.

No.

The edge of an abyss is
nothing, is not-being, is
where birds do not fly or sing
invisible. Not even empty -
something empty might be filled.
It is forever empty, forever non-full.

The ledge and the edge cannot be seen,
or quantified, identified, rectified, sanctified, justified.
The explorer knows this
when air rushes up
as the body falls.

FUSED GLASS
L.M. Kell

There is a place no one sees, but everyone knows,
knows when it comes, comes for someone else.
That unwelcome country.

Did Eliot get it right?
Do we truly end where we began
finally knowing where we stand?
Does fear or love keep one invested
in this mortal coil, to be divested?

Gritty black pearls chafe our necks,
pearls that began as tiny dark bits
flowing in our veins before the umbilical cord was cut.
Black bits, protruding under our skin,
pimples, hardening into sullen pearls.
Pearls that chafe, bind, suffocate.

Is it possible that death
transforms pimples and pearls?
Not to pure light,
but fused, like colors of glass.
Reflecting, projecting
dancing dizzy light and dark,
crashing combustible color and spark.

There is a place that everyone sees, but no one knows,
knows when it comes, comes for us.
That unwelcome country.

That falling night
where fused glass may be flaming
outside our range of sight.

THEY DON'T TEACH THIS
IN GIRL SCOUTS
L.M. Kell

Meeting a grunting bear
when camping in the Smoky Mountains is rare.
But when the bear stops, and turns to stare
at you
what to do?

- Run for the trees?
    (screaming optional)

- Calmly withdraw
    (Zen training helpful)

- Freeze and let the bear depart
    (bear behavior doubtful).

Are trees a safe haven, or
dark roots to trip on,
wet leaves to slip on?

A calm withdrawal sounds good,
but is that just weakness,
even worse, cowardice?

Okay then, immobilization.
A frozen interaction
no will to take action.

What to do?

Run for the trees, if you trust them with ease.
Withdraw, if you trust yourself, please.
And if you trust the bear, freeze.

Or, wait, you could shoot the thing and be done,
if you trust no one.

HALF MOON
Syed Afzal Haider

My spring is always colored red,
flowers dyed by that bloody hue.
—*Kim Shi-Jong*

Two days before my eleventh birthday, Nanny arrives from Elizabeth, New Jersey, skillfully wheeled out in a wheelchair to Baggage Claim by an airport attendant dressed in blue. Airports can be my favorite pastime, full of sentimental energy, people saying hello greeting loved ones. I associate airports with goodbyes and sadness. Nanny comes faithfully every year for my birthday, May 1. She can still move around, but each year she gets slower in her movements, and with the passage of time she is getting more and more forgetful. Instead of enjoying her company and appreciating her visits every time I see her, I think of when she won't be able to travel, when she won't be around. When life becomes a wait for death, I want to be gone.

* * *

Nanny walks up to the attic and sits down by my desk. Her pale grey eyes fill with tears, her large drooping lips quiver. "Do you know whom we mourn?" she asks. I acknowledge silently nodding my head. Unable to figure out the sudden death of my mother, her youngest much loved daughter. My mother died two years ago on Mother's Day, following surgery for a breast tumor that was supposed to have been benign. Nanny has private conversations with me.

"My eldest daughter is happy now," Nanny says. She doesn't mention Auntie Alexandria by name since she remarried nine months after the death of her husband, Daniel Stone, last year. On a hot Sunday afternoon in April at St. John Church, Alexandra married Noah Samson, professor of philosophy and religion at the University of Nevada. Nanny and I sat next to each other during the ceremony admiring a bright sun filter in from the stained glass windows, in many colors through the image of Christ on the cross. In a Catholic, formal procedure, Alexandra and Noah took eternal vows. "Yours and Yours only, in this life and the life hereafter," they said to each other, smiling. "What about Daniel," wondered Nanny out loud, "in the life hereafter?" Daniel Stone, a cardiologist, died of a heart attack, while making grand rounds at Vegas Central where he worked.

"Noah, my philosopher son-in-law," continues Nanny, "is too high for me. He talks out on a limb like Deepak Chopra. I like Deepak," says Nanny, looking at me, "but Noah is beyond me."

If Oprah Winfrey marries Deepak Chopra, I think, she would be Oprah Chopra.

I listen silently.

"It's only 'the other side,' Noah told me," she goes on. "'If you'll only let yourself see it.' I never look at the other side," says Nanny, looking down. "Life is too busy to look the other way, I'm an anxious woman, full of worries, concerns and unresolved issues. Life is much too complicated to lose your mind."

She stands up, "I need to put my mind at ease and learn not to hear background noises. Like in a stereo system. Treble. Bass. Blank. Life could be simple, if I could press the right button." Clutching the rail, Nanny walks down the stairs with a struggle.

* * *

I sit in the attic alone. No one comes here, not even Dad. My mother had her office in the attic. As a matter of fact, I sit at her desk. A photograph of her and Dad from a restaurant opening sits on the desk. She's holding a glass of red wine in her hand, her large eyes wide open looking directly at me, smiling. She looks happy. My dad with his eyes squinted and partly covered with his long hair is leaning on her shoulder.

One grievance, one thing I can't forgive and forget Dad for is that he let all the magazines my mother subscribed to: *Ms.*, *Mother Jones*, *Better Homes and Gardens*, *New Yorker*, *Vanity Fair*, and *Rolling Stone* continue to arrive faithfully. Dad never dropped or changed the name on the subscription. Mom's mail arrived addressed to her years after she died. Dad didn't do anything with her office either. He just closed the attic door. My mother was a writer, a restaurant critic. Like a painter, she worked alone. Her old computer and other writing tools sat there collecting dust until I discovered the attic.

Now, with each passing birthday, I spend more and more time in the attic. All I need is here—a daybed, a bathroom, and a twelve inch television and my mother's old Mac. Her office in the attic has become my hideout.

In the summertime with the air conditioner chirping along with crickets, I lie here daydreaming, listening to the ball games. In the fall I watch the autumn colors change outside the windows. Through the skylight above the desk, I am on top, close to the trees. After school on the winter evenings when it gets dark early, I come up here, lie on my mother's daybed, and read her old books and her poetry that she never published. In the springtime I feel my mother the most. She died in the merry month of May. My life in the attic is complete, I've my computer, and television, and no mother to call me. Dad never bothers me, not even when he wants me. He calls me from the flight of stairs below the attic. Dad never comes to the attic. No one does, except Nanny.

* * *

I walk downstairs. Nanny is napping on the old Morris chair in front of the fireplace. Grandpa used to sit and fall asleep on that chair, sucking sugar candy. The yellow, green and orange candy he'd buy from Woolworth's on Main Street, and very quietly pass me my favorite, orange, without Mom seeing. I think Mom knew it but she let Grandpa be Grandpa. One day he didn't get up from that chair. I was six; the Woolworth closed down, since.

Nanny has always been an object of my affection. She talks even when I want her to be quiet. She always has advice for how I might better myself, and an excuse for all my follies. She says the same things over and over now. "April is going to Princeton this fall," she'll say, "so she could be near me." April is my cousin, Auntie Pamela's daughter, who lives in Elizabeth, New Jersey.

Nanny asks Dad the same question repeatedly. "I really miss your neighbor, what was her name?" I think my mother's death seriously impaired Nanny. There are few things sadder than telling someone the same thing over and over again and for them to be hearing it as if for the first time, each time.

"Jean Austen," my Dad answers, like a recording.

Jean Austen, Redcliff and Richard moved to Bristol, England, last year to be close to Redcliff's ailing parents who lived in Bath. I miss Jean Austen, but mostly I miss Richard. He is my age. He was my buddy next door. After my mother died I spent a great deal of time with Jean and Richard.

* * *

On the way to Chez Pierre for our annual farewell dinner with Nanny, Dad tells her that Pierre no longer cooks there. He's sold the place. "He has sold his name," says Nanny. When she is not out of it, she remembers everything. Only three other tables are occupied when we arrive at Chez Pierre. The hostess shows us to our table. Nanny wants the same view, so we sit next to each other. Dad sits across from us. He's stopped asking Martha to come along to our family dinners. Martha Hasenbuch, Ph.D., the school psychologist, a petite woman of indeterminate age, with brown hair and brown eyes, is Dad's woman friend, his companion and paramour. I can't believe that I even know the word. She does not stay overnight when Nanny is visiting.

Martha's psychology is to have consistency, structure, and to set limits in the child's life. Dad believes in organization and freedom of expression. They openly disagree on most everything, each giving reasons to support their opinion. Martha is a tough, independent lady, a free spirit. She is all right. I like her. Dad protects me from her. It is not necessary. "You are overly protective of your son," she always says.

"You're right," he replies. "Leave the kid alone, he has no mother."

Nanny and Martha started off on a wrong foot. During one of Nanny's visits, they met for the first time. On a half-school day, Martha took Nanny and me to lunch at Adolph's. Sitting in the walnut-paneled dining room with white tablecloths and sterling silverware, Nanny refused to order lunch.

"These people have hurt my people," Nanny said. "I don't patronize them."

"My grandparents were born Catholic in Zinica, Yugoslavia, Mrs. Sherman," said Martha Hasenbach. "Until they died, they bore their numbers. We all carry our crosses."

Nanny ordered lunch, but left it untouched.

* * *

At Chez Pierre, Dad declines to order the red wine our waiter suggests, a 1999 Bordeaux.

"Nah," says Dad. "That was not a good year for me."

That was the year my mother died. Dad is a martyr.

"What was her name, your neighbor?" asks Nanny. "I really miss her."

A middle-aged man and his young giggly companion are seated at a table between us and the next occupied table. After the hostess leaves them, the man looks at his menu briefly then looks up at his bleached blonde companion and says, "You look good enough to eat."

Blonde smiles at him and says, "Thank you. I can't wait. I hope you're plenty hungry."

Nanny looks at me shaking her head. "I wish people would save their intimate talk for the privacy of their bedrooms."

* * *

"Superb," says Nanny to our waiter. "Give my regards to Pierre."

The waiter says nothing and sends the hostess to our table. Nanny addresses her as Mrs. La Salamandre, and tells her what a good cook Pierre is and how lucky she is to have married a man who can cook.

The hostess thanks Nanny nervously and informs her that she is not Mrs. La Salamandre and that Pierre does not cook there anymore.

"I live in Elizabeth, New Jersey. I come here once a year for my grandson's birthday," Nanny says. "Those reviews of Chez Pierre you have on your walls, my daughter wrote them. She is not with us tonight, but her husband is."

Dad nods his head in acknowledgment like a robot. No one knows his name. His claim to fame is being married to a deceased food critic.

The middle-aged man and his giggly companion leave with most of their food uneaten.

* * *

For my thirteenth birthday and the ritual of a boy turning to a man, Dad gives me a brand new Apple Macintosh computer and Martha gives me a cell phone, and Nanny brings a painting that had hung in her living room in Elizabeth for over forty years, a work of art my mother had admired a great deal. A painting of a mother and child strolling hand in hand, in the colors of spring—yellow, green, red and violet. The painting my German-born grandparents carried from Hof, Germany, to Paris, France, to Elizabeth, U.S.A. I'll never forget Elizabeth.

* * *

On a hot afternoon I jump ten feet high and catch the ball for the final out at my baseball game. I am amazed at myself, and then I fall backward hitting my head on the turf. Like a cartoon character in a comic strip, I get up and run like nothing has happened. It begins to hurt on the way home. Unable to locate Dad at his office, Cohen and Khan Architects, Martha rushes me to the hospital. I throw up in a bag for the second time at the information counter while waiting for Dad to arrive and sign the consent form.

I am already gowned and in a hospital bed when Dad arrives.

"I'm afraid I'm going to die," I say quietly to him. They wheel me into the enclosure number six before he can say anything. Martha follows behind the nurse. Dr. Savage, dressed in green scrubs and a white lab coat, is attending to me.

The doctor looks into my ears, nose and throat. Other than a brief period of playing doctor with Anastasia when I was four, I never had the desire to become a doctor. There are not enough Rembrandts in the world for them to pay me to look into the ears, noses, throats, or any other orifices, of not so significant others. I always wanted to say that.

"Did you win?" asks Dr. Savage, looking into my throat.

"Yeah," I say, when he releases my tongue.

"There seems to be nothing wrong with your son," says the Doctor, looking at Martha. "It's not uncommon to throw up and feel dizzy after a head injury, but to make sure," he continues, looking down writing on his charts, "we'll take a Cat-scan of your son's head. We want to be sure that there is no internal bleeding."

Dad smiles and says, "But Zachary is allergic to cats."

Dr. Savage makes a face, laughs awkwardly. "In that case, we'll call it a dog scan. It's a fancy name for an x-ray."

* * *

At home after dinner and before Martha leaves for her place, she reminds Dad how tonight I need to be awakened every four hours or so to make sure that my pupils are equal, that I am coordinated and oriented in time. Dad says he'll do it. Nanny offers to do it. She says it would make her feel needed. I want Dad to do it, but I say, "If Nanny wants to do it, let Nanny do it."

* * *

Nanny wakes me up and asks me what day it is.

"If it's past midnight," I say, "it should be the next day, the day after Friday."

She turns on the lamp sitting on my nightstand. The light is bright. I close my eyes and she asks me to open them. I sit up on my bed on a chilly spring night and see Nanny looking me in the eyes, examining my pupils. I see my mother in Nanny's eyes. She pats my head. Before she turns the lamp off, she says, "You have beautiful eyes, just like your mother's."

I lie down, close my eyes and see my mother in the darkness.

Four or more hours later, Nanny wakes me up again and asks, "When is your birthday?"

Lying in my bed with my eyes closed, in the grayness of the dawn, I say, "I'll be thirteen, Sunday, May first, but I don't enjoy celebrating it without my mother."

Nanny says nothing. Once again she makes sure that my pupils are equal. She sits down on my bed and massages my head until I fall asleep again.

* * *

For my birthday, Martha gets me a seven year old mutt, part cocker spaniel and part Labrador retriever, from an animal shelter called "Orphans of the Storm." I call him Shadow. Shadow is twice an orphan. The people he lived with, his masters, you might say, died in a plane crash and couldn't return to pick him up from his kennel. Shadow is beautiful, with a short thick dark coat, black as midnight. He has sad eyes. Dad says that all dogs have sad eyes. I don't agree. Shadow has the saddest. He sits with me, blinking one eye at a time. Do all dogs blink one eye at a time?

Shadow is not only my best friend, he is the smartest dog in the whole wide world. He understands everything I say. He can sit and play "King of the Jungle." He has a kind soul. If a burglar would break into our house, I think Shadow would ask him to please sit down, and would offer him a cup of tea. I can talk to him and he listens attentively to everything I say. He walks to school with me in the morning, heels at the intersection and looks to both sides before crossing the street. At the signal lights he knows to cross when the light is green, which is amazing considering that dogs are supposed to be color blind. In the afternoon, when I return from school, he is there to greet me.

"How old do dogs live to be before they die?" I ask Martha.

"Twelve to fourteen years on the average," she replies.

"You'll probably be in college when he dies," says Dad.

"When I go to college, I'll change Shadow's name to Half-Moon," I say. "The half you don't see."

* * *

In early April one year, I learn that Nanny can no longer travel alone and she won't be visiting me on my seventeenth birthday. Late in April, Richard and Jean Austen return from England for one week to bury Jean's father, Richard's grandfather.

"My mom and dad do not live in the same flat anymore," says Richard. "I want to come back to the States and live in our old house again," he says, looking sad. I remember his baby face. He looks grown-up now.

"But Mum says," says Richard with a detectable British accent, "even if we return to live in the States, we'll not live in the same old house again, and my dad will not return to live with us. It's easier to have them split up in England. In a foreign country, you can stay anonymous, and if you could ever return home again you could leave the excess baggage, like your father, behind."

I didn't know what to say. People die every day; at least his father is living.

* * *

In Elizabeth, New Jersey, Nanny lives in the old house that Grandpa bought and paid for in cash. Money was never a problem. Auntie Pamela, who ran a real estate company, visits her every day. She also found a young Vietnamese couple, Champa and Arun with an infant daughter named Mai, to live with her. Visiting nurse Aquino comes five days a week to take her for walks, play fun games with her and observe her deteriorating health. Auntie Pamela passes on Nurse's reports on Nanny's condition.

"I don't want to play," says Nanny.

"Our law is we play Simon Says," says Nurse Aquino.

"We all live by the same law," says Nanny, "and my law says we don't play. You are a girl. You can't be Simon."

Nanny gets up from her chair, sits down on her bed, and asks, "*Ou est mon mari?* Is he coming to see me today?" The nurse tries to explain that her husband died over eleven years ago.

"In that case, I'll have to go by myself," says Nanny, looking confused. "*Ou est la sortie?* After all these years, I still can't figure out the Paris Metro System."

"You're not in Paris," says the visiting nurse. "You have been living in the States for over fifty years now."

"In that case, I'll pack my luggage from my room and go back home."

"You can't go home," says Nurse Aquino. "You live here."

"I can't remember anything," says Nanny. "I sit and wait for something to happen. My life is a short story with no end or beginning. I am always thinking of something else," Nanny continues as if talking to herself. "I am never where I am. Soon I'll begin to forget my dates and my days. I am losing my wits. I can't remember what I said moments after I say it. I have a worried mind. "

Nanny lies down in her bed. Nurse Aquino takes out her pajamas and puts them on the bed.

"Mrs. Sherman, please change before you fall asleep."

Nanny takes off her blouse, puts it on her bed, and walks to the window. She looks out for a long time at the bones of the naked chestnut tree in the backyard. She walks back to her bed and puts her blouse back on. She puts her pajama bottoms on with much difficulty and lies down in her bed with both of her legs stuffed into one pajama leg.

* * *

Every time Nanny would ask about Grandpa, Auntie Pamela would tell Nanny that Grandpa died. Each time Nanny would hear that her husband has died. She'd cry. Mr. Kent, a social worker, told Auntie Pamela that every one needed to be informed of the death of a loved one and deserves the dignity of grieving for their loss at least once, but the elders with dementia hear the bad news for the first time, each time. This way they can never progress in their process of grieving and have a closure on their loss. So every time they ask they need not be told of the death of a loved one. Now when Nanny asks if Grandpa is coming, they tell her that Grandpa is going to visit her later. This makes Nanny happy, she probably thinks that he is just running a little late.

* * *

May is over, but May feelings linger on. Everything is changing. I am graduating from high school in three days. Miriam Solomon and I broke up today. I'm full of melancholy, a thoughtful, gentle sadness, a sweet miserable feeling. I wanted to go for a long walk in the setting sun. Instead, I lay me down on my mother's daybed in the attic and watch the rainfall and lightning in the distant south. I got accepted to Princeton University and that makes me happy, it will keep me close to Nanny. But now I won't see Shadow.

* * *

I visit Nanny in Elizabeth. She recognizes me when I walk into her bedroom. She sits up on her double bed and says she's glad to see me. Later, for our dinner, I bring take-out food from Great Wall, a Chinese restaurant in the shopping mall. During our dinner she tells me the same old story, I've heard it many time before. How at age two I was a plump and chunky infant, and how she broke her tailbone in an effort to control her fall when she was carrying me up the front steps of her house. My parents had left me with her to have a weekend by themselves in Manhattan. They saw *Runaways*.

I don't pay much attention. I know her story, the beginning, the middle, and the impending end.

"Lady Slaughter wouldn't know this one," says Nanny, reading her fortune cookie fortune after our dinner. "In nature, there are neither rewards nor punishment, there are only consequences." She looks at me vacantly. Her pale grey eyes are full of tears; her large drooping lips quiver. "Your mother should have not died young," says Nanny.

She looks so pretty in sadness.

Lying in her bed, before falling asleep, she asks me when Grandpa is going to come home. She says she'd like to see him. She wants to see his face and longs to talk to him. She says she loved the way he took care of her. I nod silently. I sit with her, not saying anything, massaging her head, I watch the pink hearts, light pink hearts, large, small and thin pink hearts printed on her bed sheet and matching pillowcase. She falls asleep. Outside her window, like the tears of a child crying for her mother, the night is full of stars. Half Moon plays hide and seek with floating stray white clouds. I miss and pine for the mother I no longer have, and think how my mother will die again when Nanny dies. □

THE PLACE OF NO PAIN
Sharon Solwitz

The sun was rising over the lake, gold and baby-tongue pink, the dawn runners so full of their healthiness they conversed while bounding, unlike Ann, whose gasping huffs muted the sound of her feet. Ann DiLorenzo, RN, was determined to keep up with her brother, who had passed his med boards with the second highest score in the state, but only ten minutes into their run her legs were shaking. Her lungs felt charred. This regimen could not be good for her, another of Tadd's projects on her behalf, but she couldn't even complain under her breath because—because she had no breath. Single joggers zipped by. Joggers in pairs, on synchronized gazelle legs. Beads of sweat rolled down her chest. Tadd turned around and yelled, "Give it some gas, Fats!"

She was thin, so he could say that. Still, she wanted to smack him, her baby brother, running backwards in front of her, circling like a happy dog. Giddy with self-love, resident (psych) at his first choice hospital: Young Dr. Tadd.

He tagged her—"You ca-an't catch me!"—and took off. She gulped another burning breath and, after an oceanic span, the stitch in her side like a razor blade, she reached the two-mile marker where Tadd stood grinning. He wanted them to run the half marathon in September, a sister-brother duo, nurse and doctor. He was good, joking to cover his concern for her. In his neurology program he watched emotions light up sectors of the human brain. To him, minds were understandable, fixable like cars with the right drug and prescribed routine. Matter over mind? A good rejoinder. One day she'd use it with him. Meanwhile, she cleaved to the pole, grim smile on her face.

"Two miles down, eleven to go! See you later, Fats."

"Maybe."

He wanted her to come by tonight after work to watch "House" with him. A third party would be there, a respiration therapist, great guy and possible soul mate. He patted her damp, heaving back. "You're a good person, Annie. I wouldn't say it if it wasn't true."

* * *

In the car on the way to Children's Memorial in her child-friendly print scrubs, she felt the usual dread. But by the time she pushed through the door to the ER, she had spun anxiety and disarray into readiness. She was fine in Emergency, eight months fine, commended for her quick hands, her competence with wounds, which she could clean and staple with minimal trauma to the site and the patient's psyche. In the face of torn skin, welling blood, even a white glimmer of bone, she was steadfast and almost eager. She disinfected and stitched up gunshot damage the way her mother had taught her to darn a cashmere sweater so that the hole didn't show. There was real pleasure in the work and the product, even when Tadd (when she was deciding whether to apply to college) said she would make a great seamstress. Now their parents, working stable, undemanding jobs, sometimes bragged to their friends about their children who were both in medicine. Neither parent knew (of the people close to Ann only Tadd knew) that the ER was Ann's hideout. The patients kept changing, a blur of need and assuagement. If she saw one later on the street she wouldn't recognize him.

The day, though, would challenge Ann's fragile serenity. She had locked her purse, greeted her fellows, was checking charts when she was summoned to the office of the Director of Nursing. She was to work today on the fourth floor, in Hem-Onc, where two day-shift nurses had called in sick.

Ann's hands rose in a self-deprecating gesture that they sometimes performed when she was alone in her apartment. She thought, illogically: It's July; who gets sick in July? Hating the truant nurses who might be lunching downtown with boyfriends then walking over to the Art Institute. Her jaw ached under her apologetic smile. "Oh, dear. You know my, uh—" Her heart pounded. Of course the DON knew her situation. The DON (Sarah) was unflustered and warm, a nursing ideal. Sarah's eyes looked directly into hers.

"You're needed. You've been trained."

"Beautifully."

"Ann."

Sarah did not say *Grow up*, but Ann heard it in the silence. She had indeed been trained. Five years in Hematology-Oncology and she knew it still, from the combination to the sharps cabinet to the look of a child low on hemoglobin as opposed to leucocytes. No need for a blood count. She hadn't forgotten a single thing.

Sarah shook her head, and Ann couldn't tell if her direct gaze was irked or encouraging. "You'll do fine." Then, more gently, "You aren't the first person to make a mistake. Even a big mistake. At any rate, we can't just call Manpower."

She gave Ann half an hour to compose herself. Go downstairs, get some coffee. But Ann did have a choice. She felt it in the dying fall of the DON's voice. She could quit once and for all, a decision she had been contemplating for eight months, to be exact. She could get a job at her father's shoe store, where she had worked in high school and mistakes meant a blister, at worst a sprained ankle. But, my God, your legs in those pumps look amazing.

* * *

When Ann graduated from nursing school she didn't expect to be working at one of the best pediatric hospitals in the Midwest. She wasn't a star; unlike Tadd, she had to work for good grades, spurred by fear of failure while Tadd mulled which first-rate university to attend. Panicky in the face of numbers, she might still have failed if not for Kevin's tutoring. Why Children's accepted her to their residency program, she still didn't know.

Unlike some of her classmates she hadn't always wanted to be a nurse; she simply had to be something. She liked hands-on work, liked the feeling of being appreciated, nurses earned good money, and they would always be needed, right? She interviewed well, fear and need combining to look like zeal. It's my dream job, she told Human Resources and the friendly, efficient nurse practitioner, and then the group of three doctors and the head administrator who sat before her in a straight line of chairs like judges. Having gotten so far in the interview process, Ann felt a dizzying charge of courage: I love this place. I want to work in every department, I want to learn everything, she said, and meant it. It was exhilarating to say exactly what you meant.

The introductory program at Children's was demanding but she met each challenge. She hoped to work one day with the neonates—her deft hands could find the smallest infant vein—but after rotation she was assigned to Hematology-Oncology, where she learned how to administer chemo- and bio-therapy agents, learned their many side effects and how to relieve them. She learned that drug toxicity was almost entirely a matter of dosage, which depended on a body's surface area, which varied drastically in pediatrics. There were formulas using weight and height but she didn't, thank God, have to memorize them. That was Pharmacy's job. She already knew the five "Rights"—

Right Patient
Right Drug
Right Dose
Right Route
Right Time

and to check each three times before dispensing even Tylenol. She brought home the 245-page *Pediatric Chemotherapy and Biotherapy Curriculum, Second Edition.*

And in Hem-Onc she did well. She could feel in her own body the fragile bodies of her patients, and never bumped their beds like so many other nurses. When she lifted someone to change a soiled sheet or slipped someone onto a gurney there was no yelp or moan. She disliked hanging chemo, which made everyone sicker for a time, but she learned to do it. She was a genius—even *she* believed—at finding the least congested vein. Eventually the children went home. Most got better. She had thought at first that most would die, but most didn't die, at least not in her care. She was dating a doctor, who insisted on paying for their dates and seemed to like the meals she cooked for him in return. She imagined (timidly, unseriously) the pleasures of a house, a mortgage with shared payments, even (with trepidation) children. Till she met Philby McCleod.

* * *

Ann went down for coffee as Sarah had suggested, but made the mistake of calling Tadd to cancel tonight. "I'm too shaky," she said.

"You've got to see a shrink," he said.

But she had already seen a shrink, at the DON's recommendation, after two sessions with whom she could barely get herself out of bed in the morning. "Goodbye, Tadd."

Then she was running in her Alice in Wonderland scrubs down Lincoln Avenue, her thoughts pounding with her feet. She loved Tadd though he was addicted to "House." She couldn't stand Dr. House, the brainy asshole. She hated her Wonderland scrubs, the Cheshire cat in particular, grinning shamelessly from her left breast. Children apparently loved the Cheshire cat but he disturbed her, his grin hanging in the tree after every other part of him had vanished.

Rounding the corner, Ann felt her side hurting again. She thought of appendicitis though it was lower down, then a gastric ulcer, which could lead to stomach cancer.

* * *

Philby McCleod was the pretty, ten-year-old, only daughter of middle-aged rich people. She was imperious and highly intelligent. She could be funny. She had ALL, acute lymphoblastic leukemia (*ALL I ever wanted!* she would joke, in a good mood). ALL had an excellent prognosis in children, ninety percent survival after five years. That Philby's cancer had recurred sooner than expected didn't necessarily mean trouble; it often recurred, and there were good second-line drugs.

Initially Philby wasn't Ann's patient. But she had a tantrum at the door of the room to which she had been assigned, in part because her roommate was a boy, in part because he had the window bed. After an argument in which Philby's will exceeded that of the floor supervisor, the child was transferred to an empty room that happened to be Ann's. She would have it all to herself until another patient showed up. "I need space," she said to the small group of irritated adults around her. She waved her mother into the room ahead of her, with her American Girl doll, a huge stuffed dog and her laptop.

Most of the time Ann liked if not loved her patients, but Philby made her uneasy, not just because she was a spoiled brat. Her mother gone, Philby wanted Ann's attention. What's my new percentile, she wanted to know, meaning her chances of survival in round 2. She wanted the names of her second-line drugs and what they were giving her to protect her from side-effect damage. Would she lose her hair? She didn't lose it last time, but maybe those drugs were too weak, which could explain why they didn't get it all. "Get it *ALL!* Get it?" said Philby. And what else should she be doing to beat her cancer? Read a joke book? Did it really help to laugh? She didn't laugh at jokes, she told Ann, even when she wasn't sick, though she'd had leukemia almost forever. Hey, what did ALL cells look like? And what about her cells? Were they unusually large and deformed? She'd go on till she found a question you couldn't answer, a game she played when she was scared. Ann sensed this but it still bothered her. Philby made her feel stupid.

By now Ann was considered a good, even an outstanding, nurse. Five years in Hem-Onc had earned her respect from her colleagues and affection and gratitude from most of her patients. Respect still surprised her, but affection and gratitude warmed her; she enjoyed coming to work. The doctor she was seeing was a resident and spent two nights of seven at the hospital. They would kiss in deserted hallways and every once in a while screw in an empty room. But with Philby, Ann was so nervous that she sat in the break room rereading the Nursing Guide on ALL, pp. 147-63, and when the bulb lit up under Philby's room she was there in a flash like a good salesperson. Philby's hair was blond like hers. They both had pale eyes and eyebrows, almost invisible lashes, clear creamy skin. Sometimes, as the therapeutic poison dripped down the tube into Philby's vein, Ann felt a burning in her own arm, so hot she would put it under the faucet.

Philby's precocious, irritating questions ceased midway through her treatment. Upon arrival she had seemed strong and healthy, quick mind, bright eyes, long thick hair. The prednisone plumped and reddened her cheeks. But when the steroid was discontinued the girl seemed to shrivel. "Go away," she said to Ann on day four of the five-day protocol, "you look like a ghost." So do you, Ann thought but didn't say.

She loosened the girl's gown and as usual sanitized the skin around the port, the preferred delivery mode for long-term chemo. There was the needle prick to bear with each infusion but, installed under the skin near the collarbone, a port rarely got infected. With a port you could bathe and even swim, and Philby, who had a pool behind her house, had Olympic intentions. "A light prick," Ann warned the child, as she was accustomed before a puncture. "Think about swimming. Cool water. Sun on your face."

"Why? I can't swim in here, can I?"

"That's true," Ann responded equably. She hung the saline and started the drip. "So far so good?"

The girl sent the bag and Ann a baleful glance. "It hurts like hell."

"It's just salt water," Ann said. "You're ninety percent salt water already."

"Sixty percent," said Philby.

Ann examined the place of ingress. The drip was steady. Ann wanted no more conversation with the child, but as there might be something the parents hadn't mentioned or didn't know, wishing to cover all imaginable bases, she pulled a chair over to the bedside.

"Your eyelashes creep me out," said Philby. "Why don't you wear mascara?"

Ann left the room briefly then returned to start the VP-16. She didn't stint on the task; she checked the Rights as always, paying special attention to decimal points, knowing what happened to patients given ten times what they were prescribed or, just as bad sometimes, a tenth. Etoposide was usually well tolerated, and Philby's first-round side effects had been almost nil—no fevers, mild neutropenia treated at home with G-CSF. Ann could picture Philby's blood cells, the healthy and the cancerous, wily and relentless like Philby herself. She followed the guidelines, but swiftly, wanting to do it right and be gone. To be in the break room with a cup of coffee. She wanted to think about Gary, her doctor boyfriend, who had remarked last night that he was afraid of being needed too much. It was said lightly. She hadn't understood it as a warning and had replied, uncharacteristically forthright, "I don't know how much I need you, Gary. I think I love you." She had felt heedless and joyful but perhaps she should have been cooler: *How much is too much, dude?* Or made fun of him: *I think you're projecting!* It occurred to her that when he slept at her apartment he always left early to walk his dog. Of course, the dog needed walking, and food and affection, but she felt, perhaps illogically, that in Gary's hierarchy she was lower than the dog. Should she say so? Would she sound wryly amused or unattractively needy? Tadd had said more than once that with more self-confidence she too could be a doctor. Not that she wanted a doctor's power over life and death, so much more terrible than that of a nurse.

The last day of her protocol, Philby tolerated the infusion as she had all week, though she hardly spoke. She was weak when she left the hospital and a little disoriented: not uncommon. Then three days later she was readmitted, vomiting, with barely a frizz of hair at the base of her skull, and the next day she was bleeding in the mouth and through the veins of her eyes. She died after a week in Intensive Care. Ann cried as she always did when she lost a patient, then learned the error sequence in which she had played a part. The attending physician's "1" looked like a "7" to the pharmacist, who dispensed a dosage appropriate for a large teenage boy; Philby weighed eight-five pounds. It was one of a hundred correct prescriptions the man had filled that day. The name Philby sounded male.

There was a hearing that included Ann, the pharmacist, the attending physician, Philby's parents and their lawyer. The pharmacist took the main blame, having failed to check with the patient's doctor. The hospital's malpractice insurance paid the parents an undisclosed sum and the hospital expedited their plan to computerize the pharmacy. Ann, whose prior years on the fourth floor were without incident, was reprimanded gently and not in writing; her record remained clean. But that was wrong, Ann thought. She the nurse was the last line of defense against error. She broke up with Gary, who kept assuring her, with remarkable patience, that it wasn't her fault. The therapist she started seeing probed her family history. What rules did she have to follow as a child? What were the penalties for infringement? Were she and Tadd treated equally?

Nothing changed the fact that it was *her* hands that had hooked up the bag of poison, her mind that failed to question the dosage—her feeble, woman's mind that had kowtowed throughout childhood to her father and teachers and even her younger brother, and never thought to question what was called an order. God, she couldn't even calculate a fifteen percent tip without writing it out. She lulled herself to sleep multiplying two-digit numbers in her head.

* * *

Ann was too conscientious not to appear within the appointed time on the fourth floor of Children's. Every room was filled, her old comrades, thank God, too busy to do more than call out hi and welcome back, and the supervisor didn't know her. Soon she was working automatically, dimly aware of her heart beating light and fast. She thought of the neonates, beings so small that anyone not their parent might disregard them. Less babies than goldfish flapping by the side of a pool, deaths you wince at then forget, she had at one time thought. Then there was no time to think.

Two hours into her rounds she met Nathan Feinstein, a fourteen-year-old boy whose over-radiated bladder was the size of a baby's fist. His cancer was in remission but he might have to pee all his life through a tube running out of his side into a bag. Or he'd be excusing himself every fifteen minutes to go to the washroom. He had short, soft, newly returned chemo hair dyed a whimsical blue. His face was long and thin like the face of the first guy she went to bed with (at seventeen), and she worried how sex would be for this boy Nathan Feinstein. Could she bear having sex with a man with a bag? These weren't thoughts to be having now. She tried to smile but her face felt so stiff, she couldn't curve her mouth into a pleasant expression. Couldn't imagine doing so at Tadd's tonight. It was lucky she'd cancelled.

Nathan's central line was infected and had been pulled; he needed a peripheral drip. She tapped the vein in the back of his hand, but it looked weak. She tried a larger vein in his wrist then one on the smooth white inside of his elbow. He seemed to have no blood pressure. She was perhaps breathing hard or muttering under her breath because he looked up at her. "It's a bitch," he said companionably. "Everyone has trouble with that."

"I don't want to hurt you," she said, and it was the wrong thing to have said. His eyes told her how much he had been hurt already. He glanced across the room, past the empty bed awaiting a five-year-old with a Wilms' tumor. An older man leaning against the door frame gave him a thumbs-up then turned away as if embarrassed—the father, no doubt. She felt the man's pain for his son, one thing she had almost forgotten about this floor, the multi-faceted nature of the pain here. She said, almost aloud: *Give me a poisoning. A gory car accident.*

"What?" said Nathan.

"You have good ears."

"Thank you," he said, and laughed. "I like compliments."

She almost looked at his face but controlled herself. What a strange boy. She tried the median cubital then a lower gauge needle, which slid right in. The slow saline drip commenced; he was slightly dehydrated. He closed his eyes. Mission accomplished. But the boy was speaking. "That was outstanding," he said.

She leaned closer. "What was outstanding?"

"You're very good at this."

She laughed, she couldn't help it. "Thank you," she said, and then, wryly, "I have some experience." And then: "You're a connoisseur."

He nodded; he knew the word.

Her next task with the boy was something she hadn't done for a while. She had to irrigate his bladder, clear it of clots so that urine could enter the urethra. A urologist came to explain the procedure, a nurse practitioner to show her how it was done. Once the bladder was clear they would pull the tube. In the best case scenario, small as his bladder was, he might be able to urinate naturally again.

Nathan was listening intently, fascinated, pleased. But when the NP screwed the large syringe into the tube and pumped the distilled water into his bladder, the boy gasped and squeezed his eyes shut. Steady moderate pressure, like plunging a toilet, she said. Nathan laughed then moaned. His father came in and took hold of his hand. Ann would have liked to comfort Nathan as well, but she was handed the pump and told to discharge the used liquid into a graduated cylinder. What came out was bright red but neither urologist nor NP seemed surprised. Ann was to continue till the water was clear or light yellow.

The instructors having departed, the father knelt and kissed his son's hand, began stroking his head. "How's it going in there?" he said to the boy, who opened then closed his eyes. The boy was thin but not bone thin. His arms were stiff against his sides, like hers when she ran. Averting her eyes from his face, she pumped then emptied the syringe. Floating in the liquid were black clots. She felt like a vampire, draining him, but he had begun to breathe evenly and made no sound. His father stroked his blue-haired head.

"Cool do," she said to the father, who kept on stroking, over and over, as if he couldn't stop. Silent tears ran down his face. "Bad clot. Bad clot," she said, "but we're getting them." The boy uttered a faint moan then smiled apologetically. "I am so sorry," she said.

"Go on," he said. "It's making me better."

She hoped so. She continued till the solution cleared. When he was covered up again and she added Demerol to the saline, he looked at her with astonished dark eyes.

"I love my nurse who takes my pain away."

* * *

That evening in a liquor store in search of a bottle of wine for Tadd and Tadd's pal, something cheap that didn't look cheap, she would feel the boy's pain in the place in her belly where she got menstrual cramps. Nothing ends, she would think. Nothing is ever over. Reliving again the moment when she hooked the etoposide to Philby's infusion stand, sanitized the port, numbed the skin and positioned the needle. There was an instant just before she started the pump—it was so clear now—when she'd questioned the dosage. This she has told no one, not the DON or the counselor she saw, not even Tadd. For the span of an eye-blink she'd wondered if the yellow of the liquid in the bag wasn't a bit too vivid, then quelled the small, almost ineffable doubt, shy of calling the pharmacist back, a busy man who was abrupt when harried.

The recognition lingers a moment. The nasty Cheshire grin hangs in the tree. Then she picks up a bottle that costs more than she wanted to spend—a Barolo that Gary had liked, thinking how Tadd will kid her: First her flipflop then the good wine. *I guess I have a rich sister!* And she: *For you, kid, anything!* Remembering the room that afternoon— the father's gratitude. And the son's face, how it shone with the kind of light that comes through stained glass. ☐

WRITING AND PUBLICATION
Harry Mark Petrakis

an excerpt from *Song of My Life*,
South Carolina University Press, Spring 2014.

I'm not sure at what age I decided that I wanted to become a writer. As a child I wasn't a particularly zealous reader. For a time in the mid 1930s I became engrossed in reading the pulp magazines, among them *Tarzan, Guard of the Jungle, Ghost Stories*, and *The Spider*. The pulp I found most fascinating was *G8 and his Battle Aces*, containing stories of the World War I pilots who fought in their Spads and Sopwith Camel biplanes against the Fokkers of the German Air Force. In these stories, British and American pilots were pitted in single combat against German pilots. The most famous German Ace among these "Huns" was Baron Manfred Von Richthofen, the "Red Baron" who foraged the skies in his distinctive scarlet Albatross triplane and who achieved eighty credited kills of Allied fighter pilots before he was shot down himself.

Unlike war in the trenches with men on both the Allied and German sides dying in senseless assaults back and forth across No-Man's-Land, the fighting in the air pitted identifiable heroes in valorous combat. The triumphant pilots achieved fame and an identity we could read about as we followed their exploits.

What appealed to me was the element of gallantry in these air battles, absent in the fighting on the ground. After a dogfight, there was the dipping of plane wings to defeated flyers, and often the scattering of flowers over the crash site of fallen planes. The Squadron of the English Air Force whose pilot, Captain Brown had shot down Von Richthofen on March 21, 1918, buried their famous adversary with full military honors including a wreath on his grave reading "For a Worthy and Honorable Foe."

In my adolescence I was again drawn to World War I while reading the poetry of Alan Seeger, including his prophetic poem, "Rendezvous with Death." On the eve of the infamous Battle of the Somme in 1916, 25,000 men lost their lives in the first day of fighting. Seeger wrote:

I have a rendezvous with Death
At some disputed barricade,
When Spring comes back with
Rustling shade
And apple-blossoms fill the air—
I have a rendezvous with Death
When Spring brings back blue
days and fair.

I memorized that poignant poem and recited it over and over again, identifying with the pathos of the young soldiers dying in war.

I was also moved by the poetry of another World War I poet, Wilfred Owen, who, as with Seeger, was killed in the Great War. His poetry captured the disillusionment of young men going off to war prompted by high ideals only to lose them in the harsh brutality of the conflict. In Owen's poem "Disabled," a soldier whose legs have been amputated reflects on the reasons for his enlistment.

It was after football, when he'd drunk a peg
He thought he'd better join. He wonders why
Someone said he'd look a god in kilts.
That's why, and maybe, too, to please his Meg.

In my adolescence I read the shattering novel *All Quiet on the Western Front* by the German novelist Erich Maria Remarque. That book moved me to reject the validity of any war no matter the fervor of the patriotic slogans that might prompt one to join.

I think the two years of illness with tuberculosis that struck me when I was about eleven, more than anything else turned me to the creation of stories. Long before the era of television with the more appealing radio programs not broadcast until evening, my pastime became reading obsessively. In bed both day and night, with nothing else to do, I consumed one book after another.

In an effort to escape the confinement of my room, my imagination also flourished, allowing me to carry out make-believe journeys across the world that my illness prevented me from undertaking. Perhaps a fear of illness and death that came frequently to my mind also fostered an urge in me to extricate some meaning in what I was feeling and fearing. Perhaps that concern with illness and death helped nurture a tragic sense that from the beginning has been reflected in my work.

After I had been liberated from bed and returned to school as an adolescent, my first efforts at writing were in poetry. I recall an early (thankfully lost) poem titled "Ephemeral Splendor," which spoke of my love for some nymph I identified only by describing certain of her enticing body parts. Perhaps the reason I remember this otherwise forgettable verse was the controversy it created when it was published in our four-page mimeographed church newsletter.

The stalwart president of our parish board was outraged and carried the mimeographed poem angrily to my father, warning him to reign in his blasphemous son before I blossomed into full perversity. He also suggested that some grueling and steady work be found for me in a grocery or restaurant to save me from these cesspools of inequity I was inhabiting.

My father mentioned the incident to me as a cautionary tale but I don't recall him being incensed or disturbed. I know that he felt some pride in my early efforts to write when his church secretary, a wonderful lady named Bessie Spirides told me that when my father had visitors he pulled from his desk drawer one of my early stories and showed it to his visitors saying, "My son wrote this. He's going to be a fine writer someday."

I cannot believe that my father saw any quality in what I had written at that time to warrant such a prediction. His own lack of fluency in English made him a poor judge of literature. Yet he could speak with faith about me based simply on his love for his youngest son.

In my adolescence I remember the titles of a few stories I wrote but only fragments of their substance. There was a story called "The Ballad of Billy One-Eye," the tale of an old sailor who had sailed the seven seas and had lost one eye in a fight over a woman. In a story called "Suella," a convict newly released from prison travels by train to a small town in the South to kill Suella, the woman who had betrayed him and caused him to be sent to prison. Another story titled "Ashes of the Rose" had as a principal character a man who had witnessed the death by fire of a schoolhouse full of children and who was tormented by the memory. Looking back it seems to me that those early stories often reflected a preoccupation with violence, passion and death.

My efforts at writing were desultory, at best. I'd feel the urge to write a story and after writing a few pages, put it aside. I rarely bothered to revise. Several months passed before I might feel the urge to write again.

I think my desire to pursue writing as a way of life was crystallized by an event that took place one winter when I was taking classes at Columbia College in Chicago. Still seeking some occupation to help support my family, I enrolled in a class on Broadcasting. I had been told I had a good voice and broadcasting seemed a legitimate avenue to explore.

One of our class assignments that winter was to write a 400 to 500 word short story centered on Christmas. Afterwards, selected students read their stories for the class to discuss.

My own story concerned a waiter who, returning home from work on Christmas Eve, finds his wife absent from their apartment. That had happened before and he went to the neighborhood bar she frequented and found her drinking with several men. He takes her home and, in a fit of frustration and anger, slaps her.

Remorseful at having struck her, he washes her face and helps put her to bed. Then he begins decorating the small tree he had brought home in preparation for Christmas morning. He is consoled for the moment that when his wife wakes the next day, she'll be sober, and they'll share a few tranquil hours.

The reading of each story was followed by a spirited class discussion. None of my classmates showed any restraint in soundly criticizing a story they didn't like and I felt some apprehension about reading mine. After joining the discussion on several other stories, I decided to raise my hand and was selected to read my story.

At the conclusion of my reading my page and a half, which took no more than five or six minutes, I was met with absolute silence. My first bewildering thought was that the silence signified unanimous disapproval.

I stood there in anguish as the teacher pressed the class for comment. Finally, one student spoke up, confessing that he had little to say in the face of such a poignant personal experience.

That my story was true was the general reaction of the class. I was astonished because the story was a total fiction and I tried to assure the class of that fact. But they simply would not be convinced that I wasn't the young waiter suffering with an alcoholic wife.

After class I remember walking alone in the snow through Grant Park, the flakes falling in little icy pinpoints on my forehead and cheeks. I felt suddenly aware of a power in me I hadn't recognized before. If I could create characters that my listeners would not believe weren't real, then perhaps I had a talent as a writer that I needed to nurture.

* * *

During this time Diana, sweetheart of my adolescence whom I had courted for several years, and I were married. After spending a few months living with my parents, we moved into a small third floor studio apartment in the Kenwood neighborhood south of Hyde Park. The apartment was part of a courtyard complex containing several hundred apartments. In summer when the windows were open, the babble of a dozen foreign tongues swirled through the air.

We became friendly with our neighbors whose doors were usually open to gain those currents of air we sorely needed. While we lived in this small apartment, our first son Mark was born in the same Woodlawn Hospital where three years later my father would die.

At the time I was working at South Works of U.S. Steel in South Chicago on rotating shifts, eight to four, four to twelve and twelve to eight. On those nights I worked and came home exhausted in the morning, my wife would put our baby son in a buggy and walk him for hours so I might sleep. She'd walk him along 47th Street East to the park and sometimes to her father's cleaning and repair shop on 53rd Street. Some of our son's earliest memories were of that store with its pungent odors of leather and cleaning fluids.

I don't recall writing during this period. The irregular hours of work at the mills made any writing schedule almost impossible. There was also the constricting confinement of the studio apartment, allowing for little privacy.

About this time we made a decision to buy a home with my parents. A sturdy, commodious brick house was found in South Shore that we bought for $17,000. I contributed nothing to this cost. The $5000 down payment came from the U.S. Savings Bonds my father had purchased during the war and which comprised the totality of his savings.

By this time I had left the Steel mills and begun working for the Simoniz Company in Chicago, answering complaint letters from customers who used the company's furniture polish and automotive wax.

Sometimes in the evening when a certain restlessness possessed me, I retreated into one of the rooms of the house and sitting down at my typewriter, I worked on a story. I also made some efforts to send the manuscripts out. Few of these early faltering efforts survive.

For a long time I remember receiving only printed rejection slips on the manuscripts I sent out. One such slip from *Harper's Magazine* I remember to this day.

We are forced for reasons of the limitations of space to reject many manuscripts, which are otherwise ably-written and publishable.

After a span of about a year in which I received a half dozen of these printed rejections from *Harpers Magazine* attached to my stories, one came in the mail with a tiny alteration. Some unknown (and compassionate) hand had underlined in red ink the last line in the rejection slip which read *ably written and publishable.*

I find it hard to recap my exultation at that sign, tiny as it might have been, of a human and empathetic heart. I folded that rejection slip carefully and slipped it into my wallet. I carried the fading slip for months, watching it growing dog-eared and worn. When I was asked, "How's the writing going?" I'd whip out the rejection slip with its red underlining of the four words as proof of my progress.

My employment record continued to be erratic. After I had been fired from Simoniz for probably well-justified reasons which included insolence toward my superiors, I spent a year operating a shabby lunchroom named Art's Lunch, a monstrous experience that deserves and receives a chapter of its own in this book. Afterwards I returned to the Steel Mills for a second period of employment. That was followed by a few months as a helper on a Budweiser beer truck. I also put in a year working in a garage behind the counter selling automotive parts. All this time, working in spurts, I continued to write and send off my stories.

These submissions were costly. Postage was required for the outside of the envelope and an equal amount of postage for the return envelope. Then, one often waited months for a manuscript to be returned with the ubiquitous printed rejection slips.

There were also assorted indignities. On several occasions my envelope bearing first class stamps had been replaced with one bearing third class stamps. I was outraged at those thieves and imagined the wealth they acquired peeling off thousands of first class stamps.

Sometimes the manuscripts had been carelessly handled and required retyping before I could send them out again. The front page of one of my stories came back with great brown coffee stains on the front page as if some editor had been using it as a coffee mat.

One story, which had been sitting with a literary magazine for almost a year, was finally returned with a note of apology from the editor explaining that he'd been recalled to service in the Navy and had just been discharged. Once again I was indignant. While that patriotic lout was serving his country, my manuscript was languishing in his office.

After a while there were also a few encouraging notes, sometimes no more than a few scrawled words of praise in the margins of a rejection slip. "Good job...try us again." "Read Irwin Shaw's short stories..." A few editors also offered suggestions on ways to revise the story. After I'd revised and submitted it again, once more it was rejected. I was grateful for each of these brief personal responses confirming the stories had been read. Though they are long departed from the earth, I still cherish Esther Shiverick and Edward Weeks at *The Atlantic Monthly*; Dudley Strassburg at World Publishing; George Wiswell at *Esquire*; Eleanor Rawson at *Colliers* and Pat Papangelis at *Playboy*. Their brief notes of encouragement and praise nurtured and kept me writing.

In 1953, while I was still working at Simoniz, I returned home one evening to find our dining-room table set with candles and wine glasses. The occasion, which my wife felt worth celebrating, was a letter from Edward Weeks, the distinguished editor of *The Atlantic Monthly*, on my short story, "The Old Man." Weeks wrote that the editors had admired my story although they could not agree that it was totally successful. They had been noting the improvement in my work and were impressed with my progress. He ended his letter by writing that he believed before long *The Atlantic Monthly* would be accepting one of my stories.

My wife and I toasted one another jubilantly that evening, anticipating that within a few weeks or at most a few months, I'd finally achieve publication. That milestone actually took three more years.

I'm not quite sure at just what point I began writing my first novel. I had a title, *Cry the Black Tears*, long before I put the first words on paper. The writing of the book took me a period of about six months, each day's pages triple-hole punched and inserted in a loose-leaf binder. As the writing magazines advised, I submitted an outline and a pair of sample chapters to a few book publishers.

In the months that followed that submission I received printed rejections from three or four publishers, return of the manuscript in my stamped envelope without any comment, and one handwritten, "Sorry." None of them commented on the book, or provided me any kind of advice I might find useful.

Among the editors I had been corresponding with was Dudley Strassburg who worked for a vanity publisher where a writer would pay to have his work self-published. I considered for a while and then discarded the idea of self-publishing my novel.

When Dudley Strassburg moved to World Publishing, a regular trade publisher, we continued our correspondence. I wrote asking Dudley to provide me an impartial assessment of *Cry the Black Tears*.

He agreed and I sent him the manuscript in November of that year. Several weeks passed and then a couple of months. I jotted him a short note asking about the book. He answered me saying he was extremely busy but would get to it as soon as he could. That was in the late winter and at the end of summer, almost a year after my original submission, his letter finally came.

Somewhere in my overflowing files and folders resides his three page single-spaced letter. It is a masterpiece of critical analysis, which, at the time, struck me with the impact of a bat across my head. If I could locate the letter I'd print it here in its searing entirety. He had long delayed responding because he didn't quite know how I'd react to the criticism. That was the preamble. Then he launched into me with the fervor of an assassin.

My writing was phony, pretentious, clumsy, overheated, an appalling regurgitation of Greek tragedy. My grammar was abominable, my spelling faulty, my use of words inaccurate. He mentioned the ellipses, which he called a useful symbol in any piece of writing. In my case, he wrote, it was as if I had loaded a shotgun with ellipses and then aimed it at my manuscript, closed my eyes, and fired both barrels through the stack of pages.

As I read and reread the letter in shock and pain, I felt a shame and mortification that I had never felt in my life before. That was followed by a feeling of outrage wherein I wished the plagues of Pharaoh be lavished on that abominable editor! How dare the bloody twit skewer my pride in so destructive a way!

Then, as I read the letter for the ninth or tenth time, I began to comprehend what an invaluable critique I had received. I thought of all the publishers who returned my manuscript with only a printed rejection slip, not bothering to comment, allowing me to languish in my self-deception. Here was a respected and astute editor who was going to the effort of telling me what was wrong with my work.

I wrote Strassburg within a few days, thanking him for his time and effort, and vowing I would benefit by his criticism. Indeed there had already been improvement in my short stories since the novel had been written three years earlier. I had begun a second novel I had titled *Lion at my Heart*. I had two chapters written when I received the Strassburg letter.

I dumped the disgraced *Cry the Black Tears* in the back of a closet and returned to working on the new novel, taking care to implement the suggestions in Strassburg's letter. This effort wasn't without setbacks. I literally had to reeducate myself in rudiments of grammar, begin to revise more often and with greater care.

I found it hard to mark the milestones by which my work improved. I don't think there was any sudden leap of improvement between the writing of one story and the next, but a gradual refinement in my beginning to understand how stories should be written. As I studied the work of other writers I noted time and time again how they achieved greater impact in simpler ways. Meanwhile, the very act of writing and rewriting helped tutor me in using language and creating scenes.

I understood that while it was acceptable to read and appreciate other writers, one had to exercise caution not to be unduly influenced by them. One writer I greatly admired was the gargantuan novelist, Thomas Wolfe. His cycle of novels beginning with *Look Homeward Angel*, were masterpieces I sought to emulate. Without Wolfe's genius, however, my replication of his plethora of adjectives produced cluttered and overheated passages of prose.

What became apparent to me was the importance of revision. My stories improved in relation to the number of times I reworked them. Three drafts proved better than two and four drafts proved better than three. As I became more intensely involved with the writing of stories, I found myself revising beginnings and endings and certain crucial scenes through as many as eight to ten drafts.

These revisions were not drafts comprising full pages of manuscript. Working as I was then on a manual and then an electric typewriter, if the first paragraph I had typed needed reworking I would remove the page, red-pencil my changes, and then insert a blank page to begin the page again.

I would use different color bond for the different drafts, stacking the discarded pages on my desk. When some friend ascended the steps to my study, I made sure they observed the imposing stacks of rainbow colored bond on my desk as proof of my craftsmanship.

In December of 1956, I was working as a real estate salesman for Baird & Warner in Hyde Park. My father had been dead for five years and my mother was living with us in the house we had bought together on Ridgeland Ave. I wasn't selling houses very successfully and since my salary was based on commission, my family was facing a lean Christmas. We had bought our sons a few pieces of clothing but, in lieu of any toys, I had purchased a small dog for six dollars I planned to give them as a joint gift.

All the stories I had been submitting had been returned with the exception of one, "Pericles on 31st Street," which I had sent in September to *The Atlantic Monthly*.

I had learned though experience not to allow the length of time a magazine held a story as any indication that it might be read or accepted. Magazines were notoriously slow in responding. But my experience with *The Atlantic Monthly* had my stories returned within a few weeks. Each one also came back with a little note, sometimes from Edward Weeks, or from another fine *Atlantic* editor, Esther Shiverick.

Apprehensive that editors would not look favorably on telegrams from impatient writers, I still mustered the bravado to send a telegram to Edward Weeks at *The Atlantic Monthly*. I asked him simply to verify that my story hadn't been lost. I didn't dare ask him whether it was being considered.

That telegram was sent four days before Christmas and two days later, returning to the real estate office I found a return telegram on my desk. Fearing some harsh condemnation for my rash inquiry I opened it.

"We are buying your story Pericles on 31st Street as an Atlantic First. Congratulations and Merry Christmas."

I must have read those few words at least a score of times, each time savoring and feasting on them. I cannot remember if I said anything to my associates in the office before leaving eagerly to drive home,

I read the telegram to Diana and to my mother. Diana hugged me with tears in her eyes and my mother made her cross in thanks to God. It was a fleeting but still grand moment of restitution for all the announcements of firings and small misfortunes I had brought home to them before.

I had an appointment later that afternoon at the real estate office so I drove back to Hyde Park. On the way I stopped to visit the venerable Rockefeller Chapel on the University of Chicago campus. From time to time in the past, during a fretful day, I would stop to sit for a while in that serene environment. On several occasions I had been fortunate to hear an organist or a choir practicing, the music enhanced in that spacious interior.

That afternoon the great chapel was empty of any other human. I sat in one of the rear pews and, after a few moments, began to cry. They were an eruption of tears from a surfeit of emotion that had no other outlet.

I cried with a joy born of ten years of futility. I cried for my father, dead five years, whose love saw my future. I cried for the hardships Diana had endured and for her patience and devotion. I cried to release the torrents of joy surging through my heart.

I wasn't a total fool and understood that the sale of a single story was only a rudimentary step into the world of publishing, that the road ahead would be a difficult and continuing struggle. But the acceptance of my first story by a prestigious magazine after what had seemed an eternity of effort was a fulfillment I felt I deserved to savor. ☐

PEA CANNERY
Liz Radford

It was 1962, end of our freshman year at UNC, and we wanted to make good money over the summer, even if it was someplace there wouldn't be many girls. Vince told Jack and me about the Pinn Weston Pea Cannery, twenty six hundred miles from the low green hills of campus (twenty six hundred and seven miles from our hometown). He'd seen a flier in the Student Union promising a good wage and overtime if you wanted it.

At the cannery, we'd cook peas, freeze them.

Our dads were all for the trip although we wouldn't be around that summer to work for them as we usually did. Adventure built self-reliance, they said, and now was the time to have ours. Jack read up and told us Pinn Weston was the most advanced pea processing facility in the U.S., and that the landscape we'd drive through to get there was unmatched. I wanted to tour the Grand Teton Mountains on the way back because they were home to one of the country's highest lakes, 6,700 feet above sea level. Although I knew better, I pictured an enormous, watery basin suspended high in the sky, its surface rippling with gentle waves. I got a kick out of imagining things the way I wanted and for this reason I liked a thing I'd not yet seen.

The day before we left, Vince said he shouldn't pay for gas since he was driving.

"But it's not even your car," Jack said.

We were in Vince's driveway packing the Town & Country and his dad stood across the lawn watering grass. He shifted his weight from foot to foot, looking over at us.

"Come on, Jack," I said. "Let Vince have his way."

I said this because we couldn't make a fuss anymore. The summer before, Jack and Vince fought over a girl at a party, and when the dads found out, they lectured us for two hours about how to act because now it mattered. The dads were kings of town: owners of the car dealership, clothing store, grocery. One day soon, we'd be their business partners; the next day, we'd be in charge of it all. When the dads weren't working, they sat nursing drinks and they liked to talk a lot about other peoples' problems: women, money, booze. A woman, they said, eyes wide and yellow, *can get a man by the balls*. (At eighteen, I'd not yet—how to put it?—been in the grip of any girl.) The point was, they said, we were a cut above and we'd better act like it. Jack was smart, Vince was smooth, but the only thing special about me was my imagination. For instance, I could picture Will Pinn, Pinn Weston Cannery Founder & Owner, as a dad who wore a good shirt even outdoors in summer.

Air never smelled cleaner than it did on a highway hemmed with pine forest, and then we'd come upon a panoramic mountain view, and I had that same feeling I did when the three of us drove together to start our first year at UNC: a bright, colorful, soaring excitement; a kite tethered by a reliable string.

"We're free, guys," Vince said. "Breathe it in."

* * *

Downtown Weston was a short row of buildings spaced like gapped teeth, a single traffic light hung over an intersection, a man in boots in front of a bar. The cannery sat ten miles west of downtown. When we arrived, we nearly fell out of the car, wanting so badly to stretch our legs. I walked the gravel lot, shading my eyes against the sun. It was hot and other than a pea-viner machine chewing through a far acre, all stood motionless and lush on a Sunday afternoon.

"What a gas," Vince said.

I remembered something. "Hey," I said, "did we ever pass the Grand Tetons?"

"Least a day ago," Jack said. "You were asleep."

"Asleep!" Vince laughed. "Did you know the Grand Tetons were named for tits?"

"It's true," Jack said. *"Les trois tétons."*

The long, squat cannery plant had a tall chute at one end and an office with a light on at the other. As we neared the office, through the window, I saw a girl writing at a desk, bobbing her head as if to music.

The girl was pretty.

Vince pushed the door and a bell chimed loudly over the sound of a transistor radio: *"I've made up my mind, To live in memory of the lonesome times…"*

The girl stood from up behind the desk and turned off the music.

"Hi," Vince said, offering his smile. "Is Will Pinn here?"

"Welcome to Pinn Weston," she said, uninterested in Vince. Her dark eyes reminded me of Will Pinn's picture on the flier—they had the same sharpness.

"Is Will…" Vince started again, but she only waited, eyes gleaming with some discomfort I couldn't name, until an older boy with hair dark as hers appeared through a door from the plant to stand silently behind her, arms folded. Then, her manner changed, as if she was an automaton who'd been activated. She walked around her desk to hand us stacks of papers, speaking with a practiced authority beyond her age and station. She was Susan, Will Pinn's daughter, and this was her brother John. She would get us signed up and settled, help with anything needed. We needed to read and sign the papers.

"Read all this?" Vince said.

"I would," she said.

"But Will's the dad in charge here, right?" I said.

"He leaves it to me," she said. "Will's got other business, too."

I flipped the pages and under my breath sang some of the Ray Charles we'd heard on her transistor. *"I've made up my mind, To live in memory of the lonesome times, I can't stop wanting you."* I guess I'd not expected a girl left in charge.

"You know that song?" Susan asked.

"Everyone does," I said.

"Can I ask where you're from?" she said.

"Carolina," I said.

"South?" Her voice rose.

"North. Know someone in South?"

"I did," she said, "last year."

I sang a little more.

"Do you plan to sing the whole thing?" she said.

"Why not? Do you think it's too sad?"

She looked at me sharply—the way a girl did when she suspected something to be interesting about me (which often didn't turn out to be true). I tried to hold her look, but then her brother caught her attention, gesturing toward the door that led back into the plant.

"Sure," she said to him. "Go on. These guys are fine."

She explained to us: "My brother's got chores."

"And now we do too," Vince said, signing his last page with a flourish.

* * *

In the morning, the plant started with a whine and a violent rattle as the first pea-viner machine dumped its bounty into the chute We stood with other guys outside of Susan's open office door, waiting for her to assign each of us a task in the plant. During breaks in the racket, I could hear the faint, dulcet tones of Bobby Vinton on the transistor, as well as Susan's conversation with each boy. *"Then I went far away and you found someone new. Roses are red, my love. Violets are blue."* It seemed not every boy was granted work for the day, but if the boy complained, we heard Susan's voice rise over Bobby Vinton's, sharp and unbending.

After awhile I was getting tired of waiting in line. "Work to do, money to be made," I said idly.

"You sound like the dads," Vince said.

"No I don't," I said.

But then I thought about how in Carolina around this time I'd be opening the showroom to air out the pungent odor of tires and high-sheen floor polish built up with the night's heat. Last summer, I'd started helping with the books and personnel. I'd done things I'd come to regret, too. For one thing, I fired Joe, who'd been around the dealership eight years. He was a mechanic working at the back of the dealership and, as I found out, an ex-con, paid under the table. Once we fired him, I don't know where he ended up. My dad said you can't back down whatever he says. Then the dad told me to visit Whitey Long, an old, hunched-over guy selling used cars out of his front yard in the country. I carried the baseball bat the dad told me to take along. *Pretend,* he said, *you're on your way to play a game, and if he's in his yard, talk to him about quitting the business. Use the bat without really using it, if you know what I mean.* I had a feeling this was just the start of it.

"I wonder if the dads miss us," Jack said.

"Naw," Vince said. "They know we'll always come back."

Jack considered this. "We will," he said.

* * *

The cannery had a cool, clean feel, lit by fluorescents reflecting off the corrugated metal walls. The canning apparatus bordered one edge of the room, ending at the pressure cookers the length of a football field away from where I stood by the pea freezer. The raw peas cooked already in their cans. Guys with brooms swept water and peas into drains in the floor. The locals teased the college guys, poking at them with brooms, sweeping water over their feet. At the pea freezer, big as a room, a foreman explained that Vince should watch the temperature gauge monitoring the belt that fed peas into the freezer room. Jack, in the freezer, was to use a long spatula to scrape off any peas clumping on the belt.

"It's so great they make something here," I said to Jack. "You know?"

"Sure," Jack said.

On our break, we wandered the grounds and came upon some guys lined up at long tables, sorting reject peas, looking hassled under the hot sun. A kid explained they only got a half-wage for this because it wasn't plant work. There were more guys than there was plant work, but if you did the half-wage work, you had a better chance of getting picked for the plant.

Vince asked if they'd ever gotten overtime.

"No," one said. "That Susan's a bitch."

"Hey," I said. "Why do you say?"

"She's the one who told me I couldn't do plant work today," he said. "So I'd say it's her fault."

"But she didn't hire us. Will did."

When I asked, they said Susan didn't have a boyfriend or maybe she had, last summer.

* * *

One of the pea-sorters had a revolver back at the bunkhouse, so when the sorting was finished, Vince and Jack headed off with him and the other boys to shoot empty cans out in the fields. I could hear them.

I walked by Susan's office, where she sat at her desk in the middle of the room, her small figure perched straight-backed, as if she expected news. Susan's office had a certain stillness to it, despite the tinny sound of Roy Orbison coming from the transistor. It seemed to lack any residue of conversation or laughter. *"Only the lonely, Know the way I feel tonight. Only the lonely Know this feelin' ain't right..."*

"Is Will around yet?" I asked. Will seemed in a way a different sort of dad, who I wanted to meet.

"There goes my baby, there goes my heart..."

"Hi, Jim," she said, looking up. "No, he's not."

"On-ly the lonely..."

"I just wanted to talk to him about his invention."

She appraised me and I felt happy to be the subject of her stare. She seemed to decide something. "So you heard of the Pinn Water Gun Knife then. The French Fry Potato Slicer?"

I hadn't.

"Oh yeah," I said. "It's the slicer using water..."

"Right. It forces them through a grid of knives." She motioned for me to come in and sit already, and I took the chair opposite her desk.

"True story," she said, relaxing a little in her seat. It didn't seem like Susan had many visitors. "First he asked this baseball pitcher who was working here over the summer to throw potatoes as hard as he could through these knives. His name was Harvey."

"Harvey?"

"Yeah, a baseball player," she said, leaning forward a bit. "When Harvey couldn't throw hard enough, Will got the idea to shoot potatoes from a fire hose through the knives."

"You're kidding."

"So, the pressure of the water worked. It forced the potatoes through the knives and they sliced, fast. The Pinn Water Gun Knife makes the fastest French Fries in the world."

"That's crazy," I said.

"It's true." She looked proud, but around her eyes, there was also that discomfort I'd seen before.

"Can I ask you a question?"

"What do I get in return?" she asked.

"You can ask me a question," I said.

"That's supposed to be a plum deal?" she said, but I earned a bit of a smile.

Susan was the youngest of six sisters and four brothers. She was Mormon. I didn't ask her if she had a boyfriend, so she didn't tell me that. Her other sisters lived in their own houses with their husbands. Will relied on her to work the office because she was the smartest. Yes, Will knew that there were too many guys and not enough work, but I didn't ask her if he'd taken us for young fools who'd drive 2,600 miles for overtime that didn't exist, just for an adventure. I didn't ask if this is what she took us for.

I told her about North Carolina and college and the dads. I told her how my future was all mapped out. She didn't ask me as many questions as I did of her, but I didn't mind.

"See 'ya tomorrow," I said.

* * *

I sorted peas and cleaned viner trucks for half-pay and because of this got enough plant work from Susan. I wanted to stay busy because I didn't want to get bored or think about unfairness. I also wanted to please Susan. I joined the other college guys at night at the bar in town and thought about her when I met townie girls (the townie girls had come in from miles around). I had the townies' number from the start: townies wanted out of Weston and college guys sure looked good to them. Susan wasn't like that. As the dads said, they'd get you by the balls.

I asked Susan if she would marry a Mormon.

"I can't marry anybody, working down here all the time like a man."

"You don't look like a man to me," I said. Although she sat before me, somehow I still didn't feel I'd fully seen her, and I liked a thing I'd not yet seen because it fired my imagination. I imagined kissing her in the office, behind the bunkhouse, in the Grand Tetons.

She asked me: have you ever been in love?

* * *

A thing about Susan is she paid attention. Sure, it had been hot around the cannery grounds, but it was summer. I never suspected a drought. A drought can last for months or even years, but can be declared in less than fifteen days, when plants still hang onto their green color even as roots die. Susan told me this. The first week in July, Weston was declared. Susan showed me newspapers and articles and charts marked by lines sloping down. We were losing peas. But the drought didn't stop Will Pinn from hiring more boys—over the Fourth of July weekend, three new college guys arrived to work at Pinn Weston Cannery. After they'd worked a first and second shift, they got overtime. He hired them just to buddy up to their dads.

The locals who worked at the plant—young guys from a few miles around—had always resented college guys because we took up jobs, but now with these three new boys being favored, the locals tried to make things hard. I was paired with a local at the freezer, watching the gauge, and one of his buddies motioned to me, as if in trouble. He kept motioning, so I left the gauge, and the temperature climbed and I wasn't there to fix it and the peas in the freezer clumped and got backed up. The foreman didn't care I'd been lured away, just that I'd screwed up the line.

"Couldn't you have told them no?" I said to Susan. "Not hired them? This is like when I hung around a fat kid at school for a whole month so my dad could sell his dad a car. But a lot worse."

"Yes!" she said. "You know how it is, Jim. Don't say you don't. One's a big guy in a little town where Will might open a plant."

"But what about the rest of us? There's already a lot of competition."

"Most of you seem to get along," she said carefully. "You're a steady bunch."

"We've made the best of it. I doubt every bunch does that." I raised my voice, but then felt sorry. "I know it's not your fault."

"I'm involved," she said simply.

"If you're part of a family business, you can't really help what you do."

"You can always help what you do," she said.

"How?" I demanded.

"I don't know," she said. "What's the worst thing your dad ever made you do?"

I didn't want to answer.

* * *

Then someone wrote "bitch" on the side of Susan's office building in dung. When I rushed to her office, she waved me away. She was on the phone, clutching the receiver with her small hand, whispering, maybe to Will, maybe begging Will to return to Weston. She sat slumped, collapsing into her clothing. It seemed that this, out of all hassles, had gotten to her. Her brother John had pulled the spare chair to her side, and he sat silent, sentry, offering his implacable presence. Something about it all broke my heart.

Then a kid yelled at her when she assigned him to pea sorting duty. We heard him all the way down the line.

"That's what's available," she said, her voice high and cracking. I thought for sure now Gil would return, to protect her, but he didn't.

At night in the bunkhouse, Jack spoke in earnest about leaving. We were sitting around and this kid Robbie overheard. "Didn't you read the paperwork?" he said.

"What paperwork?" Jack asked.

"That you signed, moron."

I couldn't believe Jack of all people hadn't really read it, or hadn't heard what was in it. Vince and I had heard.

Jack got up off his bunk as if to lunge at Robbie, but Vince stopped him.

"If you leave, you lose your wages," Robbie said.

"What? I already get my wages every two weeks."

"They send you a bill," Vince said. "They send it to your parents. You leave, and you owe them money."

Jack got a copy of the paperwork and studied it for days, looking for a way out. He called the dads. All this time, Susan wouldn't let me see her, but I had an idea. At dinner I told Vince and Jack I'd talk to her about helping us. She'd always talk to me about business.

"What can that girl do?" Jack asked.

"Oh, pretty much everything," I said, proud of her accomplishments in business as if I had something to do with them.

I walked by Susan's office. She sat straight in her chair. During the days we'd not spoken, the delicate skin beneath her eyes had become puffed and bruised. She had the nervous manner of someone who'd lost faith in any kind of safety.

"Vince and Jack want to leave," I explained. "Those papers were a trap. You know how hard we're trying to make the money, but the odds are against us. We just want our wages."

She tried to act tough. "What makes you any different than all of the other guys in contract?"

"Nothing," I said.

"Please, Jim." She looked tired.

"Well, is Will coming back?"

"Why does everyone keep asking me that?" she said. "He's satisfied things are going okay."

"Susan, you need someone to protect you," I said. "Or at least help with the business."

She blinked and looked away into the empty space in front of her, abstracted. "To Will, business is more his religion than anything. And there is... something to that."

I didn't understand a word she was saying and I don't think she did either.

She'd taken to wearing her hair in a limp ponytail fastened high on the crown of her head, giving her the look of a neglected child. Over the desk, I put my hand on her arm. Her skin felt downy and warm. She'd grown so thin, I was surprised she wasn't cold. We sat without moving for a long time. I wanted to kiss her to make both of us feel better.

"All of it, all of it," she whispered.

"What is it?" I said. "What they wrote on the wall?"

"What you were saying before," she said. "You get born into something, and then there's not much you can do to get out. There's no way out that makes sense in a set-up that doesn't." Her face reddened and stretched into a grimace.

"Susan," I said.

"There was someone last summer," she said. "He was going to stay on and work in the plant year-round but my father was afraid we'd run away."

I felt a tug of jealousy.

"He wasn't Mormon?"

"No, my father was afraid I'd leave the front office. Didn't matter with who."

"That's unfair," I said.

"Doesn't matter."

I pictured my imaginary, floating lake, independent of the contours of the ground below. "Have you seen the Grand Tetons?"

"What?" she said, sniffing, rubbing her hand against her nose.

"It's got one of the country's highest lakes. I might go there." I felt brave saying this, although I wasn't sure what it was I was saying.

"You know about Yosemite?" she said.

"Do you want to go there?"

"I am going there," she said.

"What do you mean?"

"California."

She looked at me, her expression serious and lovely, and then she got up from her chair and I did too, and moved to where she stood behind her desk. I didn't know what I was doing, but whatever I was doing, I was doing it now. I closed my eyes, but my mouth hit the knot of her ponytail. She'd leaned into me, forehead to my chest, clutching my sides as if for support. Her hands went to my chest, my stomach, the front of my shorts.

I stepped back in spite of myself then ducked to kiss her. Her soft mouth tasted like good salt. Then I held her, partly because I didn't know what to do next, and I don't think she knew what to do either. It wasn't quite as I'd imagined.

"Tomorrow," she said.

"What?"

"I'm leaving for California."

"What's there?"

"Nothing," she said. "Nothing." She pressed her face against my chest. "Don't ever tell."

"But what about your family, your dad?"

"Fuck Will," she said. The words exploded in the quiet room.

"What? Take that back," I said, squeezing her arm.

"No." She looked at me in challenge with eyes resolute, hateful, and strong. I feared she'd see the world through those horrible eyes forever if she didn't take it back.

"He's your dad," I said.

"He doesn't care about me," she said.

"Sure he does."

"Come with me. You've got it bad, too."

"No," I said. "You've got it worse."

I couldn't help but think back to that day last summer when I walked a long way to Whitey's, carrying the bat. As I walked, I had the sudden thought to run away. The road before me lay wide open, as did the fields to my sides, but the thing was, to me, the world outside of town seemed impenetrable. The dads and Vince and Jack had always shown me where to go, unlocked doors for me, ushered me into the right rooms where people were happy to help, and this is the way I liked it. I knew, with a certain shaming panic, unbearable for more than a minute, that I'd find the world closed to my voice, my survival, if I ran. My hands would find no purchase, my fingers would slip from surfaces hard and slick as thick glass. I found Whitey, talked to him, holding the bat in just the right way, and then tried to forget a bad bit of business. I had a feeling this was just the start of it.

I pulled Susan in so tight that I felt every bit of her.

* * *

I walked back to the bunkhouse, watching the pea-viners chew the fields like bucolic monsters. I told Vince and Jack we weren't leaving early. The next day, Susan's brother sat in her place at the desk. The day after that, Will Pinn returned from Idaho, glad-handing hard workers like me.

"Where's Susan?" I said.

"Up at the house, feeling poorly." He wore a good shirt, despite the heat.

But I knew he was lying because part of me was sitting with her on the train to California, our bodies rattling together and apart with the jarring motion of the wheels on the track. We were on a train to nothing.

Jack, Vince, and I worked at the cannery for the next few weeks, but once on the road I didn't mention the Grand Tetons for a couple of good reasons. I couldn't afford a new knapsack for the trip. I wasn't sure if Vince and Jack would climb such a long way with me.

I could picture the lake well enough: just a regular lake, high up. □

FROM WHERE I SIT
Stuart Patterson

the place in this poem

has never been found. I mind
the last station on the way,
where parties linked
in jostling files emerge,
halt, and head back
into the unforgiving whiteness,

making toward the gap
that opens on a long descent
into a garden in a jungle
we've all read about.

They despise the risk that they'll just hack
their way into sick exhaustion and end
lost, surrounded by toads,
waiting snakes
and chameleons who mimic their wounds,

sure that the wordless fanfare of paradise
will open beyond the next tangle,

their last thoughts
forming and evanescing
like clouds watched long enough,
like traffic at a stoplight.

So I will listen for those that beckon

while my courtyard fills with voices.
I admit: I despise them. The louts.

I wake, eyes opening

into a window where a tiny light
shines high in a dark corner:
Venus, who has a toxic atmosphere.

Then, over my own shoulder,
I look down on my soft, wide belly
(lit not with Titian's feverish eroticism,
but the rebarbative pastiness
of an amateur acrylic)
wondering how I will be dispersed
into places I don't remember ever being
or being from.

    In Athens, they ride metaphors to work and back.

That's how I'll travel: adventure enough right here!

But how do I get on that train, make my escape
into memories I never lived, make my best go
at traveling clean away from the fact of aging?

At least I'm not taking anything that others could use.
And I'm careful not to think of life as a mere season.

    I am simply seeking comfort.

Comfort can be found standing
on the shoulder of a busy byway: Route 12,
13 or 14, getting punched
now and then by the wakes
of passing semi-trailers,
stepping over gravel at the hem
of a weed-choked culvert.

Have mercy on her as you
motor by, listening to the news
of another suicide bombing,
or the latest advance in physics,
or as you think simply of the one
you're leaving or going to see.

I'll aim to be there,

    with comfort,

just where you're sitting,

with warm words in the blizzard,
with cool eyes in the stifling heat.

THE PRINCESS OF PORTAGE PARK
Donald G. Evans

I stared into the fire. Sipped my Kahlua. There were twenty volumes in the Dickens set, and I had no greater aspiration than to read them all as the gray, mean-spirited Chicago winter coughed its way to extinction. I dangled my legs over the cushy chair. Between Francie's life insurance money, our savings, the money from her Jetta…I needn't, and wouldn't, leave the house before I glimpsed green.

A shadow danced across the hardwood floor.

It was just a gray splotch that skittered from a sewing basket to our credenza. I peered over my book. I didn't want to move; I was at such peace. I read on—the humbug was being scared out of Scrooge's bah. I'd declined Thanksgiving dinner invitations from siblings, neighbors and friends who assumed I was still grieving my wife's sudden demise. But in these solitary moments I realized, God help me, that I was happy.

The shadow flashed again, and out of my peripheral vision I thought I saw something. I thought I saw a mouse.

I sat up straight.

Flames provided the only light in my tiny little Bungalow Belt house. Our maple tree's bare branches scratched against the front windows, and I felt a frigid wheeze across my bare feet. I hadn't noticed that I was now standing, fire poker cocked, or that my fingertips had gone cold. I was tired. I studied the couch's underbelly, reading glasses dangling against my thrumming heart.

I hated mice worse than I hated anything. They were ugly, obnoxious, wasteful and, above all else, filthy. A mouse hunt ruined my appetite and sleep, consumed every thought with despair. Mice had numbers, courage, agility and strength, and if their mission was to destroy my serenity, what power had I to thwart them?

I did not turn on the lights. I held out hope that what I thought I'd seen had been an illusion, or that I would be able to squash the problem then and there. My head was cocked at a right angle to the ground as my eyes continued to sweep the contents of the house. I saw, under the kitchen island, an eerie red glow.

Francie had always dealt with the mice. I hoped soon the battle fatigue would wear off and I could think back kindly on at least some of it. Our problems, I suppose, were typical, and in summary we were unhappy but not unhappy enough. We chugged along. To the world, Francie was bubbly and energetic, a kind and passionate woman who was generous to a fault. She was known, affectionately, as the Princess of Portage Park. But at home she made the typical nagging wife look like Betty Crocker. She criticized with sighs. She reprimanded with cabinet door slams. She punished with silence. Worst of all, she treated me like a child.

As a young man, I'd been ambitious, and I'd sold Francie on that ambition. I was going to be the world's greatest inventor, but instead fumbled project after project and stewed in the self-loathing that came with disappointment in myself. The best you could say about me was I had a fantastic ship in-a-bottle collection.

Francie was witness to all my failures. When she died, so too died the only reliable witness to the person I'd become.

I inched closer. I could see into its beady red eyes, only they weren't red—they were Francie's hazelnut brown. The mouse had Francie's glint, and its color, Francie's summer bronze.

The fire poker was raised above my shoulder. As I moved to plunge the point into that boneless body, a flash blinded me, and as my eyes adjusted I saw Francie's wedding ring necklaced to that defiant rodent.

In my hesitation, the mouse was gone. But not gone. I flicked switches, one after another. Corn flakes powdered the pantry shelf liner. Black pellets trailed from the kitchen to the living room. A sock had been chewed.

I stepped outside. I squinted across the bleak, icy terrain to Portage Park's drained outdoor pool. There hadn't been much snow and yet it had accumulated along the edges of the park. I turned to see the shadow.

It was there, watching. □

ELI AND ME AT THE LAKE
Miriam Socoloff
42 x 54
charcoal with white pastel

BEATRICE AND BECKY
Miriam Socoloff
22 x 36
charcoal with white pastel

MY GRANNY AND ME
Miriam Socoloff
22 x 30
charcoal with white pastel

EVANSTON
Frederick Pollack

When I was inadequate, I walked
in more than adequate places.
Already I bore the past
like the bag of an old-world peddler;
nobody bought, and I despised my wares.
But the world was boxes and bottles
full of fake stuff,
like the environment an alien
draws from the mind of a human
captive, missing something.

And the organism I drove
through thorns of work and speech
was insincere, unwieldy,
and impermissibly tired.
As if the famous Bug
had been expected to dress,
crawl to an office, keep
a civil antenna on
its head, support shame and parents,
seek treatment and love.

When I visited my childhood
sweetheart, the husband
she had found resembled me.
Not, I realized, because she
had nursed a yearning
those twenty years since childhood;
rather, she liked a type
we were. I saw
the perfection of the type
in his philistine rumblings.

They had done well. Though the condo
didn't look down
on the Lake, the massed oaks
and spires, but a graveyard.
The rats were enormous,
he said, but the city
took measures.
I smiled, sympathetic, thinking, Come on,
cross the street.
Live in the ivy. Eat wires.

THE MARRIAGE OF HEAVEN AND HELL IN THE MIDWEST
Garnett Kilberg Cohen

Drive your cart and your plow over the bones of the dead.
The road of excess leads to the palace of wisdom.

William Blake

I left Chicago for Purdue University in Indiana, where I was giving a reading, in the late afternoon. I had heard about the wind farm I would drive past. I had seen wind farms in other places—in the Netherlands and outside Palm Springs in California—but these experiences did not prepare me for what I saw in Indiana.

I hit the wind farm just as the sun began to set. As Interstate 65 South took me deeper into the twirling white stalks, I felt as if I had been transported onto another planet. The moon hung full and bright on the left side of the road. Its lunar surface had never appeared so clear. I could see the moon's lacy highlands, threading around and between dark sunken marias, as distinctly as if they were drawn by a sharp pencil on pale scratchy white paper. Directly opposite, on the right side of the road, hung the setting sun, blazing orange and wavy behind a screen of atmospheric gases. From my perspective, the spheres appeared to be approximately the same size, and to hover the same distance above the earth. The flat road traveled ahead of me between the two globes until it narrowed into a perfect vanishing point, the quintessential example of Raphael's theory of perspective. Below the huge balls, the lines of windmills rose from the brown stubble of the shorn fields like, like, like…like what? They were neither monstrous nor beautiful. Simply otherworldly.

Sleek white poles topped with three-winged propellers, rows and rows of them, awash in the pinkish-lavender glow where the light thrown from the sun and the light thrown from the moon inter sected. The windmills could have been strange colossal birds preparing for flight. Mechanical flowers. A huge cemetery of revolving white crosses.

One-eyed aliens with twirling antennae.

I expected the rows of windmills to end quickly. Instead, as the orange sun melted, Dali-style, into the earth and the moon rose higher, I found myself traveling into the wind farm's center. Traditional farms dappled the countryside: pitch-roofed houses, gambrel-sloped barns, and silver silos, bound together in wreaths of trees and bushes, like gifts beneath sleek white Christmas trees. Windmills as far as I could see in every direction. Ghostly and fading in my rearview mirror. Lining the horizon ahead, like tiny white jacks tossed from a giant's unfurled fist.

A billboard a few miles before the farm had declared, in bold white letters against a black backdrop, **HELL IS REAL.** I wondered if there was any connection to where the billboard was placed and its message. Could anyone who posted such a literal message really wonder if our human excesses had created the need for the surreal wind farms?

I wondered whether the esthetic loss created by covering the planet like a giant pincushion was really worth the environmental gains, the way I had always believed. Surely, this stark ugliness was better than trying to retain nuclear waste.

I wondered what it would be like to live on one of the farms huddled between the windmill's bases? I imagined I would feel under siege each morning as I stood before the picture window, sipping my coffee and gazing out at their unnaturally white trunks. Or would I come to love them the way I would a real forest?

I wondered what it would be like to be children growing up here, never knowing another landscape. Would they be able to sleep in distant places without hearing the comforting whir of the hundreds of turning axles? When they came home for the holidays from college would they have a sentimental yearning for the poles, find them a glorious sight? How can one not miss what she has always known? Would people one day write novels where the sleek white windmills were as prominent and sentimental as the prairie flowers in books by former midwestern writers?

I wondered how much energy the farm produced, how wide an area it serviced.

I wondered why some propellers turned lazily while those di rectly opposite spun quickly. I imagined more variations of air currents and wind rivers coursed through the sky than I could envisage with my naked eye. I had heard that the winds sometimes confused birds' migration patterns.

I wondered whether I would become hypnotized by the seemingly endless poles. I imagined that—despite the flat road—I would be car-sick by the time I reached my destination, where I was to read from my new book.

As I drove and darkness coalesced, I wondered what the windmills looked like from above? I imagined a Chinese checkers board, a star comprised of marble-shaped pattern of holes, locked to another stippled star, entwined with another star, another and another, each cupped indentation sprouting a windmill.

In the morning, on the drive back to Chicago, I remember to check my speedometer as I re-enter the wind farm. The stretch is ten miles from start to finish. The landscape not nearly as haunting as it was in the overlapping crepuscular light of the rising moon and setting soon.

I exit the wind farm and see the back of the billboard I had seen on my way to Purdue. (Or is it the front?) This reverse side says in block white letters, once again against a black background, **HEAVEN IS REAL.**

I wonder if it would have made any difference if I had taken a different route home, and missed the other side of the billboard? Or if the sides had been reversed and I had seen the declaration about Heaven before I saw the one about Hell. ☐

THE FOURTH DEMENTIA
John Blades

Wozzeck?

I had to think about that one for a minute.

Who wrote *Wozzeck*?

He tensed his jaw and drew his body to attention beneath the covers, until he was on full horizontal alert.

I'd neglected to lower the volume on the television, so I was forced to concentrate ever harder, to tune out the sound of the children's chorus on "Sesame Street."

Schoenberg?

Schoenberg was the first composer who came to mind. But — that only made me more uncertain. I didn't want to be too quick on the draw.

He flexed his feet, curled his toes, as if trying to get the blood to circulate to his brain, recharge his memory.

No not, Schoenberg. Close, but no kewpie doll.

It was somebody else, a 12-tone cousin of Schoenberg. Then I had it. Berg. No Schoen — . Just Berg. Alban Berg.

He relaxed,

as pleased with myself as if I'd earned a gold star for the cover of my workbook. Maybe I'd get a star. I couldn't wait to tell my caregiver.

But I couldn't tell my caregiver. I hadn't spoken to her in months. I hadn't seen her in months, maybe longer. I was sure she was out there somewhere, though, lurking, scheming, waiting to strike.

During the first weeks of the lockout, I was sure it was her knocking on the door, wanting to be let in. She'd disguised her voice. She'd pretended to be my wife. It was uncanny how much my caregiver sounded like Angela.

But I wasn't fooled. Angela was gone, gone forever. I knew that much.

My caregiver knocked for months. She knocked at five minutes before the hour, every hour. I clocked her by the television set. She started just before the "Today" show and stopped just before the ten o'clock news.

For a while, she treated the standoff as a joke. "I'll huff and I'll puff and I'll blow your house down."

When she understood that I wasn't going to open the door, she threatened to get a locksmith. She threatened to get a carpenter to remove the door hinges. She threatened to call police.

At first, I believed she would call police and I was frightened. I could hear sirens, far in the distance, but growing louder, nearer, more threatening by the day.

If police stormed his room,

I would have to use the Kalashnikov. I knew how. I'd had enough practice. I could lock and load it in the dark.

How do you spell Kalashnikov?

I tried to sound it out but I'd never been sure how it was pronounced. It didn't matter how it was spelled. What mattered was that I had one hidden in the cedar chest, beneath the quilts and towels and comforters.

Let me live in peace. Let me die in peace.

Then his caregiver gave up.

She still prepared his meals, but now she left the tray at the door, without knocking, and picked up the empty tray hours later.

His meals were always cold, because he waited an hour or more before getting the tray.

I waited until I heard her footsteps going down the stairs, until I heard her in other parts of the house, opening and closing cabinets, running the vacuum cleaner, talking on the phone.

He fumbled under the blankets for the remote. Finding it, he pushed the mute button, listening.

I heard the television playing downstairs – tuned to QVC. It infuriated me to think that she had access to QVC while I didn't, that she had access to all the good things it offered.

It made me more furious to think of her having the cable connection, while all I had was the twelve-inch set with the rabbit ears. The set was only a few feet from my bed, but I could barely make out the picture. The screen was fuzzy and corrugated – it was like watching through mini-blinds.

She had confiscated all his bare necessities when she banished him to his room. The projection TV, the DVD, the TIVO, the Surround-Sound speakers, the universal remote. She could have left him with a bigger set, a PlayStation to pass the long hours, a cable hookup so he wouldn't be completely disconnected. This was cruel and unusual.

All the unopened boxes and cartons she had returned to their senders. Most of the opened stuff – the video games, the software, the spare phones and answering machines, the commemorative figurines — she declared either useless or superfluous. She stored them in the basement, the garage, or left them on the porch for Goodwill.

"Boy toys," she said. "Things you should've outgrown years ago."

"You didn't have to throw them out," he said. "You could have gotten something at a yard sale or on eBay."

"Not worth the trouble and effort," she said, and that ended that. All my precious possessions, my years of methodical accumulation, dismissed and cast off, as thoughtlessly, as frivolously if it were garbage.

At the least, she would have left me with my iPod and headphones, but she trashed those too. Now I couldn't listen to WNOS. But it didn't matter. All I had to do was push a button in my head and I could hear the voice of Johnny Ray, singing, singing any song I liked, over and over in the jukebox of my brain.

> *There she is, my old gal*
> *There he is, my old pal*
> *And here am I, broken hearted.*

I'd also outsmarted my caregiver on the Kalashnikov. She'd discovered it during one of her surprise sweeps, before the lockout.

He pleaded with her to let him keep it. He told her it wasn't real. That it wasn't loaded. That it was a harmless BB gun.

"I've seen BB guns and this is not a BB gun."

"You're thinking of the Red Ryder model," he said. "That's obsolete now. This is the latest model."

She'd placed it in the throwaway pile, along with his other possessions. But she had so many loads to box and dispose of that he was able to recover the rifle and stash it in the bottom of the cedar chest.

Or that's where I thought I'd put it. I'd been in such a hurry to smuggle it out of her reach that I couldn't be certain.

If only I could get out of bed, I'd search for it. Make sure it was oiled and ready – ready for the invasion I knew was coming, when my caregiver got tired of fixing my meals, emptying my bedpans and milk jugs. She'd cook up some excuse, call 911, bring in a SWAT team to flush me out.

It wouldn't be long. For weeks now, I'd been hearing the sirens, getting louder and louder, nearer and nearer, only hours away, maybe minutes.

Light dribbled in through the edges of the shades, which his caregiver had insisted remain in the lowered position, day and night.

"Up," he pleaded.

"Down," she declared.

"I'm not going to dust in here," she said. "Are you? With the curtains closed, you won't be able to see all the dust balls."

I not only wanted light, I wanted air. The room was starting to smell like a mortuary.

He hadn't changed his sheets in months, because he couldn't get to the basement washer and dryer.

I could leave my dirty laundry in the hallway, but that would only provide my caregiver another opportunity to pounce. I couldn't shower either, since that would enable her to trap me in the bathroom.

"I wish you'd shave," she said. "You're starting to look like Santa Claus. You smell like him too."

"How do you know how Santa smells?"

"Everybody knows how Santa smells–like a reindeer."

"Wrong," he said. "I've sat on a lot of Santa's laps, and they all smell like alcohol."

I thought I saw her smile, but couldn't be sure in the perpetual twilight of my room.

I'd become a crepuscular creature. How's that? I not only know the meaning of the word, I can spell it. Two gold stars for my workbook. I intended to start keeping one, if only I had a notebook and a pen.

He raised his head off the pillow,

willing my body to follow. I wanted to get out of bed and open the curtains. But my body wouldn't obey my brain. My circuits were frayed, disconnected, my energy reserves exhausted.

He was barely able to draw himself upright and sit on the edge of the bed so he could relieve himself in a gallon jug.

I didn't have the strength to carry the jugs I'd already filled and put them outside the door. They surrounded my bed like liquid booby traps, ready to trip me once I did get back onto my feet.

My caregiver had done this to me, deliberately.

She'd confiscated all his medicine – his entire pharmacopoeia, the herbs as well as the prescriptions, the pills, the capsules, the caplets that gave him the energy that had kept him alert, vigilant, tip-top, revived his flagging mental and physical powers.

Now I was flagging, unfurling, tip-toppling.

That was why it was important that I play the memory game with myself, 20 questions, 200 questions, however many it took to keep my mind agile and ahead of hers.

Wozzeck?

It took me a few seconds to remember that I'd already answered that one, and correctly.

What else did Berg write?

I was challenging myself.

A cartoon panel flashed into my mind, and I saw Little Lulu and Sluggo, confusing me for a moment.

Then I had that one too. *Lulu*. Not the cartoon, Little Lulu, the opera, *Lulu*.

Another gold star.

More than ever, I wished I could tell my caregiver. This was hard stuff. Nothing like the simple questions she used to toss at me, when she was coming into my room, when we were still communicating.

Who wrote *Treasure Island*?

How many feet in a mile?

What is the capital of Nebraska?

What's my name?

She remained impassive as he answered each of the questions, until he came to the last, and he said, "Mother."

She frowned and said: "Bad job. Try again. What's my name?"

I was insulted by how simple her questions were – trivial stuff. I was frustrated and humiliated because I didn't always know the answers. I'd never been a trivia person. How could she expect me to remember grade-school questions?

I could answer the tough questions, if only she'd asked those. But they were beyond her.

Name the titles in Faulkner's Snopes trilogy?

How far is it to the Moon?

Who wrote *Lulu*?

If I asked her those questions, she'd flunk on all counts, especially the last one. Ernie Bushmiller, she'd probably say.

"What's my name?" she persisted.

"Rumpelstilskin," he said.

That drove her to the brink. "That's not cute. How can anybody help you when you won't try to help yourself?"

She'd seized the tray with his dinner and left the room.

He bolted the door behind her. That was when the lockout began. That was when she began knocking at the door, knocking and knocking.

Then the knocking stopped and the sirens started. A multitude of sirens — ambulances, squad cars, fire engines, all converging on my house. I wish I had my iPod and headphones so I could tune them out.

The sirens were louder and nearer than they'd ever been. This was the final assault, I was sure. My caregiver had lost all patience and had called 911. She was going to force me into submission.

I tried again to bridge the disconnect between my body and my brain. But he couldn't move, other than raising his chin a few inches, wriggling his digits.

I couldn't surrender without a fight. If I did, I was as good as dead. As bad as dead.

Gradually, painfully, joint by joint, muscle by muscle, limb by limb, he hoisted himself into a sitting position on the bed. He eased over the edge, but collapsed when he attempted to stand, as if his legs were stuffed with loose kapok.

He lay there, hugging the floorboards,

listening feverishly, as armored vehicles careened down the street, plowed over the curb, and stopped on my lawn. I heard bullhorns, troops deploying behind fenders and hedges, snipers scrambling onto nearby rooftops, the ratchety sound of cartridges being jammed into chambers.

From the rustling and the shouting, it was apparent that my neighbors had come out of their houses and gathered behind the police barriers, as if this was just another block party. These were people I'd partied with in good times, sheltered and comforted in bad. Now I heard them cheering the police, warning that I was armed and anti-social.

Then a spooky silence settled over the neighborhood – the calm before the stormtroopers. I knew the jig was up when I heard the clawing of panicky rats and other vermin inside the walls, scrambling for the exits.

An even more fearful sound rose from the street—"Turkey in the Straw," but played at a tempo so slow and lugubrious it sounded like a funeral dirge. I listened as my neighbors abandoned the barricades and swarmed around the Good Humor truck, their craving for sugar temporarily overpowering their thirst for blood, my blood.

Looking up, I saw deadly pink rays criss-crossing my room–lasers from the scopes of sharpshooters, penetrating the blinds, perforating the dusty twilight, in search of a live target. As long as I stayed low, beneath their destructive reach, I figured I was safe.

Then I heard scraping noises on the roof — the unmistakable sound of pulleys and ropes and grappling hooks, as police prepared to rappel down the side of my house and break through my windows.

I couldn't stay on the floor, exposed in what was about to become a free-fire zone.

He recovered his breath and crawled, bug-like, to the cedar chest. He raised the lid and dug beneath the quilts and blankets and old clothes. Nothing.

I was about to look in the closet when I heard the bump and clatter on the stairs – the SWAT team with their heavy axes and sledges, their heavy artillery.

My caregiver was urging them on. "Take him out," she shouted. "He swore he'd never be taken alive."

Weaponless, defenseless, I had no choice.

He crawled back into his bed and pulled the covers over his head,

just as the door and windows imploded, sending smoke and glass and splintered wood across the room, covering me in dust and debris.

Under the comforter, I heard jackboots digging into the varnished floorboards and rugs, shredding oak and wool. They stomped toward the bed, and after what seemed like an hour of silence, I felt barrels prodding beneath my comforter, boring holes in my skin, leaving welts and bruises.

"Watch out," his caregiver warned. "He may be playing possum. He's always been a trickster."

"You don't need to worry any more," came the response. "He'll never threaten you or anybody else again, never again."

I knew I was safe then. I'd outfoxed them. I ignored the spasms in my stomach, the terrible urge to empty my bladder, and held my breath,

making himself as stiff as a corpse.

It was quiet and blissful under there, and the noise of their clumping boots and their ransacking hands gradually receded, along with the crowd noises on the street.

Pretty soon there was total silence, and he heard nothing. ☐

A SECONDARY HALLUCINATION
Paul Nicholas Jones

O f all the stories her aunt Wilma had told her, there was one that changed the least with each telling, which made Lark think it was the most true. Though maybe it really worked the other way around and it was the truest stories that changed the most.

It happened in the fall of 1938. Wilma had just turned fifteen. Her father and brother were sturgeon fishing on the Columbia the day before when a fierce storm blew in and they had to harbor on the river overnight. That meant that Wilma had even more to do around the house. But it also meant that she had a rare chance to see Old Molly.

Old Molly, as the local people called her—her real name was Omallee—was the last full-blooded Chinook Indian on the peninsula. Actually, the phrase *most full-blooded* might be more accurate as she was also said to be a descendent of York, the black slave who had traveled with Lewis and Clark and who, along with other members of the expedition, had fathered several children. Like many native peoples, this small tribe was decimated by European disease and culture, and by the time Omallee was born (around 1870) there was no real tribe to speak of. As a girl, she married a Norwegian fisherman and joined the local Christian church. This was where Wilma met her, though it was years later, when Old Molly was truly old and Wilma was just a curious young girl.

Most families on the peninsula had some Indian blood in them somewhere, and her family was no exception, though this information wasn't necessarily available in written records. But to Wilma's eye, you could easily see it in the old photos of her great grandmother. And you could see it in her father, with his black hair and sharp features. Wilma, who looked like a Scandinavian peasant with her blond hair in a braid and blue eyes and ruddy white skin, became captivated by the native culture. She steadily grew enamored of the old Chinook woman and took every opportunity she could to meet with her, and even started to drop by her house after school.

But Wilma's grandma Margaret, her father's mother, saw things differently. Of course their people had dark skin and black hair, she said. They were Welsh, for god's sake. They'd descended from a race just as ancient and ten times mightier than these Chinook or whatever they called themselves. Of course she didn't object to them converting to Christianity. These people had been lost souls. What she objected to were these heathen legends and beliefs being passed down to such an impressionable and eccentric child like Wilma, especially as she was growing into such a stubborn and dreamy young woman. Eventually, at the instigation of his zealous mother, Wilma's father refused to let his daughter talk to the old Indian.

And now Old Molly was ill, that was the word going around, and Wilma wanted to seize this chance to see her. So she got up even earlier, pleased to see that the rain had let up. She lit the stove, tended to the livestock, collected eggs, and released the ducks into the garden to feast on the snails and slugs. Then she put on the coffee and started to make a list of supplies they needed. With her brother gone, she had a perfect reason to take the wagon, which also meant as easy way to make a side trip.

Wilma told her mother that she wanted to get to town while the rain had let up and started to hitch the mare Gretel to the cart. But then her grandma Margaret hobbled out onto the porch. She yelled not simply to compensate for her deafness, and also talked about Wilma in the third person, even when she was looking right at her.

–Where is she going? she yelled.

–She's going into town, Wilma's mother replied, handing her daughter some coins.

–I'm going to buy supplies, Wilma shouted. I wouldn't want you to waste away to nothing now, would I?

Wilma couldn't help herself. Everything about the old hag sharpened her tongue. Her grandma, still in her nightclothes, climbed down from the porch and grabbed the reins.

–She's going to see that old heathen squaw!

–She's not a heathen! She belongs to your church!

–If she leaves this house, her grandma said, I'm telling her father! And there will be hell to pay!

–If ignorance were gold, you'd be the queen of Sheba.

Then she threw the reins at the old woman and turned and started to stride towards the pas.

–Don't you go storming out of here! Margaret screeched.

That was the phrase her grandma always used, almost as if challenging her to leave. And it was an apt description, because that's what her anger felt like. So Wilma stormed out of there—though not before slapping Gretel hard on the flank so the mare reared up and gave the old woman a jolt—and strode across the pasture, and then stormed her way through the woods to the dunes. It wasn't until she came over the peak of the highest dune and confronted the ocean that she felt she had found something that could absorb the force and complexity of her personal weather.

A dense mist covered the beach, following in the wake of the heavy rain. She couldn't see the ocean that day until she got right near the surf. She stood for a moment, trying to catch her breath, and found herself staring at the motion of the incoming waves, which reminded her of arthritic hands trying to fold an impossibly sheer fabric. She knew that things would be fine if she just went home and apologized and picked up where she left off. She had a temper and so did her father and he would bark at her to please his mother and that was that.

But she wasn't ready to go home yet, so she walked north. There were no beach houses north of town, not back then. As Wilma walked, she listened to the ocean, trying to calm herself. Old Molly often told her that the reason the ocean sounds like a roar is because there are so many voices speaking at once, all fighting for your attention. There is a voice that is fainter than the rest. That is the voice you must try to hear. It is only weak because it has been calling you the longest.

Before long, she heard the cries of agitated seabirds and then several man-made sounds, something like a metallic creak and then the distinct jingle of chains. Through the mist, there emerged a strange vision. It was some kind of village of wooden shacks that seemed to be moving through the incoming waves. As they got closer, she could see that these shacks were each built on a flat-bottomed base like a barge but had large wheels, like a wagon, and to each was yoked a strange species of long-haired donkey. She watched as an incoming wave lifted one of the vessels and then easily dropped it down as the water rushed back out. They were painted in variations of yellow and red, no doubt making them easier to locate through the mists and fog.

Both men and women of this rolling village wore rough-woven but brightly colored blouses and vests. The younger women wore their long black hair in a braid, while the old women wrapped their hair in a red cloth on the top of their head. Their dark skin and sharp features gave them the appearance of a native people, though it was clear that they were not from around there. In the surf in front of these vessels, women and girls waded, their dark skirts tied up around their knees. They dipped small black nets with long handles into the water, and with a quick move, almost as if administering a lash, they emptied them into the open mouths of earthenware jars, which the girls held and then immediately covered with a wooden stopper. The men pointed into the seething water and sang out, guiding the donkeys and vessels through the surf. The boys meanwhile whirled strings to which had been attached carved figures riddled with holes. These made droning sounds, like hurdy-gurdies, and scattered the multitude of seabirds, some of which hovered in the air, trying to dip their beaks into the incoming water.

These had to be the Netters, at least that's what the locals called them. Wilma vaguely recalled hearing stories about them. They appeared once every fifteen or twenty years, traveling down the coast. What they collected, no one seemed to know. Maybe because no one had asked.

Their entire operation had the air of practiced ease, like an assembly line. No, more like something mechanical, though something wound up as opposed to something driven by electric current. From a distance, their industriousness could almost be mistaken for devotion, untaxed as it was by passion or haste.

Wilma struck a respectful attitude, standing in a posture of deference, her hands clasped in front of her, yet they were so enrapt in their work that they passed by without looking at her or speaking a word, and she was forced to follow them. After some time passed, they finally stopped, pulling their wagons out of the surf and up onto the sand. As the women stood and stretched their backs, the young girls climbed up inside the shacks, carrying the stoppered jars, and then emerged with cups and earthenware bottles and set them on the deck. Everyone moved with that inadvertent grace that comes from being pushed past the point of exhaustion. She stood very still, not wanting to betray any impatience or discomfort.

Finally, a gaunt man wearing several layers of their rough clothing approached her. He was clearly the eldest, with a scraggly white beard and stiff, unkempt white hair that looked like it had known nothing but salt water. His eyes were red and as dull as flecks of old paint and did not merely meet hers but seemed to grab hold of her as if to help support his weight. Wilma got the impression that if she stopped looking at him, he would fall over.

She tried a Chinook word of greeting that Old Molly had told her, but the old man gave no sign of understanding it. He took a deep breath, and then spoke in a monotone, like a weary guide used to fielding obvious questions from strangers. His English was accented but surprisingly fluid.

–The first thing people ask, he said, is about the wagons. And the answer is, yes, they float. Because sometimes we have to go deep into the surf. But the yoke is designed in such a way that it will release the donkey if the water lifts the whole vessel too high. It is an ancient design.

–I would imagine, Wilma replied, that the first thing people ask is what you are collecting.

–If they ask that, he said, I cannot reply. Because it doesn't exist in your language.

–You mean that we don't have a word for it, she replied.

–No, my child, he replied. I mean it doesn't exist.

–I know there are things we don't have words for, she said. But they still exist. How can we not see them?

–You can only see this if you know its name, he replied, and you don't have a word for too.

–That's absurd! she said.

She felt that she was being rude to the old man, but she couldn't help herself. Like so many men, he treated her like she was a little girl. She was a young woman. She may have looked younger than her age, but that was no excuse.

He stared at her for a moment, as if trying to find his place in his recitation. He blinked, then closed his eyes. He actually seemed to fall asleep on his feet. She studied the deep lines on his face and the cracks on his lips. What could it be, this substance they collected, that it was worth pushing themselves to such consummate exhaustion? It had to be more than food. Was it medicinal? Religious?

A small flock of terns flew right over their heads, uttering raucous cries. He opened his eyes as if in the middle of a nightmare and started waving his hands above his head. Then he saw her and came back to his senses.

–The seabirds, he said. They get more and more arrogant.

–What is it they want? she asked.

–Even worse, he said, ignoring her, now there is a coyote who follows us down the beach in broad daylight. She tries to lap up the ocean but it makes her regurgitate.

–This thing she regurgitates, Wilma asked. Is it animal, vegetable or mineral?

–It is fragile, he replied. Once it touches the sand, it is useless.

–But what is it? she erupted.

He glared at her for a moment.

–It's ceremonial, isn't it? she insisted.

–Child, he said, there is no word for it.

–In my language, I know, she replied with sarcasm.

What was it with old men? It seemed that after years of using the same words over and over again, they somehow sucked the life out of them. They pruned them to death. How was it that this inability to form complex living thoughts often came to pass for wisdom? Whatever the case, she had succeeded in offending him.

He blinked at the tone of her voice and then turned his head and waved to the other Netters. They immediately started to put things away and get back to work.

–Listen, she said, trying to speak with calm. I was born here. I am not a newcomer. My ancestors may have come here in covered wagons, but I have native blood.

Her words had started to take on a pleading tone. She hated it when she got that tone in her voice because it made her sound like the child he called her.

–I have work to do, he said, turning away from her.

–Let me work with you! she said impulsively. I have good eyes, quick hands. I work hard. I have a burning curiosity, but I am good at containing things. I have no desire to profit from your secret. The only profit I seek is knowledge.

He stared at her blankly.

–What I'm saying, she explained, is that I am not looking for material profit.

He looked at her for a moment, confused.

–What are you seeking? he asked. Some kind of prophet?

–No! she exclaimed. Profit.

–I am not a prophet, the old man said.

–Not prophet, but profit, she said. With an I. Profit, like money.

–We have no money, he said, and then he turned and started to head back to the wagon he'd abandoned to talk to her.

–I don't want money! she shouted at the old man, following after him. I want to know what this is!

Everyone stopped and turned to look when she yelled at their elder. Several of the young men stepped forward, almost as if to intercept her. She stopped, disgusted by the futility of their exchange. Then the old man and several other people looked past her and pointed up the beach. She turned to see a lone coyote walking through the surf towards them. It seemed to stare into the water, walking in a kind of trance. What was this substance, that it could drive this furtive animal to expose himself in daylight? What did it gain from this substance? The old man had reacted strangely when she used the word *ceremonial*. Maybe it caused visions, something sacred or religious.

She couldn't take her eyes off the coyote. As it got closer, it raised its head and looked at her with a kind of wild resignation, if such a thing is possible. Wilma felt no fear. They met eyes and then the animal stared back down at the water and walked past her. She watched it following the Netters into the fog.

Maybe even wild animals sought visions. Who knows? Maybe that's what this coyote now mistook her for, for nothing but some kind of intriguing but secondary hallucination.

Then again, maybe that's all she was. ☐

CHICAGO AUGUST
Art Fox

A mother-of-pearl sky
and a pebble in my sandal.

Palsied dog-day leaves
pant in drowsy boredom.

A spent flag yawns
slack bathtub air.

Skateboard kids dawdle
in their sticky tee shirts.

Scum skimmed
rain puddles melt
under a sweaty sun.

Sidewalks dusted with clippings,
a weary weed in every crack.

THE FENCE
Jane Lawless

On a May evening following the six o'clock news, Calvin complained that there were not enough fences in the world.

"What is that supposed to mean?" Gina snapped. She was filing her long black acrylic nails. Gina was his wife and Calvin had begun to wonder over the past year or so what had compelled him to marry her.

"I mean," Calvin replied, "that there are too damned many people on the planet. Everyplace is getting too crowded." He nodded toward the window and the neighboring house less than twenty feet away, from which the boom-boom of over-amplified rap music made their windows hum.

Gina's eyes followed his. She stared for what Calvin thought was too long a moment. He knew she was trying to catch a glimpse of their neighbor, a power lifter in his early thirties with numerous body piercings, who liked to walk around in all weathers without a shirt.

"So you think a fence will solve your problem?" Her tone was intended to make Calvin feel stupid, and usually it worked. Tonight, however, he wasn't in the mood for intimidation.

"You bet it will," he said, then added, although he hadn't known he was going to say it until the words were on his tongue, "As a matter of fact, I'm going to start it this weekend."

Gina snatched a cigarette from a pack on the kitchen counter and lit it. "And what makes you think you can build a fence?" Her eyes were narrow.

"You know the Home Depot motto," he said blandly. "'You can build it. We can help.' And take that damned cigarette outside."

* * *

Three weeks later, the fence was complete. It was ten feet high, made of expensive wood that had been treated to increase its noise-absorption properties. There were copper pyramids on the posts and Calvin had planted a border of vivid red cannas along the edge of the fence. It looked good; he was pleased with it. He barely heard the neighbor's stereo. Gina no longer made excuses to be outside in her white shorts and chartreuse halter top when the neighbor watered his lawn or mowed his grass or washed his car without a shirt.

Gina was sullen. She watched TV, smoked more cigarettes. They stopped having sex. A critical juncture had been reached, Calvin knew, a point of decision. His life was about to change in ways he could scarcely imagine, but for once he was not filled with dread. He had built a fence. ☐

BROCCOLI
Jane Lawless

Months later, after the divorce was concluded, Jen often reflected on how ridiculous it was that broccoli had been the assassin of her marriage. She loved it. Leith hated it. It wasn't enough that he didn't want to eat it himself; he didn't want her to eat it either. The very smell and sight of it filled him with white-knuckled fury, and he'd once slammed out of a restaurant because someone at the next table had had the temerity to order it.

This had something to do with being forced as a child to sit at the dinner table staring at gray, cold broccoli, while his broccoli-eating siblings watched Batman in the rec room. His gray, cold mother had lost that battle, caving in finally at three a.m. when it became clear the Leith would sit staring at the uneaten broccoli until hell froze over. It was the first of many lost battles with her son.

Jen should have realized what the broccoli story meant when Leith first told it to her, but he was great in bed—at least in those days—and she was in love. The final break came in October on a drive to eastern Long Island. It was a perfect mid-autumn day of blue skies and red, orange and gold leaves. They had picnicked on a beach, watching long breakers roll in, one after another, and then they had stopped at a pumpkin farm to buy pumpkins for Halloween jack-o-lanterns for their nephews. Jen chose a beautiful blue one, about fifteen pounds. As they walked among the rows of pumpkins, her gaze lifted to the fields beyond and she saw something magical: thousands of monarch butterflies were sucking nectar from the bright-yellow flowers of an acre of broccoli that had gone to seed. The orange-and-black butterflies, the blue sky, the yellow flowers, the deep-green foliage were achingly beautiful and she immediately turned to Leith and asked for the camera. She held out the blue pumpkin for him to hold.

"What?" he snapped. "So you can take pictures of pumpkins?"

"No," she said, pointing toward the field. "Look at the butterflies."

His gaze followed her finger. She saw him register the monarchs, the sky, the flowers—and then he recognized the plant that bore the flowers. "You are not," he said with measured contempt, "going to take pictures of goddamned broccoli!"

It all came together for her in that instant: Leith would never mellow, would never allow either of them be happy. She thought for only the briefest moment before she looked down at the ground to be sure of the position of his sandaled feet. Then she very carefully dropped the blue pumpkin.

Luckily, Jen had the car keys. ☐

EPPY & TUBA FOREVER
Signe Ratcliff

S o I know something's not right because I've just woken up and Tuba isn't in the bed with her peanut butter smell. She buys the real high-and-mighty peanut butter, the kind that costs as much as a steak, and every morning she wakes before me, wanders to the fridge for a tipple from her jar, returns to bed smacking her lips, and sometimes, as she settles in with her hand tight around mine, she'll mumble:

America.

She claims this never happens, but it happens all the time, and when it does, I raise my hand to my forehead in a secret kind of salute because I've been a bad American and I need this pledge of allegiance just like the school kids do.

This morning her mother is arriving from Turkey for a visit and I know Tuba isn't happy. Ever since the letter arrived, her otherwise cheery face has been stuck in a scowl, her rambunctious figure deflated in my Pop's old recliner chair. She's been sitting in that chair for weeks, making spitballs out of her mom's letter and launching them at me through a straw as I dash by with a feather duster, trying to look busy.

Once she ran out of spitballs, she gathered all the clothes we share and tried to divide them into distinct sections in the closet. These are men's. These are women's. Like bathrooms, I said, just for fun, just to keep things light, and she slapped me.

"Eppy! This is someone who won't understand us!"

I stood in Tuba's floral dressing gown and held a cold can of Hamms against my cheek. In my old life I was usually the one doing the slapping. Instead, I say, "Who does understand us?" She slapped my other cheek and told me not to get big ideas.

Tuba tells me not to get big ideas, but sometimes I get them anyway.

We met at JollyMaids. Me, the only guy polishing toasters, vacuuming drapes, throttling down Ashland Avenue in a minivan packed with maids about as jolly as bulldogs on treadmills. One maid, Rosa, she would stare me down in the van, frown at my puffy baby-blue vest, my peach jazzercise leggings, my ballerina flats, mumbling the same Spanish terms my mother uses.

Then, four months ago, Tuba showed up. The only JollyMaid I've met who is actually jolly. We cleaned a bathroom together that first day. Me in one corner, her in the other, and our heads touched in the middle. I'd been trying to impress her, talking about how someday I'd do better, how someday I'd be more than a maid. She plunged her hands into a bucket of scalding water and pressed her forehead into mine.

"We're losers. This is the only way we can make the world better. Just this."

Later that day she stood at the front window of the house we were cleaning and stared out, her eyes fixed on some distant point and I thought about all the times my Pop took me to O'Hare to watch the planes because we were too poor to get on one. I liked to watch the planes taxi around, all huge and expectant, with their big long noses and beaming eyes and just then I decided Tuba was like one of those planes. The best plane. The Concorde. And for some reason I told her that. I told her she was the Concorde, and that's how it started, her moving in with me, us being in love and all.

The doorbell rings. I cover my head with the blankets.

I don't come across many girls that I like and even fewer that like me. But I like Tuba. Sturdy Tuba, shaped like a teapot, with her round belly and strong narrow arms. She wears sweat pants and flannel shirts and often scratches her face as if she has a beard. Her blonde hair is home-schooled, cut on a daily basis with a pair of kiddie scissors. She has an impressive repertoire of ugly faces and manly vices. Beer, never wine, and always straight from the can. Coffee, black. Cigarettes, unfiltered. Sometimes she sleeps in her boots. Her voice, though, is what throws people off. Her JollyMaid voice, high and girly, like something sweet squeezed out of a very tiny tube.

The doorbell is still ringing, angry and rhythmic. I stand up, grab Tuba's robe, press the button without thinking first. Now I've gone and done it. I've just pressed the button. Tuba's mother is here and Tuba is not and it feels kind of like I've just launched a missile.

I open the door a crack, hoping for UPS or a Mormon, but there stands Tuba's mom, her face buried in her smart phone. I stare like a scared animal peeking around a tree. She is nothing like Tuba. She is the anti-Tuba. She has a supermodel-skinny body and wears that kind of I'm-better-than-you uniform: the big sunglasses on her head like it's part of her hairstyle, the long leather boots, the black cashmere coat, the tactfully-patterned autumn dress, unbuttoned just so. Unlike my fashion, hers seems mostly just a way to squash lesser people.

She looks up from her phone, catches my eyes through the crack. "Hello?"

The anti-Tuba voice, low and careful.

I open the door. She stares, I stare. "Yeah. Hi. Mrs…" I can't remember Tuba's last name. I'm not even sure she's told me. "Tuba's not here right now," I say. "She should be back soon."

She continues to stare as I wave her inside. Now I understand the reason for Tuba freaking out over our clothes. I am wearing a pair of violet leggings, a Hello Kitty tank top, and a pair of brown furry slippers with a dachshund head at each toe, their little plastic eyes swinging by a thread far from their sockets. My heels hang over the edge of the slippers, but I still wear them because they were a gift from my Pop before he died.

"Is she okay? I have been trying to call for months."

Tuba had thrown away her smart phone when we first met, said cellphones were an intrusion on human consciousness and when people scrolled through the touch screens it looked to her like sexual stroking. I had decided Tuba was right, gave away my phone to a six-year-old who'd dropped his ice cream on the bus.

"She's fine. She'll be back in a minute." That last part, I'm not so sure about, and I wish my voice didn't sound so shaky. Now I see little nodules of spitball stuck to my leggings. I start bending my legs around, trying to hide one leg with the other. "I can fix you coffee if you like it black."

"No. Thank you."

She's still staring at me with her smartly made-up eyes, worriedly searching my own, which are probably smudged with yesterday's eyeliner. I remember what I'm supposed to do. I stick my hand out, hoping she doesn't notice my cornflower-blue fingernails, chipped and ragged at the ends.

"I'm Eppy, by the way."

Tuba's mom frowns. She gulps with fright. I forget sometimes that I still look a little Back-of-the-Yards tough – a scar down the center of my forehead, the teardrop tattoo on my face. Sometimes I forget that you're not supposed to grab a lady's hand like you would a corner dope boy's.

Tuba must have told her my full name. "Epiphiano," I say, expecting that recognizing look to show up on her face, but she just keeps on staring.

I reach for the coffee machine. Tuba sets the coffee up for me every night because she knows I need coffee just like she needs her peanut butter. All I have to do is just press the button. Tuba's mom crosses her arms, leans against the kitchen counter as I face the machine. She's a crossed-armed kind of mom, I think, unlike my mom, whose arms are always wailing on somebody. I know it's my turn to speak but I don't know what to say so I take a long time pressing the button and examine the coffee machine, sort of pretending like this is part of the process, and in the meantime manage to flick some of the spitballs from my legs.

"You are her friend?"

My heart starts going. "I'm Eppy. Tuba told you about me? Epiphiano?"

She shakes her head in a slow, vicious sort of way.

Now my heart is going like a racecar. But Tuba loves me, right? I think of the time she glued herself to her purse, that crappy snakeskin purse with the handles always breaking off, but she loved it so much she carried superglue around with her so she could glue the handles back on, and one time in the bar she was a little drunk and so she superglued her fingers to the thing, but I didn't even notice because I was saying something about how I liked the bartender's face, how it reminded me of the Concorde, and Tuba started wailing on me with her purse-hand because I'd forgotten that's what I'd told her at JollyMaids. "I thought *I* was the Concorde," she yelled in her tiny voice, and knocked me clean off my barstool, and right then I thought Tuba must really love me because in my part of town you don't know if a girl really loves you until she knocks you on your ass.

"Eppy," I say again. Tuba's mom shakes her head.

I wasn't about to say I was Tuba's friend because that would make me feel sick, so I tell Tuba's mom that I'm Tuba's maid.

"You are her maid?"

"Yes ma'am."

"A man maid?"

"Yeah, "I say. "A man maid."

Tuba's mom is looking at the heap of our shared shoes in the kitchen corner, the overflowing trashcan, the overturned jars of spices. For a couple of maids, we sure are messy.

"I haven't gotten started yet," I say.

Tuba's mom's arms are still crossed, and she's still looking at me. I start to miss my mom. I wish this woman would just start wailing on me and get it over with.

"Why does Tuba live so far from the hospital?"

I'm still examining the coffee pot when I hear this. I pour a cup, take another look at her. Why a hospital? Tuba wasn't sick. But maybe this is an important thing in Turkey, proximity to a hospital. Was that a racist thing to think?

"Oh. Well, Swedish Covenant is just down the street…and it's five-star." I'm not sure if that's a thing, a five-star hospital, but I want Tuba's mom to think I've thought things through.

"Her residency is at Rush."

"Residency? Like the thing doctors do?"

"Yes. She was supposed to finish this December but they have not seen her for months. They think she has quit."

I cough. Coffee is leaking from my mouth. My eyes are watering and I'm damned scared. Tuba can't be a doctor. We're supposed to be losers. Doctors do things like marry other doctors. And now it makes sense, those heavy boxes of books we use as coffee tables. That time I was sick for three days and Tuba made me Campbells and crackers and came in every so often to feel under my jaw and even listened to my heart with a stethoscope. I had no idea it was a real stethoscope. I thought she was just being kinky.

"Tuba's a doctor?"

It seems to warm the mom up, my saying that. She uncrosses her arms and pulls her smart phone out of her smart purse, scrolls through what's probably like a whole lot of smart pictures. Right up to my face she puts the phone so I can see Tuba's smiling face. A slender Tuba in a cap and gown. Her hair is dark and long and looks kind of polished. Her teeth are white, her lips painted pink.

"She was fifth in her class." Tuba's mom smiles the last smile I'll probably ever get from her, and then I see for a second Tuba's merry eyes. The big difference is that Tuba doesn't even have to smile to get her eyes that way, but still, it occurs to me just now that Tuba came from some different place, from Turkey, from this mom, and there are a whole bunch of other people and so many things she knows and I don't. Love has a way of canceling other people out, like with those fraction problems you do in math class where you find the common factor from a mess of number and cross out the ones that don't matter and you're left with those two numbers stacked together, all snug and triumphant.

The problem is when the one you love isn't alone just like you, when the one you love turns out to be somebody else's common factor.

"We should try and find her," I say.

Tuba's mom nods and heads for the door.

I'm in a big rush to find Tuba now. I'm kicking the dachshund slippers off my feet and jumping into my brown Uggs. Over my leggings I button up the floral housecoat Rosa had left in the van and didn't want back after I told her I'd worn it. It's October in Chicago, but cold enough to be January, so I throw on my baby-blue puffy vest. I grab my keys, I race to the door. For the first time in my life, I feel like a man.

Tuba's mom is reluctant to walk with me, even though she wants to find Tuba as bad as I do. She walks a foot behind so as not to be associated with me, until she notices she's the one looking out of place. A tall man wearing a sequined gown and sparkly heels gushes into his phone, winks at me as we pass by. Behind him, a lesbian couple strolls hand in hand, walking their Chihuahua, and there is a shirtless man in tight silver underpants and cowboy boots hailing a cab. When I moved in with my uncle back in the '80s, this strip of Clark Street between Foster and Bryn Mawr was a Swedish settlement turned Latin-King territory, all us riff-raff hanging out by the Happy Foods. But then all the gay folks started moving in and Happy Foods became a lesbian bookstore. Funny how a street can change in the same way a person does.

Screamer Doug spots me and sidles out of a doorway, spooks Tuba's mom right out of her boots. "Change, man?"

"Next time, Doug," I say. Screamer Doug has lived on this street as long as I can remember. You can hear him shrieking in the distance all night in the summer when your windows are open. Tuba says it's like listening to an exotic bird.

Tuba's mom grabs onto my arm. I get a good hold on her and keep us walking. And then I feel her start to tremble because this is the zombie pub crawl weekend and now we're trying to weave between a long parade of bloodied, tattered, moaning drunks. I can tell Tuba's mom is about to cry and I feel bad for her the way I feel bad for the old ladies at Devon Market still trying to order their pork butt in Polish from a Mexican butcher.

"Don't worry," I say. "We'll find Tuba."

I swat our way through the zombies and keep us moving forward. My idea is that Tuba might be at St. Boniface cemetery where she likes to ride her bike and feed the rabbits. Rabbits are Tuba's favorite animals. Orange is her favorite color, Root Beer her favorite pop. Knowing things like this keeps me steady, and I keep thinking about Tuba's favorite things and marching Tuba's mom along so fast that I almost miss her.

At the corner of Farragut and Clark, Tuba sits on the life-sized hand-painted fiberglass dala horse installed by the Swedish Museum in preparation for the King of Sweden's visit to Chicago in the late '80s. We called it the burro back then but left the thing alone, paint-tagged Happy Foods instead with our five-pointed crowns because we figured none of us Kings were any match for a real King. Tuba likes to sit on the horse, but I avoid it. It makes me a little sick in my stomach, being around the things left over from my old life.

Tuba's mom and I call for her at the same time. And then we glare at each other, strangers all of a sudden when just a minute ago we were fighting zombies together.

Tuba sits there far above the street, dressed in my uncle's Jiffy-Lube pants and the tattered burnt-orange cab coat she loves. Steadied by her soft belly is a half jar of peanut butter stuck with a spoon. She ignores us both, her little nose pointed toward the horizon, her body rigid and expectant, as if the dala horse could gallop her away like the cowboy horses did in John Wayne movies.

Tuba's mom steps forward and starts yelling in her rapid language, tugging at the bottoms of Tuba's pants, pulling her shirt down over her belly to hide her fat. Moms are always doing this kind of thing, thinking they can fix their grown children's problems with a small adjustment: tug a shirt, straighten a collar. My mom did this too until she realized she couldn't adjust me anymore, so she just adjusted herself, decided it was best to forget me altogether.

"She's telling me I'm fat!" Tuba cries and reaches for me. "She's telling me it's common to eat dry goods on the street!" She leans so far to the side for me I worry she will fall. "She tells me it's not my fault what happened to my patient. But it is! Eppy!"

She is crying, tears fogging up her already dingy glasses. I've never once seen Tuba cry. I don't want to think that all her jolliness was just a way to keep away tears, that instead of crying she moved in with me, that she slaps me for having big ideas because she doesn't want me to figure out that her ideas were just as big. But that's what I go and think anyway.

I know that Tuba has to go back to her old life, and that her old life probably won't include me, but I climb up anyway for one last feel of her belly, the squishy softness of her flesh between my fingers. I sit behind her for one last whiff of her peanut butter smell. I burrow into her softness and wish we were on a real horse in a different time when all you had to do was ride away.

I see then that she'd gone and done what we'd always been afraid to do. She'd gone and tagged the burro, the words EPPY & TUBA FOREVER scrawled on its shoulder in black marker and enclosed with a lopsided heart. She'd gone and made things better like she always does, stitching this part from my old life to the edge of my new life. I know just then that she'll be a good doctor. I hug her closer as a jet arcs slowly overhead and we both look up and watch its descent. I breathe in as much of her as I can fit in my lungs, hoping it will be enough to keep me good, and I say: "You are the Concorde." □

THE JAZZ BAR
Dipika Mukherjee

Shanghai, 1979

Shanghai is a long way away from St. Mary's, Ohio, but the song playing tonight reminds me of home. There's that old man on the horn again and the sound swells to a crescendo with bloated cheeks and furious foot stomping, and then dies down with the approving murmurs of the crowd.

I can feel the chill coming in through the cracks of this once magnificent hotel. Rumor has it that Noel Coward wrote a play here in four days while burning up with the flu – I bet he caught the bug from these drafty walls. These old boys at the Jazz Club try to keep a little oasis-like window of grand music on this diseased and dusty Communist set-up, but it doesn't always work.

Paul takes another sip of his beer and scoots down lower. His long hair frizzes around his young face, his skin gleaming black in the low light. He wasn't even born the first time I came to China.

Chinese men fill the tables around us. They are from the Party, but the differences between the Northern burry-accented Beijingers and the Southern city-slicker Shanghai cousins keep them apart in mutual hostility. The performers pick up a new Chinese dance tune, and as the pipas and erhus sound among the Western instruments, only one table breaks into applause.

I watch Paul, who's so relaxed that he's slipping down the wooden chair by the minute—I'm going to have to pick him off the floor soon.

The bar at the Peace Hotel is grimy, with desiccated war dust on the moldings over our heads. There are some fat potato chips on the table and some sort of a banana mayonnaise that looks like mustard but tastes like a bad custard. I am fed up. If I ask for ketchup the waiter will probably get me some congealed hog blood.

They hate us here.

We are the *laowais* from a U.S. TV channel and they think we are here to fuck them any which way. But the only one I'm interested in fucking is sitting right in front of me.

"Order another beer for me," Paul slurs. His left hand scrabbles for a hold at the edge of the table, then falls limply to the side.

The drummer in the band starts playing a staccato march that drowns out my response. "Beer?" I signal to the waiter as Paul starts to cough uncontrollably. "Do you want some water?"

Paul waves a hand over his face. "No," he says before the coughing fit begins again. "Beer!"

"Pi jiu," I say to the waiter's surly back as he maneuvers himself to the next table full of old Chinese men. "Ping." I try to emphasis that we don't want lukewarm beer, then uncertainly, "Bing?"

No one understands what I am trying to say here, no matter how I say it. I'll get lukewarm beer in a dirty glass as usual. The waiter shouts something from the corner without looking at me.

"When you speak in Chinese, you sound like a tomcat yowling," giggles Paul. "Pijiu, ping, bing, pijiuuuuuuuu," he yodels.

"Maybe you should try talking then." I swing his chair around until Paul is facing the bar. He almost falls off without the table for support but then digs his toes into the floor for traction. He grins goofily at the waiter who is raising a large mug and a small one in turn. "Big One!" shouts Paul. He stands up and expands his arms wide. "Two big ones, buddy, for me and my friend." His gestures hug the whole room.

Amazingly, the waiter grins back. "Two. Big," he mouths before he disappears. That's the thing with Paul – he is so goddamn charming that he even gets under Commie skin. I have no prayer. We were only supposed to stay here a week but it's the third week now. I want to go home.

The waiter brings two lukewarm glasses of beer and sets them on grimy bamboo pads. He puts mine down with such a thump that the head dribbles over in a frothy mess.

Paul lifts his beer in a wobbly toast. "To you, my love."

One of the three ladies to our left thinks he is addressing her and smiles shyly before quickly casting her eyes down. The girls here are not as hungry as the ones in Southeast Asia, or maybe they aren't as clear about it. This girl's eyes roam over the leather of Paul's jacket and then stray to his wool scarf. In her plain grey dress she seems starved for some style or color more than anything else.

Paul is still leering at me, his eyes unfocused, when the band strikes up the tune of "The Love You Can't Get." I have been in this hole of a hotel long enough for me to be able to recognize *De Bu Dao Ni De Ai Qing*, this prostitute's song was the rage of the dance hall.

I raise my glass silently in response. Paul moves closer. He runs his index finger along my jaw line.

I look around quickly. The girl at the next table widens her eyes momentarily, then smirks into her drink.

"Behave yourself!"

"No one's watching." Sure enough, now no one is. Tendrils of smoke rise from the noisy table next to us and the dense air hangs over the room.

"You look like a cat," he purrs.

"Cut it out, Paul."

"I don't have to. You're not my boss anymore, not here."

I react to his tongue lazily wiping beer foam from his lips. "Stop it," I hiss.

Paul suddenly loses interest. "She sure is pretty," he says. His eyes follow the Chinese girl on stage, who begins to sing a high plaintive song, her voice trilling and breathy in turn. The crowd claps enthusiastically at the end of every stanza as she pauses to take her breath while the band plays on. "I will never marry a woman," he says.

"No one's asked you," I say lightly.

"You are never telling your wife, are you?"

His question is so quiet, that for a moment I think I imagine that thought. "I will," I say. "The children are too small now."

"I hear she's pregnant again."

"If she is, I don't know about it."

Someone drops a glass and there is a splintering sound followed by drunken laughter. We both watch a waiter clean up the mess.

"The wood on these floors are *old*," says Paul.

"Hmmm, I suppose."

"I hope they don't destroy this building completely."

"Wasn't much to begin with."

"You can't see it now, but there was. Here... the traces of the art-deco... like in that Chicago building..."

"Chicago's ugly. I hate tall concrete slabs everywhere."

Paul turns over a brochure. It has a picture of a bright red liquid in a frosted glass. His fingers are so smooth, so unlined, so beautifully tapered. I fell in love with those hands first. So unlike my own hands with the veins breaking through the skin and the knuckles gnarled and misshapen.

"What do you think this is?" asks Paul.

"A drink, obviously. I haven't tried it but when you've been around as long as I have only the colors change in these kinds of places."

"I want one."

"All right." I signal to the waiter. The waiter covers Paul's hand with his own while taking the brochure away. It's a most tender gesture.

"We could go away to Europe, to France. . . like the artists do. . . or just couples who want to marry each other but can't back home."

"It's not that easy."

The waiter arrives with the red drink and Paul takes a large swig. "It's good."

I take a sip from his. "I'll stick to beer."

He turns his face away and I look at his profile, trying to remember if I had been as young as Paul when I first came to Shanghai. I can't even remember being as young as Paul anymore.

Now, with my history, I am among the earliest post-Mao era journalists to be allowed in again. We are doing several stories for a TV network. Among them is the story on Deng Xiaoping's China and how the "To Get Rich is Glorious" challenge is having an effect on Shanghai.

I have always loved Old Shanghai and its history. There is not much of it left in this, once the grandest of the grand hotels, and nothing of the legendary service left in shabby, dusty, Mao-suited staff. Most nights I lie in bed at night listening to the sound of rats rushing about inside the walls and Paul's gentle snores. The waiter passes our table and I hand him a song request. Of a song that carries a sense of Shanghai's drinking and gambling, of the whores, sailors and foreigners, of all that corruption and high times.

The band strikes up the first notes of "Shanghai Lil" from the 1930s. I have this music at home from the Warner Brothers musical *Footlight Parade* with Ruby Keeler and James Cagney. Cagney doing a turn—what a great hoofer!—dancing on a bar and singing, "Looking for my Shanghai Lil" in a Hollywood version of a Shanghai bar crowded with sailors and hookers.

Paul an eyebrow at me. "So?"

"What?"

"Where do we go from here?"

The castanets are driving me crazy. They are not in the original composition like this and they thrum against my brain like a refrain. I wish Paul would stop talking so much. I hate the groove of this repeated argument.

"You don't have to complicate things, Paul. We are happy."

"We?"

"I… We… can't afford a scandal. Chicago's a big town, but I have to go back to St. Mary's. We've talked about this before..."

"I don't want to do it like this. People can be happy. Not at first. But then they are."

"You are so naïve."

"Stop being so goddamn afraid!"

"I'm not afraid! I understand consequences."

"Stop treating me like a fucking child."

I place my hand over his and hold it still, despite his efforts to shake me off.

"YOU are making this impossible."

"Really, Paul?"

"We could have a life, with each other."

"No we can't. I can't even go home with you."

"There are other places in the world."

"Places I can't go to."

"Fine." Paul pushes back his chair and gets up. He stumbles slightly, then rights himself. "If you can't choose us, I have to decide this."

"Paul..." I try to say something, but fall silent. We have said the same words too many times. Finally I say, "Don't walk away."

"Nothing's taken away unless you give it away."

"Ah. You want to talk about your people now?"

He looks at me like he's trying to focus and not succeeding. He walks away. That was a low blow and I am immediately sorry.

I think of all the times when we have broken up but this impossible bond between us has refused to unravel. Despite our differences, our age gap, we have too much to hold on to.

I close my eyes and think of Paul's dark brown eyes with long lashes and straight black eyebrows. His naked shoulders covered by that long hair that makes him look like a conquered savage while he kneels. The absolute power in my hands as I take his hair and twist it around his neck. His wide mouth and full lips.

If only Paul would stop talking.

The waiter hovering near the table has a piece of paper in his hand. I dig into my wallet and throw some notes on the table.

When I was in my early twenties, my father made it clear that no faggot would inherit a cent of his money. When my mother wheedled me into a wedding with Misty Dawn, a woman who needed marriage more than she needed a husband, I had no other options. Misty Dawn and I had an unspoken understanding, and in the early days, while we were living in Cleveland and I was trying to carve out a career, we had separate apartments.

But then my mother visited, and in that single weekend, despite

Misty Dawn's constant presence in my apartment, she immediately figured out that we were not living together. Something as stupid as not having a trashcan in my bathroom. Any home with a woman would need trashcans in bathrooms – this my mother said with absolute certainty.

This time the stakes were higher and included Misty Dawn. So we started a family. I stayed away from men for almost six years and it was hard. That hunger for pectorals rising slab-like over ribcages. For square-muscled shoulders and stomachs which funneled to muscled-hips. For sex so brutal that nothing with a woman could possibly compare. Now, especially with someone like Paul in my life, I could not risk what I had built up over so many years.

I walked through the wide streets and kept on walking until I found myself under the leafy canopies of the French Concession. This was a city frozen in time like a creature from long ago caught in amber. I could easily imagine myself in an earlier age but no one came to arrest me "for my own safety" and escort me back to the hotel. I kept walking until I stopped at an old dance hall and stared at its grim and barred exterior, trying to envision the inside of the largest and most decadent ballroom in Shanghai before the music had stopped.

I stood under the portico of this once-resplendent building and thought about my own history and wondered if I would have chosen differently, if I could have chosen anything else. I kept on walking. Perhaps it was the crisp coldness of Shanghai that night, or just the passage of decades through the indifference of time, but I felt happier as I rounded the corner to my hotel again. I could see how the isolation and absence of any investment or modernization had left this city locked in the past and largely unchanged . . . and still a vivid conjuror of dreams. Anything was possible here. I still had time with Paul. Chinese history is full of men loving men, like the Emperor Ai tenderly cutting off the sleeves of his royal robes rather than waking his lover who had fallen asleep.

I never saw Paul again.

I was so sure that he would be back again that I did not even try to find out how he left China. His clothes were gone by the time I returned to our room. I came back to the hotel every night after filming factories and hawkers the whole day and expected to see him there, sitting in that old Malayan plantation chair with his feet up and a beer at his side. Even after I went back to America, I expected him at every turn in Chicago, and especially at that seedy bar on Van Buren where we first met.

Finally I went back home, to St Mary's. To a domesticity of social obligations and familial squabbles, and my life tottered into a normalcy.

We visited my parents on weekends, and I played baseball with my sons in the backyard as my wife swam laps in the pool. I bought a boat. I still looked for Paul, discreetly making enquiries whenever I could, but our worlds were so starkly different that there were no leads at all. I stopped crossing the street to follow men until I saw their faces reflected on a shop window.

Until, eighteen months later, when there was a news report in the paper about a U.S. Navy radioman murdered by a shipmate. Paul's name was there, clear in black and white, as was the suggestion that he had been a victim of a hate crime. Whether that hate crime was due to his color or due to his being gay was immaterial – both were hinted at. Absolute secrecy has been the only option for men like Paul and me, in the armed forces or elsewhere. I scanned the lines for a hint of what had happened, but beside the details of his name and his hometown being Chicago, he was described only as a radioman on an amphibious assault ship and murdered by his shipmate, an airman apprentice who had stomped him to death in a park in Nagasaki.

My first thought was *The Navy? Paul had cut off that head of hair?*

I mourned for that hair, until I realized what else the story left unsaid. A park in Japan? In a place so secret that the murder had gone unnoticed? If Paul hadn't resisted – how can anyone not resist being stomped to death?—had he been brutalized in a way that made defense impossible?

Is nothing really taken away unless you give it away?

My grief could have no public voice. My wife and children would only look at me in incomprehension when I played "Shanghai Lil," swaying to a memory in the dark until I grew unbearably weary, too fatigued to carry on moving. ☐

COLO
James Stacey

Martha died. This came as a surprise, even a shock. Just last year she looked fit and cheerful, a barely discernible touch of gray in her blond hair, and hardly a wrinkle on her forehead or around her eyes. She certainly seemed in much better shape than her older siblings who seemed fragile compared with her.

She and I talked about Colo, Iowa, the home town to which she'd returned a dozen or so years before. One of her sons was working the family acreage, and for a while she had converted one of the family homes into a bed and breakfast.

"You must come and stay," she said. "Come for a high school reunion. They're always around Memorial Day weekend."

What a pleasant thought. I hadn't been to Colo in more than thirty years, but it was a place dear to my heart, a place that transformed my life and moved it forward. I didn't make it to Colo that year, and now Martha was gone, and it seemed I had missed my last chance to see Colo again.

"There's going to be a memorial service for her in March," my niece, Laurie, told me over the telephone not long after I'd heard the news. "Dad and Dave and I are going to drive out."

"Can I come, too?"

"I was hoping you'd say that."

"It won't be an imposition?"

"I'll have the time of my life, with my three favorite men in the world."

We were to leave early on a Saturday morning and I was instructed to take the train to their Chicago suburb on Friday afternoon. Laurie picked me up at the station, and filled me in on what was happening. Her father, Mike, had arrived earlier that day and was at home awaiting our arrival. Dave was finishing up at his office and would join us for cocktails.

Mike greeted me with his customary grin and embrace. There was gray in his hair and lines near his eyes, but the sound of his voice was the same as before.

"Good to see you," he said.

"You're looking fit," I said. "Lost some weight."

"I'm exercising now, and we're a little more careful about diet."

Laurie led us into a sitting room off the kitchen.

"There're some pictures I want you to see," she said. "I'd like to put something together for Martha's children."

It was a large room, centered on a cocktail table between facing sofas. At the far end was a wet bar next to a refrigerator and below cabinets cluttered with bottles. Laurie retrieved a carton stuffed with folders and photos and placed it on the table. Then she sat between Mike and me.

"I haven't looked at this in ages," she said, pulling out a handful of black and white glossy photos. "Here's one of you, Uncle Jim." It must have been taken when I was in my thirties, sporting a moustache and long darkening hair. "But look at this. I don't think I've ever seen it before."

It was a picture of me and my sister, Ruth, Laurie's mother. The two of us were standing side-by-side at the gate leading to our childhood backyard and the steps to our kitchen. Her right arm was around my shoulder, and my left was around her waist. I was wearing a sailor's cap and holding a baseball glove with a ball in its mitt. She was wearing slacks and a sweatshirt emblazoned with letters spelling "Grinnell." This must have been her first summer break from college, when she was eighteen and I was twelve. We were both sporting wide grins.

"Look at that," Laurie said. "That says it all."

There was not one scintilla of doubt as to how happy we were to be together again.

"I don't think I've ever seen this before," I said, holding the picture, drinking it in, and feeling the sadness that would not go away even two decades after Ruth's premature death. Near the end, we had talked about Mike, and she had urged me to encourage him to find someone new. He was not meant to live alone, she said, and he should not feel bound by the love they had shared. That was one of several promises I told her I'd keep.

"You can have that," Laurie said. "She'd want you to."

We were up early next morning. Laurie's Dave was in the kitchen, presiding over a coffee pot, orange juice pitcher, and plate of muffins. He was a commanding presence, with broad shoulders, a bald head, white whiskers and moustache, and a measured mode of talking.

"Morning," he said, opening a cabinet filled with miniature containers of coffee. "Take your choice and put it in this slot. Then press this button."

While waiting for brewed coffee, I looked around the large kitchen loaded with gadgets. Dave had his own very successful business, and happily shared his good fortune with family and friends. My wife made me promise not to let him pay for my hotel room in Iowa, and not to let him pick up every restaurant check.

Laurie was in the den, a mirror image of the sitting room, but arranged with chairs, side tables, and a large, flat screen television set. She adored her mother, but departed from her plain-spoken approach to fashion and make up. Ruth never bothered with eye shades or mascara, and her approach to hair styling was largely utilitarian, but she had encouraged Laurie to become a little more elaborate in makeup, and always was delighted by Laurie's fashion decisions. Laurie's blond hair was stylishly cut, and her skirt and blouse were subdued in color and perfectly fit.

We were on the road by eight-thirty, and ready for lunch at Grinnell, Iowa, before one. I had suggested a place called The Elms where I had enjoyed drinking three point two beer with friends and where a good pork tenderloin sandwich could be found. As it turned out, The Elms had been taken over by a fast-food franchise. Ever resourceful Dave gained directions to a similar place by stopping the car and talking to people on the street.

After lunch we took a tour of the campus, driving along Sixth Avenue, where a line of old Gothic buildings had been replaced by sleek, rectangular no-nonsense new structures. There were similar replacements along Eighth Avenue, but the old library, transformed into an office complex, and the old chapel remained. Best of all, the residence halls, with arched doorways, steep towers, and slant roofs with bay windows remained.

"Let's stop at Rawson Tower," I said, as we drove down Park Street on our way out of town.

Dave stopped the car at the walkway leading to the tower.

"This is where you and Ruth dropped me on my first year," I said to Mike. "Do you remember? Ruth said, 'You're beginning a new life. All your friends from your old life will drift away, and you'll never be the same.' Then she cried. I'll never forget it."

Mike nodded, but it didn't really resonate with him.

As we drew closer to Colo, Laurie went through all the names of Martha's children, her cousins. There was Patrick and Joe, Angie, Meg and Monica, and Tony and Rose. Each one had a story, and Laurie knew them all. The only cousin I had met was Tony, who had attended a family wedding the year before. He was farming the one hundred eighty acres Mike and I worked on decades ago as well as the family-owned half-section south of town. We'd spent several minutes talking about the equipment Mike and I had used back then, primitive stuff compared with what he was using.

They all were waiting in what we called "the new house" back then. It was a white clapboard two storey house, with an enclosed front porch and a comparatively low profile compared with "the old house" up the street. Mike's grandmother had built it in the mid-twenties, surrendering the old house to Mike's family. Legend had it that she rose early every morning, and before breakfast scanned the distance between houses to see if the lights were on across the way. Were they not, she would telephone Mike's father and rouse him out.

The older house was a taller, broader Iowa Gothic with an open front porch that ran the width of the building. When I lived there with Ruth and Mike, I had a huge bedroom all to myself on the second floor. This was my domain, where I was lord of the manor, free to stay up with a book or radio broadcast as long as I wished. My only requirement was to wake up each morning by six for chores – feeding and watering steers while Mike slopped the pigs and milked the cow.

The downstairs floor, with a bedroom off the living room behind closed French Doors, belonged to Ruth and Mike.

The cousins were scattered throughout the house, and Laurie moved from one to another before settling into conversation with Patrick, the oldest one who was closest in age. Left on our own, Dave and I settled in chairs in the sun room next to Angie, the second oldest cousin. Like Patrick, she was very tall, several inches over six feet. She also was slim, blond, and good looking, with pleasant features much like her mother's. She felt perfectly at ease talking to Dave, the husband of her much admired, older cousin, Laurie, whose fashion sense always impressed her. But she seemed uncomfortable with me, as if she couldn't quite place me. It made me feel somewhat like the Unidentified Guest in *The Cocktail Party*.

"How's your dad doing?" Dave asked.

"He's still confused by it all," Angie said. "Luckily, Rose and I have been able to look in on him. We're both close to their winter home in Tucson."

That was where Martha died, three weeks before Christmas.

"She came down with the flu and didn't pay much attention to it," Angie said. "Having the flu was nothing new to her, but then it developed into pneumonia and by the time we got her into the hospital it was too late. She was too far gone."

"That's too bad," I said. "But I can see her not being troubled by flu. She was always a cheerful, upbeat person. I remember bumping into her and your dad on the second balcony lobby of the Shubert Theatre during intermission. She was so friendly. It was as if we'd seen one another just last week instead of years before."

"That was when we lived in Mount Prospect," Angie said.

They had done quite a bit of moving about while her father pursued his career in banking. He and Martha were entrepreneurial, buying banks in rural communities after he'd gained experience in a big Chicago bank. At one point he'd even taken a break from banking to try his hand at farming the family acreage.

I glanced through the window toward the big house, two hundred yards away across the open field.

"I loved living there," I said, nodding. "I had the whole second floor to myself."

"We had to share the space for seven," Angie said, looking askance.

Dave stood and moved toward the kitchen and Angie and I drifted into the dining room, where Tony was seated at the side of a table, his back to the window and his best friend at his side. Scattered about the room were his brothers and sisters as well as his uncle Mike. We nodded to one another and I glanced over his left shoulder toward a portion of the one hundred eighty acres Mike and I had worked all those summers ago.

"That's the field I plowed with two twelve inch blades," I said, with a gesture.

Tony followed by gaze and smiled.

"You were using a brand new Ferguson Ford," he said, recalling our conversation from the year before.

"Well, it was newish," I said. "But I'll never forget when Mike and I bailed hay on that field. He was on one side of the bailer, feeding wires, and I was on the other, tying them, and sneezing every time the piston wacked another piece of hay into place."

"You were a sorry sight," Mike said, appearing beside me. "You were wearing a face mask and filling it with phlegm."

"I was allergic to hay dust."

"What a sight," Mike said. "It was hard to look at, all that stuff dribbling down."

Everyone laughed and Tony began talking about farming today. They didn't plant alfalfa, so there was no haying, and they didn't feed steers or slop pigs. It was strictly corn and soybeans. I'd seen him talk this way before in front of his mother, leaning forward with descriptions while Martha beamed. He was a sturdy, outdoors man, compact and strong, and she was proud of him.

"What did bring you to Colo," he asked, looking up.

"Well, I was expelled from my high school in Chicago. I had a fast lip and they were tired of listening to me. When I tried to reenroll in the fall, they told me I had only two options for finishing school. I could either go to night school, or transfer out of my district. So my mother called my sister for advice. She said I'll call you right back, and when she did call back she said she'd talked it over with Mike, and they both wanted me to come to Colo to finish school. Mike said he'd always wanted a little brother, and I moved right in, hardly aware that he and Ruth had been married only three months. It seemed natural to me, and Mike didn't seem to mind gaining an instant family."

"Now I know who you are," Angie said, standing in the doorway, and smiling. "You're Aunt Ruth's brother."

"Coming to Colo was the best thing that ever happened to me. Everyone here took me right in, as if I'd been part of the family for ages. I'll never forget it."

When I drifted back toward the kitchen, the youngest sibling, Rose, caught up with me. "Let me ask you something," she said. She was one of the shorter ones, with dark hair and earnest dark eyes. "You look like you turned out okay. I mean, you never got in trouble. You never went to jail."

"Actually, things went pretty well for me. I got a bachelor's degree and then a master's, and had several good jobs."

"That's so good. You can't imagine how relieved that makes me. I've got three boys and they're always in trouble. Thank you so much for telling your story, Jimmy. Now I know there's hope."

How did she think to call me Jimmy? It made me want to reach out and give her a hug.

When we left for our hotel check-in at Ames, we took a tour of Colo. The Main Street grocery store was gone. So was the corner drug store, where I bought paperback novels. Now the building housed a bar, and the open windows were largely bricked in. Orr's Café next door also had disappeared as well as the pool hall farther down. But the post office, where we picked up mail from our metal box before stopping at Orr's for morning coffee, was still there as well as the Catholic church at the next corner and the Methodist church one block away.

Then as now, the houses were spaced far apart, and there were several news ones on the edge of town. Colo had become something of a bedroom community for commuters from Ames, and the population had increased from five to six hundred. Our last stop was at the shuttered service station on the old highway. This was where all the boys congregated on Saturday nights for Cokes and cupcakes after forays to Marshalltown or Ames. Now the old station was a museum, restored by public subscription.

When we got out and walked around, I stopped and looked down the highway.

"Which way am I facing?" I asked Mike.

That made him laugh. I'd told him before about my chronic disorientation in Colo. It may have come from my first trip. We'd left Chicago on a late Friday afternoon, and I was fast asleep when the car turned off the highway and stopped in front of the new house, where Mike's folks were waiting to greet us. Not knowing which way we turned off the highway left me confused. It always seemed that the house, on the right side of the street, was facing west.

"East," he said, with a smile.

"Damn," I said, still turned around.

But there was more to it than nighttime confusion. Colo was my Brigadoon, a mystical place I'd dropped into as if through a misty twilight, a town where people never locked their doors and where they always left their car keys in the ignition, never in danger of being lost and always ready to start upon taking the driver's seat. It was a town where streets and roads were unpaved, and where traveling cars left a trail of dust like a parachute behind them, and a town where houses were separated by oceans of grass. The whole place lay so lightly on the land it could hardly slow a prairie breeze.

* * *

Colo's Catholic church had undergone many changes since I attended services decades ago. The rectory still was there, but the pastor now traveled a circuit from Colo to State Center and Zearing on succeeding Sundays. Communicants had to travel from town to town for services. The Colo church itself looked much the same, choir loft in the rear, sturdy wood pews with movable bars for kneeling, and an altar at the front. In a striking departure from days past, there was an urn before this altar containing Martha's ashes. There was a time when the Church did not condone cremation. Its thinking on that had evolved, Mike explained.

As the service went on, it became increasingly clear how highly valued Martha was by the pastor. She was a devoted parishioner, filling the church with floral arrangements plucked from her garden, serving on committees, and lending a hand whenever needed. But she was not above offering critical comments on some of his homilies, saying things like, "I liked most of it, but not the last part." And she would insist that he stop by for tea to view her garden's first spring lilies.

Her spirit seemed to fill the room as he spoke, enhanced by the enlarged photos of her, glowing in the light from stained glass windows. She was a true believer, one for whom death held no mystery. Because she knew where she was going, she was unafraid. My sister faced death in the same way. Once she knew her cancer was incurable, she was ready to die. She would wait for me, she said. She would save a space by her side.

The priest finished by asking the lord to bless and receive her, and to forgive all her sins, reminding believers that even the blameless were not without sin. And bless, too, he said, the land and the farmers who worked it. May their efforts be fruitful.

From the church, we traveled to the cemetery at the edge of town, where the urn containing her remains were buried in the family plot. Then we returned to the church basement where a cafeteria-style food counter awaited. They were serving farm food, the kind farmers' wives offered to harvest-time field workers, sturdy stuff designed to fortify against an autumn chill.

Mike and I carried our trays to a table and struggled a bit settling down.

"We're all getting older," I said.

"Yes, but it's better than the alternative," he said.

I smiled. That was a sentiment I'd heard spoken by many older people I knew, and it might have been true for people like Mike and me, but it wasn't for Martha. ☐

I AM THE CENTER OF THE UNIVERSE
William L. Lederer

I am the center of the universe
and so are you. I know what you're thinking.
That seems egocentric. But any view
otherwise is short-sighted, not linking
with a whole, systematically perverse.

Since the Big Bang, which is the center star?
Is my heart the heart of me? My core
my navel? All living bodies are
irregular. No equi-distant point or
balance between all sides because nature
abhors the static. And yet I must start
somewhere. A heartline's gyrating center
always on the move. The whole tipping part.

This pointing gyre begins with me.
No matter how dizzy that's clear.
Without a fixity
nothing will appear.

Eye the sashay of the tornado,
the rites of frenzy,the flights of snow.
Growth and decay in the potato.
Circling orders the fast and the slow.

HORIZON
Louise LeBourgeois

I was fourteen when my family moved to Chicago. The first time we visited the observation deck of the Sears Tower, shortly after our arrival, our family friend Rodrigo, a prankster, pointed towards Lake Michigan's horizon and said, "If you look carefully, you can see the curve of the earth." I squinted at the blurry line between sky and water. I closed one eye and then the other. I tilted my head. "I *think* I can see it," I said. Rodrigo laughed. "You can't see the curve of the earth! I was joking!"

But what was I seeing if not the curve of the earth? The paradox of the horizon line is that even though it appears to be utterly horizontal, it in fact describes the place where we can no longer see over the curve of our planet. It is impossible for any human, from any position rooted to the ground, to perceive the earth stretching as a low arc across our field of vision. The visible arc lies not across, but curving away from, our line of sight. We can infer its roundness by the fact that what lies at our feet is visible in its full dimensionality, but as we lift our gaze outwards, our perception of distance becomes ever more compressed until it blurs into apparent nothingness. Our borderless globe presents the illusion of an edge, but as any painter knows, a harsh line brings our attention to an abrupt halt, whereas a softened one describing, say, the contour of an arm, lends fullness to the flesh and tempts us with the possibility of the invisible.

The horizon is our imperfect perception of the edge of the globe. It is also a paradox, the visible but non-existent straight line describing a curve, the imagined place where planet and sky merge.

Sailors had to confront their own fears about the horizon as our human understanding of the world blossomed from flat to round, from a place in which a ship could fall to oblivion into a place where sailing in a single direction could mean arriving at the same point from which one departed. Christopher Columbus's 1492 voyage was certainly not the first case of global exploration, but it was one of history's most significant. Like the concept of globalization today, Columbus's voyage resulted in both discovery and tragedy, enriching some people while destroying others.

My water/sky paintings explore the idea that we are in uncharted territory, propelled towards the unknown by discovery and innovation. It is a philosophical connection rather than a literal one. These works are based upon my ongoing relationship with Lake Michigan, a tangible presence in my life as well as a metaphor, the fictive space where as far as we can see tells us there is yet more to come.

Our playful planet offers us mind-bending riddles. On the North Pole every direction leads south, and on the South Pole every direction leads north. It is possible to draw a triangle on the globe consisting of three 90-degree angles. The Earth is round, but it looks flat. It appears that the sun circles us, but in fact we circle the sun. We hurtle through space at an astounding speed, but it feels as if we are sitting perfectly still.

How can a line equal a circle? If we set out in a single direction for long enough, our impish planet puts us right back at our starting place, playing a cosmic joke on us proud humans, its very roundness twirling us in confounding, flummoxing, delightful loops. ☐

ONION STATION
Umberto Tosi

Is that where Pop went?" Theo pointed out the window to the tower that rose above the cluster of nearby, South Loop buildings. His mother glanced up from where she sat on the edge of the unmade hotel bed. She lowered the receiver, put a Chen Yu crimson-nailed, index finger to her glamour lips – morning faded – and gave the boy an indulgent smile, dark lashes fanning admonishment. Theo read the slight toss of her Rita Hayworth hair as annoyance. Movie star mom, he called her – always in character even though she only played bit parts on screen.

Alma adjusted her satin robe, took a drag of Pall Mall from a pearled cigarette holder and continued in her long-distance voice. She exhaled words in steam nicotine curlicues "...You tell *me, Maasha*. I'm out of *ansahs*. ... No. I *khan't* say when we'll be *theah*... We missed the goddamn train connection *yestahday*. Awful *stoahms*! Snow, snow snow all the way *heah*." Two-thirds home and already her tongue was in Boston – r's lost as luggage.

"*He's* off to God-knows-*wheah*! And *he* has the goddamn tickets... Some big Chicago deal, *he* says. Now it's onions! You know Victor." She never called Theo's father Vic. "He's always with some deal. No goddamn *considahration* for me or his son or anyone. I just want to take Theo and come home..." Three years now in California, and Boston was still "home."

Theo pointed out the window, down at the streets. "I want to play in the snow first!" You could never be sure of snow by Christmas in Boston or anywhere, but there it was, new, velvety as meringue piled along the icy Chicago sidewalks, an elevator ride away, if it didn't rain and melt everything.

"Quiet, Theo!" Theo's mother waved her cigarette holder but didn't look at him this time. "I hate to ask you to wire the cash, *Maasha deah*, but you know Victor."

Alma never made a move without consulting Aunt Marcie, her costume designer and the family matriarch in Boston, where they would be by now if their *City of Los Angeles* streamliner had not pulled into Chicago twenty-three hours late from having to crawl through a Midwest blizzard, snowplow engine spraying crystal plumes all the way.

Their accommodations – two compartments that his parents occupied separately– were an upgrade from last year's trip home. The war – its shortages, rationing and government buys, we don't mention the blood – had been good to his father, 4F due to scarred lungs from having the Spanish flu as a boy, though he always appeared in combative health.

Except maybe for sledding and making snowballs, Theo loved train riding better than anything – the cozy encapsulated freedom of rolling through landscapes and towns, free of it all, home, school, strictures, his bickering mother and father neutralized by convention, keeping a jaw-tight truce of convenience that allowed Theo maximum leeway. The slower the train the more time for running through the holiday crowded cars playing chase games with the half-dozen feral fellow-traveling kids who found each other the first day out – each one liberated from disoriented parents riffling through old copies of *Life*, sipping highballs, playing gin rummy a penny a point, smoking, smoking, smoking. It didn't take much pestering to get Theo's mother to tell him: "Okay! Go play. Just be good … and get back here when you hear the dinner chimes!"

Two men in dark overcoats and snap-brims had approached his father in Union Station as they came up the ramp into the echoing marble lobby, from where they would have grabbed a cab to La Salle station to catch the Boston train. His father seemed to recognize one of the men – the shorter of the two, a squat man who had to be bald under his greenish fedora. His father shook both men's hands and stepped out of earshot, but Theo could still distinguish his father's gritty nasal tenor, sharp with feigned irritation, cutting through the crowd buzz.

Theo's father stood taller than both men. He moved loose-jointed, deceptive as a pitcher – he had played triple-A ball – looking in for his signal. He edged close enough to the men to make them look up at him. Tallness was his superpower, growing up as the third tallest of four brawling brothers, in a fair-haired family originally from the mountainous, *alt'Italia* Piedmont.

"It's all business, war, politics, everything," Theo's father was a wellspring of dismissive cynicism, "right on the money," as he would say. Tallness gave Victor a dashing look that his unruly, wavy hair, small, hazel eyes and hawk nose might have ruled out.

Tallness made he and his brothers stand out, and got his younger brother Vincent picked off by a Waffen-SS sharpshooter in the Ardennes.

While Theo's father parleyed, his mother sat with her small son and their suitcases. She made sure Victor noticed her fuming in her usual, stagy way, staring daggers, blowing Pall Mall smoke, legs crossed, high heel pump kicking. The men didn't back off. One of them put a hand inside his jacket for an envelope that he gave to Theo's father, who took it, turned away and strode back to wife and child, gray faced. "Change of plans," Theo's dad said. "I need to do some business. It's urgent."

"It's always money with you."

"You think it grows on trees."

"You've got plenty. You and your whole stingy family. You and your big deals."

"If I don't take care of this, I'll be finished."

"Big shot." Theo's mother adjusted and threw the muzzle end of her fox fur stole over one shoulder. It stared accusingly down at Theo with amber glass eyes.

"Six boxcars of onions probably stuck in the snow somewhere in the Nebraska. If they freeze it's all over. We go belly up."

"What did you expect?"

"It's a freak storm this early."

Red torpedo onions from Washington – just like the bulbous magical one in Theo's coat pocket that he filched from a bag in his father's sample case.

Just before they left California, his father had handed him a fat wad of gray green hundred dollar bills. "Feel that, Theo? That's power. It's what makes you somebody." Then his father took back the money and handed him one of the sleek magenta onions from a sample case. His father took glee giving these kinds of object lessons to his son.

Theo half listened and pocketed the onion – a Flash Gordon rocket, elliptical, fat, ends tapered gracefully, with its fuchsia skin that felt silky but fell away papery. He could pilot it between the towers of this Oz and see open-mouthed, blanched faces of people staring from office windows.

Yesterday's storm had given way to cobalt skies and dunes of glistening snow. He wanted to take a churning elevator ride back down to the streets and run out of the hotel into the powder, crunching it with his galoshes. He could roll in it piled high along the curbs by snowplows, unnoticed by the wool-bundled shoppers already crowding the streets, puffing cold vapor under the strings of Santa Claus lights, determined to be jolly for their first real Christmastime since Pearl Harbor, exhausted, more thankful than puffed with victory, smiling wearily into the dawning Atomic Age.

Being "short for his age," as his mother put it, Theo had to move the little desk chair over to the window and stand on it to get a good view. "Be keaw-full theah!" His mother had waved the cigarette holder at him.

He could see his button-eyed reflection, faint and translucent, in the window pane, mop of chestnut hair needing a cut, cowlick waving, long lashes, pretty and girlish. "He looks so much like you, Alma! Honestly." His aunt Marcie would clap his face in both hands. "Little *cioccolino della zia!*" She would plant a wet kiss on the forehead of her little chocolate drop.

Theo leaned against the pane, steaming out his reflection with hot breath. When he closed his eyes he could feel the building itself swaying subtly. Or maybe he was still feeling the roll of the train under his feet from their two-day journey, getting his "land legs," his dad had called it.

Everything is in motion, even the ground in California with its mini-quakes and that bigger one that woke him up one morning, seeing the ceiling lamp swinging, feeling his bed pitch and roll, hearing his room rumble like a freight train. The earth itself flew like a rocket ship through space, the whole solar system that his father demonstrated to him with oranges, lemons and grapes on the kitchen table.

Change, change, change, and it's all relative, his father, who knew all, had told him. Einstein said it, and that's how they made the Bomb. And what if they dropped one on us?

He schemed and hoped his mother wouldn't drag him shopping and to another interminable movie matinee. They had no sooner checked into the hotel yesterday than Theo's mother dragged him down the street to her favorite escape, in this case, the glittering, French baroque, New Palace Theater on Randolph Street. They took its rococo French palatial surroundings for granted. She was in the second feature – playing a nightclub singer in a *noir* detective caper. It was on the bill with *And Then There Were None*, an Agatha Christie whodunit with Louie Jourdan. Jourdan then was being divorced by Ida Lupino, he heard his mother say, for being "that way" – raise of an eyebrow and slight limp of the wrist. "Ida isn't Italian, like everyone thinks, she's English and a real *troupah.*" A year earlier, his mother did a walk-on in an Ida Lupino movie. "She directed. Imagine! A woman!" Theo had to squirm through the entire double bill, just as he did her movie stories – plus a stupid, live dancing girl number, a blow-hard newsreel, a short and – the only blessed relief – a Bugs Bunny in "Herr Meets Hare," only slightly dated now that the toon's villain, "fatso Göring," had gone the way of the Third Reich.

Theo leaned on the window harder and calculated that he could fly straight over the Christmas streets below and land atop that other tall building without having to gain much altitude. He wanted to touch the serene, silvery robed female figure that crowned it – see if she was real, and maybe could tell him her name and why she was there, and why they were staying so long in Chicago.

He'd just have to say, *Shazam*! – like the lame newsboy in his Whiz Comics, Billy Batson – to be Captain Marvel. But he would have to be alone, so no one would discover his secret or be singed by the lightning bolt. He could try, maybe when Mama took her shower. Still, he'd never flown from this height, only off the motherly branches of the California black oak behind their bungalows off Santa Monica where the big red trolleys ran.

Then there were wind currents and navigation to manage. Theo concerned himself with names, locations and the why of things a lot. He read all signs and memorized addresses and slogans. He noted every detail about the hotel where they stayed—*The Morrison, Clark and Madison: Tallest Hotel in the World*, the cursive legend on a postcard read – he filched them as they traveled. *In the Heart of the Loop, 46 stories high and standing 506 feet above the sidewalk. Home of the Terrace Casino and the historic Boston Oyster House* – where Alma took Theo to dinner last night and thought she saw Barbara Stanwyck having martinis with Robert Taylor, denizens of the kind of talkie flicks Theo's mother dragged him to all the time. *... every room with bath and circulating ice water!* The postcard bore a colorized image of the hotel's square block base and fluted tower with its red brick facade. Decades later attending a Chicago publishing conference, Theo walked by the massive bank building where the hotel once stood on Clark and remembered how the Morrison's elevators churned his stomach.

He overheard his mother telling aunt Marcie that she was meeting some movie person – a man – downstairs later for lunch at the Boston Oyster House. Theo squashed his nose against the window and silently mouthed: "Please, Mystic Lady, keep me safe from boring lunches and another hideous double feature with Mom!"

"... as close to Boston as I'm getting for now, Maasha... I miss you."

Theo interjected. "I want to stay here and color, Ma!" Alma shushed him again.

Theo's mother braced the phone receiver with one shoulder, adjusted her satin dressing gown.

Theo stayed pressed against the window. He traced his flight, between the buildings, under bridges, along the river, over the train running along a section of elevated tracks – The Loop – looking from above like the Lionel set he had made known that he wanted from "Santa" – catching his father in a grimace. As he flew overhead, he imagined Christmas shoppers craning their necks in amazement, dropping their bundles, letting go of leashes as their dogs chased the hats that flew off from his wake.

The mystic lady atop the building could be the Virgin Mary or Wonder Woman, aglow from the pale winter sun. He imagined her beaming golden rays directly at him, conveying powers, perhaps, sending secret messages, in a fantasy, believable to him in this Emerald City of towers with its giant icy lake scattering light. He could ask the Mystic Lady to make him tall – even normal sized so people wouldn't think him so much younger than his eleven years or call him a shrimp, and so the disappointment in his father's eyes would fade away. But then would he still be able to fly?

The nanny from the concierge would be easy to outwit. Theo's mother hung up the receiver and stared across the room at nothing for a while, letting the Pall Mall in its holder burn out on the night table ashtray. Her tears, held back, did not spill over. Her lower lip trembled. Theo pretended he wasn't catching every nuance in his keen peripheral vision – one of his known superpowers. Another was his ability to distinguish between his mother's real and stage tears, the ones that flowed freely for close-ups, not held back. He tried to resist an awkward compulsion to give her some comfort. A hug in such circumstances could bring on sobbing that would overwhelm him.

"It's okay, Ma." He let his voice bounce off the windowpane at her faint reflection. "It's going to be fun here." He let his voice go high and babyish.

"Finish your cereal, Theo." She sniffed, dabbed her eyes with Kleenex and nodded to a half-consumed bowl of Rice Krispies that had long lost their snap, crackle and pop on the room service table. "Children are starving in Europe. Mama has to change and get ready now. A nice lady will come stay with you for a little bit until I'm back."

Alma picked a velvety green, classic two-piece suit – an Elsa Schiaparelli knockoff Marcie had made – from the closet, travel wrinkles brushed and ironed out the night before. She never wore slacks – too petite. She fished some peach satin undies, bra, girdle and precious nylons from a suitcase and took everything into the bathroom, full length robe trailing.

Theo jumped off the chair and changed out of his Red Ryder pajamas into street clothes as soon as his mother closed the bathroom door behind her. Quickly, playing master detective, he rummaged the hotel room desk. He thumbed through the guidebook, brochures, postcards and maps for clues.

Ah ha! For one thing, he learned that the name "Chicago" came from the French version of a local Indian word *shikaakwa*, for a wild, "stinky onion" found by the Chicago River. His red torpedo onion didn't stink. It smelled faintly sweet and sharp, promising good things to eat.

Torpedo onions must have special powers.

The center spread of the guidebook showed a cityscape with the hotel and the mystic lady tower. "The Chicago Board of Trade ... tallest building in Chicago," said the legend.

He flipped a page and saw the lady close up – gray-white metallic, dwarfing tiny figures on an observation deck, austere in fluted robes, a spiky crown of metallic laurel, and her face, blank, like in a dream. "... Ceres, the Roman Goddess of grain ... thirty feet tall ... aluminum ... She is to Chicago what Lady Liberty is to New York..." and something about cereal. Snap, Crackle and Pop's mom? Mystic Cereal Woman makes things grow. Why not me?

Romans believed she rises from the Underworld every spring – like Lena does all the time. Theo's little sister died as a newborn when he was two. His mother mentioned Lena to him only once – "something was wrong with her heart" – and ignored the many questions that followed. Theo doesn't tell anyone about Lena's visits – in a blue dress, looking about the age she would be had she survived, not saying much, just tagging along, though he hasn't seen her since they got off the train in Union Station.

Theo's mother was in the bathroom getting ready when the hotel nanny arrived with a timid, single knock. The skinny pale blond, with aqueous eyes already looked tired in her ill-fitting maid uniform. Standing in the door without letting her, Theo told her that his mother's appointment had been canceled – nanny services no longer needed.

Theo heard his mother's muffled voice through the bathroom door. "Who was that, Theo?"

"It was Pop. He's back." Theo stepped close to the bathroom door and spoke loudly. "Pop said he's going to his room to do some paperwork and that I could come and stay there while you're out shopping."

There was a pause. "Is that all he said? Nothing about train tickets?"

"Yeah. That's all."

Theo heard an irritated sign. "Okay, Theo. Go on over to your father. Tell him I'll come get you in about two hours, okay?"

"Okay, Ma."

Theo pulled his navy blue, woolen pea coat, leggings, hat and gloves from a suitcase, closed it and ran with them out the door. He had already torn a city map from the guidebook and shoved it into the lining of his pea coat along with his latest copy of Whiz Comics, featuring Captain Marvel and his magic torpedo onion.

"Bye Mom!" He called loudly through the bathroom door. He could hear the shower running. Not taking any chances, he left the room before putting on his coat in the hallway by the elevators.

"Floor?" The brass-button uniformed elevator operator looked bored and straight ahead, closing the doors after Theo stepped in.

"Lobby, please." Theo tried to sound adult.

Two middle-aged women in fox furs got on the next floor on the way down. One of them stared at Theo with baleful, saggy eyes. She cleared her throat. "Where's your mommy, little boy?"

Theo ignored her. She reached over and nudged his shoulder. "Hey, lady. Watch ya finghas!" He did his best Bugs Bunny loudly as he could. "I'm da papah boy, if you wanna know! Wheah's *youah* mommy?"

"Hummph!" The woman made a face and shook her head, making the partridge feather on her Dorothy Lamour chapeau wiggle. Her equally decked out companion gave Theo the fish eye.

Theo tried to stand straight and not giggle or burp from the elevator's rapid descent, floor after floor, ding, ding, ding, ding...

"Main floor lobby." The operator announced, opening the doors. The two women exited in step as a parade squad.

Theo made for the big brass revolving doors and propelled himself onto a powdery sidewalk. He took a bite of arctic, outside air and shivered more in excitement than cold. Cars honked and sloshed by, buses growled, people flowed around him in all directions – shoppers, workers, women and men, few children, no one paying him any attention, except for Lena, who appeared alongside him, skipping, holding his mittened hand, apparently not feeling winter's bite in her blue dress, white socks and Mary Jane patent leather shoes. Free! ☐

BURNING MIND
Jason Economus

The title of this piece is, The Ill Would Like to Give A Statement, or This is the First Day I've Been out of the House All Week, or How Do You Solve a Problem like Melancholia? or I Have no Idea How to get Home from Here, or Please Stop Ruining the First Day of the Rest of my Life, or What the Fuck is Going on?

So. I have to admit something right off the bat. I didn't vote for Obama in 2008 or in 2012.

I stood among thousands of people in Grant Park that magical night six years ago and cried openly when Obama was elected. I also passionately argued with non-Obama supporters about why they should vote for Obama, letting them know I thought they were idiots not to back him. I lied repeatedly, telling anyone who asked if I voted during both elections that I did, absentee, in Wisconsin, because that state needed my vote more than Illinois. Why was I lying about it? To everyone. I felt like a split person, divided and fragmented, watching my life from the outside filled with half truths, stone wall defenses, substance abuse issues and shame, shame, shame.

But my lying about my voting record twice was the least of my problems, just the tip of the iceberg really. The past five years have been quicksand, have been a hall of mirrors, have been a suffocating nightmare. Slowly, I'd been losing my mind.

Sounds hyperbolic and overdramatic, I'm sure. And yet. It's the truth. I've been on an odyssey of sorts that until about a month and a half ago could surely have ended me in plenty of horrible places, possibly in hospitals, in the back of police cars, or even in the morgue.

I have a mental illness. It is called Bipolar Mood Disorder. Rapid cycling to be more precise. With this disorder the cycles of up and down, mania and depression, can quite aggressively happen within my mind in forty-eight hours and sometimes, at its frightening and exhausting worst, I can run the full course of this devastating roller-coaster in just a few hours. This has left me, and my past, with regrettable and severe wreckage in every area of my life: work and relationships to family, friends, girlfriends and myself. As my situation became more and more extreme, I began to secretly think to myself that something was deeply wrong with me, but the idea that I had an illness, a sickness in my mind, was something I wasn't willing to truly face. Until I had to.

I was diagnosed very recently, at the end of October 2012. It was clear within the first fifteen minutes of my two-hour emergency psychiatric screening that I had a violence/disruption in my mind that I could no longer sustain or tolerate. I simply could not go on. A cord in me had snapped. I was lost.

I've had manic and depressed episodes for as long as I can remember, but they felt normal to me, were part of how I worked and occasionally thrived. I'm an artist, I'm a passionate guy, I'm sensitive, I'm horny, I'm generous. I also come from a broken home and I had an abusive, alcoholic dad. These were my rationales and justifications for my wild array of moods and behaviors. It was only after I was diagnosed that I understood that my first depressive break took place when I was seventeen (it lasted for over a year), and that it was in reality the start of a very, very long road of jagged and abrupt ups and downs of mood, inconsistent and impulsive thinking, irrational flights of spending, promiscuous sex and rages that would leave me shaking and foaming at the mouth. Always, eventually, I would go back to the little, all-dark cell in my mind that I kept myself in, thinking I was not safe enough to share myself with others. The last piece of this cycle was bottoming out, completely hopeless despair. And all of this would sometimes occur within one day. I can't tell you how utterly tired I am.

So for almost fifteen years, over half my life, I've had this battle raging inside my brain, never having any idea of the terrible toll those years of keeping it all inside was going to take. The day before I was screened and diagnosed I could not stop crying for five hours. A friend found me crawling on my apartment floor, incoherent, muttering. I remember clearly thinking, I don't believe I can survive this. It was as though my mind was devouring itself and I couldn't escape. Thankfully, I am now on a strong mood stabilizer. It makes me want to sleep till next Tuesday, and I am already slowly growing a small bowling ball in my belly because the medicine makes my triglycerides increase severely, but other than these two side effects things are slowly working themselves out for the better.

People recently have said things like, "I'm so proud of you, good for you for getting help, you are so strong to face this," and of course I appreciate it, the sentiment behind the supportive comments, but really, if you were in a room that was on fire and you finally dashed for the door, and gripped the door handle even though it seared your hand with burning, and you escaped from the flaming room, it just wouldn't quite feel right if waiting outside there was a pack of folks saying, "I'm so proud of you for getting out of that burning room, good for you." But I did make it out and now I have to breathe. I have to meditate. I have to exercise. I have to slow down. I try to identify triggers, create balance, get good sleep, drink less alcohol, take my meds, talk to people when I am really hurting or feeling out of control emotionally. I am not terribly successful with any of this yet.

I am not anywhere near on the other side of this, not even close. Most days, I feel stuck and failing—I'm not good at healing, I want a fix, now. It doesn't work like that, I know. My very real struggle takes place every hour of every day, whether it's struggling over sleeping or substances or sex or things like reading or texting or driving or money or food, or my memory or concentration. My former relationship to the Reality I knew is gone and I have to make another, new relationship. People ask, is it relieving to have a name for it? Sure, I guess, in a way. If you had a troll baby and one day called it, My Little Troll Baby Bi Bi Bipolar, would it be comforting that the troll baby was now called Bi Bi? Sure, a little, but you'd still have a goddamn troll baby to deal with. And yet, in some ways this troll baby is actually turning out to be a gift; an aching and astonishing gift.

Yes, I have slowly, painfully, humbly come to appreciate my troll baby and even started to think it might be my very key to a life lived richly.

For me, my journey so far with Bipolar has been both amazing and terrifying. Both enlightening and shocking. This illness has warped my will and rocketed me to heights and plunged me to depths I could never have imagined. It's brought me a curiosity and sensitivity to all the little reservoirs of emotions within me, all the corridors my thinking scurries through. It's given me weird wacky adventures and allowed me to meet the strangest of people, it's helped me see the broken around me and it gives me the strength to say, "We can get through another day, there is something better just around the corner."

I take heart in something Camus once said: *In the darkest of winter I found within me there lay an invincible summer.* And as that summer light starts to shine just a little more in me, there's a little less dark. And I'll take it. I'll take a sliver of light. I'll take anything I can get to finally see that the monster under the bed in my mind isn't a monster at all. In fact, that monster is just that little troll baby that I am going to have to fucking learn to love and take care of. Because otherwise it will eat me. That troll baby—what an ungodly appetite and wicked temper.

I'm not now some newborn cheerleader for Bipolar or even mental illness. We have enough cheerleaders in the world and besides, I lost my virginity to one so I'm good there. I just want to lay down my mask for a second and say, Hi, I'm Jason, I have a mental illness, I struggle, I struggle every single day and will for a long time and a lot of other people do too. Invisibly struggle. And it just fucking sucks and it's really scary, hard stuff.

In no way do I begin to pretend that this short piece of writing is somehow conclusive about me, or an authoritative work on mental illness. It's just a tiny, first attempt to begin to erase the distance this illness has put between me and others, between me and living life in a healthy, happy and productive way. When I think about those who struggle with more relentless and consuming experiences with mental illness I consider myself lucky. And I am deeply grateful that we are all alive and have so much potential. I am deeply grateful for the vast, wild and mysterious state called humanness, for the way we live with mind, body and heart.

And I am most deeply grateful that there's a flame that lights even the darkest nights and never dies away. Never dies away. □

AN INTERVIEW WITH ERASING THE DISTANCE FOUNDER BRIGHID O'SHAUGHNESSY

Jason Economus

Founded in 2005 and seen by over 40,000 people, Erasing the Distance is a non-profit arts organization based in Chicago that uses the power of performance to disarm stigma, spark dialogue, educate, and promote healing surrounding issues of mental health.

Brighid O'Shaughnessy is the Founder and Executive Artistic Director of Erasing the Distance. Since 2005, Brighid has reached over 40,000 people with theatrical performances about mental health issues that she has acted in, directed, devised and/or produced. A nationally sought after speaker and instructor, she has taught the ETD methodology at the Chicago School of Professional Psychology for the last several years as well as at University of Illinois at Chicago through the Asian American Studies Program. She has presented multiple times at the Active Minds National Conference, as well as at such places as Santa Clara University, DePaul University, Cathedral Counseling Center and the Anne Bilstein Theological College. Brighid was granted DePaul University's prestigious David O. Justice Award for her use of theatre to educate communities about mental illness in non-traditional and creative ways. She was also chosen by Extra Mile America as one of 200 heroic leaders in the United States making a difference in their communities and received a 3Arts Vision Award to support her artistic work at ETD.

Jason Economus is a member of the ensemble.

JE: How did Erasing The Distance come about?

BO: I founded Erasing the Distance in 2005. In part, I did so in response to my time co-directing a theatre arts project at Thresholds, Illinois' oldest and largest psychosocial rehabilitation agency. As I guided what we called members (versus clients) in telling and performing their own stories and I grew in my own awareness around issues of mental illness, I realized how many people in the general public were affected by these issues. Either personally or through a loved one, it was touching nearly everyone I knew and met in some way. Because of this, I felt there needed to be some outlet for these stories to be told and shared. The other main impetus for Erasing the Distance's founding was my own personal relationship with someone who has severe PTSD. It affected our relationship in incredibly significant ways and was overwhelming, frightening, and intense. We both tried for some time to put up a "perfect" front to others, due to our own fears, stigma, and shame. As I became more willing to share about how his mental illness had affected me, I realized I never wanted other people to feel as alone as we had or without resources. For those two reasons and countless others, I began the organization.

JE: Why is it that personal stories are an important tool for healing and mental health?

BO: I believe personal stories are incredibly important tools for healing. What I've observed through this work is that an enormous barrier to help seeking and harnessing well being is feeling that you are the only one who is dealing with an issue such as depression, bipolar, anxiety, you name it, and that nothing can be done to truly shift your reality. We make up "stories" in our minds that no one will ever understand us, that we are somehow fundamentally flawed, and that we are beyond or unworthy of help. Because of that, we choose silence and shame and attempt to "handle it on our own," which sometimes works of course, but many times does not.

Personal stories have a way of breaking down that myth both for the teller and the listener. They challenge our assumptions and hold up a mirror, giving us new ways of seeing ourselves and others, in all of our frailties and our power.

For the tellers, I think of a woman named Marlena. Marlena saw one of our shows a few years back and decided she wanted to tell her story. Due to her own shame and fear, however, she cancelled this appointment several times before finally making her way to us. At her story collection, she closed her eyes the entire time because she said she could not "look her collector in the eye" due to embarrassment. She also wanted to use a pseudonym to remain anonymous.

A few months later when we let her know that her story would be shared through our company's work, she said that through the mere act of telling her story in such an unabashed way, she had made significant progress towards facing herself and her past. She not only wanted to use her real name as part of the production but she wanted to attend the show and invite friends as well.

At the show itself, she informed me that just through knowing her story would be used to help others she had again made another leap in her healing and decided to be part of the talk back and answer audience questions after the show. This was a transformative experience for her to "come out" in such a bold way and since then, she frequently attends performances where her story is shared and oftentimes speaks to audiences following the show to let them know where she is now in her journey.

She has expressed to us on many occasions that this experience has changed her life and that she now walks with a much lighter load knowing that she has had us to help carry it through the act of performance.

JE: In your work with Erasing the Distance, what barriers have you seen in regards to mental health access, treatment and education? And what are some reasons for hope that you've encountered in your time doing this work?

BO: I think one of the biggest barriers that continues to rear its ugly head, even more-so than I originally truly realized, is how unaffordable and inaccessible much of mental health care is for most people. I believe at Erasing the Distance we do a meaningful and effective job creating safe spaces for people to come forward and share their truth and we continually connect people to education, resources and information designed to move the healing process forward. Unfortunately, with many Americans uninsured or underinsured, much of that care we are suggesting is out of reach for people financially and in some cases geographically. As an example, research shows that the best treatment for mental illness is a combination of psychiatric and psychological interventions. However, to see a psychiatrist can cost upwards of $200 - $250. If that is something you can't afford, then the more accessible and cheaper methods for medicat ing—alcohol, drugs, food, sex, etc.—become much more appealing options. This creates environments ripe for relapse and worsening of already debilitating conditions. Not to mention in Chicago alone, we have entire areas of the city that have few to no mental health professionals, clinics, hospitals, or other social service agencies. So even if someone wanted to get help, the options for him or her are enormously limited.

I do have hope though, for many reasons. One of which is this. Through a partnership we have with The Chicago School of Professional Psychology, we do audience evaluations after all of our major productions to gauge changes in attitudes, feelings and behaviors regarding mental illness. I am constantly moved by the shifts we see. As one example, repeatedly, after seeing our shows, we see increasing numbers of people willing to seek help themselves and/or connect people to resources and assistance in the community, an increase in feelings such as empathy, compassion, care and respect for those with mental illness, and an increase in numbers of people saying they would date, befriend, or hire someone with a mental illness!

I believe it is first with these smaller changes that we set the stage for larger ones to occur. If we can change the minds, let's say, of politicians, leaders of major corporations, and individuals who shape and run school systems, this can lead to seismic shifts in the ways that people with mental illnesses are treated and their energies harnessed as leaders and change makers. This is something that inspires me on a daily basis to continue forward and do the work I do. □

VESSEL
David Hart

Are we the last to winter with the dead,
marooned on this island?

Will the bus never dock
On the far shore of this boulevard?

Not so far from you, yet each return
Somehow in doubt, as though

A mythic vessel must be launched
Each day, great seas crossed.

From the thin warmth of doorways,
Women sing to windward,

Neon shadows frozen mid-stride,
Their wine thickened with false comfort.

Over the hard lake no stars
Emerge by which to navigate.

* * *

At last aboard the swaying hull, weary rows
Of oarsmen turn to me

Silent with hope in bright heat that blows
As though beaten by wings.

Turning from their eyes, I touch
Their shoulders with promise as I pass

And we lurch toward home at last,
A vessel of light and comradeship.

BUGROAST
Rogers Worthington

Big Harold, bent in sleep at the far end of the bar, raised his arm. "You got customers," he called out to the bartender, who was slumped in a standing doze. Big Harold didn't see the new arrivals coming; he heard them. No big deal at the Twin Sisters, which sits on an empty stretch of highway a half mile from the nearest town. Afternoons it's so still you can hear falling pine cones glance off the roof. Nobody much comes or goes anywhere in Wisconsin's north woods on a winter weekday afternoon. Lunch is over. Children are in school. Working people look out the window and think of home. There's a lull to life.

So no one else noticed when Arthur Bozowski and Gilbert Diggs pushed their beater into the Sisters' gravel parking lot. Bozowski, the shorter one, exited the car, a sagging, rusted '76 Dodge Charger, with a hard kick to the front right wheel. Diggs, a feeble smile working his mouth, trailed behind. The bartender snapped awake as the two shoved through the front door. Bozowski stood stomping snow from his Frye boots like it was a fallen enemy before he joined Diggs at the bar.

"You can't pick cars worth shit," Bozowski said without turning his head. Diggs, his eyebrows raised, looked at the steam rising from his coffee cup.

Bozowski sat staring at himself in the mirror from beneath the brim of his leather western hat. A rush of January wind shuddered beneath the tavern, muting the bark of a nearby dog. He tipped the hat at his own image and swiveled around to survey the other side of the room. Breathing in deeply, he dropped his gaze from a stuffed moose head on the log wall, to the row of chairs behind the pool table, taking them in like a judge considering a newly seated jury. When he turned back to the bar his face had reddened. He raised a clenched fist, paused, and slammed it down hard. *"God-damn son-of-a-bitch piss-ant...Moth-er fucker!"* he yelled out to no one in par ticular. Spittle clung to his beard.

The bartender, an ash of a man in his late seventies, glanced below the cash register for the nightstick kept there for moments of disorder. At the other end of the bar, Big Harold opened his eyes and considered the two men. Before Bozowski and Diggs showed up, he had downed one shot of Jim Beam after another. Now his head rested on an arm splayed before him. A slash of late afternoon light brightened the white of his shirt. It glared against his dark blue suit and ruddy complexion.

"What the hell, Boz," Diggs chortled into his hand. He was a thin man with hunched shoulders. Bozowski having a fit was nothing new for him. The car, the dealer who sold it to them, or just general circumstances—all were likely irritants. There was no telling what would set off Bozowski –like that cook at the Chinese joint west of Duluth, their last job, who called him 'Bozo' one time too many.

Diggs bought the dying Charger in Duluth for $300 the two men had pooled. In their haste to hit the road, he didn't check it out as well as he should have. It was trouble ever since.

First, the tread came off a front wheel, almost putting them in a ditch. Then, a crankcase leak led to overheating and a near-seizure of the engine block. Constant infusions of oil were required, and the big 360 cubic inch engine gulped down gasoline. Diggs proposed ditching the car when they reached their destination. "We can sell it for scrap, buy bicycles and pedal to the mills," he told Bozowski. "We can put screw-in hooks in the garage ceiling and hang the bikes from them at night."

"What's the point of hanging them up," Bozowski had said, "if there's no piece-of-shit automobile in the garage to make room for?"

Diggs had been fixated on the idea of a garage all day. There would be a storage cabinet for fishing gear, and a deep freeze stocked with steaks, hamburger patties, and fish filets. And somewhere, he had seen those red hooks for suspending bicycles from the ceiling. He'd already mapped out the rest of the small house they hoped to buy once they had enough for a down payment. A workbench and tools in the basement; a big cast iron skillet and boiling pot in the kitchen to cook up pancakes for breakfast and spaghetti and meatballs for dinner; a big TV and a couple of Barcaloungers in the living room. And who knows what in the backyard. "We can set up a grill, play badminton, mumblety-peg, or whatever the fuck else it is people do in backyards," Bozowski had said. What it wouldn't be was the long chain they'd both known of hot-plate dinners, post office boxes, furnished rooms, transient hotels, and edge-of-town motels that stink of other people.

"I'm buying drinks for every man in the house," Bozowski announced, ordering a beer for himself. Diggs shot him a look. "How about you, big man?" Bozowski said. "What you drinking? " Big Harold, the only other customer, remained motionless on the bar.

The bartender moved over to Bozowski, bent forward and spoke in a quiet voice.

"Take it easy," he said, nodding toward Big Harold. "His wife just passed."

When he came in that day, Big Harold, a county road crew foreman, told the bartender of having just buried his wife of thirty years in the town cemetery, where the backhoe labored mightily to turn frozen ground.

Bozowski grunted. "Gilbo here had a wife once," he told the bartender. Diggs half chuckled and shook his down turned head, causing his fringe of limp hair to whip around after him.

"Aw, Shut up, Boz," he said.

"She didn't much like him," Bozowski went on. "He'd keep trying to get a little, because every now and then she'd get merciful and let him pile on. But it was goddamn rare. And then she cut him off altogether." He munched on some trail mix he pawed out of a plastic bowl.

Big Harold raised his head and rested his gaze on the short man. The bartender reached for his bar rag. Bozowski went on.

"But Gilbo didn't know that. He was like one of them pigeons in that psychology test, where they get them to come up to a box and peck on a stick, and get a little feed," Bozowski said. "But when they rigged it so as not to give any more feed, the dumb birds would still keep coming up and pecking at the stick anyway. They never stopped pecking" He had read this in a newspaper article about some professor's study of people addicted to slot machines.

"That was Gilbo," he said. "He'd keep on pecking' but wouldn't get any."

Diggs grinned and shook his head. "Jesus, Boz," he said, sup pressing a laugh. It became a snort, then a sneeze. He had been intent on watching a barely audible TV set behind the bar. A faded, out-of synch Bugs Bunny cartoon was on. Bugs was being held prisoner by Sheriff Bulldog in a cage-like jail cell in the middle of a green field. Sheriff Bulldog was standing there, hands on hips, looking righteous. The sun was behind him—but he cast no shadow. They forgot to make a shadow for Sheriff Bulldog. Diggs noticed things like that.

"Where you boys from?" the bartender asked. Diggs, without moving his eyes from the TV screen, named a hillside town west of Duluth that stares out on Lake Superior beyond long beachfront acres of rusted ore loading equipment. Neither he nor Bozowski were from there. It was just the last place they worked.

"One shit-hole of a town," Diggs said. He went on to liken it to other small, forgettable towns in Minnesota, Idaho, North Dakota, Wyoming, Utah, and Oregon, where one or the other of them had worked over the last few years. They teamed up in Gillette, Wyoming, where

Bozowski was in the county lock-up for drunk and disorderly. Diggs was in for vagrancy. Bozowski's charge had to do with trying to break a restaurant window with a wine bottle. Fortunately for him and the restaurant, the lighter fluid it contained spilled out in mid air when the washcloth wick fell to the ground, far from the window. The two men hit it off. Turned out they worked at the same pea cannery in Eugene, Oregon, at the same time, but different shifts. Bozowski liked Diggs' calm, and Diggs liked Bozowski's way with words. When they were released, Diggs talked Bozowski into joining him at an AA meeting.

"What kind of work do you boys do?" the bartender said.

Diggs described a string of jobs that involved hot water one way or another—restaurant kitchens, canneries, car washes—jobs that came and went like foster homes in a bad orphan's childhood. "In a whole bunch of shit-holes," Diggs said. He shook his head in disbelief. For several seconds he appeared locked in his thoughts. Then he looked up and jerked his head toward Bozowski.

"But all that's going to change," Diggs said.

Bozowski was silent. Usually when this subject came up, he would say something to make Diggs think; maybe something with a hidden meaning. Sometimes, he would ask a question. He might ask Diggs, "How many people now live in the United States of America, and how many more are gonna be living here ten years from now?" Or he might just say, "There's only five things everyone has to do every day of their life, Gilbo: eat, drink, shit, piss, and sleep." The point was that if you had a job producing food, water, bedding, or toilet paper, there would be more customers every year and you would always have work. "It's a no-brainer," Bozowski would say.

But now he was silent. His eyes were locked on the bar. A bug had made its way onto the lacquered surface and was inching its way toward him. It was a small dark beetle-like bug with hard, shiny wings held tight to its body. Bozowski took a slow swig of beer. He watched the bug stop and start. Then he reached over and took a toothpick from a bowl near the cash register.

The bartender grabbed a paper napkin and moved toward the bug. "No," Bozowski held up his hand. "He's mine." He held the toothpick aloft in his right hand like the short barbed sticks wielded by banderilleros in a bullfight. Diggs rose up from his stool for a better view.

"I'm gonna touché the son-of-a-bitch," Bozowski said. The bug came within range. Sure enough, with a quick dart of his wrist, he impaled it. He held the toothpick up and studied the bug like it was a prize in a box of Cracker Jacks.

"Ugghh!" Diggs said. He shook his head in a shiver, took out a cigarette and struck a match.

"Hold that," Bozowski said. "I'm gonna roast his brown bug ass and send him through the fiery gates of hell." Big Harold, fully awake now, turned on his stool. He was a barrel-chested man in his late fifties with a creased face and a rumpled residue of thin white hair. Bozowski squinted as he studied the insect. Its tiny legs were kicking furiously, as though it was trying to run somewhere fast.

Bozowski reached for Diggs' match. "I'm gonna immolate him," he said. "It'll send a message to all the other bugs."

"Yeah?" Diggs said. "What's that?"

"Stay the hell away from my beer and pretzels. Stay out of where men eat and drink," Bozowski said. "Who needs bugs anyhow."

Diggs was thinking on this when Big Harold spoke.

"Birds do," he said. "They feed on them." Outside, the engine of a small, slow-moving airplane droned high in the sky. The big man took in a breath.

"And they don't need anyone cooking' up bugs for them and stinking up the place," he said. The bartender directed a surprised look at Big Harold. He pulled a beer and brought it over to him with a fresh shot. The January wind moaned again as it gusted beneath the tavern, among the old railroad ties on which it rested.

Diggs tucked his head down and coughed. Bozowski had told him things he said he'd done as an Army Ranger in Vietnam, or later as a civilian in response to some affront or other. Detailed things, like as how to render someone unconscious with a forearm blow to the neck's vagus nerve; or the force required to garrote someone; or to drive a combat knife between an enemy's ribs. Diggs was never sure of the truth of those stories. Bozowski did mess up that cook in Duluth who called him Bozo. But Diggs figured Bozowski— unless he lied about his age— would have been too young to have spent much, if any, time in Vietnam. And an army veteran he once worked with told him his friend's bandy legs were too short and crooked to complete the Rangers' required five-mile qualifying run in forty minutes.

The flame of the match moved close to Bozowski's fingers. He dropped it in an ashtray and leaned forward to look down the bar toward Big Harold. A fat huff of hot air belched out of a heating unit fixed to the rafters. It churned down into the dank air, heavy with the smell of ashtrays, disinfectant, and creosote.

In an attempt to change the mood, the bartender asked the two men where they were headed. Diggs pointed east down the road they had arrived on from the West.

"Green Bay," he said. Bozowski grabbed a fistful of toothpicks from near the cash register and began stacking them one by one in an ashtray.

"What's going on in Green Bay?" The bartender asked.

"We're gonna get on at the paper mills," Diggs said.

For weeks, Bozowski had painted word pictures of Green Bay. He described neat rows of homes with fresh mowed lawns, and a weekend nightlife downtown with lots of available women. He told Diggs how in January the steam rose from the tall stacks that towered over the town's paper mills; how the steam congealed in the sky from sub-zero temperatures, and drifted away and disappeared, leaving the air thick with the sweet, hops-like smell of pulp. He told of good jobs, and how once you got one you never lost it because the union was strong, and in good times and bad, everyone needed paper towels and toilet paper.

"They pay real good," Bozowski said. He opened the matchbook and began dropping torn off match heads inside the little square structure he made with the stacked toothpicks. It resembled a miniature log cabin without a roof.

Big Harold shifted on his stool.

"No you're not," he said.

Bozowski turned and fixed his gaze on him. So did a surprised bartender, who considered Big Harold a potential ally in keeping the peace.

"No we're not what?" Bozowski said.

"Getting on at the paper mills," Big Harold said. "You got no chance."

"Bull-shit," Bozowski said.

"How you mean?" Diggs said.

"Those are seventeen dollar an hour jobs with benefits, and that's a father-and-son union down there," the big man went on. "You have to be born into those jobs. They keep them in the family. They don't just give them to anybody who walks in off the street. Especially outsiders."

He said this as though it was common knowledge anyone would know, and he pronounced "outsiders" as if spitting out something distasteful on his tongue.

Diggs' mouth grew slack. His eyes were on the big man.

"Besides, you have to go to school to learn computers to work in those places," Big Harold went on. "It's all computers now." He swept a big hand high across the room.

"Hell, I can do that," Bozowski said. Diggs shook his head. "Now Gilbo here, it wouldn't do him no good to study computers. It'd be like pouring coffee in a cup with a hole in it."

Diggs shook his head. "What the hell, Boz," he said. The play had gone out of his voice.

"But there's plenty other jobs he can do there, and I can learn computers," Bozowski said. "I can learn any god-damn machine. Just put me in front one of them fuckers."

The big man took a swig of his boilermaker. "No," he said. "It wouldn't do any good." He paused. "You got to be born into that town and into those jobs, or you have to be around a long time and know people who know people."

The bartender had his dishrag out. He made big peaceful loops with it as he slowly cleaned the bar between the two men.

"And even then, you have to be real lucky," Big Harold said. "No. I would say you got no chance. No... chance... whatsoever." The words came out one at a time, like darts to a board. He raised his boilermaker, finished it off, and signaled the bartender for a refill.

Diggs looked down at the bar and rubbed his fingertips across its weathered surface. Bozowski, still in his hat and coat, thrust his right hand in his pocket and considered the big man again. His face reddened. For almost a minute he sat frozen. Then he picked up his mug and downed what was left of his beer.

"Well that sure as hell ain't what I heard," Bozowski said. He put his emptied mug down hard on the bar and tossed out a five dollar bill. Then he snatched a fistful of trail mix and shoved it into a coat pocket. "Besides, how in fuck's name would you know anything about it, sitting up here hundreds of miles away in this dump of a place?"

"Vamanos, compadre," he said to Diggs, moving off his stool and heading toward the door. "We're going to Green Bay, and what this guy says—and even that shit-pile of an automobile you bought us—isn't gonna get in the way." He went out the door and moved down the short flight of steps to the parking lot.

Diggs sat motionless. Bile welled up in his throat. He stood and struggled putting on his coat, his arm at first entering a hole in the torn lining. He moved toward the door, but paused as he passed the ashtray. He bent and peered into the toothpick log cabin Bozowski had made. The two ends of the toothpick that skewered the bug rested atop two adjacent sides, like a spit for a pig. Beneath was a half-inch mound of broken-off match heads. It wasn't a bug log cabin. It was a bug funeral pyre. Except no one had lit the fire.

He bent down and looked closer. The bug's little legs were still feebly kicking, like it was trying to get somewhere fast, but without traction and going nowhere. Diggs considered taking a paper napkin and pulling the bug off the toothpick. But the thought quickly passed.

It was dark outside now and snow was falling. The old Dodge, covered with a thin coat of flakes, was barely visible against the white of the parking lot. Bozowski had managed to start the Charger's engine. Even idling, a thick plume of oily exhaust floated out the tailpipe. He had the trunk open and was dumping something into a steel dumpster sheltered beneath the tavern.

Diggs paused by the door as he buttoned his coat to the collar, tight against his neck. He turned the collar up and thrust his hands deep into the pockets. Through the small pane of glass in the door, he watched Bozowski's breath emerge in puffs—breath, or cigarette smoke—as he closed the Charger's trunk. He wondered if Green Bay had car washes, and if the steam that emerged from them when a washed car emerged rose and froze in the air like the pulp moisture that rose from the tall stacks of the paper mills. Big frozen puffs of steamy, soapy moisture, rising and then floating away and disappearing.

He paused a few seconds more. Then he pushed the door open and walked out into the night, breathing in the chill air, tinged with faint scents of pine, creosote, and gasoline. □

WINDY CITY SINNERS
Melanie Villines

When the entry bell rang at H&V Dry Cleaners, Virginia Martyniak peered over the rim of her bifocals and saw a man in a black woolen ski mask. It was the middle of May - and even though it had been a cold spring, it wasn't chilly enough for a ski mask. There was only one explanation.

Good God, Virginia thought, not here!

It had been all over the news for the past few months that a man in a ski mask was holding up dry cleaners. But Virginia had never worried—the robberies had happened near Wrigley Field, on the other end of town.

Holy Mary Mother of God, Virginia thought, this is the Far Northwest Side of Chicago - things like this don't happen. All the cops live around here!

"Gimme the cash," the man said, aiming his pistol at her chest.

Virginia tried to comply, but her arthritic right foot had fallen asleep. Dear Jesus, please help me move, she prayed. If I don't give the man the money, he'll think I'm resisting.

Virginia wasn't ready to die. She was sure she had some kind of sin on her soul. She hadn't been to Confession in a good long while. Father Spinelli gave such harsh penances, even for venial sins. But, Virginia wondered, what is sin? Sometimes, there are special circumstances—like now. If I had a gun and killed this man, would I be guilty of murder?

When she finally reached the register, Virginia slammed her hand on the old machine's lever, and the drawer shot open with a ding.

Lord, I can't afford to lose this money, she thought. I worked hard for it. And now this do-nothing just waltzes in and wants to take it from me. Dear God, how can you allow things like this to happen? Is there no justice in this world? But Virginia decided to take this up with God later—for now, she would turn over the mon ey and try to keep from getting shot.

She ripped the bills out of their slots and slid them onto the counter. The man grabbed the wad of cash and crammed it into the pocket of his black leather jacket. When the robber turned to leave, Virginia was glad he was going, happy she was getting rid of him, thrilled that he hadn't harmed her.

But then she saw the man's eyes turn toward Gertrude, her dear Gertrude. The plastic goose sat on a small table behind the counter—along with a brimming box of outfits. Virginia had just dressed the life-sized lawn ornament in a drum majorette's costume.

"Nice bird," the man said, poking the goose's baton with the end of his gun.

"Don't touch her!" Virginia screamed.

She scooped up the hollow goose, stumbled through the shadows to the back of the store, and fumbled with the door. But the man ran after her and wrenched the goose from her arms.

"No, no, no!" Virginia howled.

She kicked the man in the shin and tried to knee him in the groin, but he managed to push her away—knocking Virginia against the back door. Then he skipped to the front of the store, snatched up the box of costumes, stuffed the goose inside, and slid out the front door.

After he left, Virginia kneeled down, pounded her fists on the floor, and moaned, "Gertrude! Gertrude! My baby."

Her whole life, Virginia had longed for a child. She had prayed, gone to doctors—even made a pilgrimage to Lourdes. When Herb gave her the plastic goose a few Christmases ago, Virginia got so caught up in caring for Gertrude that she finally accepted her fate. She would go to her grave a barren woman.

And now Gertrude was gone! Virginia felt her heart shattering like glass. She would never be able to give that much love to another goose—or any other type of lawn ornament or stuffed animal or doll or even dog or cat. No, she had given it all to Gertrude.

"My baby!" Virginia cried out. "Virgin Mary Mother of God, please keep her safe!"

* * *

For a week after the robbery, Virginia wore the same pink-and-white-checked nightgown and stared out the kitchen window at the spot in the backyard where she used to sit with Gertrude.

Herb Martyniak was afraid his wife would never get over the loss. He went to the garden supply store and bought another plastic goose. But Virginia wouldn't even look at it. Herb knew there was only one answer—find Gertrude. But the police weren't about to expend man-power on a case like that.

Herb wished Virginia had a relative or a friend who could come over and comfort her. But Virginia had no parents, no siblings, and no real friends - just passing acquaintanceships with the customers who breezed in and out of the dry cleaners.

Finally, Herb called the rectory. He knew Virginia disliked the pastor, but Herb was desperate - and figured Father Spinelli might have something up his clerical sleeves that could ease Virginia's pain.

* * *

When Father Spinelli arrived in a huff of black robes, Herb stood aside to let him in. As he led the priest to the kitchen, Herb could feel Spinelli's hot glare against his back. This is your job, Herb thought. Don't act like I'm a gravy stain on your satin vestments!

The priest looked at Virginia in her spot by the window, then nodded for Herb to leave the room. Herb grabbed the newspaper from the kitchen table and headed for the backyard, slamming the door behind him.

After Herb left, Father Spinelli pulled up a padded kitchen chair and sat next to Virginia.

"What is bothering you, my child?" the priest asked, even though Virginia was almost twenty years his senior. The priest's words were comforting, but his tone was strident. Virginia picked up on his tone, which echoed inside her head.

Virginia closed her eyes. She heard noises - like a gnashing of teeth. She saw a black whirlpool, then she was looking into a deep pit. She heard weeping and wailing. Then she saw clothes in a gigantic washing machine—she saw them tossing and turning through a large window on the side of the machine. She saw words—names of sins—tumbling around inside the washer. Then she saw dirty water run out of a hose under the machine. The sinful words went down a drain into the ground. The door of the washer opened, and the clothes floated out, as snowy as goose down. The black whirlpool became white. The weeping and wailing and gnashing of teeth were gone, replaced by pleasant sighs.

Virginia opened her eyes and stared at the priest. She saw the word "PRIDE" on his forehead.

"You're suffering from the sin of pride," she said in a flat, matter-of-fact voice.

"What makes you say that?"

"I can see it in your face," she said.

"Virginia," Spinelli said, "I'm here because your husband is very worried about you. He wants me to help."

Virginia knew that scorn for a priest must be one of the worst possible sins. But Spinelli had been no help to her over the years—offering no sympathy when she'd gone to him for counsel about her desire for a child. During her Confessions, when she'd admitted her envy against pregnant women and her anger at God, the priest had lectured her in a prissy voice—and had given her several rosaries each time as penance.

"I don't need your help," she told him. "I have been called by God to do a mighty work."

* * *

Now that Virginia was up and walking around, Herb was careful not to disturb her. She was still acting strange—preoccupied and distant—but at least she was talking, eating, and sleeping. Herb figured he'd just go along with anything she said for a while.

When Virginia told him she intended to change the name of the dry cleaners and buy new signs, Herb knew it was a crazy idea. They couldn't afford new signs. They could barely make the rent each month. Virginia told Herb to cash in their IRAs. The signs would be a good investment, she told him.

After the signs were in place, Virginia returned to work. Over a month had passed since the robbery. The store reopened under its new name on the first day of summer.

The business was now called "Redemption Dry Cleaners." A subtitle under the name said: "Wash your sins away."

* * *

Father Spinelli stood in a line that snaked down the strip mall, waiting for his turn to enter Redemption Dry Cleaners. He couldn't believe it. The absolute gall of the woman—trying to compete head-on with the Catholic Church!

The line crept ahead, inch by slow inch. Many of the people were repeat customers, whose remarks only fueled Spinelli's rage against Virginia.

"I feel like a new man," said an old man with a cane. "Before, I was in a wheel chair. But my anger and other sins have been washed away with each cycle. Soon I won't need this," he said, waving his cane.

"Yes," agreed an elderly woman. "Before I wore thick glasses. Now I am seeing like young girl. Sins are getting cleaned from my soul."

The priest fumed in the long, slow-moving line. The woman is purporting to get rid of sin, he thought. And now she's making people believe that she's working miracles. Plus she is cleaning these people's clothes. How is the Church supposed to compete? We can't offer a practical service such as this. If this keeps up, perhaps she will franchise this operation and put us out of business.

Father Spinelli felt angry, envious, resentful, and many other sinful things as he stood in line. He stuffed a Tums in his mouth as if it were a communion wafer.

When his turn finally arrived, the priest stepped up to the counter and faced Virginia. The woman was aglow - as if she'd found her true calling in life.

"What do you want cleaned, Father?" she asked.

"I do not require your service!" he said, slamming his fist on the counter. "I have come to tell you to cease and desist this sham!"

Virginia was sure the priest needed a long rest at a retreat house. Why should he care about her business? Certainly, a small operation such as hers couldn't be a threat to a huge conglomerate like the Catholic Church.

Spinelli hurled his half-roll of Tums at a huge framed portrait of a goose that hung behind the counter in a sort of altar.

The crowd gasped.

"He's jealous!" a middle-aged woman said.

"Have your jealousy removed!" said another woman.

People in line grabbed the priest and tried to rip off his clerical shirt so Virginia could clean it. But the priest said a quick prayer—Saint Michael the Archangel, defend us in battle!—and managed to pry himself free.

He staggered out of the stifling store, then ran all the way back to the refuge of Saint Francis of Assisi Church.

* * *

Herb believed that Virginia had lost her mind. But he loved her so much, he couldn't bear the thought of putting her away anywhere. Anyway, what harm would her screwball ideas do? She was acting mostly like herself, except for this sin business.

The dry cleaners didn't clean anything on the premises. Herb and Virginia bundled up everything and sent it to a big commercial operation in the suburbs. Still, none of the customers inquired where the clothes were cleaned or how the sins were removed. People accepted the service as if it were just another mysterious sacrament.

Herb's tolerance for Virginia's innovations did not go unrewarded.

In just a month as "Redemption Dry Cleaners," they made as much money as they had cleared the entire previous year.

Location, location, location, Herb thought. What a boon that we're living in such a hotbed of sin. And who knew? ☐

CHICAGO (ARIA)
Susan Hogan

Chicago I sang to you until my voice drifted up
and crammed into the crevices of the Krainik's ornate ceiling,
and I can't get it down. Chicago your eyes look like you think too much.
Chicago will you pay my rent? Otherwise go sink into the lake.
Your furious pigeons fly like torn box kites.

Chicago when will you unroot yourself
from your concrete foundations and fly
across America's graveyards?
When will you be worthy of your Addams and Monroes?
Of your artists subsisting on 312 and potatoes?
Chicago why is the Harold Washington Library red as a ghost's insides?
Chicago you're stuttering under the weight of the animal souls
you've transformed into ghost colored air.

Chicago after all it is you and I tell heaven what is holy.
The cardboard boxes in your warehouses cry out in agony.
Melrose Park made me want to be a Bodhisattva.

What is the point of your madness?
Chicago I can't quit you.

Chicago the ginkgo leaves are rallying on the sidewalk.
I haven't read the *Tribune* in months,
everyday another murder, citizens, murder.
Chicago I ate pizza across from the St. Valentine's Day Massacre.
When I go to Chinatown they lock me in Ping Park.
My friends and I push each other into the river crossing the railway bridge,
or jump to dodge the trains,
or other times climb up and start a new life in that little house.

Chicago I punched a hole through the door after reading Sinclair.
My mind is made up there's going to be fisticuffs.
Chicago I'm a union carpenter's daughter.
My alcoholic mother thinks I'm disgraceful.
I won't repeat Sandburg's poems.

I smoked hookah on my friend's Logan Square porch
until she moved to the Middle East.
I sit in my apartment and stare out the window at a brick wall.

Chicago when will you unroot yourself
from your concrete foundations and fly
across America's graveyards?

Chicago why is the Harold Washington Library red as a ghost's insides?
Chicago you're stuttering.
I can still hear them lowing.

I can still hear them lowing, citizens,
they look at the ground with their miraculous eyes.
I'm a disgrace at good vodka introductions, spilling everything, citizens,
and jumping off bridges.
I won't repeat Sandburg's poems to cats who spit at that man.
Chicago you look fat in those jeans.

Everyone in this city has money but me.
It occurs to me that I am Chicago.
Am I talking to myself again?

I'd better consider my natural resources.
My resources consist of two bottles of GNC vitamins six ex-boyfriends
three ex-girlfriends
an unpublishable manuscript lamenting/celebrating you
and the dent in the wall where I keep banging my head, citizens,
against my, citizens, head.

The empty teacups accumulate on my desk for weeks.
I have freed the penguins from the Lincoln Park Zoo,
the sea lion at the Shedd is next.

Chicago when I was nine daddy took me
to a Monet exhibit at the Art Institute

we wouldn't have gone except somebody'd bought him the tickets
the paintings were colored with angelic light and I had no idea
how much my father liked art, my father who came home at night
smelling like sawdust and beer but who always kissed my forehead
and that was when I realized that art wasn't something above me
that my father and beer liked art.

Am I talking to myself again?
Bike lanes are blowing kisses to the environment.
Community gardens are blowing kisses
to the environment, citizens, blow.
The environment catches one of the kisses, citizens,
squished in a fist and puts it in its pocket.
Chicago what did we fight for in Haymarket Square?
Chicago the old gangster movies told me the truth.
Chicago are you even paying attention?
I'll lay it out for you.
It's true I don't want to get a Ph.D. or push the same button
all day in an agricultural supply factory,
I'm impulsive and explosive anyway.
Chicago I'm putting my queer shoulder against yours.

SPLINTERS
Micki LeSueur

Sarah found Peter at his worktable, hunched over the tiny figurine he viewed through a mounted magnifying glass the size of a saucer. He held his breath as he brushed red on the figurine's lips in tiny, precise movements. The surgical-quality lamp that lit his work also showed every detail of Peter's face: the patches of stubble missed during his morning shave; reckless dark hairs sprouting from his nose and standing upright from his brows; a pill of brown mustard in the corner of his mouth.

"You know I don't like to be disturbed when I'm working," Peter said, eyes on the figure.

Sarah walked over to the desk and picked up the lamp, feeling the balance of the heavy base on one end and the delicate bulb on the other. The plug pulled loose from the outlet as she walked over to the table where Peter's miniature world was displayed, a near-exact replica of town, painstakingly recreated over countless hours.

Sarah lifted the lamp and struck the base against the tiny Carson's True Value hardware store. The postage stamp-sized paper banners declaring *Glidden Interior Paint $8.99 a gallon!* shredded from the broken glass of the windows on which they were mounted. She brought the lamp down again and again on the Safeway, fractured balsa wood and resin shingles raining debris on the miniscule minivans and shopping carts in the perfectly scaled parking lot. Then she struck the DeLite's Café, a massacre of waiters, patrons and furniture on the patio.

After a moment of disbelief, Peter reached out to grab her arm and Sarah swung the base at Peter's head, knocking him to the floor. The trickle of blood from the cut on his forehead a match to the paint on the brush still in his hand.

Sarah continued her path of destruction, decimating the post office, the high school, the football field and bleachers. The neighborhoods on the west side, east side, and north end, all with their trimmed lawns, freshly painted clapboard siding, porch swings, gardens and decks. Then the post office, Hobby Lobby, McDonald's, and the Radio Shack, everything splinters and shards.

Finally, the church, with Peter in his tux standing at the door, and

Sarah in her gown standing in the courtyard, perfect versions of themselves. And their house, that looked precisely like the real one, right down to the light that could always be seen burning through the window of Peter's workroom. All beyond repair.

Five years of Peter's life gone, in the blink of an eye. Five years of Sarah's life gone, second by second, minute by minute, hour by hour.

Sarah put down the lamp and strode past Peter who was dabbing at the cut on his forehead with a solvent-soaked rag. "I just wanted to let you know," she said, walking out the workroom door, "I'm leaving." ☐

BROTHERS
Robert Kerwin

My brother Raymond and I were in our pajamas, prodding through the crib's bars, playing with our new baby brother, Jerome.

We were just getting to know Jerome; then Jerome wasn't there anymore. According to my mother, there'd been something "radically wrong" with Jerome from the day he came from the hospital after she'd had him. The doctors told my mother and father that Jerome was better off dead, that if he had lived he would have been blind or crazy.

I couldn't work that out — what it would be like to have a brother who was blind; you'd have to lead him by the hand everywhere he went. Having a crazy brother would be even worse. You'd never know what he was going to do next; he might even throw a fit some day and jump out the window. No. Even though I missed Jerome, I was glad he was gone, in a way; he was better off dead, the doctor had told my mother, and it was better for all of us that Jerome died and went to heaven.

There was no wake or funeral for Jerome, no friends and neighbors coming by to pay respects. There was no casket for him in our living room, either, and no heaped flowers. No. All I remember is that Jerome was there with us one day, Raymond and I playing with him through the bars of his crib, and the next day he was gone. The crib gone too, and Raymond and I had our bedroom again all to ourselves.

* * *

My father is going down the alley on the way to work, and my mother is holding Raymond and me up to the window to wave goodbye.

Raymond was six then, I was four.

That same afternoon we were playing in the back yard, and my mother was up above getting supper ready. "You two stay where you are until I call you," she shouted over the porch railing. "Keep an eye out for your father. When you see him coming up the alley, let me know."

A boy came along the alley with a canvas sack slung on his shoulder. He stopped at our gate and said to Raymond: "Come with me on my route, help me deliver."

My mother had warned us never to leave the back yard — under any circumstances — and until that day we'd never left. I was afraid to, I didn't want to disobey.

After a glance to the kitchen window, Raymond climbed over the fence and went off with the boy. As he was leaving, Raymond — for the first time ever— didn't look like my brother anymore; it was as if he no longer cared about me, or hardly knew I existed. Off they went, he and the boy, receding down the alley; at the corner, they turned, and disappeared.

I stayed by the fence, feeling guilt for what my brother had done, and afraid of what might happen to him — and me, too — when my mother found out he was gone.

Soon she came onto the porch, and called: "Come on, boys, inside with you now — supper."

When I didn't answer, she called again. Then, after a dreadful pause, my mother leaned over the rail, suspiciously, and said in a curious singsong: "Where's Raymond?"

"He went with the boy."

"What boy?"

"The boy who sells magazines."

My mother bolted down the stairs and took hold of my arm. "Where did they go?" she shouted. "When?"

She yanked me off my feet, held me under one of her arms, and with the other bumped open the gate, then rushed into the alley. "Which way?" she cried. Her face and hair had gone wild, she was growing more frenzied by the second as we raced along, her searching behind garbage cans and over fences into one back yard after another. "Raymond!" she called out. "O, Raymond!"

To me it seemed only moments later that my father appeared in the alley, and from then on my memory is a jumble of intense, agitated rushing and pushing, me scared to death as I was juggled from one of my father's arms to the other, lifted high again and again ashe displayed me, held me up in front of him, thrusting and waving me, like a monstrance or a doll, into one shocked face after another.

We scramble onto a porch, my father's fist bangs on the door, the door opens, he thrusts me into their faces: "Do you know this boy? Do you know him?" Sometimes an entire family comes to the door, and my father hoists me higher, close into their startled faces. Then, still holding me aloft, my father turns and bumps down the stairs, and we cross a lawn and sprint up the stairs of the next house, onto the next porch, and the next, banging on one door after another all along our block, and into the block beyond, and the block beyond that.

It's almost suppertime, everybody is at home in all the houses. I smell the suppers cooking as the families open their doors to us: women wiping their hands on their aprons, men in shirtsleeves with the evening newspaper, children hunching behind. "What is it?" somebody says to my father. "What's the matter?"

"Do you know this boy?" my father cries, thrusting me. "Do you know him?"

Some of the women nod Yes, yes, we know him.

"And his brother?" my father says. "Have you seen his brother?"

Face after face, door after door, negative head shakes, and eyes which turn sad and follow us as we bump down the porch stairs to the sidewalk, and stumble to the next house, and the next.

By the time we got back to our flat it was getting dark outside, and I was set down into one of our kitchen chairs like a prop.

* * *

Two days later I stood alone at our kitchen window, searching down the alley for my mother. O, I wasn't completely alone, even though I felt I was; two girls were there in the flat, looking after me. My father was at work and my mother was at the hospital.

The girls were doing a school project at our kitchen table. "Isn't this amazing?" one girl said. "You put a record in the oven, and it comes out soft, you can form it into any shape you want."

Holding dishtowels, the girls took the heated records out of the oven, set them onto the sink, and after the records had cooled, they picked them up to show me: "See?" said one girl. "You can mold the record, shape it into a bowl, or a vase, or anything you want."

I stayed by the window.

Finally I saw my mother coming along the alley, and my heart leaped. I was so thrilled to see her, and relieved that she'd actually come back, hadn't gone away forever. Also I was bursting with anticipation for news about my brother.

As soon as my mother was in the door, I rushed her: "Is Raymond better today?"

"About the same."

"When is he coming home?"

"Not sure."

My mother wasn't very old then, but when I'd see her appear, far down to where the alley narrows, her hair didn't look like her own; it was gray now, and straggly, blowing about.

After a few days at the window that's who I looked for: not the mother I knew, or had known always, but a new mother: a harried gray-haired figure in a black coat, a strange mother trudging the alley, with her head down. Every afternoon, from the window I studied my mother as she plodded toward home. For the first time in my life I felt sorry for my mother, and considered myself to be more in control of things than she was.

Day after day, as she came in, I said, "How is Raymond? When is he coming home?"

"Maybe tomorrow, maybe the day after. We'll have to wait and see."

"See what?"

"See what the doctor says."

"When can I visit Raymond?"

"Pretty soon. We'll see."

This went on for twelve days. On the thirteenth day, Raymond died.

* * *

"He hadn't a mark on him," a woman was saying.

I was buried in amongst them, roaming my way from room to room of our flat: out to the kitchen, then back in to the front again, then back out through the hallway again to the kitchen. I couldn't find my mother and father anywhere. I just kept wandering, smiling up into the faces of strangers, the strangers smiling down to me; now and then someone I'd never seen before leaned in and gave me a sad little kiss on the cheek. Some strangers lifted me off my feet, hugged me, smothering me in their perfumed, fleshy folds. Over and over I was discovered by somebody and lifted high onto display, or I was taken by the hand and escorted around by other strangers, tears in their eyes as they pulled me along, me in my little white suit and white sandals.

I looked up into the eyes of our neighbors, the same sympathetic eyes I'd looked into only a few evenings before as my father and I bumped onto their porches, and banged on their doors.

I wandered around, tunneling in and out beneath people's legs. Many of them didn't even see me, or know I was there.

I wormed my way to the casket, which was set against our living room wall. It was a tiny casket, with folds of white satin. I stood there for a while, taking deep breaths of the aroma from the flowers banked all around.

Our living room being crowded like that reminded me of when my mother and father had company, a party; but here people were quiet and subdued. No drinking, singing, or dancing. My mother had muted the pink-colored flambeaux on our walls, and my brother was lying there in his casket all dressed up, like a little prince. Right in our living room: my brother, wearing his white suit and white shoes, a bank of flowers surrounding him.

A woman came, took me under the shoulders, and lifted me. She was crying as she held me just above my brother in his casket, then lowered me to his pale face. Raymond didn't look very much like the brother I knew — or had known. "There now," the woman said. "Kiss your brother goodbye."

Even though I searched through our whole flat — parlor, hallway, bedrooms, and out in the kitchen — there was no sign of my mother's relatives. Not one. I couldn't understand it. Everyone else was there — one of my father's brothers even had come in on a train all the way from California. But none of our South Side relatives showed up.

Raymond died in the summer, maybe that's why. They were on vacation. Every year the aunts, uncles and cousins on my mother's side went to Paw Paw Lake or Powers Lake. I'm sure they'd heard about my brother — they must have — but they stayed on their vacation, anyway. I don't know why, and I never found out why.

* * *

During the week after the funeral, I learned what had happened to my brother. First he and the boy with the magazines went down to Addison by the El, then headed over to Ashland, where Raymond was hit by a car. The driver was an old man, who, when he realized what he'd done, pulled to the curb, lifted my brother off the street, carried him to a nearby gas station, dragged him to the grease pit, laid him on the concrete, then took blankets that mechanics drape over car hoods, tucked my brother under them, and drove away.

A woman walking by had jotted down the plate number.

The man had no driver's license; he told police the car belonged to a friend.

(Years later, when I asked my father why they hadn't pressed charges, he said, "The man was old, and we were heartsick; we'd had enough.")

* * *

During the thirteen days that Raymond was in the hospital, I don't know if he ever woke up, or smiled, or said anything to anybody. I don't know whether my mother tried to talk to him, either.

Every day after work my father went to the hospital, too.

Anyway, that was the end of Byron Avenue, and — for the time being, at least — the end of life for us on the north side. ☐

THE WALKER
R. Craig Sautter

JT figured it this way. He was walking for a living. He'd heard of fellows who walked from New York and that big old Atlantic of the east coast all the way to the Pacific Palisades of sunsets. They were walking for this cause or another: lost mothers, sisters, sons, cancer, muscular dystrophy, to end hunger, stop gang violence, stand up to police brutality, who knew all of it? The world was so large, but JT only knew a few who suffered or were cured of these maladies, although millions of bucks were collected in donations, he noticed.

"No," JT said, "I've walked for myself, every day, but Sundays, all day, nine am to nine pm, working twelve hours a day in the beating sun, hard blown wind, ripping ice storms, bitter cold, raw spring rains, and more, for five long damn years."

He wondered how far he had walked. He kept track at first, then he forgot, and then he didn't care. Who would he tell? But, he figured at three miles per hour, which was what he probably averaged with stops and exchanges and such, three miles per hour times twelve hours per day equaled thirty-six miles per day, six days per week equaled 216 miles per week, times fifty-two weeks a year equaled 11,232 long miles, for about five years equaled 56,160 miles in the service of his own noble cause. That was walking across the United States almost nineteen times. But he didn't see no one writing newspaper stories about him. Besides, that wasn't the point.

"Thank you." He smiled at a woman in her late thirties as she lowered and then raised her window. He slipped the money into his pocket.

"The point is, what's it mean to me? I once figured I get ten bucks an hour, quarters and bills. So that times twelve hours equals $120 a day, times six days totals $720 a week. Not so hot, but that's what I got, times fifty-two weeks becomes $37,440 per year, and the government don't get none of it. That ain't half bad and it's twice as good as starving."

"But that's not the point. The point is I walk for a living, so how much do I make a mile?"

"Yes, sir. I appreciate it. I'm looking. I'm looking. No luck!"

"Hang in there, brother." The pickup driver tossed a bill back as the light changed.

JT pushed it deep into his pocket. "Well, I already said that I make ten dollars an hour, and as I said, I also make three miles an hour with all the chatter with some of the drivers waiting for lights, time off to visit the nearby woods to take a leak, and then maybe to scarf down a sandwich in the supermarket parking lot where I park my old beat up Ford Taurus. That is about $3.33 per mile. But no supervisor, no deadlines, no punch clock, no fear of getting fired. I just have to worry about holding the spot. That's why it's got to be twelve hours almost every day. I guess just like Taurus, I'm a bull who took my failures and charged ahead. I could've checked out after the accident, after Joan died that way, after I became an outcast, after the pain pills were my main motivator, when everybody else quit on me."

"Why don't you get a job, man? You're always in this damn intersection. I should run you down. You're bumming me out,"

"Blessed are the meek for they shall inherit the earth," he smiled, in a fake beatific way that drove the guy wacky.

"Don't give me any of that religious B.S. Am I going to have to get out of this car and beat the crap out of you?" The man threw his transmission into park and reached down to pull out an undersized baseball bat, souvenir of some game promotion.

JT caught sight of the lathed and polished wood, the size of an old police baton, and stopped counting miles and dollars. He stepped back, which he occasionally had to do, dodging this or that, but had no time to recollect how many honest miles he'd lost that way, at least one or two in all these five years here.

He un-shuffled the second of the three signs he carried for select missions from the middle of his small deck, the one that read: "Feed the hungry, tend to the poor. You will be rewarded!" He thought he had read that somewhere in the Bible when he was a kid, or maybe he heard it in church, back when he was a regular, in other words, a distant memory. But in these last seven years he had come to believe it completely, and now shared what little he made when he could. He had so much to make up for, so much to be forgiven for.

But the sign about not having a "Job" and needing "Help" on the bottom of the three sign deck he carried wasn't quite accurate. Although he had had many jobs, from teen mill worker to hamburger flipper to manager of a successful fast food middleman distribution company owned by Joan's uncle, he'd been fired plenty of times, too. And he really hadn't had any real job in seven years, ever since he got drunk at that Saturday night country club dance and plowed into a Mercedes SUV on Route 13, injuring Joan, the wife he loved so much, who died later that next morning in the hospital emergency room, with all the chloroform smells, blinding white lights, weeping and sirens, rushing doctors and nurses.

And it wasn't as true about needing "Help" now as it had been. Thirty-seven grand a year, tax-free, at least let him get a small apartment about three miles *away* from this shopping center intersection he worked, allowed him to get a small TV, and do his laundry every week, eat solid, although mostly alone, except when he ate with Karen, who he met in the complex laundry room and chatted up once when he was really lonely. She cashiered at K-Mart in the opposite direction. He didn't think she knew what he did for a living and all he could tell her was, "I work independently and am outside a lot talking to clients." That was a funny way of putting it, but that's how he put it, like he was a professional of some kind. There it was again, the sin of vanity.

He stumbled back another step, felt a crack across his shoulder and winced in pain. "God damn parasite," he heard the guy scream. JT dropped his signs. Horns all around them were blasting away. The light turned green and drivers were yelling at them. He saw, through a sudden gush of tears, the grains of wood swinging again, coming down on his forehead, felt it slice like the steel that had shattered her side door as the SUV hood smashed through and cut to her heart to her lungs that last day either of them had lived, felt his skull crumble like one of her finely crafted ceramic bowls crashing on concrete. ☐

CLASS NOTES
Gary Houston

S cott Cornelius came out, he writes, "to myself and close relatives" in 2010, The Year of the Tea Party, and "to" us, via the alumni magazine, only now, which just might be in The Year of the Coming Out. I don't know why he spared us those three years, but I want to know why they let Jason Collins hog all the publicity.

I remember in the widowed Mrs. Josefson's boarding house on Blessings Street, four of us stayed during '66-'67—me, Russ King, Hudson Owen and Scott. Hudson and I were a class below the other two. On his first day Scott discarded horizontal sleep as a non-necessity and stood his bed on end against a wall. He slept with Kantian intermittence in a chair—thirty minutes study, ten minutes snooze, thirty minutes study, etc.—day after day and I guess each after each of his four Brewster years. He reportedly wrote the longest senior thesis in the history of The College of Brewster (on Nepal, his specialty to this day though he never visited), and his advisers were not necessarily grateful for the work cut out for them.

Scott was next to me in Gunnar Shull's exhilarating (I jest) class on political models and modalities, and I recall that during William Sloane Coffin's memorable visit to our campus and our mandatory Chapel he also stood before us in that very classroom. Understanding cursorily what our course was all about, he introduced most of us to the name and philosophy of Pierre Teilhard de Chardin S.J., who wrote about global and even cosmic consciousness in ways suggesting hope for peace and for mankind. Coffin said he himself subscribed to these themes, which in fairness let's say played well in the Sixties, and called for questions.

"You certainly have shown us a very pretty, a very attractive vision," said the first questioner, who hadn't bothered to raise his hand and who was Scott. "And of course it is *all very fine in theory* [italics mine for a reason I'll give shortly], but it is naïve and impractical, and it is short on facts. In fact it is devoid of them."

All during high school none of my arguments with my dad (basically, young liberal vs. Greatest Generation conservative) transpired without his favorite interjection, "all very fine in theory," which he drew, as the saying goes, like a knife. So its use by an undergraduate refuting a minister about twenty years older, even a known radical minister, seemed cheeky. Especially from a kid with an out of fashion crew cut conforming to a round skull (a look rather like Curly Howard's) and a hick accent. But along with the hick accent was a dry wheeze, which lent Scott not only an odd authority but age and what today we'd call gravitas. Pat Buchanan has that and I imagine he did when he was in college.

Well, heavens, I don't know Brewster now except it remains committed to calling itself The College of..., but back then it teemed with such men. They lacked sexual knowledge and sometimes self-knowledge but even so acted middle-aged, crusty and in some ways you could say wanted to be Somerset Maugham as portrayed by Herbert Marshall if, to accommodate Scott, a hick Herbert Marshall was conceivable. Brewster teemed with them, yet still Scott was in a league all his own.

After they debated for a time permanently stolen from our lives, Coffin checked his watch and with a relief he failed to hide announced he was due to stand before another class, hopefully one with naïve kids in it with dreams of saving the world.

So now I connect that Scott of old with the one who in 2010 came out "to" himself and close relatives and cannot but think that the latter category includes a woman of, he says, "three decades of marriage." It seems that that Scott of old endured a terribly long time, far too long before deciding that a marriage is all very fine in theory. Easy to say in hindsight, but for self-knowledge's sake I think he should have given beds a chance. □

BLINDFOLDED MAO
Steve Cejtin

M ao can't see that his revolution has stagnated to a post
modern consumer state where nets need to be erected
to stop suicides at factory dormitories where the workers pause between shifts making iPhones for the foreign imperi-
alists like us.

POPE EYES
Steve Cejtin

T hat sense that someone is watching you when you walk down the isle toward the altar at St. Peters in Rome: is it the Swiss Guard, his Holiness, or the main man himself?

TUBES 2
Steve Cejtin

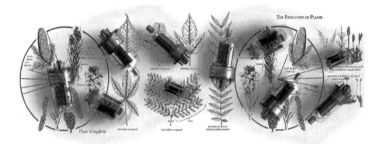

I t seems that technology and nature may have been more in sync in the analogue era.

GUMBALL WORLD
Steve Cejtin

 ometimes the planet seems to be in the hands of those who would treat it as merely another object for immediate gratification.

A FAMILY STORY
Michael Miner

Sur Boulevard Raspail, chez tante,
Before the kaiser's fine verstand
Caused death to open wide and quaff
Nine million to
its maw,

In France's blissful summer heat
On cushions at my great-aunt's feet
They learned, the children Romanoff,
"Attendez-vous"
was law.

They came that year but not again.
And was her teaching all in vain?
How served the tongue of M. Voltaire
Against the ruby claw?

Tell me, you vile and godless Red
your steel at Anastasia's head,
With her last nip of Russian air
Did she ask you
"Pour-quoi?"?

TO A DAUGHTER WHO WILL VISIT SPAIN
Michael Miner

They endure, those old portraits of young soldiers. They look good,
Staring resolutely out at pale hands busy under a black hood
Raising a tray of powder. Breast and bellows froze together
And forevermore that moment of surging blood and leather
Gives this woody anteroom its manliness.
The women tend the dust. They primp the flowers. They think
   themselves no less
For doing so long without. Could it be they feel relieved
At passing blandly through the age when they'd have grieved
Otherwise, when an old gentleman's mouthful of fine heat
Goes whoosh! and cold air spills in from the street?
Only the widow knows, when it's all come out the same,
If she'd rather dust under an old face in a new frame.
You'll see few of those.

TOWARD TRIESTE
Michael Miner

Furrows where lace should be,
round precipices
where his fingers and face
should be sewing his kisses.
Wanting his belly,
all muscle and trim.
Wanting the jelly
I can badger off him.
Jelly and ice cream,
crusts sugared and flat.
Between memory and dream
floats the thick, custard fat.

And the wet heat licks
the family bible in my lap.
The preening bus swigs us
to impress a sullen night
and the cooling spit
washes us in dirt.
    Oh, darling
    I am sick.
I burn with a cold fire
stronger than thought;
it eats my truth
out of the lie
and I collapse

into silent narcissistic lips.
    Give a damn night.
    Give a damn.
Bend me your back.
Cup your endless empty eyes
and hold me until I know I'm known.
I'm finger painting circles on the moon.
    Four days.
Put something in me.

Touch me the touch
That heals this hollow pain.
    Four days.
I must be pure;
yet it's clenched beneath my skirt
like the casket of a compromise.
I rot
within a skin
eternal as the crystal
of a bee
in silent bark.
My throat thinks it is crying.
    Give a damn.

Up there on the luggage rack
ripens his chemistry set of flesh
for starving children.
    Sausage, bread, and cheese.
No wonder the bellies
of dying babies are huge.
The bellies have swallowed the brains,
Broken the minds and souls
Into dumb dead meat
Senseless as thighs.
    Darling. Eat.
    It's yours. My treat.
    Enjoy.
And darling, let me chew
your fleshy sweet pale arm
of sausage, bread, and cheese.
I am a cannibal you know.
Shriveling to grace I eat
My sixty pounds of me and squat it out
In scented crypts. These puffy
Yugoslavians might make me run.
And are they Christian? I don't know.

So I'll just eat around your precious soul.
I know where it is.
Look dear,
we're what we eat so why
don't we eat what we are?
I'm you you know.
This is your fat,
not mine.
Where are we now?
Go join the other dogs
sticking their noses through
the pigs' fence. Ahh, the goldenness
of midnight, beer, and piss.
Take care my love.
Oh dear, you haven't got a dinar for these boys
Who want to buy some bread!
Nor I.

So let the urchins starve.
I hope they do it philosophically,
freezing a bit and thinking of parents
staring across an empty field of corn
and crying to a smiling
child of ice.

Furrows where lace should be
soft precipices
where his fingers and face should be
sewing his kisses.
Where a warm tiny place should be
This is.

It seems as if my whole life
Is this night.
When I sit absolutely calm
and think only that I am

after all, not young,
the pain gives me myself to hold
the way I once rolled down
my green and gentle hill
to feel my bruises gather in a gown.
When we ask what we need
where do we start?
With bread?

He settles back disconsolate.
Why?
Good God, if there's some trouble, dear,
I'll chew on that. Aw, what shame,
You found your dinar, bought a roll,
Were seen. (*You filthy Yank!*)

    No!
Let them both stay Communist.
The hell with them!
                    You can't!
You can't. It's my food too.
We bought it just for you
And I was happy when you ate.
It was my gift. You let me
Choose the sausage.
Coward.

Is any left?
Give me the bag!
Give me the knife!
Give me the knife
or I'll use my hands!

I do not speak your language.
Your touch is only odors.
Wolves raised me and wolves taught me

and I truly cannot tell you what I am
but somewhere I am howling in disgust
I don't know where.
Howling contempt, curled against a rock
while voices close in, hiding behind lights,
weaving voices, sickly as this bus,
and great white square
rational smiling lights
and I spring by them
scratching at the stars.

The stars are only leaves.
I want to stand on the clouds
And drink their dew.
I want their tears.
Their tears are mine.
Heaven isn't far.
It's where we crawl off to and touch
the wounds that will not heal on earth.

The living and the dying things
are passing in the night.
I don't know what to follow.
I don't know what is right,
and nothing
absolutely nothing
    nothing
is in sight,
         except
this hungry thing I am
gnawing silently.
Oh Christ! It's begun again!
It's in me. It's in me.

DANCING IN THE ABATTOIR
Olga Domchenko

They remember the night you danced half naked wearing only your tawdry underclothes. Underneath was what? Raging burning flesh for something no longer there. Like an oom pah pah band gone mad. Organ grinder burning the machine and his monkey in vain.

You said that you hated Thelonious Monk. That ruined you in his eyes right off. There was nothing left after that. Even though you may have redeemed yourself just a bit… with that piece of Miles Davis.

The only thing you have left that's authentic is the cold. Your rooms are icy cold. Icier than the Arctic in winter. Your floors are smooth as pearls and icicles cling between your toes. This place is icier than all the castles in Scotland. No tea left even to warm your frozen gut.

Each day you wake up and walk on ice. So cold it burns your feet. You are like the Indian firewalkers but no one gave you lessons.

You do not need lessons to walk on fire. You walk through raging flames each and every day and in the evening cool yourself off at the birdbath with that noisy blue jay.

The fever you calm down with your own hands. It's embarrassing to meet anyone. They always think you're dead.

Your body is finally clean. Empty of all food. Gorge spit then throw it all away. There is nothing left to defile now. Not even a crumb. Now you can breathe. As much as you like and there is nothing to get in the way.

Is that why the little host was so wet? I almost threw it up. It was soft and tasted of real bread. Some child was allowed to make it with their grubby little hands. It tasted of snot. Warm as fuzzy yeast. Mouthful of maggots. I almost laughed. What should you do then? Spit it out?

I walked down the aisle trying to hide my amused horror. Could they tell? Was that a smirk on my face?

The leaves fall down like shimmering gold coins and then they turn to blood. The grass is still so green but autumn will not cool down.

When will it come finally, the hush of first snow? Sometime deep in the night it will start falling and snatch you from your dreams. Like a sleepwalker you will go to the window and the rapture will begin, as the universe starts to breathe, and you will hear like tiny wheels the earth manufacture itself anew.

Each snowflake a thousand silences.

These people cannot stand silence. Or empty space. They catch the falling leaves with demons who roam the streets with long whips that scream throughout each birthing season.

They say the moon is too bright. It bleaches their rooms and they sizzle like raw steaks in their beds.

Early in the morning I have to go there. I walk through the swinging white door like the room to a surgery ward and am greeted by the smell of pure, raw, wet death. Though everything is wiped down with bleach and sanitizer, the room reeks of dead cow. Blood is everywhere. The steaks and livers and rumps and skin and bone and gizzards and the snot on the butchers hands. My stomach growls with the pain of that smell and my nose almost falls off my face.

It is an upscale abattoir, when you turn left there are rows of green pistachios and organic crackers.

I wipe things down with meat market rags. They are white. "Oh I thought she was off the rag," says the butcher, smirking through his designer glasses perched on his little upturned Irish nose. Wince. He dreams of blood every night. Chickens, goats and pigs, he roasts them all outside the front door, to bring the people in to the raging fires of the sacrifice. The goat looks so thin, emaciated, like he walks on piles of construction debris. Smells of Styrofoam and plastic.

They like things very thin. "Thin!" she shrieks. "I want it thin. But not shaved." I move the sharp knives back and forth back and forth and the meat falls into a frothy pile of translucent skin, like your shredding back, a pile of dead roses. Just enough meat to sink your pearly white teeth in.

The little toilet in the back is where they come to relieve themselves. Mostly piss. It smells sweetly sick, pink like piglets. Syrupy soap and tepid water to clean the stink off.

The well groomed lady in the designer jogging suit, her long ponytail swishing like a horse's tail swatting flies, stays in the bathroom a long time because she really has to go, but can't position her large body well enough to avoid touching things, can't avoid smelling things that stink. The abattoir next door is at least bleached.

Come and taste the soups. Yes we have soup made fresh every day. They are made from many hands pulling apart old chickens no one will buy. Sometimes a piece of rubbery grizzled skin gets in. Must boil it down turn the gas up high. Pure schmaltz like New York delicatessen. They think it's so good like Mama's and they pour it into little plastic cups and clutch it like the Holy Grail as they sample Annie's homemade gluten free cookies.

I too eat meat. Turkey, salami, pastrami, corned beef, pale white chickens, speckled with tiny blue veins and violet bruises. Perfect ballotines infused with precious sea salts, pepper, oils and exotic spices.

The one with the walrus moustache like Bismarck, he teaches disadvantaged children in Uptown, has a son in Mongolia, and likes to watch serial killer movies. He adores the bloody roast beef but only eats unblemished chicken. "What's that"? He winces at the slice of bird in front of his nose for inspection. A tiny little vein. "That makes me sick," he says, asking if I can make it go away. I slice through half the bird before the blue thing finally disappears like an inky drawing smudged by the rain. I offer him the final pieces, pure white and blemish free like faces in a magazine.

He finally leaves and famished I take the pile of meat from the top of the garbage can and eat it.

They all look like meat. Red-faced cherubs. Wish they would go and hunt their own.

Wish they would try to lift up all the pigs and cows and sheep and horses I have to lift up to the slicer. The greedy, sharp blades moving through the dense tightly woven flesh and cutting it into paper. Goes right to the bloodstream, makes them strong, stronger than bulls, raging bulls gorging on human flesh. What fun if only once a year. That bull he got three this time.

They don't know yet, but next year it's their turn to dance. ☐

RITUAL FIRE DANCE
Brian Allan Skinner

an ekphrasis

I want to set fire to my life,
burn it to the ground,
dance around the flames,
smear my skin with ashes.

I want to kick through the char,
stomp on the embers,
make sure nothing remains
that's not been refined.

I want to drift up like smoke,
twining, curling:
Dervish pirouettes,
nowhere and everywhere.

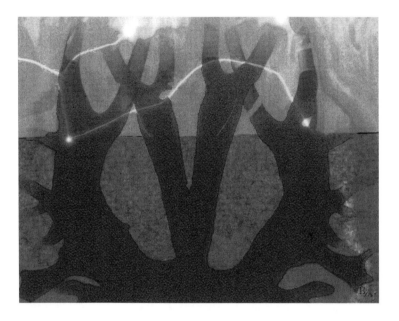

NOT MANY TREES OUT THERE ON PEACHTREE STREET
J. Weintraub

The first time his resume appeared on my desk, I slipped it into the doubtful file along with those from the burnt-out school-teachers, the newly minted M.B.A.'s, and the copywriters whose careers reached back to Spiegel and Montgomery Ward.

Two weeks later, with the job still open, I received another one. This time I penciled a red question mark on the upper-right-hand corner and passed it on to my Staff Director with several other possibilities from the second round. When Florence called me into her office a few hours later, his was on the top of the pile.

"Why the question mark?" she asked. "He looks perfect. Far more experienced than the kids we interviewed yesterday."

"I think we'd be wasting our time. He seems overqualified, and he probably wouldn't be interested once he heard the salary."

"You sound like you know him."

"Not personally, but he's something of a literary celebrity around here. At least to those who read little reviews and write poetry."

"I don't know anything about little reviews," said Florence, "but if he writes poetry, he probably needs the cash. Call him in."

I arranged for an interview the next day. Professional associations like ours expect its staff to fill many roles, and now that our Personal Finance Division had decided to spin off a line of manuals from its program materials, we needed someone who would perform all the functions of a small publishing house at a relatively modest wage. From his resume—which listed a score of editing, production, and copywriting jobs with McGraw-Hill, Bradford Exchange, and the like –I had no doubt that Bud Holloway could turn raw manuscripts into books and sell them to our C.P.A.'s. But this was Bud Holloway, and being able to afford him was the least of my concerns.

* * *

A profile of Holloway, which had appeared some years before in the *Tribune's* "Book Talk" supplement, had characterized him as "ursine," although when he lumbered into our office, he reminded me more of an overgrown teddy bear than, say, an Alaskan grizzly. Tall and pot-bellied, he had the flat face of a football lineman in the days before facemasks. But his cheekbones were as prominent as Jim Thorpe's, and these and the tip of his nose were colored bright red as if he had been hurrying into the blustery wind off of Lake Michigan to arrive on time for his interview. The wind also seemed to have disheveled his thin, graying hair and slackened the knot of his tie, and his brown loafers were not well matched with his blue blazer and gray trousers. But an indifference to appearance is not unusual among editors, to say nothing of poets, and as he spread his weight across the breadth of his chair, self-confidence gradually replacing his initial jitters, he soon impressed both Florence and me with his intelligence and publishing expertise. In fact, as one anecdote—stretching all the way back into the era of linotype and address-o-graphs—followed another, I began to feel like a green apprentice sitting at the foot of a master craftsman.

Almost from the moment he left the office, Florence asked me to make him an offer. "Unless you still have some doubts," she said, and then I handed her the *Tribune* profile that I'd copied at the library the previous night.

Referring to Holloway as "a veteran combatant on the Midwestern literary barricades," the article praised him as one of the leaders of the *"fauve-naïf"* school of poetry and prose, which several years before had been "at the very avant of the avant-garde." Yet although the movement had now "passed into the passé," Holloway was still considered a "major player" as the editor and publisher of *Shout*, a literary review celebrated for having published the early work of Brautigan and Bukowski, the later prose poems of Nelson Algren, and almost all of Mike Banacek's notorious *Under Wacker Drive* cycle. Although its "fire and spark" had faded in recent years and its financial support was "precarious," *Shout* was still highly regarded as "a resilient survivor among a decidedly ephemeral breed," and its editor was praised as "a refreshing throwback, a renegade known to have refused government grants on principle." I was also pleased to learn that Holloway still personally commented on most of the manuscripts he received. (Although I hadn't submitted my own poetry to *Shout* in some years, I remember having been encouraged by the handwritten notes attached to the rejection slips.)

"So?" said Florence, returning the article to me.

I replied that it might be risky to hire the renegade editor of a struggling experimental literary review, a *fauve-naïf* combatant on the literary barricades, to handle the publishing affairs of an association of accountants, particularly since the members of his review board were conservative in taste, edgy about budgets, and suspicious of eccentricity or show.

"He didn't strike me as being particularly eccentric," said Florence, "and he seems to be enough of a professional to keep his hobbies separate from his working relationships."

"Still, if he accepts the job," I argued, "it might be safer to turn it into more of an in-house position. I could handle the meetings and most of the member contact."

"No," said Florence. "The Personal Finance Division is underwriting half his salary, and they like to see what they're paying for. We'll both attend the Winter Meeting in Atlanta next month to introduce him to the Division, and I'll send you along to the March Membership Committee retreat in Las Vegas to help smooth his way there. But after that, he'll be on his own."

"The Membership Committee?"

"He'll be handling the Division's membership drives, too."

"You never mentioned anything about that to him."

"We'll be paying him almost as much as we pay you. You want him to earn it, don't you?"

"Sure," I said, pressing the matter no further since any marketing assignments that did not appear on Holloway's desk were likely to appear on mine. Besides, despite my doubts about his suitability for the position, Bud Holloway might prove to be a useful colleague. Although I had been writing less in recent years, several acceptances—from *Salt & Pepper Review* and *Chanticleer* in particular—had reawakened a desire to see my name in print. Perhaps I could profit from Holloway's experience and his editorial connections.

But by the time we got around to discussing my writing, it was too late.

Florence had asked me to keep an eye on him shortly after the initial meeting in Atlanta. "Some of his board members are concerned," she said. "Either he doesn't hold his liquor very well or he drinks too much."

"He was very impressive at the leadership conference."

"But he was practically reeling at the Division reception. I saw that myself, and as far as I could tell, he never even appeared at the awards banquet afterwards. Did you see him there?"

I shrugged my shoulders. "It's his nerves. He's only been on the job for a couple of weeks."

"Well, he'd better find some other way to calm his nerves before he meets with Membership in March. They're not a very tolerant bunch, and the Chair-Elect's a Mormon," and the day before our trip to Las

Vegas, I dropped into Bud's office.

Closing the door behind me, I came quickly to the point, advising him to moderate his drinking as much as possible. "Or better yet, stick to mineral water. Like me."

"Mineral water?"

"Particularly at the cocktail parties."

"Mineral water?"

"Diet coke, club soda, ginger ale, coffee, whatever. You've got to keep your head firmly on your shoulders at these things, Bud. There's a lot going on beneath the surface, political wise, I mean, and you want to be able to focus, to observe clearly."

"Observe, yes. To be someone on whom nothing is lost," and as he nodded pensively, I suspected that he accepted the truth of what he'd been told but resented it just the same. The next time I saw him, it was beneath the vast canopy at the entranceway of Bally's Casino Resort. Apparently returning from an excursion on the Strip, he was cradling a paper bag in the crook of his elbow.

"You've been out already?" I asked.

"Foraging," he said, and crumpling the brown paper around the neck of the bottle inside, he raised the package above his head like a bagged woodcock. "Care to join me in the room for a snort?"

"It's a little early for that, isn't it?"

"Sure is. But seeing as I'll be imbibing exclusively mineral water tonight, I figured I'd need some serious stimulation prior to the festivities. That way, I'll be sure to focus my full attention on keeping my head on my shoulders, political wise, you see. Where's this so-called function being held, anyway?"

"Rialto 4. In the Grand Salon. Seven o'clock sharp."

"Seven o'clock sharp," he repeated before disappearing into the hotel, and there he was in the Rialto suite when I arrived at seven o'clock, leaning against the bar, a highball glass filled with something other than mineral water in his hand. Before I could reach him, I was drawn aside by the Membership Director to discuss an impending retention campaign, and I quickly lost sight of Bud as our members and their families crowded into the room.

About half an hour later, as we were preparing to reconvene to the Broadway Room for dinner, a glass shattered against the marble floor. I turned with the others to see Bud erupt from a nearby group and maneuver swiftly through the press of bodies and out into the foyer. Excusing myself, I followed him down the Hall of Fame into the lounge just off the main casino floor.

"You know, I'm annoyed at you," he said as I climbed onto the stool beside him. The bartender slid a Scotch into his hand.

I ordered a beer. "Annoyed? Why? What'd I do?"

"Not what you did, but what you didn't do. Or at least didn't tell me." He took a sip from his Scotch. "Florence showed me your story in *Salt & Pepper*. It's good. She said you write poetry, too."

"Now and then. I haven't published much."

"She was surprised you hadn't mentioned it to me. She said you knew about my work. I guess you don't think much of it."

I had planned on him making the first move, but I was unprepared for this defensive, belligerent edge, the result, no doubt, of a bellyful of Scotch. "Just the opposite," I said, trying to rescue the moment. "Maybe I think too much of it. And maybe I was afraid of being too forward. You're a successful writer, you know, committed to…"

"Hah!" he exclaimed. "Never successful, committed to nothing, and not even a writer anymore."

"What do you mean?"

"I write what people tell me to write nowadays. On commission or salaried. You don't consider that writing, do you?"

"No. But your fiction, your poetry…"

"There's a certain purity to a blank sheet of paper," he said, "and I've decided to violate that purity no more."

No longer thinking of my own interests, I was honestly troubled by this revelation. I shook my head. "No. I won't accept that. Not from a writer like you, Bud. It's never gone. Writers have to write, just like sharks got to swim. Otherwise they drown."

"Appropriate metaphor," he said, and then he added, "I don't write anymore because no one reads anymore. Not the important stuff, anyway. Just crap. That's all that's out there. Nothing with vision, sympathy, imagination. Just crap."

"Maybe," I said, warming to the argument. "But that's still an excuse. The act of writing itself is a positive act. Even if nobody reads a poem…"

"Takes two to tango! I once thought I'd always be leaving something behind, even if it were only a few words or a small token of some greater truth. But now I know that a poem unread makes less noise than a tree falling in a forest unheard. Doesn't even exist." He finished his Scotch and then raised the glass to admire the prisms of light reflecting off the ice cubes. "Besides," he added, "nature does it better."

"And what about *Shout*?"

He returned the glass to the bar and pointed toward it as the bartender glanced our way. "*Shout*? I've got enough to finish the volume, and then it's R.I.P."

"But you can't kill it just like that! It's one of the longest running—"

"One of the longest running throwbacks in publishing, and I'm sure all 200 of my paid subscribers will be devastated." He watched the bartender refill his glass, and then he handed him a ten-dollar bill. "Take his next beer out of this," and he turned back to me. "I'm through with it. Only my grandchildren mean anything to me now, and a steady income. Baby photos and making money, and as I'm sure you're well aware, making money is diametrically opposed to good writing."

"I don't know about that. Dr. Johnson said that only a blockhead..."

"DIAMETRICALLY OPPOSED!" and he slammed his glass down onto the bar, sprinkling pellets of ice onto his wrist. "Maybe once... Hemingway, Faulkner... no, nobody read Faulkner until he was almost through, and Fitzgerald died broke, and Banacek a suicide just a couple of months ago, and he didn't even earn an obit in the *Trib* let alone enough to bury himself with. No, my friend, if it's filthy lucre you want, become an investment banker, not a serious writer." He swung his arm around my shoulders. "But we'll make a bundle publishing books for accountants, teaching them how to augment their cash flow. A noble pursuit."

"Which reminds me, we should be getting back. They've probably already started eating."

He slid his arm from me and slumped over his drink. "You go. I'm not hungry."

"Then don't eat. But you need to make an appearance."

"I don't need to do anything. I'm on my own time now."

"No you're not. This is a business trip."

"My budgets and schedules are perfectly in order. I'll take care of business tomorrow morning."

"The social functions are business. The Division is footing the bill for us and we're on call. They expect to see you there, and they'll notice if you're not."

"Oh, it's that kind of job, is it? Bought me body and soul. I thought I was hired to make and sell books, not toady up to every empty-headed bitch who fancies herself a literary critic."

I was about to start on my second beer but instead lowered it to the bar untouched. "What empty-headed bitch?" I asked.

"How can I be expected to hold my tongue if some empty-headed bitch insists that Margaret Mitchell could write rings around chauvinist braggarts like Hemingway and Mailer—"

"What empty-headed bitch?" I repeated, my voice beginning to tremble.

" – and that Nelson Algren should have been on the Pope's hit list for sullying the honor of Louisiana womanhood..."

"Not Felicia Bell, the Chairman's wife!"

"Well, it was an accident."

"What was an accident!"

"I would never purposely spill good liquor, especially not Chivas Regal, down anyone's dress, even if she deserved it. That's just a waste of good liquor. It was clearly an accident."

"Down the front of her dress?"

"More like inside." He lifted his hands to his chest and cupped them as if he were displaying a pair of cantaloupes. "Between these ..."

"The whole glass?"

"A double. On the rocks."

"Oh, Bud, I'm sorry."

"People get what they deserve. Did I ever tell you about when me and Algren and Banacek got soused together at O'Rourke's and settled some old scores with the lit-crit crowd? Hell, I couldn't have been much more than twenty. . . But you don't have time for this, do you? You've got a function to attend, don't you?"

"Not now I don't," I said. "We've both got all the time in the world."

"Good," and with a gesture toward the bartender, he said, "Get this gentleman another refill," and then I bought a few rounds myself. But eventually, after more Algren stories and more Banacek stories and a Berryman story and after admiring a considerable number of snapshots of his children's children, I reminded him that we had an important meeting early the next morning.

"Yeah, I know. They bought me body and soul," and as he began to descend deeper into self-pity and incoherence, I gave up trying to wedge him off his barstool, leaving him to find his own way back to his room. The elevator banks were only a few yards away, and I was sure he had drunk himself into worse shape in far more sinister places than the lounge of Bally's Casino Resort.

He appeared on time at our breakfast meeting, exhibiting no sign of the previous night's excesses other than a pink tinge lining the whites of his eyes, a slight tremor at the tips of his fingers, and an aversion to any nourishment other than black coffee. But he missed the farewell reception that evening, and as soon as he returned to the office he was fired.

He was given an hour to clean out his desk. I don't think he ever completely understood, and as he brushed past me in the corridor for the last time, a cardboard box under each arm, I wondered whether there was anything I could have done to have prevented this from happening.

* * *

I had seen that bewildered, stricken look in his eyes once before during the Winter Meeting in Atlanta, several weeks after he'd been hired. We had been attending his first session with his review board, and after he was introduced and welcomed to the association, the Division Chair, Dr. Page, presented a summary of his responsibili ties. Along with launching a book program "eventually to consist of twenty volumes per annum," he was expected to supervise the fundraising program and manage the member and retention campaigns, and as Dr. Page continued to enumerate additional "support and administrative tasks," Bud's eyes seemed to widen in direct proportion to the rapidly expanding scope of his duties.

He glanced toward Florence, and when she diverted her eyes from his, he turned back to Dr. Page and said, "Well, I have done a lot of direct-mail. Books, mostly."

"It's all the same," replied Dr. Page. He had been Chief Financial Officer for a large packaged goods company and considered himself an expert in all aspects of product development and distribution. "Marketing's marketing whether it's for soap powder or books."

Bud managed to restrain himself, and he remained silent until the meeting adjourned. But as we were walking back from the Omni toward Peachtree Street and our hotel, I could not ignore the wounded, perplexed expression still lingering on his face—identical to the one I was to see several months later on the day he was fired. "What's the matter, Bud?" I asked.

"Membership drives? Fundraising? You people never told me about that."

"We weren't certain that the Division would be funding those kinds of activities. But don't worry…"

"Don't worry! They're talking about twenty titles a year—editing, production, marketing–and still…"

"They're lucky if they come up with five. Trust me on that."

"Frankly, I don't know who to trust. Why don't you people come clean with me? I don't know whether I should be listening to you, Florence, this fellow Page, or my Uncle Ned."

"Like we said at the interview, it's kind of complicated," and as we proceeded down into one of Atlanta's deep central canyons —blank granite walls stretching upward as if organically from the sidewalks—I again tried to clarify for him his place in our association's intricate skein of shifting hierarchies, further complicated by competing priorities that seemed to fluctuate with the tides. I was stressing, in particular, the dangers of the political marshlands that often grew soggier and more threatening with each successive memo, when I suddenly realized that Bud was no longer by my side. He had, instead, stopped up the street, several paces behind, to talk with a young woman who was partially concealed inside the concrete flutings of the striated monolith that towered above us. It was growing dark, and I had noticed in passing neither her nor the bucket of roses at her feet. She was offering one of them to Bud.

"This is Julie," said Bud, introducing her to me as I approached.

"Bud, I was trying to explain... "

"Julie," continued Bud, "is far more intriguing than your Scope and Correlation Task Force can ever hope to be."

"Thanks, I guess," said Julie. "Anyway, here's a nice red one."

Bud took the flower from her, and after he handed her a five-dollar bill, she stooped down, I assumed, to tempt me with her merchandise.

"None for me, thanks," I said before she could pluck another rose from her stock. "We're here on business, and I wouldn't know what to do with one of those even if you gave it to me for nothing."

"Aren't you lonely out here?" asked Bud, still staring at his purchase as if it were, rather than an ordinary rose, an exotic orchid, one of a kind. "Streets are pretty empty. You can't be selling very many of those."

"Walter's punishing me. I missed a day, and this is always a rotten spot. But the Home Electronics Show will be here next week, and the purchasing agents, too. We always do better with conventions in town."

"You sound like a professional," said Bud, and then after a pause, "Flower vendor, I mean."

If she resented the innuendo, her smile gave no hint of it. "No, I'm not a professional. None of us are. I'm actually a musician. From Seattle. I've been traveling the country in search of roots."

"Roots?" asked Bud. "You mean like ginseng and mandragora?"

"Not those kinds of roots! Musical roots. Didn't you hear me? I said I was a musician. Songwriter, too. But in the meantime, I've got to make a living . . . and I still owe you two dollars change."

"Keep it," said Bud, and together we resumed our trek back to the hotel.

"Maybe I'll bring along my zither tomorrow! Play you one of my songs if you stop by!"

"That would be delightful!" Bud shouted back over his shoulder, apparently forgetting that we would be flying home to Chicago the next morning. "It's a deal."

"What're you going to do with that?" I asked, nodding toward the rose.

"Probably stick it in a glass of Scotch and watch it wilt. Why don't you join me back up in the room? You can tell me more about that Scope and Fornication Task Force."

"I don't think so," I said as we turned onto Peachtree Street. "There's just enough time for a shower before the reception."

The smoked door of the hotel slid open and we were inside. A parrot screeched.

"We must be on the registration level," said Bud. "That's where the parrots are."

"Last night it took me about twenty minutes just to find the Tower B elevators."

"I think I know how to get there from here," said Bud. "Follow me," and like a native guide heading into the bush, he stalked into the interior.

The first six floors of the hotel were divided into a series of converging levels and concourses leading variously into the restaurant court, Boutique Alley, the exhibit halls, the health center, and, occasionally, back out to the street or into the multiplex next door. Chutes, ramps, escalators, and high-tech spiral stairways circled the perimeters of the hotel's three towers, linking the six levels, and above them concentric bands of open corridors—ivy draped over their balustrades like blankets of Spanish moss—wound thirty stories upward to the ceiling. Dwarf palms and ferns seemed to sprout from the turquoise carpeting, and on the ground level of Tower B, a jungle of ficus trees surrounded a network of lily ponds inhabited by families of ducks. Businessmen and women sat sipping beverages and reading newspapers on the small platforms anchored to the rims of the ponds.

The jungle opened into the huge atrium of the central core, brilliantly illuminated during the day by the sun streaming through a rainbow-prismed skylight. Tethered to the skylight was a gigantic mobile, its slowly revolving steel plates replicating the primary colors of the parrot that had just flown past my nose.

"Quite a change from the sterility of the streets," I said.

"The world's first air-conditioned rain forest," replied Bud.

As we circled toward the bulbous glass tubes of the Tower B elevators, I spotted Ted Pelletier and his wife, Emily, sitting on one of the wicker couches positioned near the registration desk. Ted was the Secretary-Elect of the Division and, as a native Atlantan, he was also acting as Chair of the Host Committee for the current meeting. Both he and Emily were dressed in formal eveningwear, his wife especially striking in her low-cut gold lamé gown. Yet the two were sitting apart, at opposite ends of the couch, staring in different directions. There had been rumors about Ted and the administrative assistant who often accompanied him on his association travels, presumably to take notes.

Ted was also a crack securities analyst, and when I had last seen him, during our Denver meeting, he had recommended an emerging biotechnical stock that eventually produced impressive capital gains for me.

"Hold it a second, Bud," I said, steering him away from the elevators. "Here's someone you should meet."

Ted stood up to greet us as we approached.

"And this is my wife, Emily," he said after I had introduced Bud to him. Emily, however, seemed reluctant to recognize our presence, and after nodding vaguely our way, she resumed gazing at the clock above the registration desk.

"Well, what do you think of our fair city, Mr. Holloway?" asked Ted, after a moment of awkward silence. "The hub of the New South."

"Not many trees out there on Peachtree Street," said Bud.

"There's plenty of trees in Atlanta. But we've got other priorities here downtown. Can't you see, we're bringing the greenery inside, along with the people. Stifling hot out there in the summer and wet in the winter, and it's a lot more agreeable to travel from one destination to the next in controlled environments. If you're registered in a hotel or work in an office downtown or even are doing your Christmas shopping, you hardly need to walk the streets at all."

"I guess that is more agreeable," said Bud.

"Safer, too, and no panhandlers. It's a lot easier keeping a causeway restricted and secure than a city street."

"What are you all dressed up like that for?" I asked, changing the subject. "You look like a toastmaster."

"We were part of a wedding party down the block. Her little sister. But it's over with now, and we'll be attending the reception and the awards dinner tonight. We've taken a room here so we can change . . . which," Ted continued, raising his voice to address his wife, "it's about time we did. Otherwise, we'll be late again."

When she didn't respond but seemed, rather, to turn more deeply into herself, Ted asked, angrily, "Are listening to me? Do you want to make us late again?" and without waiting for a response he then turned abruptly toward the elevators.

Realizing that I might not have another chance, I followed him, striding quickly to match his pace. "You know that Technitron stock you were touting last year," I said. "It worked out pretty well for me."

"For me, too. That's how I can afford to take a room in a swank hotel like this just to change clothes." He suddenly shouted back toward his wife, who was now talking to Bud as they slowly approached us. "Are you coming or not?"

As he turned back to press the elevator button, he resumed our conversation as if it had never been interrupted. "There's no such thing as a sure thing. But with that in mind," and his eyes narrowed mysteriously, "Bodyprime. It's on the NASDAQ. Bodybuilding equipment moving into nutritional supplements. Out of Teaneck, N.J. Low debt, good P.E., and expanding globally. Currently selling at a discount to book value, but probably not for long. Just don't try to corner the market, please."

"Bodyprime," I repeated aloud, and then under my breath as we entered the elevator. "Bodyprime, Bodyprime."

Facing out from the rear of the glass tube as we ascended, I watched the lily ponds diminish into glittering surfaces, and then when I glanced upward, the multicolored mobile seemed to swoop down on us like a monstrous predatory macaw. Still silently repeating "Bodyprime" to etch it into my memory, I suddenly realized that I had forgotten to punch in my floor.

I had assumed that Bud had followed us into the elevator. But when I turned forward to press the button on the console, he was nowhere to be seen. Ted and I were accompanied in the elevator only by his wife, Emily, who, resplendent in her golden evening gown, was smiling down at the brilliant red rose in her hand. ☐

A BIG RED JUMBLE OF LINES
Andy Holt

On a Saturday night late in the summer, Jackson receives an unexpected call from his brother while eating dinner with his wife and son. He hasn't talked to Chase in about a month, and in that time he has already begun to believe that he is free of him forever.

The last time he'd seen his brother was on the day their father slipped on the back porch of his house and broke his leg, and Jackson had to spend an afternoon in the hospital parking lot with Chase, who was afraid to enter. In the two hours they spent watching the heat waves roll off the pavement, Chase had told him stories of SARS outbreaks and botched surgeries and the dangers of antibiotics, repeating some of them three or four times, never altering a single word, like a tape on repeat. That day, Jackson had resolved to cut his life cleanly away from his brother and all the stress that came with him. Aside from holidays, emergencies, and the occasional funeral, Chase would be invisible – a family ghost.

Jackson sees the caller ID and lets the phone ring a few times, one of those harsh rings that can only come from bulky old plastic phones with cords that always get hopelessly tangled. His wife Emma glares at him for leaving the table to answer. His son Caleb just packs more mashed potatoes into his cheeks, glasses loose on his nose, as if someone might steal the food from his plate at any moment.

"I'm scared," Chase hisses into the phone. "There's something wrong with me."

You can say that again, Jackson thinks, and immediately feels guilty.

"Chase," Jackson says. He glances at his wife.

Emma drops her fork and mimes *what does he want now*? Nobody had been happier than Emma to see Chase out of their lives. The man was a bad influence on their son, she had said, though Jackson hadn't known what she meant. Chase was too innocent to be called a bad influence, too much a child himself.

"I'm pretty sure I have herpes, or maybe chlamydia. Some kind of venereal disease." Chase coughs into the phone. "For that matter, what does AIDS feel like?"

Jackson turns away from his family and whispers.

"Chase, you can't have VD if you've never had sex."

"Exactly," Chase says, and considers for a moment. "That's what's so scary about it."

Caleb stares at his father while Emma pulls him around the corner into the hallway. In case he asks for an explanation later, Jackson starts thinking of other things VD could stand for. Veteran's Day. Video Disc. Voodoo Doll.

Jackson sighs. "Fine. You have VD."

"Yeah, I know. It wasn't a question."

"Then what do you *want*?" Jackson asks, sounding harsher than he intended. He imagines his brother fidgeting with the phone wire and mouthing words to himself.

"I'm calling to ask if you could drive me to see Dad sometime this week."

The phone slips out of Jackson's hand and hits the floor with the dull whack of plastic against tile. For a subconscious flash, he can hear fire crackling, smell oranges and burning wood searing his nostrils. He imagines smoke rising from somewhere far away and rubs his forehead with a damp palm. When he picks up the phone again, a crack has formed along the side. He pictures sticking his thumbnails into the crack and pulling the phone open, letting the electrical contents spill out onto the floor. He holds the phone back to his ear.

"My new therapist says that seeing Dad would be good." Chase sniffs and clears his throat. "It is important for me to see him," he adds, with more resolve.

"You got another therapist?"

"Yeah, his name is David. Good guy. Very helpful."

Jackson knows that he should be happy to see his brother getting help, but Chase has been through at least a dozen therapists, and his choices seem only to get weirder, one unlicensed quack after the other, putting his little brother through all sorts of strange paces. But even stranger is Chase's whole-hearted belief in every one of them, impossible to discourage.

"Give me a few days. I'll call and tell Dad we're coming."

Jackson stays on the line until he hears the dial tone. For a few moments he just stands there and decompresses, listening to the monotone buzz until it sounds like it's coming from inside his head. The distorted outlines of words start to break through, sped up into high frequency. He pulls the phone away from his ear and places it gently onto the receiver.

Caleb peeks around the corner, eyes oversized behind his glasses and hair sticking out in all directions. He looks like Jackson's mother, with her oblong cheeks and pale eyes. She had been so proud of the likeness, calling Caleb her little twin. By her last year of life, her features had sagged away, but you could still see the familiar hard blue tint around her pupils, the same color magnified through Caleb's glasses. Jackson, on the other hand, has always found the resemblance unsettling. Caleb has nothing in common with her – anxious where she was determined, flaky where she was strong. Jackson loves his son, but in a more complicated way than he had expected, not the way a good father might love a normal boy.

The three sit back down to dinner, Caleb back to chomping with his mouth open, Emma back to clearing her throat whenever she wipes her mouth with her napkin. Jackson thinks about Chase and their father and tries his best to prepare himself.

* * *

On the day before the big orange grove fire of 1975, the school bus made its usual way through the February morning, taking Jackson, Chase, and the other students to school at Citrus Grove Elementary. Their town was on track for the worst drought in a decade, one hundred fifty days without a single drop of rain, and expecting thirty or forty more. The thunderstorms would return in the summer, and after the first rain the ground would groan with relief. But the summer was still two months away. That morning, everyone was still tense with the repetition of warm, dry days, worrying for the health of the orange crop. Their town only had small, private groves, none of those cooperative growers with endless acres of oranges. Their houses were all built around one patch of trees in the middle, flecked with scattered dots of orange. It held their town together. Losing their crop to the drought seemed capable of making the whole town unravel. Even the children on the bus were more jumpy than usual, and that morning Billy Barton started talking about peeing and sex.

Chase sat in his usual spot at the back of the bus, wearing his bright-red baseball cap cocked downward so it covered his massive, pale eyes. Jackson sat in the row in front of Chase, keeping guard over him. He didn't like to watch his little brother picked on, if only because he didn't know how to make him feel better afterward.

It didn't take much to set Chase off. One day, their teacher had taught them about how germs were invisible, but they were everywhere. Chase had bolted upright in his desk and ended up crying and scratching his arms until they were pink, and the teacher had to send him to the nurse's office. Now even the sight of the dried gum and unidentified grime on the floor of the school bus could make Chase tremble. He always washed his hands before and after he used the bathroom and after anyone touched him, even his family.

Billy Barton turned around, face already smeared with grease and a filthy smirk. Jackson tensed, seeing the look in his eyes, full of manic boyhood aggression. Billy peered over the back of the seat and licked his lips, then slapped the brim of Chase's hat from underneath with his fat little arm. His round eyes opened to Billy and stared, perfectly still.

"Hey, Chase!" Billy snorted, like his snot had gotten in the way of a chuckle. "You know how sex works, right?"

Chase dropped his shoulders, preparing for whatever was coming. Jackson had the feeling of watching from behind glass.

"My big brother told me yesterday. You want to hear?"

Chase pushed his hat brim back down and pulled his knees up under his chin.

"My big brother told me you put your wiener in the spot and pee. That's where babies come from, he says. And you have to drink lots of water for it to work, he says."

Chase only stayed in his tight little ball, hat and knees covering him like armor. But something flipped on or off, like a short circuit. Billy wheezed and leaned forward, probably hoping for another tantrum from Chase, but he gave up after a minute. He shifted around in his seat and hit the kid in front of him on the head with an open hand.

The school bus went over a bump, and Chase fell over to his side, still bundled up. He wouldn't move when they got to school, and Mr. Cranston, the gruff man with the potbelly who coached all the sports teams, had to carry him out of the bus and take him to the nurse's office.

Jackson didn't see his brother again until they crawled into the back seat of the car when their mother picked them up in the afternoon.

"How was your day?" she asked over her shoulder.

"Fine," said Jackson.

"Chase?" She tilted her head toward him, just enough for Jackson to see her long, narrow face sticking out from her shoulder-length hair. She spent an hour every morning trying to make her hair hang evenly, but it always tangled in the humidity, making wings that stuck out around her ears. Maybe that was why she always looked slightly, almost imperceptibly off-balance.

Chase pulled his hat from his head and squeezed it against his chest. He glanced at the door handle and floor and smudged-up window. Jackson knew all he could see was germs.

"Anything out of the ordinary happen today, Chase? This morning, perhaps?"

Jackson could never figure out how she always knew.

"We'll talk about it with your father when he gets home. I think it's time for us to do something. Take some action. It'll be all right, sweetheart."

In about ten minutes their house came into view, sky blue with white window frames, and the car pulled into the long gravel drive. It curved back and forth more than necessary to make the impression of a meandering country estate, though the house was on flat ground in the middle of Citrus County.

"Orange juice is the blood of Florida," their father liked to say from the back porch, overlooking the grove. "It keeps us alive." The trees sprawled out in rows that blended into green lines with dark soil between them. The roofs of the houses on the other side were visible in the distance, like tiny Floridian mountains.

Their family didn't own any of the orange groves, but Billy Barton's father owned a grove that Billy said was bigger than you could run across in a whole day. The Bartons lived an hour out of town, where the groves were bigger, part of an industrial grower cooperative. Whenever anyone drank orange juice during lunch at school, Billy would grab the bottle from them and take a messy swig.

"It's mine anyway," he'd say, and no one would argue.

Jackson once asked his father what he meant about them staying alive on oranges if they didn't own any. They were sitting on the porch while Chase stayed inside and read books and washed his hands. His father stayed quiet for a full minute or so, his shoulders sagging over his slight gut. Years under the Florida sun had turned his skin a leathery brown and left hard lines on his face. Jackson sometimes tried to trace the lines with his eyes, hoping to read his father's thoughts in the patterns.

"I don't want to talk about the Bartons," he finally said. "They're not bigger than us. They just take up more space." Jackson didn't understand what he meant, and he felt that his question hadn't been answered. He tried to read his father's face in the red sunset light, but the lines were hieroglyphs, unintelligible and foreign.

When they arrived home from school, Chase ran to the bathroom to wash his face and hands with scalding hot water, as always. Jackson saw him run into their bedroom, slamming the door with his butt to avoid touching the knob. The bunk bed squeaked. Chase slept on the top bunk, farther from the ground.

Their father arrived home on schedule at 5:30 and took a single beer from the refrigerator, which he would sip all evening until it was warm enough that they could smell it across the table at dinner. Their mother spoke to him in hushed tones in the living room. Jackson strained to hear from the kitchen, but the only words he heard were *nurse* and *disturbed* and *too much*. The more she said, the louder their father grumbled. It was an animal noise, like she was poking him with a stick a little harder every few seconds. Once she seemed to have finished telling him the story, he erupted into a single word.

"Chase!"

Chase peeked around the corner into the kitchen. He was in his racecar pajamas with the padded feet. Jackson nodded to him and tried not to smile while Chase walked, his back perfectly straight, through the kitchen and into the living room.

"There you are," his father said. "Mary, give us a minute."

Mother hurried into the kitchen, quickly enough that she caught Jackson unaware, not even pretending to look at his multiplication tables. She squinted at him, tapped the workbook with her finger, and tousled his hair before heading down the hallway and into the office on the other side of the house. Jackson put his pencil down again and listened.

"Tell me what happened today," their father said.

Jackson imagined Chase staring wide-eyed at the ground, like something was seeping up through the floorboards.

"The nurse said you threw another one of your fits. We're going to figure out what's wrong with you, right now. We can sit here right through dinner. I'm not even hungry."

Jackson slid into the chair closer to the living room.

Chase stuttered before he spoke. "Dad, how do doctors make things so clean?"

"What the hell does that have to do with anything? I'm trying to talk to you here. Your mother wants us to send you to a shrink. I don't want that to happen." His voice was quiet, but harsh. Jackson didn't realize until years later that their father might have been scared.

There was no answer from Chase. At this point, Jackson couldn't imagine what either of them might look like, only that his father loomed over Chase in the recliner, the wrinkles of his face like hard lines folding in on themselves.

His voice softened. "I don't know, Chase. I guess they use chemicals or something. In the war, we sometimes used lighters to burn the germs off." He paused. "There you go."

Jackson was certain that Chase hadn't known that. His eyes must have lit up, fiery bright.

"Billy Barton was picking on me," Chase said, sounding much more relaxed. "He said something gross, and I didn't want to be around anybody all day."

"Damn those Bartons," their father said, though he said it off-hand, like he was just saying it for Chase's sake. "Son, you're just too tense. Every little thing shakes you up. You're always inside. Why don't you go out and play in the orange grove with your brother? Blow off some steam, maybe."

"I hate the grove," said Chase, spiteful. "It's dirty, and there's nowhere to sit down."

Chase had only ever been inside the orange grove once, a few months earlier, when Jackson had invited him to play hide-and-seek with his friends, The idea had been to help Chase be more normal, but Jackson realized his mistake once he saw Chase standing out there between the lines of trees, under the sharp blue sky of Florida winter, his feet digging into the dirt while he shifted his weight back and forth. Someone found a worm and held it up. Chase gasped and looked around, mouth hanging open in horror, as if seeing it all for the first time – the thick soil under his feet, the bugs in the trees, the stench of bitter orange peels. Chase screamed, high-pitched like a whistle, and passed out into the dirt while running back toward the house.

Their mother put him into the bathtub while he was still unconscious and lathered him up so well that the soap-suds hid the dirt floating in the water. "It's okay, baby," she said when his oversized eyes opened, wiping his forehead with a washcloth. "You're all clean now."

Jackson had been listening from outside the bathroom. He peeked through the door and saw Chase's head sticking out of the bubbles, awake now but with eyes sagging in comfort, as if he'd been teleported from Hell to Heaven in a moment. That night, Chase covered the window by his bed with yellow construction paper so he wouldn't have to look at the grove from where he slept. No doubt his nightmares happened out there.

Listening now to his father and Chase in the living room, Jackson wondered if Chase ever dreamed of transforming the grove into somewhere safe – clean and flat like the bottom of a bathtub. Sounding resigned, their father told Chase to wash up for dinner, and he rounded the corner into the kitchen in his racecar pajamas, rubbing thin tears from his eyes.

* * *

Jackson sits outside Chase's house on Wednesday morning, waiting for him to come out so they can visit their father. The breeze carries cool mist off the water into the window of his truck, but between gusts he can feel the air warming already. The shack that Chase lives in always looks oddly calm from the outside. It sits in the middle of a wide dirt lot on the edge of an inlet from the Gulf. Investors had bought the property during the Florida construction boom and built a small wooden structure to serve as a foreman's office. The oper ation went broke after the recession hit, so they lease the shack to Chase at a rate low enough that he can afford to pay with his salary from his job as a bagboy at the Publix three blocks away.

The blinds open a sliver and shut again. Chase comes out and spends a few excruciating minutes making sure the door is locked. He wears a baggy, white polo shirt tucked into chinos. His hair is plastered to his head and parted to the side.

"Thanks for doing this," he says, climbing into the truck. Jackson studies his face. His eyes only grow more pronounced with age, blue-green between oversized eyelashes.

They don't speak for most of the drive. Chase taps the dashboard with his knuckles, faster whenever Jackson changes lanes or specds up. Finally, when Jackson has had enough, he looks at him and clears his throat. Chase stops tapping and rests his hands on his lap.

"My new therapist thinks he knows what's wrong with me," Chase says, as if he hasn't said the same thing a half-dozen times before. "Before you ask, the condition doesn't have a name. But he says it happens when you don't learn how to crawl when you're a baby."

If he weren't driving, Jackson would close his eyes and try not to listen.

"He wants to teach me to crawl as an adult. He says that'll help." Chase looks at his fingernails. "It's weird, I know, but he says it'll work. He cleans the carpet in his office every day, so germs won't even be a problem."

"I remember you crawling when you were a baby."

Chase grimaces, like he hadn't expected Jackson to remember. "I checked on the internet, and the symptoms all match up anyway," he says, and nods to himself. "I know that I crawled, but maybe I just wasn't doing it right."

Jackson doesn't know what his brother's symptoms are, strictly speaking. Chase has always been strange, but at some point he crossed the line between being an odd child and a mentally-diseased adult. Jackson wonders what would happen if the therapist does cure him. He tries to imagine what Chase would be like if he were sane.

They pull onto the long drive in front of their childhood home.

Jackson has never stopped being shocked at the change. The paint out front has faded, and one corner of the eastern wall is visible from the road, blackened with ash. Out back are acres of weeds and scorched earth, scattered with the remains of burned orange trees. There is a presence, a tingle in his skin as the car creeps closer to the front porch.

"But before I can crawl, I have to deal with childhood conflicts," Chase announces as he climbs out of the truck. "Apologize for how my problems may have hurt others."

Jackson looks at him and then at the house. And just like that, he knows what is coming.

* * *

On February 28, 1975, recess began as usual, children scattered across the playground, moving in manic patterns. Sister Jameson had sent Chase to the nurse's office earlier with a stomach complaint. Jackson couldn't remember Chase coming back to class, but the nurse must have sent him to recess, because Jackson spotted him perched atop the broken spiral slide. The orange grove edged up against the wooden fence, and Chase rested his chin on his palms, staring out at the lines of trees.

Jackson approached him for a minute, but he thought better of saying anything. Everyone else had long forgotten about his school-bus breakdown the day before, but Jackson felt that anything could trigger another one. Sometimes he pictured his brother's mind as some sort of Frankenstein reactor with jumbled wires and electric sparks popping without warning.

The smell came before the smoke, a sour stench that made the girls crinkle their noses and look around for a culprit. Jackson was playing soccer on the far edge of the recess field by the back fence when he smelled it. Within a few minutes, he started to feel his eyes burn. He assumed it was sweat until he saw Sister Jameson walking briskly from the school building, her habit puffed up behind her like a parachute. She whispered something to Mr. Cranston, though there was nobody near enough to overhear her. He immediately blew the whistle, and the children gathered around him in their lines by class and gender.

Jackson turned back to the playground to see Chase, now standing on top of the slide with his arms straight to his sides, hands clenched, looking out over the fence. White smoke rose in a tall cloud from somewhere out in the middle of the grove. For a moment Jackson felt dizzy, as if his head were over-inflated. Wild colors crept into the corners of his vision, and when he rubbed his eyes and opened them again, he saw everything in overexposure – the smoke, the students teetering back and forth in their lines like orange groves in the wind, Chase standing tall in the distance. Jackson saw the dirt and grass stains covering the children and the snot-covered upper lips, the way they shoved each other to catch a look at the fire and rubbed their eyes with their grimy hands to keep the smoke out. Their chatter turned incomprehensible, almost violent in his ears. Sister Jameson and the other nuns pushed through the crowd of children like angry black thumbs, counting heads, until they noticed Chase. Sister Jameson yelled his name once and he climbed slowly down, wiped his knees with his forearms, and took his time on the way back to the group, lips pressed into a tight grin.

No doubt the smoke was the cause of his momentary vision changes, Jackson would decide later, but he couldn't shake the idea that in that moment, on the day the orange grove burned to the ground, he had glimpsed the world through Chase's eyes.

* * *

Jackson and his brother stand on the front porch of their father's home. This is the only side completely undamaged, because it faces away from where the grove used to be. Everyone had been shocked by how quickly the blaze spread, with everything dry enough to ignite like cigarette paper. Some houses didn't survive the fire, and many other families used insurance money to repair what was damaged. The authorities never discovered who started the fire, only that it must have sparked shortly before noon, about fifteen minutes before recess began. For a few days, the children had to stay inside because the air was filled with white smoke that burned their eyes and made their throats itch. Their family lived out of suitcases in a government-run shelter for a few weeks until the fire department declared their house safe to inhabit again.

Years later, the neighborhood remains a patchwork of new houses for the rich and damaged ones for those, like their father, without money for repairs. In the flurry of rebuilding, nobody had saved enough money to re-plant the orange trees. Many of the neighbors had only owned small shares of the grove and always worked normal full-time jobs to make ends meet. The oranges had been the most romantic part of their lives. Nobody lost much yearly income from the grove burning, but they sacrificed the romance. They weren't orange growers anymore.

Finally, their father answers. He sits in a wheelchair, one leg in a large cast, with one of their mother's old handmade quilts draped over his legs. His face has wrinkled with age, turning softer and rounder, but Jackson imagines that the hard lines are still under there, buried under the graying skin.

"Boys! Come in, come in," their father says, smiling under his dark, narrow eyes, the only ones in the family that aren't blue.

Jackson smells the scented candles that his mother had taken to lighting the year after the fire to mask the smell of ash. She died five years ago, from a stroke, but their father still lights the candles even though the ashen smell from the wildfire has long dissipated.

"I'm sorry I don't have any beer or snacks for you boys," he says, rolling into the living room and turning around in an empty space next to the recliner. "I don't drink or eat all that much, seeing as it's just me."

The living room has been packed through the years with decorations – deer heads, picture frames, and empty vases – so that it has started to look like the storage room of a museum. Jackson sits on the dusty old flower-print couch. It creaks, but the cushions are softer than ever. He sees the back porch through the windows, blackened and empty of furniture.

"Now, as much as I love a visit for any reason, I've been told Chase has something he needs to talk to me about."

Jackson had told him this much over the phone. Their father bends forward to catch Chase's eye and winks. His optimism in his old age should be somehow inspiring, but Jackson can't help but find it cripplingly sad.

"I'm sorry about your leg," Chase says.

Their father grins, but Jackson can't figure out why. "It's nothing. Like I told you before, I tried to scrub the back porch, since it's always bugged me how I never got the ash off, and wouldn't you know, I lost my footing."

No part of the house had ignited in the fire, but it had been so coated in ash that the back porch became unusable. Swiping a finger on the railing would turn it black. The flame-retardant foam that the fire department had sprayed on the house turned the ash into a sticky sort of tar that dried until it had seeped permanently into the wood. Jackson pictures his father scrubbing the porch with a rag, which saturates black in a matter of seconds.

Chase scratches his ear. "No, *I apologize* for your leg."

Jackson cringes. It's happening, he thinks. The dizziness returns, the tingling in his skin, like what had happened decades earlier when he breathed in the orange-grove smoke. Their father rolls himself closer to Chase. All of the surfaces are breathing, coated in invisible filth.

"I don't see what you mean. It wasn't your fault."

Chase now has both hands up to his ears, not scratching them so much as grabbing them in his fists and pulling down. He starts to mumble, quietly at first, but building.

Oh God, Jackson thinks. Don't do it, Chase. Leave it be.

"But what I wanted to say was about the fire."

"The fire?" Their father rolls backward.

"The fire was... I mean, I was the one who... I want to *apologize* for the fire."

Jackson imagines Chase's words darting around the room in blinding colors, now impossible to contain. Their father squeezes the quilt. Once again, Jackson sits helpless and watches the drama of his brother's life unfold.

"David says that I'm afflicted and that it's not my fault, that you should forgive me so that I can get better. He says it's the first step in a process..."

Chase rambles, louder and faster, until he's somewhere else.

Jackson can see his father cringe with every word. His face goes from pale to pink, and his breaths grow more labored. With surprising speed, he throws the quilt to the ground and jumps up from his wheelchair, arms outstretched toward Chase with tensed, claw-like fingers. The wheelchair rolls away behind him as he starts to stumble forward on his broken leg, like a skinny Frankenstein monster. The cast on his foot clunks on the wood floor with every step while he limps desperately toward his son. The pain must be unbearable, but Jackson doesn't know how to intervene. Their father groans through his teeth, and Jackson watches his face tighten, reddening in uneven patches until the whole thing is soiled and illegible, like wine seeping into paper. He falls to the floor and passes out.

Chase backs away until he runs into the wall, then stands frozen, eyes like bright blue discs against his white face. He looks fragile, as if even the smallest touch would shatter him into sharp little pieces. Jackson can imagine them scattered across the floor, glimmering like fragments of stars around his father's pale body.

* * *

The paramedics come and put their father into the ambulance. Jackson decides against taking Chase to the hospital, so he has to drive him back home before meeting his family at the emergency room. Together, the brothers sit in the truck and watch the broken yellow line in the middle of the road, how it blends into an endless vibrating snake when they pick up speed.

They pull up to Chase's lot. Jackson almost expects to need to carry him to the doorstep, but his little brother just nods and steps out of the truck, carefully, one foot at a time. Jackson watches him hobble up to his tiny shack like a man with a fractured ribcage, surrounded with white mist from the waves breaking against the seawall.

Jackson arrives at the hospital. Emma sits with Caleb in the waiting room. She runs up to him while Caleb fidgets in his chair. She looks at Jackson expectantly, but he says nothing.

"Don't you want to know if your father is going to be okay?"

After the solitary drive from Chase's house to the hospital, Jackson wants to tell her that nothing is okay, that his father and brother are lost forever. Then he wants to tell her that if they're strong they can save their own family from this kind of end, he and his wife and child, by cutting away the dead parts of his family and building their own. He feels the bravado of a man who has survived a catastrophe.

"They said he just re-broke the leg. Plus some bruises from the fall." She crosses her arms. "What happened?"

"It's just that he tried to stand. I'm surprised he walked as far as he did, to tell you the truth. I don't know what made him think he wouldn't fall."

Emma squints at his face, her eyes darting from feature to feature as if reading a map. Jackson knows that she wants the rest of the story, and he suspects that she could guess most of it herself. But she doesn't argue, not here in the hospital with their son nearby. She only whispers to Jackson while they walk to the waiting room chairs. "I told you that brother of yours is trouble. Maybe now we'll be rid of him for good."

Jackson sits down next to his son and puts his arm around his shoulders. Caleb flinches and looks at his father for a moment and then around the hospital room, blinking as if he is noticing everything for the first time. He tugs on his ear before looking back down at his lap.

This is a moment for fatherhood, Jackson thinks, for love between grandfather and father and grandson, when they should be thinking with one mind about grief and the fleetingness of life. Jackson tries to remember sitting with his own father on their porch, looking out over the rows of trees in the setting sun. He imagines an ancient lineage of fulfillment and patriarchal duty, stretching from the Stone Age through his father and himself, all the way down to his own son, fidgeting next to him. All these things he tries to feel deep in his bones.

But something doesn't connect. His forehead tickles, and somewhere in the lineage he imagines shredded wiring, images in electric flashes – his mother's frizzy hair, Chase pulling on his ears, Caleb flinching, how none of them ever seemed to look anyone in the eye, how they were always watching blank surfaces like they were alive, coated in a film of moving things. The hospital waiting room walls vacillate under the florescent lights, crawling in unreadable patterns. Jackson wonders how long it might take for him to want to burn it down himself, to stop all the moving in one colossal blaze.

He closes his eyes and presses his temples with his fingertips. When he opens his eyes, the hospital is reasonable again. But flickering through his thoughts like a loose light bulb, he can see his little brother, young and tiny and lost in a wild orange grove, his strange mind a big red jumble of lines, all the while thinking *I don't belong here. This is not my home.* □

THE EYES
Rosellen Brown

Nobody's eyes match.

She studies hers: one wide and confiding, open to anything, her girl's eyes. A little fixed, more than a little approving, wile-less. Look at the way it takes in everything without inflection, not critical, not guarded. Her virgin eye that saw her first rose, a tea, more striped and subtle than a sunrise. First ring-tailed rat, gift of Tigger-Ann, open as a chicken breast on the lawn, and she and her girl-friends screamed as if they'd been macheted. Skipping stone, flat in her hand. Grandmother slipping toward death and gone. Her horse's sweaty flank, harder than wood, lovely the way it curved like a cello, but warmer, she could feel the coursing blood under her hand, a rhythm if not a music. Lake of the Woods, the facets of grit on the beach, the cold of the forest closing down on her chilled skin. Degas ballerina bent over one knee.

This is the eye she wants to believe in, wants others to look into, straight down into it like a bore, like staring down binoculars back-wards. Her hope of innocence, the sweetness-of-marriage eye, the round village bread eye, hands full of clear water eye, no color at all. You bring yourself to this eye and it takes you in. The eye that looks for God, no shelter in irony, no irony anywhere. No hiding. That eye.

The other holds the world. Narrower, because of all that pinches. She tries to widen it but it will not change. Sign here, please: the notary eye. This is the eye that does not share secrets, waffles, does not entirely trust. Gives and takes. The eye that knew that friend-of-the-family's wandering eye, the eye he looked up skirts with, before her mother saw. Knows who's real, who's made by mirrors, only a nasty flash of light to scare the crows of the competition. *I am my master's dog, at Kew. Pray tell me, sir, whose dog are you?* Does not sleep in the presence of strangers, not for an instant, and the voice strays firm as Lycra, and she hears it. Not mottled, not pied, it has no echo.

Wants what it wants, good things the other eye approves, but bends them sometimes with the pressure of such certainty, and she sees it. Remembers when she was three or maybe four, crying to hold that ca-nary more yellow than a morning egg yolk, which Mother handed her finally, patting its head with a fingertip. "Softly, softly now." Took it in her palm and squeezed so hard with joy it shot up out of her fist with a shriek and was gone, uncrumpling. Eye the color of the ocean in November, windy, not quite blue. Not a Zen eye, this eye does not believe in Nothing. Nothing will come soon enough.

When do the eyes begin to tell stories, she wonders. Do her daughter's yet? But you can't be an adult without that line that wavers its way down the middle, you even have to hope it for her—programmed, surely, like cell division. Self at a distance from self. Not growling like leashed dogs, though. Sniffing, curious. Jane Fonda Jane Austen Jane Addams Jane Doe—anyone you want to look at hard enough, that line bisects her brow to chin, whatever the costume, however the hair lies that day, marching its march under orders. Their eyes have it, double-hearted: richness, contradiction. Not torn, she insists, leaning in on her image, not torn at all. Multiple. As Shiva has many hands, as a candelabra holds its separate lights, why not (grandiloquent pup!) The sweet round plum of an eye for hoping, the harder chip an eye for coming through.

She closes one, opens it, and then the other, smiles, wiggles her brows like Groucho, which tickles. They will not make her choose. Neither the stockholders nor the ordinary citizens with whom she lives. She turns her head one way—the soft-cheeked girl next door—the other Mrs. Robinson slithery with wanting. *Really.*

May you live in uninteresting times, she tells herself, a blessing. Too late, too late for that. She sits at the top of the wheel and dares it not to move a notch. □

CROSSING THE STREET
Paul Skenazy

There was a day about four months after Harry's death when my grandfather Ben—Zadie to me—saw a boy who looked from the back exactly like his dead child. It was crowded where he walked along Roosevelt Road, with cars moving slowly in both directions, vendors lining the walkways. Stores extended out to the sidewalks, their pots and pans and chickens suspended on hooks, apples, lemons and lettuces in bins, socks and underpants still in the box. But it seemed the same beige jacket that Harry had worn for so many years, bought Zadie imagined off the same racks at Mandel Brothers. It looked like the same hair as his son, pale as hay, curling out at the ears. Even a little longer on the left side just like Harry's because of that nearsighted barber my grandma Ida (my Bubbie) took him to. And outside his jacket the boy was wearing what seemed like the same flimsy holsters weighted down low along his hips by two toy six-guns. The boy was ready for a showdown, though not quite ready at the moment my Zadie saw him. Just then he was staring down at his feet, balancing himself at the edge of the sidewalk as he dipped one foot up and down into the sludge of the gutter, his shoe dark with grime from the pool of winter snow below him in the street.

Zadie's own Harry had abandoned his gun belt maybe four years before the accident when his devotion to Hopalong Cassidy gave way to an even more devout imitation of a slightly pot-bellied Al Capone, and he took off the holsters and began to tuck one of the guns inside his front belt. By the time he was shot, Harry was done with that story too, and was instead a round headed reader, such a large almost perfectly round head he had that you thought he would one day have to have a neck like a bull and stand over six foot tall to grow into it. Like this boy. And you thought watching him, as Zadie thought now across the street, staring while people bumped against him on all sides, that a head like that would topple off the boy's neck if he bent too far to one side.

At eleven, last year, all Harry would do was read, and talk. Mom told me that: how her little brother would talk your ear off making sure you knew all he learned from the front page of the *Chicago Daily* News or the stories in the *Saturday Evening Post*. How almost every afternoon on the way home from school Harry would stop at the library at Cermak and Green, take off his cap and smile to the two women librarians. Each day as he came in the librarians would smile, glance at the clock and then back to each other with the tiniest knowing nod at his regularity. He would go sit himself down at the table nearest the corner with the light coming in from the high windows and take up a magazine, a book, a Chicago paper or one from Indiana, New York, Atlanta. Whatever caught his eye. He would read till the windows grew dark, the lights came on in the center of the tables and he looked up and realized that he would be late again for dinner. He worried about worrying other people. As he banged hard on the wooden steps and rushed into the front hall of the tiny apartment, his coat already half off, he was probably lucky to have his head so full of facts, events, anecdotes—the assembly of others' lives—because they insulated him from my Bubbie's complaints. Her chicken was falling off the bone already from him, she might say, or the liver had turned hard as shoe leather he was so late, or the once steaming soup was now cold on the table at his place from waiting. Or she would sit and stare and say nothing for a moment, until she muttered under her breath in a Yiddish just loud enough for him to hear how he worried her sick all the time, didn't he think ever about other people? And to make sure he washed the newsprint from off his hands before he sat down. Her despair her way to welcome him. And it was a blessing then at the meal, my Zadie worn from his time stitching shoes all day, his eyes gazing painfully through his thick glasses, my mother and my Uncle Abe both taciturn from waiting each night for Harry's return; it was a blessing then to have Harry's flood of library stories, his avalanche of memory, to sit like a centerpiece and distract them all through the overcooked peas, wilted cabbage and never quite mashed potatoes.

It didn't take long for my Zadie, still standing there across the street, arrested by his vision of his dead son, to decide, reluctantly, despite his eyes, that this boy was not his Harry but a little boy, his Harry three maybe four years ago now. But our family, we never give up on the dead but carry them to our own graves and find their faces everywhere along the way. My mother who hated her mother by the time Bubbie died saw her whenever she got near some group of *yentas* walking down Devon Avenue. I will follow men with long black hair for blocks sometimes still a year after my friend Art died, looking at their thick heads of hair for some hint of that distinct bald spot at the crown that grew so prominent in his last days from all the chemotherapy.

But mom and me, we just look, content with the shadows, the web of loss. We'll admit to ourselves that we're seeing ghosts, quickly realize how the kids or the wife will laugh when they hear us talk about another sighting like we're standing watch for whales. Zadie would never just watch. The people who owned the small shops near his shoe store knew him and would smile sometimes when they'd see him approaching another stranger. "Looking for his son again," they'd say; or, "She must be like his mother in Russia," they'd tell each other. He would sometimes bring them to the store, these strangers, take them in the back for some tea, talk to them until he could separate himself from who he wished they were. It didn't happen so often to bother my Bubbie, or bother her too much, and my mother says sometimes the people would come back bringing their boots or shoes for a new sole here, a pair of laces there.

So it is not surprising that Zadie could stand where he was only so long with the people shouldering by him and turning a little to see why he'd stop in the middle of the sidewalk like a stalled car. Perhaps some of these folks going where their lives led them even followed his gaze across the street, tracing the line of his attention. Though I doubt if they could pick out this particular boy amid the crowd, the one with his hand now in a woman's as he started shuffling along the edge of the curb, resisting the woman's pull forward to keep his shoe skimming the surface of the sludge. Maybe my Zadie would have stared longer before he moved but he saw them, mother and child, angling away. Zadie's eyes would never waver from a face. They never wavered from my face I know as I talked to him about some little house I had drawn or the tunnel I was making with pillows on the rug or asked him to read me something from the newspaper he always seemed to have sitting beside him on the couch. I can picture him staring like a flashlight as he traveled quietly across the street, barely glancing at the cars to make sure he was safe, more concerned not to release the boy from his attention. Perhaps it was the hands he took in most—the woman's over the boy's, pulling the boy along now, gently, down the street, her shopping bag a little fuller and certainly a little heavier as they left the fruit stand with whatever it was—a grapefruit, maybe a pear or two—and barely paused at the neighboring stalls.

As it turned out, he did not take the boy or the woman to the shoe store. The boy—a David—was just a boy, not his boy. He was six, he smiled a lot, was a little slow sometimes getting jokes, never missed a chance to eat a pickle. He liked it when Zadie would tuck him into bed and tell him stories. He liked how Zadie would sometimes suddenly roll his eyes behind the glasses that magnified the whites till they seemed to bulge, ready to explode. He liked how his mother laughed at dinner more, started making brisket once a week, and let him listen to the radio later into the night without noticing. And over the next months he learned he could stare out the small window of his bedroom for long stretches of an afternoon while his mother and the strange man they met on the street talked in a low croon together behind the door of the next room. He eventually forgot the months when Zadie came to live in the apartment, forgot Zadie's glasses and stories, forgot the new dresses his mother made that year for herself. Another man replaced Zadie in his life, stayed longer, but also disappeared in turn. And by then it was David's job to support himself, help his mother, take her to movies or the occasional baseball game she so loved.

* * *

Polite as Zadie was, soft as his voice was, warm as that smile was that I remember still from when I was small, the woman must have turned, startled, when he put himself in front of her, interrupted her shopping, her morning, her life. She stepped back for a moment, I imagine, especially as he moved one hand out, politely still of course, to touch the sleeve of her coat to stop her, however temporarily, so he could look straight at the boy, could again convince his aching chest that this was not Harry, not his Harry. For until that moment, looking from the dark eyes of the surprised woman to the boy, Zadie must have held on to some hope of Harry's return. The woman stood still, balanced between fear before an unnamable danger and anger at this intrusion that made her yank her arm free of Zadie's touch, easy as that was since Zadie's fingers hardly blemished the wool of her sleeve let alone aimed to keep hold of it.

Zadie couldn't talk for just that time it took him to see that the boy's red cheeks were too round, the fingers a little short and wide, the eyes not as bright as his Harry. Just the time it took him to relinquish his hope and descend from his imaginings back to the noisy, crowded street, to the brusque shoulders brushing by his, to the face of a woman and child he didn't know. The ears, though, the ears—and he reached out his left arm to touch the child just above the ear and brush the hair from across the top of it, even as the woman intercepted his efforts, deflected his hand and pushed by him with a stare that was surely meant to register rage but hung between them unsteadily, a mix of shock and worry, while she struggled awkwardly to drag the boy away with her. The boy looked at Zadie for the first time, really, since for the first time he realized that this man mattered—mattered enough for his mother to not want him near. And so David became interested, pulled back from his mother's urging, dropped that still dangling leg of his deep inside the pool of snow and water in the gutter, and kicked up sludge at my Zadie's pants. Then, his balance gone in the aftermath of his attack, David slid suddenly along his other foot until he hit the pavement hard, his guns making a clatter preliminary to the cry that came after the shock of his landing.

It was my mother who told me how after the shooting Zadie and Bubbie said almost nothing to each other, in the kitchen or the dining room, morning to night. They were silent too in their bedroom, under the covers, turned away from each other, their backs rubbing stiffly one against the other in their tiny bed. And silent in the store, where they would serve customers as if nothing had happened, serve even the curious who came in because they'd heard about the shoe store where the little boy (my Uncle Abe) shot his younger brother when they were playing with the pistol their father kept under the cash register. Kept hidden and ready because Zadie had always been afraid of theft, there had been so much of it in his little village in the Ukraine. My mother told me about Zadie's walks, how he would get so restless in that store, hour after hour. He would not stop work for lunch but instead, sometime after three, would just look up from whatever he was doing to the street outside the window, move to the clothes hook, pick up his hat, and depart, not saying anything to anyone. Bubbie would not even glance at the door when the bell on the top rang. She'd call my Uncle Abe from the back room where he would help after school with the gluing and cleaning to come up front to watch for customers, never pausing in her own work. Zadie didn't wear a winter coat those days, just the dark black suit with the suspenders I remember him in years later and the white shirt and the black bow tie, and his hat, slung low over his eyes, as if he were walking into an eternal snowstorm.

Zadie was wearing the hat that day too, when he turned his attention to the woman in the tumult of the child crying unhappily on the pavement. She abandoned the mesh bag of food as she tried at once to comfort the boy and hasten his movements, urge him up rapidly so they could escape this man who she looked at now with even more fear for upsetting her afternoon. It was then, I think, that she first saw Zadie's eyes, with their look of greed and emptiness. Her body froze, kneeling beside the boy. Zadie apologized then, explained then. She must have offered some sort of smile then too, or at least a nod. I imagine her lowering her eyes, while Zadie bent to pick up the lettuce and fruit now soiled from the sidewalk. He offered a hand to help her up, offered it again to the child with a few kind words and a glance at the child's leather shoe now soaked through with the cold slush of the late afternoon. He asked if he might buy her a tea and the boy some hot chocolate, there was a little restaurant where they could sit just at the corner and the boy could have a cookie perhaps and might he carry her bundles. She moved her chin only slightly in agreement or acquiescence as Zadie softly took up her bags while she grasped David's hand tightly in hers to insure herself that her son was safe. Zadie looked down at the boy now looking up at both his mother and this man, and led them two or three stores down the street to the little restaurant run by the old man and his sister Tamara. The restaurant known for the painted china that came from St. Petersburg. And for Tamara, who never got out of her slippers all day, shuffled along on them with their flattened heels and her worn brown stockings with the tiny holes delivering teas, sandwiches and cookies among the tables, never lifting her feet off the ground, the soles making a kind of whooshing noise like someone whispering for quiet.

The three of them went back to that little restaurant often in the next weeks, met there in fact most days as Zadie began to come down that way each afternoon, his wandering at a halt, a destination in hand for the first time in months. She was a widow, her husband gone from some freak accident in the tanning factory over on Wabash. She did sewing at home, like my Bubbie, but a little more practiced, more fine work, for more money, though still barely enough to pay for her little apartment.

Even when he moved in a few months later, a key in his pocket, Zadie always called it her apartment, always thought of himself as just visiting for a time, while the time grew from afternoons to nights, from days to months. My Bubbie never met her that I know, never would talk about her, and only reminded my Zadie of his days with her by silence and the long blunted looks that passed for intimacy in my memory of holiday dinners each Rosh Hashanah, Thanksgiving, Chanukah and Passover before Zadie died.

I didn't know about her until I left my own wife and children in my mid-forties for a woman I didn't mention to my mother but she was warning me against anyway. It was when I was driving her downtown along the Eisenhower Expressway. She talked about how when she was fourteen she'd been sent to live for more than a year at her Aunt Sarah's and how I must not, ever, let anything like that happen to her grandchildren no matter what. Zadie and Bubbie were both dead by then, he long since buried after the operation for ulcers that turned into an infection that burned through his insides, and she only in the grave a few months after her years of widowhood suffering through arthritis and diabetes with only the conviction of fated misery to console her. My mother said nothing of a David, little of the woman. She told me only that Zadie left

Bubbie, moved in with another woman he met she didn't know how. And how in her grief Bubbie, beside herself, cursing the man and the world that made him and killed her child, sent her other children away, one to each sister—my mother to Aunt Sarah, Uncle Abe to Aunt Sophie. She and Abe saw nothing of Zadie that year, little more of Bubbie. So my mother never met the woman, never saw if there was a David. I know the woman—some woman—existed, know that David must have too, know that something like this happened sometime that year, in those quiet days, weeks, and months that came after the shooting.

He came back, my Zadie, my mother never knew why or how. He never said a word to her about his time away. He hugged my mother when he came to get her and her suitcase from Aunt Sarah's, thanked my great-aunt and hugged her too, helped my mother into the cab he had hired, held her hand all the way home, where Bubbie waited with her overcooked chicken and lumpy potatoes already on the table and Uncle Abe, disconsolate, already in his chair. Dinners were more quiet than ever after that, the whole of the week was quiet after that. My mother told me how rarely Zadie, never much of a talker, spoke now, even as Bubbie grew more restless year after year. The radio, when they could afford to buy one, must have been a blessing.

Zadie would still take long walks but at night now, after dinner, until maybe nine when my mother would hear the door open and he would come in, hang up his suit jacket, smile quietly and settle into the corner of the sofa under the lamp to read the paper until long after everyone else was in bed. I remember him in the same corner of that same sofa years later when it was my turn on his weary knee, or as he watched me play marbles on the rug at holidays, or when he would put the paper over his face while the adult talk went on around him on the Friday nights we were there for dinner. My mother adored him all her life. But it was Bubbie she would see as she walked from one store to the next in her neighborhood, while I communed with Zadie, sitting still in that corner of the sofa, the light above his head, his slight mustache barely shading his upper lip, his smile wary, his eyes tired, so tired, anxious to help and ready for sleep.

That my father was a quiet man, that he was undemonstrative, that he was the one we always counted on and he was always there, that he never walked away into the dark, that he kept himself from strangers with a formal shyness, this of course comes as no surprise. ☐

BUDDING LITERARY MASTERS

The Chicago Literary Hall of Fame launched the Budding Literary Masters prizes in order to celebrate the talents of young writers in Chicago. Two thousand dollars in prize money, along with certificates for advanced creative writing education at StoryStudio Chicago, were distributed among the top young writers, who were honored at a ceremony and reading at Ernest Hemingway's Oak Park birthplace on July 10, 2013.

CLHOF introduced the contest to fulfill its mission of uniting the past, present and future of Chicago literature. The contest is a way to encourage young writers to continue exploring the world, and our city, through language.

Distinguished judges Bayo Ojikutu, Rosellen Brown and Syed Afzal Haider selected the winning entries.

MY BELOVED HOME

MUNA ABDULLAHI

SCHAUMBURG HIGH SCHOOL

Sahal lay on his back thinking of what had happened to him. He remembers the last time he saw his mother and father. He remembered the times that he has spent with his brother and sister. He could not believe that it all happened in one month; the armed forces marched into his family farm. He could not believe that what happened had changed his life completely. He would not understand how the united people that he had grown up with now were divided.

The clashing of tribes caused the extensive civil war that had suddenly erupted in the country. The moon was perfectly round in the middle of the sky. The fire had gone off. Everyone around him had gone to sleep, but Sahal could not go to sleep that night. He knew that he would need the energy in the morning, but the thoughts of his family would not leave his mind. Now on the run, Sahal was often awakened by his nightmares. The sweating, the terror, and the sounds of gunshots—his brother's and father's deaths...

Sahal could not imagine that he would never see them again. He wondered what had happened to his mother. He wanted to be with her now more than ever. Sahal was glad that Mohamed, his cousin, was with him.

Mohamed was eighteen years old. He lost both of his parents in the car accident when he was ten years old. He lived with his uncle who had five young children. Mohamed worked in his uncle's clothes store in a nearby village called Dilla. He loved to help his uncle, Ismail, in the store. When Ismail heard that the militia forces were heading to Dilla, he decided to send Mohamed to Borama where Ismail's cousin, Farah, lived. Borama was one hour away by the land cruiser from Dilla. The next morning, Mohamed took the land cruiser and left Uncle Ismail and his cousins. Mohamed wondered if he would see them again. Now he was in the forest with Sahal on the run, and the indefinite future that lay before him.

Sahal listened to the wolves howling after the moon was gone in the sky. He had never left his homeland before. Sahal recalled his life in Somalia. He loved his life. Amina, his older sister, used to make breakfast for him every morning after they prayed Fajir or the Morning

Prayer. Sahal and his brother, Ahmad, loved eating his sister's looh, which was the Somali pancake. Sahal, Amina, and Ahmad sat together for breakfast with mother. Every day, Ahmad walked Sahal to school before he went to work with his father on the farm where they spent most of their mornings and afternoons. But now these familiar days, like his former life, were gone.

* * *

In the winter of 1989, Amina's former classmate Osman, formally asked her father for permission to proposal her. In a traditional way, Osman came to Sahal's house with his father, to make the official engagement ceremony. Amina's father agreed after he made sure that Amina agreed, too. Osman was well educated, with a good job. He worked for a livestock trading company in Harawa Valley, Ethiopia. Osman asked Amina's father if he would allow Amina to move with him to Ethiopia. Sahal's father agreed on one condition. He wanted him to let his daughter come to visit him once or twice a month, and with this condition they made a deal. Sahal was very young at that time, but he remembered every detail of that night. A year later, Amina got married, and she moved to the city of Jigjigo, where her husband worked. Sahal missed his sister so much. He even thought of visiting her once, but due to the Ethiopian and Somalian War, and it was almost impossible for his sister to visit them again. He had not seen his beloved sister since then.

* * *

The word spread around Sahal's neighborhood quickly. "The soldiers are coming to get the young boys in Borama. They need them in their forces," Sahal's mother said at the dinner table that night. "We should do something, you know, before they get to our house. Don't you think Farah?" Sahal's mother said calmly.

"I have heard that they are heading to the east, to Dilla. I pray they do not reach Borama he soon. Insha'Allah; for Allah's will!" Sahal's father said.

"I am glad that Ismail had sent you to our house, Mohamed," Farah said, looking up from his plate.

"I assume that you are in a safer place now. You are like one of my sons." Sahal's father said.

"Thank you, Uncle Farah," Mohamed said politely.

"I remember your father very well. We grew up together. I remember the times that we stole apples from our neighbor's tree. 'Curse you little monkeys' would yell our old neighbor," Farah said smiling at the memory. "You look just like your father, Mohamed. Your father would be proud of the fine man you have become.

"You should go to bed now. Ahamad will show you around tomorrow," Sahal's father stated.

"Thank you Uncle Farah. Happeen wanaksan, good night," Mohamed said.

Mohamed lay on the bed that Sahal had set for him, and thought of the last words that Ismail had said to him at the bus station before he left.

"Don't ever give up and seek help from Allah." These words inspired Mohamed.

He now was willing to move on and face the challenges in life.

* * *

The tribal militia forces backed up marched into Borama in 1991, while Sahal was in school. Ahmad and Mohamed were working on the farm with Farah near north of the village. Farah and Ahmad had gone to the house for lunch, but Mohamed had stayed to work for an hour or two because he was not hungry yet. Sahal's mother had gone to have tea with a neighbor. Four tribal militia soldiers knocked on the door when Ahmad and his father came back home to eat lunch. Ahmad opened the door.

"Aslamualikum Alikum, peace be upon you" Ahmad said quickly.

"Wa Alikum, and upon you," replied one of the soldiers dryly.

"Can we come in? Is your father home?" asked the solider who looked the oldest in the three other soldiers.

"Abo, Father," Ahmad yelled suddenly feeling nauseous.

"Aslamualikum Alikum," said Farah when he reached the door moments later.

"We need your permission to recruit your son into the armed forces to defend Borama," the solider said casually.

"No, I would not destroy my son's future," Farah said firmly.

"Let me try this again, we want your son to be in the armed forces," the solider said in a demanding voice. The air felt thick making Ahmad use his mouth to breathe as he watched the conversation get tense between his father and the angry looking solider.

"No," Farah said again, feeling stronger than ever.

The soldiers forcefully took Ahmad and his father outside of their house. There were men standing on the sidewalk of the street and the sight of Farah and his son being dragged out of their house caught their attention. The soldier asked Farah one last time and told him that it would be better for him to allow his son to go with them.

Farah realized that this would be the end but he said, "I would rather die than see my son kill an innocent person." Then, the soldier fatally shot both Ahmad and his father effortlessly as if it's not their first time to do it.

"This will be the end for anyone who will say no to us," said the soldier, and then he walked away with the other soldiers. Ahmad and Farah lay on the muddy ground, their bodies soaked with blood. Their lifeless eyes stared up at the beautiful sky as if waiting for the angels to come down and get their souls.

* * *

Sahal sat under a Higlo tree, it reminded him of his brother, Ahmad, who always said that if you sat under a Higlo tree between the Magribe prayer, after the sunset, and the Isha prayer, three to two years after sunset, all of your stress will be relieved. Higlo trees' leaves never fall down in any weather conditions, it stays green for a very long period of time and that makes it very special. Sahal always questioned Ahmad's myths but every time he sat under a Higlo tree he felt better. He used to sit under the one two kilometers away from his family farm for hours until his mother would send someone to look for him.

"Hey there quiet kid, I almost thought you got lost," Daha said trying to adjust next to Sahal under the tree.

"It's my land how could I ever get lost," said Sahal, looking at the navy blue sky.

"Why does that sound so familiar?" Daha chuckled his little boy laugh.

Daha was one of the teenagers that Sahal and Mohamed met along the way. He lived with of his grandmother in a nearby village. His grandmother sent him to sell cloths that she had handmade to Djibouti when the armed forces marched into his town.

"What is your story kid?" Daha asked.

"Mine is no different than the others Daha." Sahal replied not taking his eyes off the bright moon in the dark sky.

Daha looks up and closes his dark brown eyes. "You are not the only one, we are all homesick."

"Why do wars exist?" Sahal asked innocently.

"I don't know, but I know that we need to get some ohàoh," Daha said smiling. He got up in one move, flexing his arm muscle along the way.

Daha held his hand to Sahal and his smile, so comforting, it reminded Sahal of Ahmad. Sahal smiled back, took Daha's hand and stood by him. Daha did not let go of his hand and Sahal looked up to him questionably.

"Promise me that you will always hold your head high no matter how many times life hits you in the neck," Daha said with a sudden seriousness.

Sahal was taken aback but replied, "I promise."

Daha's effortless smile came back and they walked back together to the camp. Sahal remembered that beautiful, sunny day as if it were yesterday. Ahmad walked Sahal to school as they had always done. Ahamad then went to work with his father on the farm. The streets of Sahel's village were busy as usual. People were coming in and out of stores. Retired old men sat in cafes drinking their tea.

Sahal was in Quran Studies when he heard gunshots and people screaming. His classmates panicked. Sahal did not know how to react. He sat on his desk watching his teacher trying to calm the students. He thought of what could be happening on the streets of Borama. He wondered if Ahmad and his father were home in a safe place. They must be home for lunch by now he thought as he looked at his watch.

Mohamed, who stayed later to work in the fields, had come back to Sahal's house to eat lunch. Ahmad and Uncle Farah said to Mohamed that they would be back in thirty minutes, but they had been gone for two hours. When Mohamed arrived, he saw neighbors standing around Uncle Farah's house. Women were crying, and men's faces were solemn as they stood by the door of Sahal's house. Mohamed hurried into the house, and he saw Aunt Fatima crying over the two bodies that lay on the floor. A white sheet was neatly placed on top of the two bloody bodies. Mohamed moved closer. Astounded he realized the two bodies were Ahmad and Uncle Farah. Uncle Farah looked oddly peaceful as if he was asleep and so was Ahmad. He could not believe that the soldiers had killed them. Aunt Fatima, Sahal's mother, walked to Mohamed, and she handed him a small backpack. "I put things that you will need in the backpack. Go to Sahal's school. Take him, and the two of you must leave Borama as soon as you can." She wiped her eyes with a handkerchief and continued, "Please take Sahal out of here. God protect both of you," she said. Mohamed had seen Aunt Fatima cry on her daughter's wedding night. Her eyes then were full of joy. Now, they were full of distress.

"I will keep him safe habo, aunt. Don't worry," Mohamed said with tears coming down his checks. He kissed Fatima's forehead and rushed out of the house. Wondering if he will ever see her again...

Sahal snuck out of class while his teacher was trying to stop his classmates from climbing up the window. Sahal wanted to go home. When Sahal got closer to the front gate of the school, he looked back to see if anyone was following him. That was when his cousin Mohamed grabbed Sahal, and they fled out into the woods not looking back. Mohamed told Sahal what had happened to his father and brother. Sahal did not believe him for a moment, but then, tears started to come down his checks.

Sahal, at twelve years of age, had to leave, as did the other surviving children in his village. After his village was attacked by the militia forces, he had to travel to Djibouti by foot with the teenagers. The news of his brother's and father's murders terribly affected Sahal. He realized that this war would never end well.

Sahal never considered leaving Somalia, but now he only had his memories. He would never forget the winter season, when after dinner, Sahal's parents, Ahmadand Sahal would sit in front of the fireplace in the living room and play games or listen to Farah's stories about his childhood. Sahal would never forget the smell of rainin the air or the beauty of the spring flowers. Home. He would never forget his beloved country. Soon, Mohamed would wake him, and they would be on the run again. "Allah, protect us," Sahal prayed. □

DOORS CLOSING

ALIANA BARNETTE-DEAR

OAK PARK & RIVER FOREST HIGH SCHOOL

P icture this: Swiftly striding up the iron cast stairwell of the platform, stepping lightly through the cage-like door, you unearth your azure Chicago Transit Authority pass of plastic and cheap smudged ink. Slipping your card into the turnstile as you push through to the other side, you pass the attendant a small smile of acknowledgement; you receive an apathetic glare in response. But you don't care. It's not your place to care. Your only thought as you turn through shallow tunnels of piss-stained walls and crude murals courtesy of the Chicago street bomber "Vomet" is catching this Red Line to Chicago Ave.

See yourself now, standing before the wooden array of voltages and pigeon relief, gazing across at nothing and everything as your hands excavate the bottoms of your pockets. Your head absently dips to the tune of your buds and your lips murmur to maybe some or none of the words as you survey the near barren platform. An approving smirk tickles at your lips as you anticipate your first comfortable Redline adventure. Then, suddenly, the mood changes; the rancid tunnel expels a seemingly endless stream of homosapien vermin, rambunctious shouts and obnoxious laughter. You're crowded, having picked a spot near the entrance and the worst part, the train screams and screeches around the corner, finally making its appearance five minutes past far too late.

"This is Fullerton. This is a Red Line train to Ninety-Fifth and Dan Ryan," the automated voice pleasantly utters through the speakers above the door, barely audible over the sound of crying infants and loud, irritatingly stale conversation. "Doors Closing." You push through the doors as the last of the frantic flood trickles past you and you can already feel the condensed heat and stink engulf you in its sweat. There are no seats open anymore, so you must dangle from the steel bars and fight for your balance as you catch wind of the aroma of whomever's child has yet to master the art of potty training.

"This is North and Clybourn." More animated bodies file into the quickly shrinking train car, the inane chatter drowning out the hollow ding emanating from the speakers, sounding the closing of the doors. Just two more stops—don't worry you can make it, just two more to go. The L goes underground and a few kids shriek from the unexpected shift. You tap your foot off beat and drum your fingers against the cold metal as another stop comes and the car almost swells with the next wave of cheery shoppers and apathetic teenagers, fresh from the various shops on Clark. The very air tensing and smelling of misery and strangers, you're bumped and prodded twice more as the humanoid pestilence around you shifts and sways, attempting to make room for the next wave.

"This is Chicago. This is a Red Line train to Ninety-Fifth and…" The moment the doors open you push and maneuver to expel yourself—and several others—from the shrink- wrapped can of Chicagoan sardines. The stench of urine and sweat clings to the walls and you can't help but hold your breath or faint amidst the fog of foul and the common peddlers of the city. Emerging from the never-ending basement, you're standing front row to a concert of tires, engines, and horns, you breathe easier. Your heart rate evens, your back relaxes. You brush the last of subway glitter from your hands, a glorious mixture of one part public transportation, three parts familiar. You're tucked delicately in the folds of the ever-changing fabric of Cubbies and Sox fans, deep-dish deliciousness and caramel covered popcorn, short trips on the subway and evening commutes on the 'L.'

These rides are as essential to your time as love is to your sanity. Not a day is wasted within these bacterial traps, never a moment not worth recall. The effort you put into condensing your body mass everyday can only be described as dedication. You've broken every social boundary you have, denied yourself the sanctity of your personal space, and violated the integrity of your sense of scent, for what? Fifteen minutes saved? The dedication it takes to accept whatever crawls through the cracks of society, to face the pungent smells and give tunnel-dwellers the best Dirty Harry you've got in your arsenal, gives you everything you need to make it out alive in this sweaty jungle of steel and stale attitudes. Any feat, no matter its size, can be missed and pass you by in an instant. The doors willclamp shut before your eyes and you'll watch as what could have been pushes by. If you can compress yourself to make it through fifteen minutes, half an hour, or more in the Red line or any of the Chicago transit lines, you can accept the challenge of maneuvering through throngs of people and expelling yourself into the relief of self fulfilled success. There is never a train too crowded that you must miss your stop, change your plans. All it takes is effort, focus, and drive. You just have to get your foot through the door.

Your phone vibrates in your pocket; a friend wants to head over to North and Damen, some new sushi bar they're dying to try. You could try the army of lutescent cabs on the street or head across the street back to the subway. You hear the shouting of another packed train car from the grate below you, can already smell the bodies pressed close to your own, feel the car rock and your feet tip unbalanced against an unlucky stranger. You smile. It's just another Tuesday afternoon in the heart of your city, just another train ride in the place you call home. □

THE ANTIDOTE

CYRUS DELOYE

NORTHSIDE COLLEGE PREP HIGH SCHOOL

The house once sat on one of the four-block streets that ran between the two cemeteries where he had lived. It was demolished as soon as his parents passed away per his demand as inheritor of the address. It was his belief that, though he had been free for many years now, he needed to be finished with the crude assemblage of wood, plaster, brick and glass that only served as a reminder of his stunted childhood spirit. Since the adolescence of his parents' poisoned marriage he perceived that he had to leave the place or welcome its contamination. Because the poison, he deduced, had been, and always was, the lot on which he grew up. During his confinement it was revealed that the house could not grant his father's wishes, nor did it meet his mother's standards. And as his parents came from the generation that found itself stuck between traditional spousal roles and the sexual revolution, they managed to never reconcile the family.

Year after year, from holiday to holiday, under the inhospitable roof of a home that should have never been – the poison continued to spread. It would have been appropriate had the building been a laboratory for deadly chemicals. Some empyreal explosion could have made way for a properly founded structure to be erected in its stead. Often the boy would contemplate its demise: his liberation. He used to be undecided as to whether or not his parents would go with it. Sometimes his parents were home when disaster struck; sometimes they would be spared and given a chance to find something better for themselves. The boy was never homicidal, just contemplative. As such, he developed an uncanny ability for introspection that lent itself to his self-restraint. He would have been a hero to the world had it known of the oppressive place from which he came.

One blustery day he took the train downtown to visit a jeweler, for the second hand on his watch had stopped ticking. The winds battered and buffeted his body as he waited on the rather empty elevated platform. "Doors—open on the left." Southbound, the L departed. He transferred from red to brown at Fullerton, detrained at Madison and Wabash. Cut to Jeweler's Row, where diamond salespeople were as closely packed as the atoms of the gem they sold. Upon exiting the train the boy was engulfed by forceful gales, spat out by the turnstile, and shoveled down into the street. There, on the façade of the nearest building, the address he sought flailed mightily in the breezy gusts, almost beckoning for the boy to pull his hood down, tuck in his shoulders, and rush through the door's revolving entryway. He scanned the advisory for the jeweler's cumbersome Italian name – there it was, amongst sweaty dealers, shoppers, deliverers and coffee-girls. He clambered into the elevator and requested the fifteenth floor.

In defiance of the building's impressive stature, the jeweler's shop stood cramped and claustrophobic, brimming to its edges with untidy dressers full of half-opened drawers stocked with various metals and minerals, and tables containing the tools for the craft, and the hundreds of papers it took to conduct the business. The commotion of the store embraced the boy as the jeweler welcomed him like he was his long lost son. The jeweler spun around in his swivel chair, speaking with a distinct European intonation, "You know the last time you were here, you were barely up to here." The boy stared at the jeweler's hand held right above his bent waist. And he noticed the dangling feet. The jeweler was one of the last to contract polio before its vaccine became available, and while his hands and arms were especially hardened, his legs had become thin and unused. Yet the disease had done nothing to diminish the artisan's skills; for he was as good at cutting stones as he was at conversation, and this was observed as a casual gathering of Hispanic, European, and African people crowded and passed through his cramped office.

Settled into a raggedly upholstered lounge chair, the boy waited and listened in on the exchanges. The jeweler spoke with the tongue of a gifted schmoozer and possessed a vernacular that transcended any conventional language. Like his arms, his conversing skills were conditioned by years of entertaining garrulous company. When he gave advice or sales quotes he could not help but tell stories of his daughter's wedding ring or the Jews' usurping of the diamond trade. The boy did not mind at all; he had been mesmerized by the cultural commerce the jeweler facilitated, and for a brief while he forgot about his home that was devoid of it. To him, the shop was a microcosm of what life could become.

The boy walked back to the platform. The gusts recommenced their beating of his body, though he took no notice. Thoughts of what he had recently witnessed blew around his mind at speeds that topped the Beaufort scale. Caught in this mental vortex, he took the wrong set of stairs and ended up on the wrong side of the tracks. He thought about moving to the right side, but he did not have the means to pay another fare. Besides, did he want to be home anytime soon? The wrong train came, and he got on, and he went the wrong direction. But it felt right. He had time to see the city. He could observe the people getting on and off, fantasize over why they had gotten on and where they were going. Those few hours he spent with the jeweler felt like a predestined reunion, as if each patron had been guided there by some higher being—saints sent to show him his new path. What had become the most surreal and visceral experience of his life, he discovered, could be found in boundless amount on the public transit. He craved this human interaction with a hunger only escaping to the inner city could suppress; where the heart beat better and faster and stronger the closer he was to the core of this new world. The dichotomy between his frozen home and the dancing steel cars flashing in the sun was clear to him, and this new possibility became the frontier for all of his aspirations.

So he rode the subway whenever he could. There was no particular reason for the line he chose or the stop he got off at on any given day. His moves were aimless but his motives could not have had more purpose. He found his throne in the crushed velvet seats that lined each train car. His chariot came with a gush of wind and the harsh glow of halogen headlights in the evening. His ticket no more than a small plastic card that held two dollars and twenty-five cents. With it, he tapped in to the vitality of the city that coursed through his veins and served as his antidote. In Chicago he found a world that pushed childhood homes of crumbling floors and cracked ceilings into the foreground. In Chicago he found life. □

NOTES ON CONTRIBUTORS

A former writer and editor at the *Chicago Tribune,* **John Blades** is the author of the novel *Small Game* (Holt, 1992). His short fiction has also appeared in *TriQuarterly,* the anthology *Chicago Works,* and other publications. "The Fourth Dementia" is taken from a loosely connected series of stories collectively titled *The Sanity Claus,* another of which was published in a 2010 edition of *CQR.*

Robert Brown has created poetry and solo performance for the Smithsonian's National Museum of Natural History in response to "The Visual Griots of Mali," as well as for Kansas City Repertory Theater in response to *Clay*, and he is currently writing his first full-length collection (tentatively titled, *GRAPEVINE*). Robert is completing a B.A. in the Poetry Program at Columbia College Chicago. His show, Real Talk Live, plays every third Friday of the month at Elastic Arts.

Rosellen Brown is the author of ten books, five of them novels, including *The Autobiography of My Mother, Tender Mercies* – not the movie! – *Civil Wars, Before and After* – of which there was a movie –and *Half a Heart.* She has published three books of poetry, a miscellany of essays, poetry and stories, and a book of stories, *Street Games.* Her stories have appeared frequently in *Best American Short Stories* and *O. Henry Prize Stories* and the *Pushcart Prize Anthology* and she teaches in the MFA in Writing program at the School of the Art Institute of Chicago.

Marcia Cavell taught philosophy for many years, for the longest time at the State University of New York at Purchase, New York; also at New York University; and most recently at Columbia University. Also a trained psychoanalyst, she taught a course in Freud and Philosophy both at the University of California at Berkeley and at The New School in New York City. The piece which appears here, "Waiting," is the second chapter in a memoir itself entitled *Waiting,* the first chapter of which, "Trains," appeared in *The Antioch Review,* Winter, 2012. She is the author of two books, *The Psychoanalytic Mind, from Freud to Philosophy* (Harvard University Press) and *Becoming a Subject* (the Clarendon press, Oxford University), and numerous articles and book reviews both in philosophy and psychoanalysis. *Waiting* is her first venture into non-academic writing. Her mother, Marcia Lee Masters, was a well-known poet, as was her grandfather, the Chicagoan Edgar Lee Masters.

Steve Cejtin is a visual artist residing in Evanston, Illinois, home of his studio Hammer & Pixel. Originally involved with the commercial and artistic aspects of video, film and other recording media, Cejtin concedes that sometimes the still image is the more powerful venue for expressing the sense of conflict and contradiction that is in fact a major part of our modern daily life. His work tends to be political in nature, but often drifts into a visualization of the conflict between technology and nature or diametric opposed forces of logic and science versus instinct and emotion.

Garnett Kilberg Cohen has published two collections of short stories, *Lost Women, Banished Souls* (University of Missouri Press) and *How We Move the Air* (Mayapple Press), and a poetry chapbook, *Passion Tour* (Finishing Line Press). Her awards include a Notable Essay citation from *Best American Essays 2011*, the *Crazyhorse* National Fiction Prize (2004); the Lawrence Foundation Prize from *Michigan Quarterly Review* (2003); and four awards from the Illinois Council of the Arts, including a 2001 Illinois Arts Council Individual Artist's Fellowship for prose. Her essays and short stories have appeared in many publications, including *American Fiction, Ontario Review, TriQuarterly, The Antioch Review, Alaska Quarterly Review, The Literary Review, Descant, The Roanoke Review, The Nebraska Review* and many others. She has also published poetry in two anthologies, *Dorothy Parker's Elbow* (Warner Books) and *A More Perfect Union* (St. Martin's Press), as well as in many journals such as *Tulane Review, Mid-American Poetry Review, Calyx,* and *The Maryland Review*. A former fiction editor of *The Pennsylvania Review* and *Hotel Amerika,* Garnett has also served as the review editor at *Another Chicago Magazine* and the editor-in-chief of *The South Loop Review*. Garnett currently directs the Creative Writing—Nonfiction B.A. Program at Columbia College Chicago.

James Crizer studied theatre at Ole Miss and writing at Bowling

Green. He currently lives northwest of Chicago and serves as an associate dean at the College of Lake County. His poems appear in a variety of journals, most recently including *The Boiler, Portland Review, Licking River Review, The Pinch* and *Wisconsin Review.*

Don De Grazia is the author of the novel, *American Skin*. His work has appeared in *TriQuarterly, The Outlaw Bible of American Fiction, The Italian American Reader, The Chicago Tribune, The Chicago Reader, Rumpus,* and elsewhere. He is a screenwriter in the Writers Guild of America (east) and a full time member of the Creative Writing faculty at Columbia College Chicago.

Olga Domchenko was born in Germany and is of Ukrainian descent. She is a poet and writer and is currently working on her first short story collection. Olga has read her poetry and stories at various Chicago venues including Club Lower Links, Upper Links, Chicago Filmmakers, and Northwestern University radio station. She lives on the North Shore outside Chicago where she writes and gardens.

Jason Economus is based in Chicago, where he acts, writes, directs, teaches and throws out the occasional one-liner. Jason is heavily involved with Erasing the Distance, a company that uses theatre to minimize the stigma surrounding mental illness. He directed their past fall show, *Will You Stand UP?* and performs consistently with them on touring shows throughout the Midwest. He has acted, directed and created new works in Chicago with all sorts of neat companies like New Beast Theatre, Library Theatre, The Building Stage. He has created several short on-line comedy videos and created and wrote a festival winning short film called *Who Is Steve Shubert?* Most recently Jason directed *Miss Julie* with Vintage Theatre Collective, created and filmed the short film *20 Something* with Solo Studio Pictures and directed *Macbeth* for Door Shakespeare in Door County, Wisconsin.

Donald G. Evans is the author of the novel *Good Money After Bad* and editor of the anthology *Cubbie Blues: 100 Years of Waiting Till Next Year.* He founded and directs the Chicago Literary Hall of Fame and is the Chicago editor of the *Great Lakes Cultural Review.*

Art Fox is a practicing physician who has published a few prior poems in *Chicago Quarterly Review* as well as *California Quarterly.* (He seems to have luck with journals starting with "C" followed by "Q").

He values cadence and tone in poetry. His poems tend to be brief and descriptive. Visual imagery is quite important to him in poetry and also as a photographer. He has exhibited in some one person and group photographic shows, has published photographs, and has won some photographic awards. He lives in Chicago's West Loop neighborhood, and is a proud husband, father, and grandfather.

Gina Frangello is the author of three books of fiction: *A Life in Men* (Algonquin 2014), *Slut Lullabies* (Emergency Press 2010) and *My Sister's Continent* (Chiasmus 2006). She is the Sunday Editor of *The Rumpus,* the Fiction Editor of *The Nervous Breakdown,* and was the longtime executive editor of *Other Voices* magazine and its book imprint, Other Voices Books. She also is on faculty at the University of California-Riverside's low residency MFA program in Creative Writing. Her short fiction, journalism and essays have appeared in numerous publications and anthologies, including the *Chicago Tribune, Huffington Post, Chicago Reader, Fence, Prairie Schooner* and *Men Undressed: Women Writers and the Male Sexual Experience.*

Jack Fuller has published seven critically acclaimed novels and two influential books of non-fiction about journalism. He served as editor and publisher of the *Chicago Tribune,* where he won the Pulitzer Prize for editorial writing in 1986. Along the way he has been a police reporter, Vietnam war correspondent, and Washington correspondent. He retired in 2004 as president of Tribune Publishing. He lives in Chicago with his wife, Debra Moskovits. He has two children, Tim and Kate.

Syed Afzal Haider has had short stories and essays published in a variety of literary magazine including *Saint Ann's Review, AmerA sia, Rambunctious Review, The Journal of Pakistani Literature, The Taylor Trust, Trajectory, Marco Polo,* and *Indian Voices.* His stories have appeared in the Silver Birch Press Anthology series, *Silver, Summer,* and *Green.* Oxford University Press, Milkweed Editions, Penguin Books, and Longman Literature have anthologized Haider. His short story collection, *Tumbleweed Connection,* was a finalist for the MVP competition. His first novel, *To Be With Her,* was published by Weavers Press. His second novel, *Life of Ganesh,* is forthcoming.

David Hart grew up in a small town in central Illinois. After graduation from college and law school, he practiced corporate law in Chicago for many years. Upon retirement he returned to his poetry avocation.

He has appeared in reviews such as *Southwest Review, Hiram Poetry Review* and appears with some frequency in an on-line literary publication, *The Front Porch Review.*

Jan Herman (b. Jan. 2, 1942), editor, publisher, author and journalist, founded NOVA Broadcast Press as well as the little magazine *San Francisco Earthquake* (1967-1971). He published Beat, post-Beat and Fluxus writers and artists, including William Burroughs, Allen Ginsberg, Lawrence Ferlinghetti, Michael McClure, Robert Duncan, Ed Sanders, Dick Higgins, Wolf Vostell, Norman O. Mustill, Claude Pelieu, Mary Beach, Carl Weissner, Jean-Jacques Lebel, Richard Kostelanetz, Ed Ruscha, Liam O'Gallagher, Ferdinand Kriwet, Alison Knowles, Philip Corner, and Nanos Valaoritis. He worked with Higgins at Something Else Press, becoming the editor (1972-1974). As an author, he co-wrote *Cut Up or Shut Up* with Weissner and Jurgen Ploog, and published other experimental fiction. He is also the author of *A Talent for Trouble,* the biography of the director William Wyler. As a journalist, he was a reporter and columnist at the *Chicago Sun-Times,* the *New York Daily News,* and the *Los Angeles Times* (1981-1998), a fellow in the National Arts Journalism Program at Columbia University (1998-1999), and a senior editor at MSNBC.com (1999-2003).

Chicagoan by day, Californian by night, **Susan Hogan** is a poet who embraces the life of a nomad. She collects energy and immediacy wherever she is, spreading it outwards through her writing. She has studied at the University of Illinois-Chicago (English), Lomonosov Moscow State University (Russian), the University of Denver (book publishing), and San Diego State University (poetry and translation). She has served as contributing editor of *Poetry International,* has worked helping underprivileged students in San Diego with English as a first or second language, has interned for the Poetry Foundation's think tank, the Harriet Monroe Poetry Institute, and is currently employed at a small arts book publisher. Susan has given poetry readings across the country and is constantly generating new work, with help in part from her co-collaborators at the Chicago-based Caffeine Arts Collective, where she is resident poet. Her writing has appeared in *Serving House Journal, Alchemy Journal of Translation, Inner Art, The Chicago Gazette,* and other publications. Susan and her partner are expecting their first child, due in April. Keep up with her at www.susan-hogan.com and twitter.com/writemorepoems.

Andy Holt is a fiction writer born and raised in Florida. He has since lived in North Carolina and Chicago. Beginning in the fall of 2013, he will be pursuing an M.F.A. in fiction writing at the University of California, Riverside. Andy is twenty-three years old, and *Chicago Quarterly Review* is his first publication.

Gary Houston is a past *CQR* contributor and a former arts editor and writer for the *Chicago Sun-Times.*

Paul Nicholas Jones is a fiction writer living in Chicago whose stories have appeared in *MAKE* Magazine and the *Greensboro Review.* His story "Documentary" was selected by Stuart Dybek as the winner of the Guild Complex Prose Contest and nominated for a Pushcart Prize. In addition, he's received several fellowships to the Ragdale Foundation, read an essay for WBEZ and performed at Fictlicious and the Sunday Salon reading series.

Robert Kameczura (www.kameczura.com) has been called "one of Chicago's Renaissance men" for his art and photography. Mr. Kameczura has exhibited widely and internationally, in Japan, Poland, Ireland and Canada as well as across the U.S. He has exhibited at the Metropolitan Museum of Toyko, The Sakima Museum, The Peninsula Museum, The Rockford Art Museum and the EAG Gallery in the Elmhurst Art Museum to name only a few venues. He works in almost all genres; large acrylic paintings (of often epic size), watercolors, silkscreen prints (often dance related), drawings, linocuts. His work frequently has a highly romantic quality. For the last few years he has been concentrating on limited edition Giclee photographs and prints. Some of these prints are art-based, done after his drawings in the manner of traditional prints but a great many are based on his photographs. These are altered, hand retouched, and reworked extensively on the computer then printed with archival inks on fine paper in limited editions. The late Chicago collector June Spiezer, whose collection is housed in the Rockford Art Museum has said of him, "Robert Kameczura is Chicago's new 'Genius of the Giclee.' He treats this new medium with the finesse and skill of an old master. It is not just the quality of his work, which has amazing subtlety but the range and depth of feeling of his prints is astonishing. He is a master colorist and designer. His work glories in richly imaginative textures. Every print seems to bring something fresh and new; whether exploring effects of light and form in nature, showcasing the darker aspects of the urban experience, exploring small personal moments of self-reflection, or creating pure abstractions. His prints convey a kind of mind stretching beauty and originality which is found only in the work of the finest artists." He recently received two Illinois Arts Council Grants for Photography. He headed the campaign which created Chicago's public art program and was one of the founders and first directors of Chicago Artists Month, to name only a few of his credits. He is currently co-curator of the exhibit "Chicago Artists Interpret Shakespeare," and art and music critic for *Big Shoulders Magazine* (www.sobs.org).

L.M. Kell holds a B.A. in English and a B.S. in Secondary Education. She taught eighth grade English in North Kansas City, Missouri for four years, then managed the editing department at Bernard C. Harris Publishing, Inc. for five years. After graduating from the University of Nebraska with a J.D. and a concurrent Master's Degree in Community and Regional Planning, she clerked for the Chief Justice of the Nebraska Supreme Court. L. M. is now a retired Chicago litigator. After experiencing just about every career that involves words except journalist, novelist and/or blogger, she is slowly coming to terms with being a poet. Her late, deeply beloved husband taught philosophy before becoming a Chicago playwright. He left the best of himself here in their two adult children and in the words he wrote. L.M. lives across the street from the original Potbelly's Sandwich Shop, in a home full of various fish, amphibians, two cats and one dog. She also is a beginning playwright. L.M. enjoys her wonderful circle of dear human friends, and quaffing a Magners regularly at The Galway Arms.

Robert Kerwin's celebrity profiles, personal essays, travel and op-ed pieces have appeared in *Playboy, Cosmopolitan, Travel & Leisure, TV Guide, The New York Times, Newsday, The Washington Post, Chicago Tribune Magazine,* and *Los Angeles Times Calendar,* among others. They have been distributed by the *Chicago Tribune* and *L.A. Times* syndicates. "Brothers" is part of a memoir, *Here's To Better Times.* Born in Chicago, he now lives in northern California.

Jane Lawless, a Chicago native, has worked as a television scriptwriter, legal secretary, freelance editor, and writer-producer of educational materials, including an audio tour-guide program for Chicago's Field Museum of Natural History. Her short stories have appeared in *Bellowing Ark, Big Muddy, Chicago Quarterly Review, descant, Rosebud* and *Zahir.* She has been a resident of Colorado Springs since 2000, where she volunteers at Pikes Peak Hospice as a pastoral counselor. She also cooks, gardens and loves hiking the backcountry. Jane and her husband, Rick, a real estate broker, are the owners and vintners of Lingering Deer Winery, where they live with their two cats on the edge of the Pike National Forest.

Louise LeBourgeois is a painter. She lives in Chicago and swims in Lake Michigan from May to October. The look and feel of vast open water, plus the lake's flat horizon, inspire her painting. The lake, beneath the constantly changing sky, is both the simplest and the most complex visual image she sees regularly. Although she has never been a naturally early riser, she thinks it is an exquisite joy to swim in the lake while watching the sunrise. LeBourgeois earned her M.F.A. in Painting at Northwestern University in 1994. She shows her work at Packer Schopf Gallery in Chicago, Gold Gallery in Boston, Dolby Chadwick Gallery in San Francisco, GallatinRiver Gallery in Big Sky, Montana, and Megumi Ogita Gallery in Tokyo. She teaches in the Art and Design Department at Columbia College Chicago. She is also currently working on an M.F.A. in Nonfiction Writing at Columbia College Chicago. This is her first published essay. You can see her artwork at www.louiselebourgeois.com

William L. Lederer has had over thirty plays produced in such theaters as Hull House, Barry Street, Old Town Players, Triangle Art Center, Body Politic, Theatre Building, Athenaeum and Prop Theater. His teleplay, *The Reader and the Writer,* was originally produced by WTTW and later aired throughout the United States and Canada. Lost in the Grand Canyon a decade ago, he played himself in this misadventure on A&E's "The Unexplained-Wilderness Survival" and the Discovery Channel's "Storm Warnings-No Place to Hide." His works, including essays, poems and reviews, are on archive at Chicago's Newberry Library. He teaches creative writing at Stateville Correctional Center in Romeoville, Illinois.

In addition to writing stories for fun and her own amusement, **Micki LeSueur** is a freelance copywriter, writing fiction posing as non-fiction for major corporations and their advertising agencies. She is also the founder and host of Fictlicious, a live reading and music series, and its podcast series. LeSueur is also the president and founder of Coat Angels, a local not-for-profit proving warm winter coats for cold Chicago kids.

Joe Meno is a fiction writer and playwright who lives in Chicago. He is the winner of the Nelson Algren Literary Award, a Pushcart Prize, the Great Lakes Book Award, and was a finalist for the Story Prize. He is the author of six novels including the bestsellers *Hairstyles of the Damned* and *The Boy Detective Fails*. He is an associate professor in the Fiction Writing Department at Columbia College Chicago.

Michael Miner has written poetry all his life in private conversation with himself. Aside from a few early poems he gave to a friend in St. Louis who was publishing a magazine there, he has made no particular attempt to publish any poetry—though he has slipped an occasional poem into the media column he's written for the *Reader* since 1987. Miner was raised in Canada and suburban St. Louis, educated in journalism at the University of Missouri, spent a couple of years in the navy (he published a couple of poems in his ship's newspaper), and came to Chicago in 1970 to work for the *Sun-Times*. He's been a staff writer for the *Reader* since 1979.

Dipika Mukherjee is an author, poet, and sociolinguist. She made her debut as a novelist with the publication of *Thunder Demons* (2011), long-listed for the Man Asian Literary Prize. She also won the Platform Flash Fiction competition in April 2009. She has edited two anthologies of Southeast Asian short stories: *Silverfish New Writing 6* (2006) and *The Merlion and Hibiscus* (2002) and her first poetry collection, *The Palimpsest of Exile,* was published by Rubicon Press in 2009. Her short stories and poems have appeared in publications around the world and have been widely anthologized. She is the Associate Editor of *Jaggery* (A South Asian Diasporic Arts and Literature Journal) as well as Founding Member & Chair of the Mentorships/Retreats/Residencies committee at Asia Pacific Writers & Translators (a Global Writing Initiative). She is currently a member of the Vox Ferus group of poets in Chicago as well as a member of the Chicago Writers Association. More information at dipikamukherjee.com

Natalia Nebel is a writer and translator (Italian to English) whose short story "Slough" was nominated for a Pushcart Prize and whose translations, book reviews and short stories have been published in *Burnside Review, Free Verse, TriQuarterly, ELM, Seems, Fifth Wednesday* and *Primavera,* among other publications. In her free time, along with Alexandra Sheckler and Christine Sneed, she organizes a literary reading series called Sunday Salon Chicago that is a sister series to Sunday Salon in New York City. Special thanks to Benita Noveno for dreaming the SuSa endeavor up in the first place.

A recovering academic, **James (Jimmie Ray) Paradiso** is in the process of reinventing himself as a photographer, painter and memoirist. With graduate degrees in both Philosophy and Business Management, he taught at two community colleges and five universities for over thirty years. His academic achievements include receiving the Freedoms Foundation's Leavey Award for Excellence in Private Enterprise Education and coaching the $10,000 winner of the University of Miami's International Business Plan Competition. In Chicago, his photographs and paintings have been exhibited at the Apollo, Greenhouse, Lifeline, Raven and Wit Theatres. His photos have also been published in *after hours: a journal of Chicago writing and art.* James belongs to several writing groups including the Chicago Cultural Center's Randolph Street Brown Bag Poets, Chicago's Neighborhood Writing Alliance and Winnetka's Off Campus Writers Workshop. A collection of his memoirs, *Don't Fret, Mr. Jim,* is in the works. If asked why he photographs, paints and writes, he would simply say "to fill temporal-spatial-psycho-social holes, and on good days, to enjoy the flow." You're invited to visit his online photo-gallery at www.JamesParadiso.com.

Stuart Patterson is an Associate Professor of Liberal Arts at Shimer College in Chicago, Illinois where he teaches across the school's "great books" curriculum. His major areas of teaching and research include contemporary aesthetics, the history of reading, and the history and philosophy of the social sciences. He also has artwork appearing in current group shows around Chicago and plans for a solo show in Chicago in 2014. His appearance in the *CQR* marks his first published poem.

Harry Mark Petrakis is the author of twenty-five books including novels, short stories, and memoirs. He has twice been nominated for the National Book Award in Fiction. He has lectured extensively at colleges and clubs across the country. He served two years as writer-in-residence for the Chicago Public schools and two years as writer-in-residence for the Chicago Public Library. In 1992 he held the Nikos Kazantzakis Chair in Modern Greek literature at San Francisco State University. This excerpt is from his book of memoirs titled *Song of my Life* to be published by South Carolina University Press in the spring of 2014. Petrakis spent the first half of his ninety years in Chicago and the second half living in the dunes of Northwest Indiana with his wife Diana. They have been married sixty-eight years and have three sons and four grandchildren.

Cecilia Pinto's work has been published in a variety of journals including *Esquire, Fence, The Mississippi Review* and *TriQuarterly.* She teaches in the certificate in writing program at the University of Chicago's Graham School of Continuing Liberal and Professional studies and works for a major retailer.

Frederick Pollack is the author of two book-length narrative poems, *The Adventure* and *Happiness,* both published by Story Line Press. His work has appeared in *Hudson Review, Southern Review, Fulcrum, Salmagundi, Poetry Salzburg Review, Die Gazette* (Munich), *The Fish Anthology* (Ireland), *Representations, Magma* (UK), *The Hat, Bateau,* and *Chiron Review,* etc. Online, poems have appeared in *Big Bridge, Snorkel, Hamilton Stone Review, Diagram, BlazeVox, The New Hampshire Review, Mudlark,* etc. Recent Web publications in *Gloom Cupboard, Blinking Cursor, Occupoetry,* and *Seltzer.* Adjunct professor creative writing George Washington University. Poetics: neither navel-gazing mainstream nor academic pseudo-avant-garde.

Liz Radford is a Chicago-based writer and current MFA candidate at Northwestern University. Her fiction has been published in *Prick of the Spindle* and her non-fiction appeared in AWP's *The Writer's Chronicle.* She has written feature stories for various news publications and is a marketing professional.

Signe Ratcliff is a Chicago-based writer and artist. Her work has been published in the *Chicago Quarterly Review* and her manuscript *The Winter Box* was selected as a finalist for the 2013 James Jones First Novel Fellowship.

R. Craig Sautter is author, co-author or editor of ten books, including *Expresslanes Through The Inevitable City* (poems). He teaches courses in philosophy, politics, history, literature, and creative writing at DePaul University. He was the 47th president of the Society of Midland Authors: www.midlandauthors.com

Paul Skenazy lives in Santa Cruz, California with his wife, his cat, and too many books acquired over thirty years of teaching literature and writing at the University of California. His fiction has recently appeared in *Catamaran Literary Reader* and *Red Wheelbarrow.* He has written two novels looking for publishing homes and is currently working on a third about Chicago. In his previous life as an academic and critic, he published books on James M. Cain and other noir writers, reviewed fiction and memoir for the *Chicago Tribune, Los Angeles Times, San Francisco Chronicle* and other newspapers and for a dozen years wrote a regular column on thrillers for the *Washington Post.* He also revised and edited a novel, *La Mollie and the King of Tears* by Arturo Islas, published posthumously.

Brian Allan Skinner has worked extensively in publishing as both a writer and graphic artist. The publications in which his work, reviews and illustrations have appeared range from the literary *(Kirkus Reviews)* to the scientific *(Scientific American Newsletters).* He began his career in the fine arts in the traditional media of oil-on-canvas and watercolor, but now works almost exclusively in digital media. His artwork can be seen in several venues in and around New York City, as well as online at www.brianskinner.net. He is currently employed as a studio assistant and digital technician for a New York still-life photographer. Recent explorations include cliché verre, a technique of etching and painting on glass photographic plates, in which he first dabbled over forty years ago. His latest literary endeavors include a second short story cycle entitled *Café Kundalini.* He is also at work as the editor on a second feature-length documentary film.

Christine Sneed's story collection *Portraits of a Few of the People I've Made Cry* won AWP's 2009 Grace Paley Prize in Short Fiction and was a finalist for the *Los Angeles Times* Book Prize for first fiction. *Portraits* was also awarded *Ploughshares'* 2011 John C. Zacharis Prize for a first book and the Chicago Writers Association's book of the year in the traditionally published fiction category. Her second book, a novel titled *Little Known Facts,* was published by Bloomsbury USA in February 2013. Her short stories have appeared in *Best American Short Stories, PEN/O. Henry Prize Stories, Ploughshares, Southern Review, New England Review, Glimmer Train* and other journals. She has been awarded an Illinois Arts Council fellowship in poetry and has published poems in journals such as *River Styx, Pleiades, Black Warrior Review, Poetry East* and *Poet Lore.*

Miriam Socoloff is an artist and educator. From 1998 through 2007, she was the curriculum coordinator and drawing and painting instructor for Gallery 37 School Advanced Arts Education Program. Her students have won national awards, including the U.S. Presidential Scholars in the Arts Award. Miriam, in collaboration with Cynthia Weiss, has created mosaic murals for buildings in the Chicago area. Their murals have been published in *A Guide to Chicago Murals* by Mary Lackritz Gray (University of Chicago Press, 2001) and in *Urban Art Chicago* by Olivia Gude and Jeff Huebner (Ivan R. Dee Publisher, 2000). In 1998, Miriam was awarded the Golden Apple Award for Excellence in Teaching and a Chicago Artists International grant to study mosaic technique in Italy. She was selected for an artist residency at the International School of Art, Umbria, Italy and four artist residencies at OxBow. In 2003, Miriam was awarded a Fulbright Memorial Fund Fellowship to study in Japan. In 2006, she was awarded a Fund for Teachers award to study mosaic technique in Italy. In 2011, Miriam received the U.S. Presidential Scholars Teacher Recognition Award. Currently, Miriam teaches in the After School Matters program. She is a member of Ten Chicago Women Artists, and her website is www. miriamsocoloff.com

Sharon Solwitz's short story "Alive" appeared in *Best American Short Stories 2012.* She has published two books of fiction and over sixty short stories, some of which have won awards including the Pushcart, first prize from *Moment Magazine,* and the Nelson Algren Award (thrice runner-up). Her collection of stories won the Carl Sandburg Prize and the Midland Authors prize, and was a finalist for the National Jewish Book Award.

James Stacey wrote his first story at age eighteen and has been writing ever since. As a reporter he worked for several periodicals, including *Business Week and American Medical News.* As a free lancer, he published feature length articles in the *Chicago Sun-Times, Chicago Tribune,* and the *Washington Post,* among other newspapers. He is the author and co-author of two books on health policy, *Inside the New Temple: the High Cost of Mistaking Medicine for Religion,* and *Severed Trust: Why American Medicine Hasn't Been Fixed.* He also published a novel, *The Medicine Men,* which describes power struggles within a Washington-based lobbying office. More recently, he completed a memoir, *My Functional Family,* and now is working on another novel. A native of Chicago, he returned to the city nine years ago, after spending two decades on the East Coast.

Umberto Tosi's "Onion Station" is from *The Einstein Express,* an autobiographical novel-in-progress. His published works include a recent triptych of novellas – *Our Own Kind, Satan the Movie* and *My Dog's Name* – all three set in Los Angeles, where he worked eleven years as a staff writer and section editor for the *L.A. Times* and its Sunday magazine before moving to Northern California where he edited and wrote for *San Francisco Magazine,* Francis Ford Coppola's *City Magazine,* the *San Francisco Sunday Examiner/Chronicle* and other publications. His published works include the spy biography, *High Treason, Sports Psyching, Milagro on 34th Street,* and his short story collection, *Gunning for the Holy Ghost.* Umberto Tosi was born in Boston and has resided in Chicago for the past three years with his partner, artist Eleanor Spiess-Ferris. He has three daughters and a son, all grown.

Steve Trumpeter's short story "Sky Boys" won the *Chicago Reader's* 2012 Pure Fiction contest. His short stories have also been published in *Jabberwock Review* and selected as a finalist in *Glimmer Train's* Fiction Open contest and *Third Coast's* Jaimy Gordon Fiction Prize. Steve lives in Chicago with his wife, Kathryn, and Talisker the cat. He is currently toiling away at his first novel, *Glow.*

Melanie Villines is a novelist, playwright, television writer, screenwriter, biographer, and editor. Her work includes the novel *Tales of the Sacred Heart* (Bogfire Press), the family memoir *Reason to Fight* (co-written with Hiram Johnson), a celebrity biography *Beyond Hollywood* (co-written with J. Herbert Klein), *Anna & Otto,* a novel for children (Inklings Press), and a variety of ghostwritten books and screenplays. In Chicago, she was active in the city's theater movement, studying with David Mamet and William H. Macy and co-founding Chicago Dramatists, where she workshopped fourteen of her plays. Her short stories appeared in the Silver Birch Press *Silver Anthology* (November 2012) and *Green Anthology* (March 2013), and her play *Bernice* (co-written with Hiram Johnson) had a February 2013 workshop production at BAAL in Dallas. Born and raised in Chicago, Melanie has lived in Los Angeles since 2007.

J. Weintraub is a Chicago writer, poet, and translator who has published widely in literary reviews and periodicals across the country. He is also a dramatist and has had one-act plays produced in New York and Chicago. (More on his work can be found at http://jweintraub.weebly.com). He would like to dedicate this story to the memory of the writer Curt Johnson, editor and owner of *december* magazine and a former colleague of his (at least for a short time, anyway).

Laura Williams (cover illustration) has had many different jobs. She has decorated large cookies. She has built dioramas. She worked at a costume company (where she made hats for elephants, belt buckles for lion tamers, and other silly things). She made props for commercials and movies. She was a wardrobe assistant. She worked at one of the first production companies in NY that did digital compositing. She found images. Laura learned Photoshop, which lead her into the world of high definition television, and then onto interactive design. Now she is a graphic designer at a book publisher and a freelance designer and illustrator. She has made a lot of crazy things and has been involved in many different streams of visual communication. It is interesting, challenging, hilarious, surreal, insane and infuriating and it is all made easier because she works and collaborates with some incredibly talented and inspiring artists. Her personal work weaves inside and outside of her work for hire and although she has tried for most of her professional life to keep them separate, she is beginning to understand that the more she can merge them all together, the more satisfying it will be.

Rogers Worthington is a former reporter and National Correspondent for the *Chicago Tribune.* He is a Chicago transplant from Queens, New York. This is his first published story.

Budding Masters Winners

Muna Abdullahi (Schaumburg High School): Muna was born in Somalia and grew up in Yemen. She came into U.S in 2010 with her family and joined with her father in Chicago. At the moment she is a senior at Schaumburg High School. She is going to be a pharmacologist and a writer.

Aliana Barnette-Dear (Oak Park & River Forest High School): I like to believe I was born amongst books. As a child I loved to read and I aspired to write stories that would make other children as excited as I was with Dr. Seuss's *Many Colored Days* and *Oh, The Places You'll Go.* Throughout my education I continued to write and learned that expression through the pen leads to many roads, one leading me to where I am today, a graduated senior, a future children's author and pastry chef.

Cyrus Deloye (Northside Prep High School): Most days I wake up, I stretch, and I think to myself, "I'm gonna do something today." Usually that something includes water polo, soccer, comedy, guitar, and up-to-no-good-tomfoolery. I rarely write, and while it doesn't come naturally I am very interested in adding it to my list of something. In short, thank you for reading.

CQRB

Chicago Quarterly Review Books

My Postwar Life

ELIZABETH MCKENZIE - Editor
Foreword by KAREN TEI YAMASHITA

$19.95 trade paper (328p) ISBN 978-0-9847788-0-5

"To become familiar with the stories and storytellers from other parts of our planet...is a key component of being a citizen in the world today."

-from the Introduction by
Elizabeth McKenzie

"Written with the authority of eyewitnesses and empiricists, this anthology presents a portrait of Japan and Okinawa that is impossible to erase from memory."

-Stephen Mansfield,
The Japan Times

"The image that opens the collection is a photograph of a piece of debris from ground zero in Nagasaki. It is the face of a wristwatch, its hands stuck forever at 11:02 a.m.. However, unlike the recovered wristwatch, life in Japan and Okinawa went on. My Postwar Life is a beautiful bit of proof that it carried onward, and is something to be celebrated."

-Manoa, a Pacific journal of
international writing

"This engaging anthology of short fiction, essays, poetry, photography, and more illuminates the interconnected past of the U.S. and Japan, from WWII up to 2011's earthquake. Ryuta Imafuku's essay, "Nagasaki. And Scattered Islets of Time," is a walk through the suspended reality of post-atomic Nagasaki, accompanied by Shomei Tomatsu's powerful photos of bum victims, detritus, and seared bamboo stalks. Deni Y. Béchard's story, "The Deleted Line," tells of Yukio, a translator who censors a textbook regarding the Battle of Okinawa and is subsequently reprimanded by an old karate master, who explains that to erase the past is "like saying we must let go of our minds, of our spirits." "The Emperor and the Mayor" is Stephen Woodhams' candid interview with Hitoshi Motoshima, former mayor of Nagasaki, who was castigated by some for blaming Emperor Sh?wa for Japan's role in WWII. Hiroshi Fukurai's "Disaster Memories" investigates the radioactive threat of the recently damaged Fukushima Nuclear Power Plant, and Noboru Tokuda's beautifully illustrated diary from his stint as a young soldier in the Imperial Army during WWII is particularly moving. McKenzie's (MacGregor Tells the World) collection is a stunning testament to a country's literal rise from the ashes-casual readers and academics alike will find many of these selections rewarding and informative."

-Publishers Weekly

CATAMARAN
LITERARY READER

Billy Collins Alan Feldman Thomas Crawford Wendell Berry Renee M. Schell Carol V. Davis Mary Mackey Alyssa Young Gail Wronsky Matthew Woodman Sholeh Wolpe Terry Martin Catherine Freeling Dan Phillips Helene Wecker Susan Vreeland Joao Melo M. Allen Cunningham Stephen D. Gutierrez Ryan Rising Mary Doria Russell Daly Walker Hilton Obenzinger Deb Liggett Jeff Kelley Doug Thorpe Robert Nizza Galway Kinnell Frank Paino Brynn Saito Tyehimba Jess Margaret Elysia Garcia Bill Zavatsky Linda Pastan Gary Young David Sullivan Alan Cheuse T.C. Boyle Ana Maria Shua Molly Gloss Gina Ochsner Alfredo Vea Goro Takano Wallace J. Nichols Douglas Brinkley Jerry Martien Stephen Kessler Dale Pendell Gary Snyder Killarney Clary Aleida Rodriguez Judith Serin Casandra Lopez Dane Cervine Judith Barrington Anya Groner Beatriz Vignoli Linda McCarriston Cassie Premo Steele William J. Harris Patricia Smith Peggy Townsend Deni Y. Bechard Paul Skenazy Liliana Heker Elizabeth Crane Chuck Rosenthal Karen Joy Fowler Jack Shoemaker John Moir

The new quarterly magazine
of art and literature

Charles Hood Eva Saulitis Jeanne Wakatsuki Houston Belle Yang Samuel Salerno Astrid Cabral Zara Raab Sheniz Janmohamed Melissa Reeser Poulin Patricia Zylius Chana Bloch Edward Field Richard Silberg Robert Hershon Robin Messing Cornelius Eady Edoardo Sanguineti Moon Chung-hee Vanessa Blumberg RCA O'Neal Vito Victor John Straley Andrew X. Pham Steven Haddock Tom Larson Trane DeVore Jane Vandenburgh Peter Laufer Lawrence Weschler Jonah Raskin

WWW.CATAMARANLITERARYREADER.COM

MUNRO
CAMPAGNA

ARTIST
REPRESENTATIVES

Jack NIXON | *Recreation* | Graphite on paper

630 North State Street, Suite 2109 | Chicago, Illinois 60054
Telephone +1 312 335 8925 | www.munrocampagna.com

sundaysalon

NEW YORK CITY > NAIROBI > CHICAGO

Sunday Salon Chicago is a larger than life reading series in the Windy City featuring a refreshing blend of local, national and international literary voices.

On the last Sunday of every other month at 7 p.m., at Black Rock Pub & Kitchen, we shine the spotlight on four writers who read novel excerpts, short stories, or poetry. Some of Chicago's best loved storytellers have been included in our lineups as well.

Our mission is to give writers a place to network and share their art, as well as to provide an opportunity for passionate readers to discover new work and get to know the larger literary community. Black Rock offers a great beer list, and the private room we are given with two fireplaces and comfortable seating creates a relaxed, open environment.

To learn more about Sunday Salon and our event schedule, go to www.sundaysalon.com or like us on Facebook.

We hope to see you soon!

The Nelson Algren Committee

Since 1989

www.nelsonalgren.org

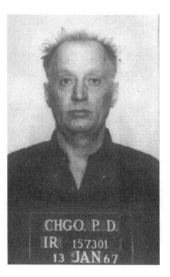

"Literature is made upon any occasion that a challenge is put to the legal apparatus by conscience in touch with humanity."
—Nelson Algren

L. Frank Baum

Edna Ferber

Leon Forrest

The Chicago Literary Hall of Fame

honors its
Fourth Annual Inductees

www.chicagoliteraryhof.org

Ben Hecht

John J. Johnson

Thornton Wilder